*T. Harrell Allen*

# LEE'S LAST MAJOR GENERAL

## Bryan Grimes of North Carolina

Manufactured in the United States of America

Lee's Last Major General: Bryan Grimes of North Carolina
by T. Harrell Allen

Copyright © 1999
T. Harrell Allen
Maps Copyright © 1999 Theodore P. Savas

Includes bibliographic references and index

Printing Number
10 9 8 7 6 5 4 3 2 1
(First Hardcover Edition)

ISBN 1-882810-23-6

Savas Publishing Company
202 First Street S.E., Suite 103A
Mason City, IA 50401
(800) 732-3669

This book is printed on 50-lb. Natural acid-free paper. It meets or exceeds the guidelines for permanence and durability of the Committee on Production Guidelines for Book Longevity of the Council on Library Resources

To Mary-Ann,
Jackson, and Maston,
with love

*Bryan Grimes*
*Maj Genl*

*2nd Corps*
*A.N.V.*

Major General Bryan Grimes

## TABLE OF CONTENTS

## LIST OF MAPS & ILLUSTRATIONS

### Maps

continued. . .

continued

# $\mathcal{P}hotos$

The Civil War always has fascinated Americans, but never before has it enjoyed such steady popularity. An apparently insatiable Civil War audience has provoked and fostered thousands of new books in this decade alone, including a great many needless and insupportable biographies. It is, therefore, a considerable pleasure to introduce the life story of a general who undoubtedly deserves a life study, an officer whose career actually is of interest and importance, not just to some admiring biographer, but to historians and serious students as well.

Bryan Grimes saw about as much war as any man in the Army of Northern Virginia. He spent his entire career in units associated with the renowned Second Corps, fighting beside men like Robert Rodes, John B. Gordon, Dodson Ramseur, and Jubal Early. Grimes experienced diverse action on varied fronts. He served on the Peninsula in 1862, invaded the North twice, participated in all four battles around Fredericksburg, fought up and down the Shenandoah Valley in 1864, survived the daily gloom of life in the Petersburg trenches, and lived to see his army's prideful last day at Appomattox.

T. Harrell Allen shows in this biography that even in an army noted for its high concentration of successful citizen-soldiers, Bryan Grimes stands out as a distinguished example. Dr. Allen fully chronicles Grimes' pedestrian record as a student and his rather more productive antebellum career as a cultured gentleman planter in North Carolina. But this background hardly fitted Grimes for commanding a division in his country's premier army. It is interesting to ponder the environment in which men like Wade Hampton—who still needs a good modern biography—John B. Gordon, and Bryan Grimes flourished. One wonders too why other Confederate generals with similar backgrounds and opportunities—Thomas F. Drayton and Roger A. Pryor come to mind—failed as spectacularly as Grimes succeeded. Allen argues here, convincingly, that in the case of Bryan Grimes, bravery, discipline, and above all a single-minded devotion to duty, made that difference.

This first biography of Bryan Grimes is especially welcome because it is the only book to draw extensively upon the general's unbelievably rich war letters. A sizable selection from those letters, mixed together with some important unfinished memoirs by Grimes, appeared in Pulaski Cowper's *Extracts of Letters of Major-General Grimes to his Wife Written While in Active Service in the Army of Northern Virginia. . . .* That volume appeared in 1883, only three years after its subject's death. The tantalizing potential of the letters is evident to even the most cursory browser. Nearly all the extracts published in 1883 transparently avoided controversy.

Cowper must have labored mightily at his editing, because the full Grimes letters as revealed here are frank and forthright. Often they are critical of other units or officers (Grimes especially disliked the Stonewall Brigade and fellow Tar Heel General William R. Cox). The unvarnished bluntness and irreverence of the Grimes letters makes the very best kind of reading for students of the war. They surely are among the most quotable letters I have ever encountered, and are the backbone of this biography. Because Grimes wrote to his family nearly every day, Dr. Allen has been able to use the letters as a sort of hat rack upon which to hang his other discoveries from secondary sources.

Readers also will come to recognize Grimes' long connection to the 4th North Carolina Infantry—both directly and obliquely—as an historical boon. Like most low-numbered regiments in the Army of Northern Virginia, the 4th North Carolina was an especially literate and articulate collection of men. Those soldiers left behind a large and scattered research base in the form of letters, diaries, articles, and other first person material. Diligent mining of those resources adds another layer of contemporaneous perspective to the story of Bryan Grimes' life.

*Lee's Last Major General: Bryan Grimes of North Carolina* is a biography of unusual relevance. Because he was neither a career soldier nor a bombastic politician, some readers may reach an empathic understanding with the general. A man of modest background and firm beliefs, he found himself sucked into a situation in which his natural talents emerged to an uncommon degree. The fascinating story of that blossoming, together with Bryan Grimes' singular battlefield record and tragic postwar death, unite here in a meaningful and deserved biography.

Robert E. L. Krick

Richmond, Virginia
October 1998

**M**y interest in Bryan Grimes began in the fall of 1994, when I noticed a silver highway state marker just outside of Grimesland, North Carolina, that mentioned the general's nearby plantation home. My interest kindled, I rushed to my university's library at East Carolina to read more about this obscure Confederate officer. Other than passing references, there was nothing to be found. My curiosity piqued, I drove to the University of North Carolina at Chapel Hill, confident that I would find scholarly articles and perhaps even a book or two about him. Much to my surprise, I found only a single source, that being a 1961 Master's Thesis by James Douglas Daniels. Daniels' work, while excellent, focused primarily on Grimes' Civil War career. After devouring that, I wanted to know more, much more, about the man.

Despite the lack of secondary sources, I soon discovered a treasure trove of original letters written by Bryan Grimes to his brother, daughter, and wife, the bulk of them during the Civil War. They were primarily donated by Grimes family members and have become part of the magnificent Southern Historical Collection at the Wilson Library, University of North Carolina at Chapel Hill, and the state archives in Raleigh. Both collections also contain correspondence addressed to Grimes as well. Some of these letters I subsequently discovered were published in a small and heavily edited book two decades after the war and four years after the general's death. Most of it, and other pieces I would eventually find, remained unpublished.

This primary material reveals a distinct American type, a true Southerner who was the product of an old social-economic order and its subsequent Calvinistic values. He was a staunch patriot for his Country's cause, a man of stern morality based more on the Bible than political doctrine. Grimes' overriding personal value was duty. Indeed, it was his personal compass all his life. From these frail but vibrantly-written letters flows a true sense of the man. These primary sources, the key to the historian's search for truth, flesh out and humanize the image in the photograph who, cloaked in a Confederate gray coat trimmed with a general's wreath and stars, stares forth with a steady iron gaze. His writings confirm that he was one of North Carolina's most remarkable sons.

Though not a professional soldier, he enlisted early and soon was leading a regiment in action. He continued to learn the craft of war and developed into an extraordinarily good combat officer. In early 1865, he was given a division and promoted to major general—the last officer of that rank appointed by General Robert E. Lee. And it was Grimes who directed the Army of Northern Virginia's last attack at Appomattox Courthouse on April 9, 1865. After clearing the way for the army's wagons, he was ordered—to his utter shock—to withdraw his command. Fearing a mistake, he refused and continued to refuse until General Lee's order accompanied the directive. The army was to be surrendered and the troops were to stand down. Although he considered flight, Grimes realized his duty was to obey Lee's order and surrender with the rest of the army. Grimes was a fighting general to the *last*.

In November 1864, Grimes wrote his beloved wife Charlotte the following words: "Some people at home think that we have not done our duty up here, but when the history of the war period is to be written, and the disparity of the forces employed considered, we will come out with flying colors and honor; and if justice is done, it will be shown that we have done our duty." Grimes has deserved recognition for his remarkable career, but is has taken one hundred and thirty four years for him to receive it.

Despite his courageous war record and high rank in the Confederate army—much less his place in the history of his native state—not a single book or lengthy monograph has been written about him until now. Certainly he was deserving of a full-length study, but history and those who write it ignored him. On May 9, 1882 in a letter to Col. W. L. Sanders, North Carolina's Secretary of State, Jefferson Davis offered an astute observation. "Men live in the estimation of posterity not by their deeds alone," penned the former president of the Confederacy, "but by their historian also."

This is Bryan Grimes' story.

T. Harrell Allen
Greenville, NC

# Acknowledgments

As always, there are those who deserve special thanks for their assistance to me in writing this biography. I apologize in advance if I forget to mention someone.

Dr. Rick Williams, professor of classics at Southern Illinois University, helped translate the worse of Grimes' handwriting and added helpful ideas, encouragement and advice during this long process; Maston Allen, the historian in the family, read the manuscript in its several variations and offered helpful suggestions; Nelson Allen assisted in proofreading and offered corrections; the Late Gene Williams, ECU librarian, assisted me in locating obscure sources; John R. Woodard, archivist at Wake Forest, shared sources with me; John White, the reference assistant with the Southern Historical Collection at UNC, offered advice and insight, all with good humor and patience; John Bass willingly offered suggestions and shared materials from his private collection; Robert E. L. Krick offered suggestions and wrote the wonderful Foreword for this book.

And of course, I must thank my publisher, Theodore P. Savas, for his help in turning my manuscript into a book.

Thanks also to the Grimes family members for their many contributions—in particular, Bob Grimes, John Grimes, Al Purrington, Bill Mordecai, John B. Grimes of Virginia, and others who wrote and shared information and insight. Thanks also to John Patterson, who pursued medical leads in trying to determine the scientific basis for Grimes' observation that the Yankee corpses turned black, and the Confederate dead remained natural in appearance.

Thanks also to my two sons, Maston and Jackson who, each in his own way, contributed to the book.

And a special thanks to my wife Mary-Ann, who encouraged me to "saddle up" and take these long rides to and from Raleigh and Chapel Hill in search of the general. To her I owe the most. She alone understands the soul of this book.

## "Our cause is just, for it I will fight;
## even for it I am willing to die"

*A* slim, handsome young man with dark hair, firm jaw and penetrating gray eyes stood before the people of Pitt County in eastern North Carolina in February 1861. Gathering his thoughts and probably with some nervousness, he delivered his first political speech. The North Carolinian was campaigning as a delegate to the proposed state convention that would decide if the Old North State would remain in the Union or secede. He was not a politician and routinely shunned the public eye, even though he was a gifted speaker, his oratory skills honed as a debater at the University of North Carolina in Chapel Hill. He had argued various points of the day often and well as a member of the Philanthropic Literary Society, and he now drew on that training to express his views on secession. His goal was to be elected as the delegate from Pitt County—should a state convention be called to settle the secession issue.

He began with a straightforward statement of his position on the issue of secession, declaring, "No man more ardently desires the preservation and perpetuation of this Union than myself, but I ask for the Constitution at the same time. I wish for the Union as it was formed by our forefathers and handed down by them, but I ask for us no Union when we cannot have our Constitutional rights at the same time."

The crowd stared intently at the young college-educated planter from nearby Grimesland, a sprawling plantation where he and three generations of his family had resided. "A fanatical spirit hostile to the institutions of the South pervades the whole Northern population," he asserted. "Corrupt politicians and fanatical preachers have united in an unholy alliance, and the control of the Northern State Legislatures has passed into their hands and has been evidenced by bitter hostility to our institutions."

The intense young man, intelligent, cultivated and wealthy, was representative of the young Southerners who believed themselves destined to lead their region—and their society—in the approaching cataclysm. The crowd looked to him and others like him for insight and leadership. "This fanatical spirit is steadily increasing," the young man orated, "and ere long the power of the Federal Government will come under their control."

The recent election of Abraham Lincoln the preceding November underscored the speaker's comments. "With a President committed to their fanatical views, a judiciary and both Houses of Congress of their own selection, what can the South do to defend her right when she is thus tied hand and foot!" he exclaimed, now playing comfortably to the crowd. "In the first place, let us demand and insist upon a final and just settlement of this bone of contention, or upon a final and eternal separation between the North and the South."

The mass of citizens was by now clearly aroused by his passionate prose. The speaker underscored his eloquent convictions by sealing his delivery with a bold and courageous personal statement, one drawn from a well of character and strength from which he would drink from often in the coming years. While I prefer a final settlement of this important issue, he contended, "I am willing to meet the consequences if forced upon me," he declared, "Our cause is just, for it I will fight, even for it I am willing to die."[1]

The people of Pitt County reacted to the young man's rousing speech with an equally rousing chorus of applause, electing Bryan Grimes soon thereafter to represent them should a state convention be called to settle the question of secession. Grimes' eloquent passion and staunch secessionist posturing reflected the values and beliefs of many in Pitt County, and his fellow North Carolinians would not forget him in the turbulent times that lay ahead of them all.

It took three months before a state convention was finally called in the state capital at Raleigh, and Delegate Grimes travelled ninety miles from his ancestral home at Grimesland, in eastern North Carolina, for the occasion. If there was any real doubt as to the convention's outcome on May 20, 1861, the delegates ended the speculation by unanimously passing an ordinance of secession: North Carolina would join ten other Southern states and leave the Union. Appreciating the import of the action—but certainly not the consequences—the young orator kept as a keepsake the pen with which he signed the ordinance. After the vote was announced, cheers rang throughout the capital. On the west end of the building, word was passed to a young artillery captain to fire the artillery pieces to salute the occasion. Stephen Dodson Ramseur, a recent graduate of West Point, gladly complied with the directive and a deep thunder rolled over Raleigh, signaling North Carolina's independence from the United States. Although Grimes and Ramseur did not yet know one another, their lives would eventually become deeply intertwined.

Given his background it is not surprising that Bryan Grimes took such an ardent stand for North Carolina's independence. In fact, many of his ancestors had shown similar revolutionary zeal and fighting spirit. The current resident of Grimesland was descended from William Grimes, his great-great-grandfather from Norfolk County, Virginia. His ancestors had migrated to Virginia from England about 1660.[2] William and his wife Anne had settled in Norfolk in the early 1700s, but one of their four sons, Demsie Grimes, moved to North Carolina in June 1760. Demsie married Penelope Coffield and settled in Edgecombe County in eastern North Carolina. He was appointed justice of the peace for Edgecombe County in three years later by Governor Arthur Dobbs. After moving to Pitt County, Demsie—Bryan's great-grandfather—purchased several farms on the Tar River and combined them into a large plantation he called Avon. Desmie was one of the signers of the Pitt County Resolution and Declaration of Rights on July 1, 1775, a form of opposition to the British Parliament.[3]

Demsie's wife Penelope gave birth to a son, William, on March 29, 1766. William, at the young age of thirteen, served as a private in the 10th Regiment of the Continental Army in 1779. His steady work ethic, farming abilities and keen business sense combined in 1786 into the successful acquisition of several farms near Avon on the Tar River. William named the large track of land "Grimesland," the plantation Bryan would be born on in 1828. Four years later in January 1790, William married Anne Bryan, the daughter of Col. Joseph Bryan of Craven County.

William's industrious nature continued to develop, and by age twenty-one he was the tax collector for Pitt County. Politics also ran in his blood, and a few years later he represented the county in the House of Commons, 1793-1794. He was also a devout Christian, a vestryman of the Episcopal church and a delegate to the first convention of the Episcopal church, which was held in North Carolina at Tarboro in May 1794. Willam was one of the signers of a constitution of the Protestant Episcopal Church in North Carolina. It had evolved from the Church of England and had been the established church in the South. Even though the Baptists and Methodists had become by 1800 the largest denominations in the South, the Episcopal church still remained the church of the planter class. These deep roots all but guaranteed that the descendant Grimes children would remain devout members of the Episcopal faith. Unfortunately, William died in October 1797, a young man of thirty-one. He left behind one 4-year-old son, Bryan, who had been born on July 13, 1793.

In August 1815, Bryan married Nancy Grist, the daughter of Gen. Richard Grist. Although Nancy bore Bryan six children, only three lived into adulthood. The youngest, born on November 2, 1828 at Grimesland and also named Bryan, would eventually beome Maj. Gen. Bryan Grimes. Just four months after his birth Nancy died of pneumonia on March 2, 1829. Bryan's father remarried in 1831 to Lucy Olivia Blount, and thus the rearing of baby Bryan was left to his older sister Susan, and his stepmother.

Bryan Grimes, Sr., appreciated the value of higher education. He had attended the University of North Carolina for two years and was very proud of his college training—even though he was forced to return to work the extensive farms and take care of his family prior to graduation. Contemporaries described him as as "one of the most upright, honest and enterprising farmers in Pitt County."[4] Throughout the region he was known as a man of "uncompromising integrity and lofty character."[5] He accumulated great wealth during his lifetime, which included numerous slaves. Politically, the elder Grimes strongly supported Henry Clay and fiercely opposed Jacksonian Democracy. He was strong-willed and did not like opposition to his views on any front. Yet, despite these unyielding traits, he was known as a generous man and viewed as the person to approach if a family member was experiencing financial troubles.

His oldest, Susan, married Dr. John G. B. Myers in 1853. Little is known of her life thereafter other than that she passed away nine years later in 1862. Only bits and pieces of correspondence exist between Bryan and his older sister, and these mainly encourage the youngest Grimes to study harder. Bryan's older brother, William, attended the University of North Carolina for two years before transferring to Princeton, where he graduated.

Despite the loss of his mother when he was an infant, Bryan appears to have adjusted well to the tragedy and led a normal life for someone of his circumstances. He was fortunate to be part of a loving and large family, as he had several half-brothers and sisters, one of whom, John Gray Blount Grimes, would serve with him durng the Civil War.

As a youth he rode horses, looked for a mysterious cypress tree that Blackbeard the pirate was rumored to have climbed, swam in the area streams, hunted the plentiful wild game and fished in the nearby Tar River and Bear Creek. Although little is recorded about his early years, there is nothing to indicate that his life was atypical of children of that time and region and, in particular, those born of wealthy parents.

The traits he would later display as an soldier—an indomitable fighting spirit and leadership by example—were evident even in his youth. One boyhood incident aptly demonstrates Grimes' mettle. A friend, Daniel G. Fowle, managed to get in a fight with a boy larger than either himself or Grimes. Fowle was getting the worst of the encounter when Grimes stepped forward and ordered Fowle away. "Stand aside," he instructed. "This fellow is a bully, but I am nearer his size, let me make the fight for you."[6] An associate recalled that Grimes "would fight in a minute, without regard to the size of the boy who had insulted him. He would make friends and quickly forgive when the fight was over." The result of this particular altercation went unrecorded.

As a young man Grimes attended the socials and balls both at his home and those of other prominent families. In addition to Grimesland, his family owned a summer home in Washington, North Carolina, on the Pamlico River about ten miles away, and a winter home in Raleigh. Life at Grimesland was good, and in later years he would often say that the only vocation he was interested in was that of a farmer.

The wealth possessed by the elder Grimes provided significant advantages for his three children included a superior education. His father valued academics and saw to it that his sons received the best instruction possible. The revenue generated by the family plantation allowed Grimes to send both William and Bryan to the best private preparatory schools in the region. Bryan's first brush with school came in Nash County, a positive experience

Bryan Grimes as a young man. His exact age in this image is not recorded, although he was probably around fifteen. *Southern Historical Collection, Wilson Library, The University of North Carolina at Chapel Hill.*

followed by a sojourn at an academy in Washington, North Carolina. He then attended Bingham School in Hillsboro, a respected institution founded in 1806, where he studied under the tutelage of William James Bingham. Bingham, the second principal, had graduated from the University of North Carolina in 1825 with first honors. Bryan was a favorite of his old teacher not just for his good lessons but for his "undaunted spirit, generosity and perfect integrity." In a letter to William in August of 1842, Bryan Sr. commented on young Bryan, now fourteen, during his tenure at Bingham. "I am informed that Bryan applies himself pretty assiduously now," he wrote. "I am pleased to hear it, for he has been doing but little since he left Hillsboro [Bingham]. He has no time to lose, but that seems to have but little weight with him. I fear unless his progress is better he will not complete his course at one and twenty, and that is as long as any youth ought to be at school."[7]

It was at Bingham that Bryan met his close friend, James Johnston Pettigrew, who would be a classmate at the University of North Carolina and later a brigadier general in the Confederate army. After building a solid academic foundation, young Bryan entered the university at Chapel Hill in 1844 at the age of fifteen.

During his childhood Grimes developed a taste for literature as well as a deep interest and apptitude for writing poetry. One of his early and undated poems, "My Heart is at Jones," was probably written shortly before he left for either the Bingham School or the university. Its title refers to the owner of a resort in Warren County where the Grimes family often vacationed during the summer. Its theme throughout was his having to leave home.

> My heart is at Jones, oh would I were there.
> My heart is at Jones, where alls bright and fair—
> Walking with Willy, and talking with Joe,
> My heart is at Jones, wherever I go.
>
> Farewell to the ladies, farewell to the girls,
> Farewell to the children with their pretty curls,
> Farewell to Miss Alden, who dresses so neat,
> And farewell to Steven, who looks at his feet.
>
> Farewell to the young folk at whose merry calls
> I have hied to the alley to roll off the balls,

Farewell to the sofa, where often I sat,
And watched Mr. Grimes twirl his cane & his hat.

The ladies at Jones' are just to my mind,
So gentle, delightful, obliging and kind.
The gentlemen too are so very polite
Im astonished to see such a wonderful sight.

Farewell to Miss——-her bright hazel eyes,
Have cost the young men several thousand of sighs,
Farewell, lady fair, all to thee homager bring,
And beauty proclaim thee, the belle of the spring (Miss Stennis)
Farewell to the muses, to the lyre farewell,
Farewell to the pleasure, which poetry imparts,
Alas, for inspiration, you've told its death knell,
Alas, for the muses, you've broken their hearts.

[signed] B. Grimes[8]

Intelligence, however, which Bryan possessed in abundance, does not always equate to being a good student. While attending Bingham in September 1842 his father felt the need to chastise him for not hitting the books hard enough. "Remain at the Hill during vacations with attention to your books," advised the elder Grimes. Apparently Bryan promised to study harder, for in May 1843 his father wrote that he was "pleased at your promise of more diligence in your studies." Unlike Bryan, his older brother William was more studious and possesed the more serious personality of their father. "William is in Raleigh," noted Bryan's father in a letter to the boy in 1842, "[and] I wish I could say he was enjoying himself. I do not think he gets on very pleasantly. He visits but little, but rarely [attends] the dancing parties, and I think he cares but little about the society of ladies."[9]

At least some of William's social shyness may have been the result of the severe head injury he had suffered as a youth that forced him to use a cane.[10] Despite his health problems, William would eventually join the Confederate army, only to be discharged after one day because of his poor health.[11] Though he could not carry a musket, William supported the Confederacy by growing crops and shipping them to the Virginia army.[12] Young Bryan, on the other hand, was healthier, more sociable than his older

Bryan Grimes, Sr., the father of William and Bryan Grimes. *Southern Historical Collection, Wilson Library, The University of North Carolina at Chapel Hill.*

brother, and enjoyed a strong attraction to the ladies. His good looks, quick wit, humor, and charm attracted them to him as well.

Unfortunately there is little preserved correspondence between Bryan and his father during this period. Letters between William and his father, however, are more plentiful and shed considerable light on the relationship between the father and his sons. An interesting and rather detailed exchange of letters between Bryan Sr., and William during the latter's college years (1840-1844) is particularly revealing, and demonstrate the influence of the father on the sons. William became unhappy while attending the University of North Carolina and asked to transfer to William and Mary. His father, however, objected to relocating to Virginia.[13] In a letter to his son, Bryan Sr. listed his particular reasons why William should remain at UNC, but left open the possibility of transferring to Princeton or Yale.[14] Eventually, William left UNC for Princeton—his father eventually gave in and paid for the education—where he graduated in 1844.[15] This part of the Grimes family historical record evidences the perspective of a father interested in the burgeoning affairs of his sons, and that of a wealthy and influential member of the planter class in eastern North Carolina just two decades before the Civil War. His strongly held Whig views influenced his offspring as well. So too did his dominant traits, which included a strong character, a firm will, a deliberative mind, and a propensity for action. These attributes were evident throughout Bryan's entire recorded life—and especially evidenced themselves on several fields of battle.

Just as Bryan Sr. had a telling impact on the development of his sons, so too did William play a distinct role in shaping Bryan. The siblings enjoyed a close relationship, and Bryan was quite fond of his older brother. He routinely sought his advice and counsel—much like a son seeking wisdom and guidance from his father. But who the young men were and what they would become was inextricably tied to the land upon which they were raised and the traditions underwhich they were brought up.

For more than two hundred years agriculture had been a dominant force in the economy of North Carolina. The planter class, as its name suggests, literally arose from the tilling of the soil. This group of families produced men of wealth, education, and culture. Generations of this class produced men of self-reliance, independence, a strong sense of duty and a willingness to take up arms to defend their freedom. Their way of life or culture was sacred to them and just as clear and dear to them as they thought revealed in the scriptures of the Old Testament. They firmly believed their society and the members of it were God's chosen people. It was, for a small number of the South's citizens, a chivalrous society based on an idealistic notion of Greek democracy.[16]

William Grimes (left) and Bryan Grimes (right) as young men, circa 1850. Note that William was photographed with his cane, which he carried as a result of a riding accident he suffered as a young boy. *Southern Historical Collection, Wilson Library, The University of North Carolina at Chapel Hill.*

For generations Grimes' had worked the soil of eastern Carolina, producing abundant crops and acquiring huge tracts of land that evolved from small farms into opulent plantations. By the 1850s Bryan Sr. paved the way to transfer his lands and power to his two educated and resourceful sons.

Bryan and William welcomed and understood their inherited role as members of the planter class. They had been taught that responsibility was unseparable from their power and influence. During the 1850s both developed their inherited estates and William, showing a business aptitude, began to acquire considerable real estate in Raleigh. Their station in life allowed Bryan to travel to Europe in 1860, as many young men of his class did. Both would probably have continued in their agricultural roles had the country not fallen into civil war. Fiercely patriotic and loyal to their region, state and, in particular, their way of life, both would become unwavering supporters of the Confederacy and risk their lives and fortune in defense of it. Before William had graduated in 1844, Bryan Sr. had written him of these things and offered fatherly advice about his future vocation.[17]

The same year William left Princeton (1844) young Bryan entered the University of North Carolina at Chapel Hill. The fifteen-year-old freshman was one of twenty-seven pupils. While intelligent, academic excellence was not his strong suit. "I am sorry to hear you were deficient in some of your studies," scolded his older sister Susan soon after the first round of faculty reports were issued. "You must not mind a little hard work. Strive for the first. . .everybody will think a great deal more of you, particularly the girls that you care so much to please." Bryan's reply, if there was one, is not recorded.[18]

In all fairness, the teenager's course of study was difficult and thorough—and certainly a substantial change to what he was used to. The curriculum was largely based on Latin and Greek, mathematics, French, geography, rhetoric, and law. His first series of classes that fall included the ancient languages (Latin and Greek), algebra, ancient geography, elocution, compulsory prayer, recitation and chapel. His marks demonstrated moderate academic success, and certainly were no cause for serious alarm. He received a "VR" (very respectable) in geography, a "T" (tolerable) in languages (the lowest passing grade at the University), and an "R" (respectable) in mathamatics. His attendance record showed that he missed prayer four times, recitation twice, and chapel service not at all.[19] His father was probably displeased because he had not received the higher grades of "VG" (very good) or "G" (good). In 1844 at UNC, however, the faculty rarely awarded the highest grade (excellent), and typically the best a student could earn was a mark of very good, at least according to a faculty ledger of recorded grades.[20]

Bryan's grades slipped somewhat the following spring 1845, when he earned "Tolerable's" in math, language, and geography, and a "Respectable" in bible studies. His attendance also declined, with more absences in prayer (18), recitation (17) and chapel (2). Bryan had earned what today would be considered the equivalent of "C," and his father was not pleased. On March 7, 1845, the elder Grimes penned his son a letter that many fathers today could have written. "You were marked as deficient in your studies," he reprimanded. "Would it not have been better for you during vacation to have made up your deficiencies than to have spent your time as you did in a round of frolicking? Study by day and by night. Never let me see you marked deficient. I fear you are just dragging along through college."[21]

Bryan Sr. was probably reacting to mid-term reports by the faculty and young Bryan's activities while home at Grimesland during spring vacation. Bryan, to some degree, must have followed his father's advice. "I received your report of the faculty," wrote his father on April 16, 1848. "The report in the main was not very bad, yet it was not one calculated to give me pleasure." The mixed chastisement from his father continued. "Your scholarship was marked tolerable and deportment not objectionable, still there was complaint of your inattention to study. Let me ask you what is the use of my laboring as I do to afford you the means [of an education]," he inquired of his son. "Look at me laboring by day and by night for your benefit and then suppose what my feelings must be." Without equivocation Bryan Grimes' father warned him what would happen if his academic career did not get on track. "I will say to you in plain language that if you do not change your course, I shall be compelled to take you from college and put you to work on the farm."[22]

Heeding his father's advice—and perhaps reacting to his none too subtle threat—Bryan, by now a sophomore, improved his fall 1845 marks to two R's in bible studies and Greek and two T's in Latin and math (Geometry and Trigonometry). This improvement did not endure. Although his grades for the mid-term of the 1846 spring session included three R's and only one T, his final grades slipped to four T's in Latin, bible studies, Greek and math. In the fall session of 1846, Grimes took rhetoric, French, Latin, bible studies and math. It was a better semester for him, and he received "Respectables" in every course except for a "Tolerable" in Latin.[23]

"You are now approaching manhood," observed Bryan, Sr. to his son during the fall session of 1846. "Now the question is what business will you be best qualified for in life. I expect you will have to follow in my footsteps and become a farmer," he wrote, reflecting on his son's apparently weak grasp of academics and on his own aspirations for him. "This is a business that requires no big intellectual powers," he noted in an offhanded and probably unintentional slight of the boy, "but depends primarily for success on industry and a judicious economy. The farmer in North Carolina has never received the rank in society he ought. It will be necessary for me to purchase a farm for you before you begin business."[24]

The father's speculation about Bryan's vocation is similar to the letter he wrote William when he was at Princeton. However, he believed William intelligent enough to become a lawyer—a possibility he did not raise with Bryan. Interestingly, Bryan, Sr. seemed unaware that young Bryan desired most of all to become a sucessful farmer. In fact, Bryan never mentioned a desire to enter a profession. In fact, in an undated letter written about this time, Grimes agreed with his father:

As you implied, I do not think that I can rise to distinction in any of the professions. I have and always have had a low estimate of my abilities. I think it by far the wiser plan to settle down and be a plain but honest cultivator of the soil . . . and maintain the stature in society that I now hold through you. My natural propensities would lead to farming, and it shall be the desired object of my heart to please and rival you in the respectability of your occupation.[25]

In this same letter young Bryan mentioned to his father that he hoped Grimesland, his birthplace and home, would be given to old sister Susan so that it would stay in the immediate family.[26]

In the spring of 1847 Grimes enrolled in French, Greek, math, history, Latin and bible studies. The undistinguished session brought about another round of mixed grades. His best mark was a "Very Respectable" in history, a "Respectable" in bible studies and double-pairing of "Tolerables" in Greek, Latin, French and math. The faculty recorded twenty-four absences from prayer, twenty in recitation and four in chapel.

The fall of 1847 witnessed the beginning of his senior year at the university, and Bryan was tiring of academic study. Eager to graduate, he enrolled in several difficult courses, including Latin, calculus, French, Greek and a course in law. His presence in a law course was somewhat ironic, for he was suspended for two weeks in October by the faculty for having been engaged in "disturbing the [Chapel Hill] village by indecent and outrageous noises."[27] Apparently he did not engage in the shenanigans alone, for a short time later four of his classmates—including his good friend James Johnston Iredell, who would fight with him in the Confederate army—were also suspended. Bryan did not deny the charge. A short while after his suspension a friend wrote that he was "sorry to hear that you had been suspended, but was glad to learn that you, after having committed in the eyes of the faculty an unpardonable act, shrank with disgust from telling that which is but too often in college considered as an excusable lie."[28] Despite the suspension, Grimes earned "Respectables" in French, calculus and law, and "Tolerables" in Latin and Greek.[29]

The final session of school in the spring of 1848 found Bryan enrolled in French, Latin, chemistry and law. Mired in academic mediocrity, he earned "Respectables" in three courses and a "Tolerable" in Latin. His four years of toil garnered barely passing grades, and he never received a mark higher than "Very Respectable." Nevertheless, he did graduate in June 1848 at age 20, earning his degree before the age of 21, a concern that his father had worried about for some time.[30]

"Let me hear what amount you will require to pay off your debts against you," wrote his father on April 6, 1848. "You must not leave Chapel Hill in debt." Bryan obviously agreed, informing his father that the amount necessary totaled $220. Although Bryan, Sr. paid the large sum without much question, he was not pleased. The amount," he informed his son in May 1848, seemed "a pretty considerable item for only one-half a year."[31]

Although young Grimes was not a scholar, he did engage in other intellectual pursuits during his years at the university. The most influential of these extra-curricular activities involved his membership with the Philanthropic Literary Society. He joined the society during his freshman year on August 23, 1844. The literary society was actually one of two at the university, the other being the Dialectic. A favorite question on campus was, "Are you a Di or a Phi?" At Commencement, the Dis wore blue and the Phis wore white, the colors of the university. The Societies performed several important functions for the students by providing social activities, meetings with visiting young ladies, speechmaking and, the most important of all, intellectual growth through formal debating. As one UNC president cogently observed, "Many young men who neglected text-books obtained here a valuable education, while those who were candidates for offices learned here what they could not learn in the classroom—how to manage men." Without question Bryan Grimes was one of these young men.[32]

The two societies held their meetings in their respective library rooms on the third floor of the South building. The students took a great deal of pride in their libraries, which when added together, were larger than that of the university's. In fact, they were widely considered the best collections in the state.[33]

For the formal debates, parliamentary law was strictly followed. This meant the strict rules of order had to be learned by the young men, who also had to develop the ability to speak extemporaneously, write well, and do research. As part of their forensic training the chief debaters studied their subjects thoroughly and argued them with intelligence, zeal and sometimes eloquence. The rigorous demands of the societies helped shape them for future positions of leadership in any number of callings.

Grimes participated in his first debate on September 27, 1844, shortly after joining the Philanthropic Society. He assisted another debater on the topic "Should every free white man be entitled to vote?" Grimes and his partner assumed the affirmative side of the issue and the minutes of the society show that the debate was decided in their favor.[34]

Usually a topic was assigned about one week in advance, which gave the debaters but little time to research and prepare their arguments. This was one of the reasons why the members were so intent on maintaining a good library replete with reference works on a variety of topics. Since the university refused to pay for these books, a tax was levied on the members to obtain them. On November 22, 1844, Grimes—having assumed the role of principal debater—argued affirmatively on the question whether there should be a union of the church and state. The members, who typically voted at the end of the debate, decided against him. Several months passed before he had another opportunity to engage in debate. On April 18, 1845, he argued the affirmative side of the issue of "Should the right of search be prohibited?" This time the members of the audience agreed with Grimes and declared his side the winner. Although his grades may have been marginal, he seems to have dedicated himself to the art of debating, winning two of the three sessions during his freshman year.[35]

Activities in the Society other than debating provide an insight into how Grimes' spent some of his time as a college student. Members were allowed to check out books from the Philanthropic library, and Grimes took advantage of this opportunity. For example, during his freshman year he checked out *Roman History, Stories of Sea, Last Days of Pompey, Murray's Naval Tactics, Buccaneers, Goldsmith's Rome, Arabian Nights, Homer's Iliad, Tales of the Sea, History of England, Shakespeare, Wonders of the World, I Says, Says I,* and *Locke's Works,* among others. He also devoured reference works, probably in preparation for upcoming debates, including *Encyclopedia Britanica, Democratic Review, Political Quotations, Library of Useful Knowledge,* and *Georgia Review.* History, geography and stories of the sea were his favorite topics. Indeed, the highest grade he earned in college was a "Very Respectable" in history and geography.[36]

In addition to teaching members rigorous thinking and oratory skills, the Society also instilled a certain amount of composure and discipline. Meetings followed a strict decorum, and members who talked or disrupted others were fined by the treasurer. Grimes liked to talk, and his conduct, while not bad or disrespectful, brought about a series of fines. For instance, he was cited seven times in the fall of his Freshman year for "talking," misdeeds that cost him (or rather his father) 75 cents. Grimes' recidivism was high, for he continued to talk and continued to be fined. He was cited eleven times during the spring session of 1845 and fined appropriately. On several occasions he was also fined for going over his time limit in the debates.[37]

During his junior year Grimes actively campaigned for one of the most prestigious offices open to students, that of Chief Marshal at Commencement. The position's prestige ranked only behind those of the state's governor, the university president and the Orator for the occasion. The Marshal was conspicuous for good manners, a handsome person and savoir faire. The contest between Grimes and Thomas J. Person was one of the most heated in the university's history. According to one source, Grimes' chances were ruined by the charge that he was the candidate of the aristocracy, while

Person courted the democracy.[38] Jealousy of his wealth may have doomed his chances. Despite these flashes of interest in campus politics and oratory, Grimes never ran for public office as an adult.

A significant part of Grimes' collegiate tenure centered on his close friendship with James Johnston Pettigrew. Like Grimes, Pettigrew—who would later become a brigadier general in the Confederate army—was also from a prominent eastern North Carolina family. They had known one another since their days together at the Bingham School, and both were members of the Philanthropic Society at UNC. Like most enduring friendships, theirs was built on a foundation of compatability. Their temperament, personal values, and chivalrous attitudes combined with a mutually combative spirit to forge a bond that would last throughout their lives. It is no coincidence that both men would later recognize in the other a pair of traits: character and leadership.

Pettigrew, who was born on July 4, 1828, in Tyrrell County in eastern North Carolina, entered the University of North Carolina in 1843, one year ahead of Grimes. Pettigrew's family structure was indicative of the closeness of the familial ties in the eastern part of the state in the mid-1800s. His two sisters, Anne and Mary, were first cousins to Charlotte Bryan, Grimes' second wife, and both were reared by Charlotte's mother in Raleigh after their own mother, Ann, died during childbirth.[39]

While similar in many respects, Pettigrew's intellect was clearly superior to Grimes'. Pettigrew earned a rare "Excellent" in math courses and mostly "Very Good" in his others, easily graduating as the Valedictorian of his 1847 class.[40] In fact, while eulogzing Pettigrew, President David L. Swain spoke of him as "the most accomplished scholar who ever went forth from the university."[41] The retiring and sensitive Pettigrew, who had something of a "reputation for stand-offishness," had few friends, and Bryan Grimes was probably his closest companion. When Pettigrew was elected President of the Philanthropic Society during his junior year, he shared with Grimes the reason he refused to accept the position: he did not want to appear to be currying favor.[42]

Both spirited young men were ready, if necessary, to defend their honor (and their family names). Young Pettigrew embarked on a fist fight with a classmate at UNC that almost escalated into a duel. Similarly, Grimes would also come within a hair's breadth of fighting a duel early in his career with a

Confederate captain. In a June 16, 1847, letter to Pettigrew, Grimes described a near-violent encounter brought on by his friend Tom Myers. Apparently notes written by Myers offended a girl's family. Grimes, however, refused to reveal the name of the person who wrote the notes, and an angry male member of the supposedly transgressed family informed Grimes that he was going to physically whip him. Grimes, in a move somewhat out of character, verbally worked his way out of the brewing controversy. "I don't believe that consistency in love affairs is one of my redeeming qualities," he later reflected.[43]

An exchange of college letters between Grimes and Pettigrew reveals something about their deep friendship, future plans and vocational interests. Because of his outstanding ability as a mathematician, shortly after his graduation in 1847 Pettigrew was offered a professorship at the National (Naval) Observatory in Washington, D.C. His salary was $1,200 per year. A few months later on July 27, Grimes returned to Chapel Hill for his last year, obviously dejected at the thought of facing a school year without his friend. "I have returned once more to the Hill of service," he wrote, "but surely not to the same place. I am no longer the happy indifferent youth I was want to be. A change has come over the spirit of my dreams." He continued in the same vein with an even greater outpouring of candor and forthrightness. "You know not the extent of my friendship for you. It was more than is conveyed in that simple word. It has more the resemblance of what is described to be love. I would call it love, but man cannot love man. It was more than friendship and little less than love." Finally, he advised his friend to continue his pursuit of the law. "Study the law where your talents can have full success . . . in a few years you will be among the brilliant lights of the land." Obviously Grimes was lonesome without his fellow soul mate. It is interesting to note that Pettigrew left the observatory after only six months to study law in Baltimore.[44]

Although he might have followed Grimes' advice, the study and subsequent practice of law soured Pettigrew's opinion of the profession. Pettigrew joined his cousin's law firm in Charleston after his return from Europe in 1852, and practiced in the lovely historic city for nine years until the eve of civil war. From the beginning his view toward the legal profession was critical. "Studying in the City with a person who has a large practice is entirely a farce. You. . .learn nothing except what you ask, and you do not know what to ask." If his former classmates wished to study law, he advised, do it at the UNC law school.[45]

On the eve of his graduation in 1848, Grimes received a letter from Pettigrew which reflected a growing maturity mixed with his growing-cynicism for the profession only recently chosen:

> You are now. . .about to launch your little bark upon the great water, and before you have been sailing six months, you will be completely overpowered with disgust. You will see vanity without any foundation: ignorance, nothing but ignorance . . . Lawyers, who never poked their noses out of the door without having a precedent, except perhaps to smear on it a little of the mud of politics. . .And the Baltimore bar think themselves at the head of the country.[46]

Despite poor grades and the absence of his dear friend, Grimes managed to struggle through his final year. He wrote Pettigrew on June 9, 1848, "Would you believe it, I have graduated and have the privilege of attaching AB to my name. I am now on the banks of the noble old Tar [River] and what occupation would you suppose that I follow?" He thought he would rejoice upon leaving Chapel Hill, but instead noted candidly "how different were my feelings from what I anticipated—all were weeping and I wept too."[47]

As noted earlier, Grimes returned to Grimesland and earnestly began his occupation as a planter. He excelled as an agriculturist and was more than content with his chosen vocation. He met a beautiful young woman, Elizabeth Hilliard Davis, daughter of Dr. Thomas Davis of Franklin County, and they were married in the spring on April 9, 1851. She was eighteen and he was twenty-three.[48]

Mimicking what he had already done for William, that fall Grimes' father gave him sufficient land and slaves to start his own farm.[49] Hard and consistent work absorbed the hours and days in the years that followed, and in October 1851, the elder Grimes presented Bryan with the Grimesland plantation. This must have been particularly pleasing to prospering young planter as he had always cherished that particular piece of land. Bryan Sr. had built the current Grimesland home in 1818, and it remains occupied today. The beautiful large white house with its extensive porches was the birthplace of Bryan, Susan and William. Thus at twenty-three Bryan inher-

A pre-war image of Bryan (left) and William (right) Grimes. Although this outstanding image is undated, is was probably taken in the late 1850s. *Southern Historical Collection, Wilson Library, University of North Carolina at Chapel Hill.*

ited a considerable estate and the responsibility for successfully managing it.[50]

The success and happiness that Bryan had enjoyed since graduation spriraled into a lengthy period marred by tragedy and heartache. In January 1852, Elizabeth bore Bryan his first child, a son also named Bryan. Unfortunately, the sickly infant died within a month. The sorrow that filled their house gave way to joy on New Year's Day 1853 when a daughter, Bettie, was born. A third child, Nancy, followed in June 1854, but like her older deceased brother, she too lived but a short while and died that September. "You have lost the little one that was dear to me," mourned his father on October 11 in a heart-felt letter of condolence to his son. Bryan and Elizabeth conceived a fourth child, another son also named Bryan, who was born in 1857. Unfortunately, the emotional and physical cost of bearing four children in five years, coupled with losing two in the interim, took its toll on Elizabeth. She passed away in November 1857, only eight months after Bryan's birth. A pervading sadness enveloped the planter. On his young shoulders now fell the burden of rearing two motherless children, Bettie and Bryan.

Despite these crushing personal losses, Bryan refused to buckle under the strain. Instead, he turned his attention to physical labor, becoming in the process a successful planter. He increased the productivity of his lands, his personal wealth increased, and he eventually grew content to live his life as gentleman-planter.

On March 18, 1860, tragedy again touched the Grimes family when William received a telegram from Pulaski Cowper, a brother-in-law married to his half-sister Mary. Their father, Bryan Sr., had died the night before on the steamer *Louisiana* in the Chesapeake Bay on its return to Baltimore. The cause of death according to the Tarboro *Southerner* was apoplexy (stroke). Cowper requested that William send someone to Plymouth, North Carolina, with horses and a "barouche" (four-wheeled carriage) to gather the remains.[51]

Seeking solace in travel, Bryan went abroad in the late spring of 1860, where he spent six months traveling in Europe. He carried with him a letter of introduction written by Chief Justice Thomas Ruffin, a North Carolina planter and distinguished jurist. The letter of reference, addressed to "Honorable C. J. Faulkner, U.S. Minister at Paris," described Grimes as Ruffin's "friend. . .a gentleman, well and favorably known in our State. I take great pleasure in introducing him to your acquaintance."[52]

After crossing the Atlantic on a steamer and just before it docked in Ireland, Bryan wrote William on July 14 about his intent to trek across the British Isles. "My first intention was to have landed at Liverpool," he explained, "but upon my learning more about the typography of the country I have decided to travel through Ireland and then down Scotland and enter England, taking it leisurely until I reach London." He described his voyage as "very pleasant," and that he managed to accomplish it "with but little of the horrible sea sickness which I had so much dreaded."[53]

Grimes found Dublin, Ireland a city of stark contrasts. "I had thought that I had seen poverty in our own country, but nothing to compare with that by which I am now surrounded," he wrote on July 19. "What would you think to be followed at every step by 10 to 15 beggers? Dublin is a city of varied interests to strangers. It has both the antique and the modern to enjoy."[54] After reaching Paris in mid-August, Grimes bought a beautiful watch that he would one day give to his second wife, Charlotte Bryan. Charlotte described the time piece as "a blue enameled heart set with diamonds, and was, the loveliest watch and chain I ever saw."[55]

Shortly after Abraham Lincoln was elected president in November, 1860, Grimes returned to North Carolina. Though he had been abroad, he quickly sensed that the political climate—both nationally and in his home state—had changed dramatically during the months he was absent. Like many other Southerners, he anticipated civil war. When South Carolina fired upon Fort Sumter April 12, 1861, Grimes hurried to Charleston to witness the historic event. The fort's garrison, however, capitulated quickly and he arrived too late to see any of the actual bombardment.[56]

Whipped up by the excitement of the moment, Grimes embarked on an odyssey across the new Confederacy. By train he travelled to Montgomery, Alabama, and thence on to Pensacola, Florida, where Gen. Braxton Bragg's forces were rumored to be on the verge of engaging the enemy. Disappointed with the lack of action in the panhandle of Florida, Grimes moved on to New Orleans and then up the Mississippi River to Tennessee. Before long he was on a train filled with the first troops sent from Alabama to Richmond. Ironically, he occupied a seat immediately in front of Andrew Johnson, who would eventually be President Abraham Lincoln's vice president during his second term of office. According to Grimes, he "heard the first groans given in contempt of his [Johnson's] treachery to the South, which were repeated at every station, when it was made known that he was on board the train."[57]

An exhausted but elated Grimes returned home in early May 1861, where he soon discovered that his friends had nominated him during his absence as a delegate to the state convention. The election was held May 13, and he was elected without opposition. Almost immediately he left for Raleigh for the state convention and took his seat amongst the pro-secessionists. While in the capital he also took an active role in promoting a series of war measures designed to support the state's efforts to raise an army.[58]

Events moved forward with dizzying speed. The firing on Fort Sumter triggered President Lincoln's call for troops to put down the rebellion, which in turn led to the secession of Virginia. The withdrawal of that state paved the way for North Carolina to follow suit, and she voted unanimously on May 20, 1861, to secede. Grimes did not continue dabbling in politics, preferring instead a hasty resignation from the convention in the hope of obtaining a position in the army. With wartime fervor pulsing through the state it was not difficult—even for someone without any military experience—to obtain an appointment. His turned out to be a major in the 4th Regiment of North Carolina State Troops. His commission, signed by Governor John W. Ellis, read as follows:

The State of North Carolina

To: Bryan Grimes

We, reposing trust and confidence in your patriotism, valor and military skill, have appointed, and do hereby commission you a Major of the 4th Regiment of Infantry in our State Troops: to the rank from the sixteenth day of May, 1861, and we do hereby vest you with the authority appertaining to said office, to the end that you may promptly and diligently perform its duties, as prescribed by law, in the discharge of which all officers and soldiers under your command are required to yield you obedience.[59]

The planter-turned-soldier was now prepared to fight for what he believed, and fight he would to the last.

# The 4th North Carolina Infantry

## "Shot guns with buck shot is my desire"

**T**he 4th Regiment of the North Carolina State Troops, formed in May 1861 at Camp Hill near Garysburg, Northampton County, was mustered into the Confederate service on June 28, 1861. The first commander of the regiment, Col. George B. Anderson, was born on April 12, 1831 near Hillsboro, North Carolina. Anderson was more than qualified to lead the regiment, having graduated from the U.S. Military Academy in 1852. Thereafter he saw service on the frontier until he resigned his commission on April 25, 1861, and joined the Confederate States Army. His appointment as colonel dated from May 16, 1861. The North Carolinian was, according to one source, "the first officer of the old army, then in service, who proffered his sword and his life to North Carolina." He was a "splendid specimen," was how one recruit described him, "tall, erect, brown-bearded, deep-chested, round-limbed, with a musical voice." Anderson's jovial yet professional attitude made him a popular officer with his men. Edward Porter Alexander, one of the Confederacy's leading artillerists, recalled Anderson after the war:

> Of the officers killed I was a very great friend of one G. B. Anderson of No. Ca. He was a six footer of fine figure with specially good legs which gave him a very graceful seat on horseback, & his face was as attractive as his figure, with brown hair, blue gray eyes & general good nature in every feature. I had gotten to know & to like him at Ft. Leavenworth in 1858.[1]

Another up and coming officer, Stephen Dodson Ramseur, who would later achieve distinction within the army and become a friend of Bryan Grimes, also admired Colonel Anderson. After Anderson's prominent display in the Battle at Seven Pines, Ramseur wrote "[I am willing] to give my life to have my [regiment] behave with the same glorious gallantry as did

FOURTH REGIMENT.

1. Bryan Grimes, Colonel.
2. George B. Anderson, Colonel.
3. James H. Wood, Colonel.
4. John A. Young, Lieut.-Colonel.

5. E. A. Osborne, Colonel.
6. J. F. Stansill, Major.
7. J. F. Shaffner, Chief Surgeon.
8. Rev. W. A. Wood, Chaplain.

9. J. M. Hadley, Assistant Surgeon.

Col. Anderson's 4th N.C. State Troops."[2] As the testimonials from fellow contemporaries demonstrated, Anderson was a solid officer destined for higher command. He would also have a profound influence on Grimes.

Indeed, Grimes may have sensed some of these leadership traits in Anderson, for he voluntarily chose to serve under that officer. In his brief recollection written after the war, Grimes remembered that he was "was offered by Governor Ellis the Lieutenant-Colonelcy of the Eighth Regiment, or the majority [major] of the Second Cavalry, or majority of the Fourth Regiment, which latter I accepted."[3] I chose to be major of the 4th North Carolina, explained Grimes, because "I felt deficiency of a knowledge of military tactics, and Colonel George B. Anderson, a graduate of West Point, was Colonel of the 4th Infantry, whilst the others were officered by inexperienced civilians like myself, and I preferred a subordinate position with an efficient officer to higher rank with officers without experience."[4] This pragmatic decision and insight would serve Grimes well, for as a civilian he had much to learn, and Anderson would prove an able instructor.

Within eight months of the North Carolina's secession, thirty-nine regiments were dispatched for Confederate service, among them the 4th North Carolina.[5] The regiment was made up of ten companies totaling 945 men.[6] These early companies were composed primarily of young men from a local region, usually a county, and they often knew each other. The average age of the men of the 4th North Carolina was twenty-two.[7] Most often they were led by a local politician or someone with social standing, and in some cases by a prominent individual who had formal military training. The 4th reflected these tendencies. Its ten companies were formed from only six counties: three from Iredell, two from Rowan, one from Wayne, one from Davie, one from Wilson and two from Beaufort. Interestingly, Grime's home county, Pitt, did not supply any of these volunteers, so it is likely that he knew few, if any, of the men he would eventually command.[8]

The ten companies had colorful nicknames that often reflected some community connection, physical or historical. These monikers were also a strong source of great pride for the men. Company names that comprised the 4th North Carolina included the Blues, the Southern Guards, and the Wilson Light Infantry.[9] Another colorful and important element of the regiment was its regimental band. With eighteen members it was considered a fairly large organization, and its primary duty was to practice, much like the soldiers who were forced to endure endless hours of drill and instruction. During a battle the band would have additional and less pleasant duties, such as serving as litter bearers. Their typical position at the opening of a fight would be a short distance behind the regiment with the assistant surgeon.[10]

About two-thirds of the North Carolina volunteer soldiers in 1861 were unmarried and many came from families of average or above-average personal wealth. Their economic status allowed the family to forego the presence of the adult male worker or, viewed another way, the income he produced. Most people mistakenly believed the absence would be short-lived.[11]

The officers of the regiment were appointed by the state's governor. The 4th North Carolina was commanded by a colonel (Anderson), who was in turn supported by a lieutenant colonel (John Augustus Young) and major (Grimes). Other officers included the regimental adjutant, quartermaster and medical director or regimental surgeon. Two of these men, quartermaster Capt. Thomas M. Blount and surgeon Dr. John Francis Shaffner, would later clash with Grimes.[12]

Camp life with the regiment, characterized by a contemporary as one of sobriety and piety, proved agreeable to Grimes. Writing after the war, one member of the 4th described the composition of the unit as "a pious and orderly set of men. The camps often resounded with hymns and songs." He also observed that profanity amongst the officers was seldom heard, noting that "Grimes, though of a quick and fiery temper, was careful never to take the Holy Name in vain."[13]

After settling into camp, Grimes posted to his brother William in Raleigh on July 8, 1861, an early (and perhaps his first) letter since joining the army. "This is my first night in encampment, and I can assure you the sensation is numb and strange. . . .our encampment is located in a most magnificent grove gently undulating and with the tents dotted here and there looks particularly picturesque." With over 1,000 men in camp, Grimes was keenly aware of his need to evolve into an effective military officer. I will "stick close to business and increase [my] military knowledge," he informed William, "[and] I shall expect to understand something about it before the cessation of hostilities." A few hours in camp brought the realities of soldier life to the fore, and the young major clearly missed the comforts of home. Would you get "a small single mattress, as I shall be on the ground after tonight for I am now using Capt. Carter's, who returns tomorrow," he inquired of his brother. While they shared willingly of their belongings during the war's early days, Grimes' relationship with Company E's Capt. David M. Carter would change dramatically in the months ahead.[14]

Still learning to be an officer and conscious of his rank, he also asked William to  purchase and "forward right away a trumpet such as Field officers wear upon their hats with the figure 4 in the center of the trumpet. You can see what I wish by examining the hats of some Colonel or Major." The number "4," was in reference to his regiment's numerical designation.

Three days later Grimes again penned another letter to William, requesting that a local tailor make a uniform for him and also "procure some light gray stuff and make me a blouse just like the one he made for Col. Anderson." Apparently the colonel's clothes, as well as his leadership abilities, impressed the major. "Have the straps placed upon the shoulders with a leaf worked upon the ends. . . similar to what is inclined to be worn by the Majors," directed Grimes. He renewed his earlier request for a mattress for "I am now sleeping upon three camp stools with my trunk for a pillow." "We can't say when the regiment leaves," he concluded, "but not until the Colonel thinks them well equipped and drilled." Grimes also dwelled briefly on the sickness and death that plagued the early army camps, observing that while his "Camp very healthy, only 17 sick opposite is Col [Charles C.] Tew's regiment [2nd North Carolina], 240 in hospital with 3 deaths yesterday."[15]

Still adjusting to military life, Grimes on July 15 wrote William. "I think when I become fully initiated in military matters that I shall rather like it then; otherwise sleeping out last night is rather cold."[16] Within days he was expressing to William his progress and strong desire to become an effective officer. "I am learning gradually the duties attendant upon the functions of Major. At any rate I know full well that the Lieutenant Colonel is as ignorant in military knowledge as myself. Col. Anderson thinks the material of the Regiment is what it should be. Time is only necessary to perfect it."[17]

Although Grimes wished he could visit Raleigh, he knew that his position of responsibility within the unit made such a thing impossible. "Being in command at present I cannot without injury to the Regiment leave," he lamented. Like every uninitiated soldier, Grimes watched the gathering storm on the plains of Manassas with a heightened interest, fearful only that he would miss the first, and perhaps last, major battle of the war. "I am afraid that the great battle will take place before our arrival," he wrote to William on July 15. Grimes' prophesy was indeed correct. The newly-formed 4th North Carolina did not depart Camp Hill, where it continued practicing its drilling, until ordered to Richmond on July 20, just one day before the battle. Once the unit arrived in the Confederate capital, orders were received on July 29 to proceed to Manassas Junction. Much to their dismay, the North Carolinians were assigned to the garrison at that place and remained there performing post and fatigue duty during the summer and winter of 1861-1862.

As if missing the first large-scale battle of the war was not enough, Grimes became ill with diarrhea in July, as did many of the new recruits. "I have been at times quite unwell since I have been here owing no doubt to the change of water [and] also with the exposure attendant upon camp life," he wrote William. "This morning for the first time have I been absent from duty." He received permission to spend a few days in the Bull Run Mountains recuperating. The malady took many lives, especially during the war's first year. Luckily for Grimes, his case proved to be relatively mild and after a short absence he was able to return to his regiment. The same cannot be said for some of Grimes' comrades. "Almost every hour in the day the funeral dirge could be heard and the firing of the doleful platoon sounded out upon the air almost continually," observed Edwin A. Osborne, the captain of Company H, "reminding us that death was busy in the camp."[18]

After a month in camp at Manassas Grimes wrote an exceptionally long and revealing letter to William. A private, he observed, enters the service with a "superfluity of patriotism that would be greatly diminished by a trial of six months." Speaking of course of his own experiences, Grimes believed "the privatations are endurable so long as one can retain his health, but imagine a poor fellow with the measles and nothing between him and mother earth, but a solitary blanket. And many poor fellows [have] nothing but a cloudy sky to cover them." Realizing the extent to which his native state had strived to care for her soldiers in the field, he added that "her soldiers. . .have tents to sleep under which cannot be said for a great majority who fought and won the battle at Manassas."[19]

The month near the front impressed the major and altered his views on several matters. "Fighting from my opinion, is the least of a soldier's exposures," he observed. "The danger of a battle is nothing in comparison to the risks from exposure to which he is subjected in camp life." Not wanting to minimize the experiences of the veterans who had endured Manassas, he added, "Though from a view on the battlefield the risks there are not be laughed at." Although Grimes had not yet heard the whine of a minie ball fired in anger, his observation was exactly correct.

His proximity to the July 21st action allowed him to absorb firsthand the grim reality and harsh aftermath of the Manassas battle: "The stench now arising from the putrefaction of the dead is intolerable," described the North Carolinian in a letter home. "A [handerkerchief] full of whisky and an extra bottle to keep it full is the only means by which you can visit the severely contested spots on the battleground." Taking an interest in where his fellow Tarheels had fought during the engagement, Grimes sought out the spot where Col. Charles Fisher and the 6th North Carolina was engaged. Fisher was killed during the action and the unit had suffered heavily. Although the bodies had been removed, "at least fifty horses in an area the diameter of which is perhaps forty yards," were rotting under the hot July sun. The signs of battle were visible everywhere, he explained, and so was the course of the Federal retreat. "For miles you can trace by knapsacks, canteens and coats the road they pursued on their flight." In addition to the flotsam of battle, burial sites littered the devasted landscape. "Near a church I saw eight freshly dug holes and one of the wounded (still at the church used as a hospital) informed me that he counted seventy dead bodies thrown into one of the pits." The hasty burials received by many of the fallen became evident as Grimes guided his horse across the fields. "In riding now over the ground you can see the outlines of a body hardly covered by the dirt," he wrote with some disgust, "with the toes of the shoes sticking out. At another encampment, a scull, an arm, in fact, the most ghastly sights are to be witnessed all on the field."[20]

As was common among the soldiers, Grimes picked up a discarded artifact as a war souvenir. "I have a couple of sticks I expect to send home," he informed William. "(Enquire of old Utly the bookseller for them). I shall send them by a man from Iredell county with the request that he leave them with Utly in Raleigh." One of the wooden pieces was from the Widow

Henry house, or as Grimes described it, "from a badly riddled house in which that old woman was killed. She used it as a poker." The other item "was nearly cut into by a chain shot not far from where Beauregard's horse was shot under him. I also send you a ball which may be dangerous, to give you an idea of our playthings," he teased.[21]

The horrible attributes of a field of battle did not damper the major's desire for either the war or his enthusiams for meeting the enemy in combat. His confidence was growing and he appeared to be a quick study of the art of military science. "You no doubt wonder how I progress in military knowledge," he inquired in one letter home. "Somehow or another without much exertion on my part, I am acquiring a proficiency in military matters. I thought [this] was very doubtful when I accepted the appointment," he penned, revealing in the process a small streak of early self-doubt. "It may come through the pores of the skin, at any rate [I] am acquiring the habit and knowledge to converse without very much exertion on my part."[22]

The time spent around Manassas gave Grimes the opportunity to take the measure of the men of the regiment and the officers that led them. "Our officers are all pleasant and agreeable companions, sociable and gentlemanly," he noted. "Lt. Col. Young, Dr. King, myself form our mess." Young, who was second in command of the regiment when it was formed, soon transferred to Richmond to help in the manufacturing of clothing for the army.[23]

As Grimes and thousands of other young soldiers soon discovered, soldiering was largely a routine built around camp life. "The duties are onerous," he explained. "Think of being aroused by the drum at 4 a.m. and on my horse before 5 o'clock. Return at 61/2, again at 81/2 to 1 p.m., again from 4 p.m. to 6, and then wind up the day by dress parade, with general supervisory duties to perform during the intervals." In an attempt at humor he wrote that he saw a soldier "with his dormitory and kitchen on his back," a tongue-in-cheek reference to the man's blanket and frying pan. One small break in the monotony occurred when General Beauregard "came down to view the Regiment when I had them." Rumors circulated about the regiment's status. "It is said (but not officially) that our Regiment is attached to Gen. Beauregard's reserves and bodyguards," wrote Grimes, although he could not vouch for the accuracy of the gossip. "Our movements here are uncertain. We hold ourselves ready to move at an hour's notice."[24]

As is often the case when men were away at the front for long periods of time, events occur on the homefront that can only be dealt with via correspondence. Such was the case when Grimes learned of the death of his deceased wife's sister. "I have been extremely pained to learn of the sudden death of my sister-in-law, Lucy Davis," he wrote William, "which no doubt you have heard before this. It makes Bettie's [his young daughter] position there very doubtful for upon Lucy's good judgment, I asked from her proper guidance. I have written to Dr. Davis to send her to Arch Williams to go to school until they hear further from me."[25] Similar personal family tragedies would impact Grimes throughout the war. He handled each of them in an attentive and caring way, revealing much about his character in the process. Despite the difficult tasks he faced as both a soldier and commander, his letters reveal an overriding concern for his family, in particular his young daughter, Bettie.

The weeks and months fell away as the men of the 4th North Carolina continued drilling and learning the ways of military life. The summer soon melded into fall, and by early October the men began to suspect that they might be going into battle soon. "I hope to God I may come out all right, and think I shall for I now begin to feel confidence in my ability to manage the Regiment," Grimes penned his brother. The young major was growing accustomed to the life of a soldier, observing in the same letter that "It is a study I am becoming partial to and if I had not been sick I should have been much better prepared than I am. Dysentery has played the wild with me, but I believe I am slowly improving." Although he had managed to escape the grip of disease with little suffering beyond a temporary setback in his military skills, dozens of others were not nearly so lucky. "We have had a great deal of sickness and lost about 70 men," lamented Grimes. "Col. [William W.] Kirkland's Regiment [21st North Carolina] has lost about 200 out of 1300 and has not more than 100 efficient men," an insightful observation of just how badly early-war regiments were devastated by illness.[26]

Although the men did not experience battle that fall, another disagreeable task befell Grimes, that of serving on a courts martial board. "For a fortnight I have been on a court martial," he wrote in a letter to his cousin Mollie. "All are minor cases, but when it involves the life of the accused, it becomes a very serious duty, one from which most of us would prefer being excused. Pronouncing a sentence of death upon a soldier for offending in what at home we would consider praiseworthy is rather trying to a man's sensibilities."[27]

The constant drilling, drudgery of camp life and stress of serving on the court's martial board—coupled with the constant (and false) rumors of impending battle—began to frustrate Grimes. In November of the war's first year, he wrote William that "It will be useless for me to express an opinion relative to the prospects for an engagement to take place shortly for I have been anticipating, wishing and predicting a fight for so long that my patience has been completely exhausted." Nothing but a battle would satisfy the major. "I shall not rest quietly until I hear the long roll beat. Rumors are now that an engagement will take place within ten days and all hopes for winter quarters, north of the Potomac will have vanished." Grimes' view of how to treat the enemy, as demonstrated by uncharacteristically harsh rhetoric, was unequivocal: "If my wishes could be consulted and followed I should say, raise the black flag and give no quarter to invading foes." Clearly the aftermath of the fighting at Manassas had deeply affected the young officer. "If only you could visit our hospitals you would feel in all its horror the bitter cost of war. And if one drop of the milk of human kindness toward them weren't permitted to exhibit itself, you couldn't be a true Southern man at heart."[28]

Reflecting on this change in his attitude since coming face-to-face with the human side of war, he wrote:

> I did not love them [Confederate soldiers] when I left home and loved them less when my bowels were operating twenty times a day. When I hear the dead march played in escorting some poor fellow Southerner to his last home, I feel more venom in my heart that I thought possible. We have buried fifty men from my regiment. All strong, hearty, athletic men when they left home. You would be astonished to see how little sympathy exists among the men for each other.[29]

Revealing his growing attitude toward the necessity of stern military discipline and the unwavering belief that orders must be obeyed, Grimes commented, "I see by the papers yesterday that Col. Singletary has been arrested by orders of Gen. Hill. He has not learned the first and most important duty of a soldier, obedience to orders of superior officers."[30]

This last statement provides an important insight into Bryan Grimes. As a commanding officer he expected unquestioning military obedience from his subordinates, which is what he in turn offered his superior officers. As a result, the issue of insubordination soon reared its ugly head in the 4th North Carolina, and Grimes was directly in the center of the controversy.

The incident, an exchange of words between Company E's Capt. Thomas M. Blount, and Grimes, took place on November 19, 1861. According to Grimes, the exchange was uttered in the presence of several privates, thus setting an example of insubordination. Grimes called Blount into his tent for the purpose of giving him an opportunity to explain himself and reflect upon his conduct, asking the captain to repeat what he had said. Apparently Blount repeated his utterance in a manner even more insulting in tone (and perhaps substance) than before. Unwilling to tolerate insubordination of any kind, Grimes placed Blount under arrest and filed formal charges against him. The written charges were forwarded to headquarters and accused the captain of conduct prejudicial to good order and military discipline.[31]

In Specification 1, Grimes charged:

> That Capt. Thomas M. Blount, Quartermaster, upon being ordered to report five wagons to the Officer of the Day and being specified a particular wagoner to report to him did permit and sanction the ordering of said Wagoneer to start off on a private mission, when he [Blount] had been informed that the men would suffer that night for wood.

Specification Number 2 charged that:

> Capt. Blount upon being addressed by the Commanding Officer of the Regiment, [Grimes] answered in a very abrupt and unbecoming manner, without stopping nor turning his head towards his commanding officer, who addressed him, but continued his walk as if having addressed an inferior—intending disrespect to said officer.

The final specification of the three-counts read as follows:

> Blount did upon being requested by his commanding officer to be more respectful, replied, and "I will thank you to be more respectful when you address me," in a very angry tone and offensive manner. Upon being asked,

what did you say? replied, "I will thank you to be more respectful when you address me if you are my superior officer.[32]

Like many young Confederate soldiers, Blount was not used to military life or its demanding rules and orders—especially orders delivered by other young men near his own age and social standing, men who would in other circumstances be regarded as his peers. Blount had only been in the army about six months when Grimes brought the charges against him. It is probable that Grimes' service on several courts martial panels instilled in him a clear sense of the absolute necessity of obeying military commands at all times, as well as the importance of rank within the military hierarchy. In addition, the regiment had been under the command of West Point graduate Col. George B. Anderson, who had imbued its senior officers with the importance of conventional codes of military discipline. Thus two hot-tempered young officers, both new to military life and its unique set of demands, clashed within the system both were forced to operate within.

It did not take long for the situation to deteriorate further. On the following day, November 20, Blount formally escalated the tension between the two when he wrote Grimes the following note:

I understand that in narrating the occurrence of the afternoon of the 19th (November) which led to my arrest, you made use of the following or expressed, "had I (you) not been bound up by the position I (you) held in the Army, I (you) would have taken up something and given him (me) such a frailing (or wacking?) as he (I) would have remembered for a long while!" An immediate resignation of our respective commissions will afford you an equality of positions and an opportunity of openly inflicting the above or any other form of chastisement you may desire![33]

Blount, in no uncertain terms, was challenging his superior officer to a duel. It would be more than a month before Grimes even saw the note, and other events during that time served to provide a context which likely influenced Grimes' reaction to Blount.

As the case with Blount aptly demonstrates, the implementation of discipline was a problem, especially for commanders who had to struggle against the reluctance of many to adapt to military life. Grimes' discipline problems, however, were not limited to Blount. Before long another officer of the regiment, Capt. David Miller Carter of Company E (which, coincidently, was Blount's company as well), ran afoul of Grimes' strict adherence to military protocol. The day after Blount penned his challenge to Grimes, Carter received a written inquiry from Grimes via Lt. Thomas L. Perry, the 4th North Carolina's adjutant: "Maj. Grimes directs me to require of you in writing why you were not at Batallion drill this afternoon." Carter's rather tart reply the following day did not sit well with Grimes. "The purpose of my absence from camp on the occurrence referred to," he retorted, "was duly explained by me in writing on the slate in your office, and that I had received no notice official or otherwise of an instruction to resume the drills which had been suspended for several days—previously to leaving camp." It is unknown whether Grimes had been informed of the message on the slate board or whether indeed the message had in fact been left as Carter claimed.[34]

Not satisfied with Carter's response, on November 22 Grimes sent another inquisitive missive to Carter via Perry: "I have been directed by Maj. Grimes to request of you your reason (in writing) for absenting yourself from Company drill this morning." Carter replied the following day to Perry. "I was absent from company drill yesterday morning [as I was] engaged in constructing a fireplace and chimney to my tent." To Grimes, such an admission was tantamount to blashphemy. Carter did not seem to consider drilling particularly important and did not take orders relating to such matters seriously.[35]

While Carter's rather flippant response angered Grimes—who was also serving as the regiment's temporary commander—he saw a deeper motive behind Carter's insubordination: a connection to the brewing controversy between he and Blount. " I am having some trouble with Captain Carter," Grimes wrote to brother William on November 24, "but I only have to give him rope enough and he will hang himself. Blount I have had placed under arrest and if he does not apologize I intend having him court martialed."[36]

Five days later Carter replied to a note from Perry regarding his absence from duty. Carter claimed he had been granted a leave of absence by Company K's Capt. F. M. McNeely, "commander of the Regiment," and that he had written the explanation on the slate in Perry's office. The record is unclear when or why McNeely was in command of the 4th North Carolina or why Carter was given a leave of absence. It is possible that Grimes, who had requested a leave himself to tend to his daughter following the death of his sister-in-law, had left for North Carolina by this time.[37]

Meanwhile, the thorny issue of Blount continued to fester. On November 28 the arrested officer wrote the assistant adjunct of the army complaining that he had been arrested on November 19 and had remained in confinement without being notified of the charges against him. Blount closed his request by asking for "a speedy trial." Learning of Blount's reach up the army chain of command, Col. George Anderson directed Grimes to give Blount the information he asked for, adding, "At the same time I regard it as quite useless to ask so soon for a speedy trial as the presumption is that the matter will be disposed of as soon as the interests of the service will allow."[38]

At this time Grimes was far away to the south in Raleigh, attending to family matters concerning the care of Bettie, his young 8-year-old daughter. While still in the Tar Heel capital he received a January 10, 1862, telegram directing him to return to Virginia as soon as possible because his "service may be needed." When he returned four days later he found the note from Blount dated November 20, 1861, in which he had suggested both he and Grimes resign their commissions so they could be free to pursue their differences unrestrained from military law. With his fighting blood aroused, Grimes responded directly to Blount's challenge by demanding to know his intentions. "In case of our mutual resignations or otherwise removal of legal obstacles to demand of me the satisfaction usual among gentlemen; if so, you can be accommodated." Grimes made sure his response was clear and that Blount understood that he was prepared to fight him. The direct response to the challenge was typical of the man and reflected the character and fighting spirit Grimes exhibited throughout the Civil War.[39]

In this same reply to Blount, Grimes—suspecting the role Capt. Carter played in this affair—stated, "I make this inquiry in this form for the reason that Capt. Carter, the bearer of your note, [is] not to be authorized to inform me upon this point." Grimes was attempting to remove Captain Carter from the communication chain since he believed that Carter had advised and perhaps was even encouraging Blount to press the issue with Grimes.[40]

Blount received Grimes reply on the morning of January 14 and responded that very afternoon:

If I am to understand this that you decline to execute your threat when I give the opportunity you wished, then I have to say that such is my intention—to demand of you an apology for the utterance of this threat against me, and in default of this apology, demand satisfaction for this insult and other injuries I have received from you. Therefore, if you will say that you do not intend to carry out your threat and that you will grant my demand for satisfaction, I will send you another note immediately on receiving such information.

P.S. This will be handed to you by my friend, Capt. Carter.[41]

Blount's two rather obvious points were clear: he was demanding satisfaction for the insult he believed he had suffered, and he purposely ignored Grimes' request to keep Carter out of it and, in fact, had his reply delivered by Carter with a post script to underscore his point. Blount had inserted the tip of the blade and then twisted the knife.

"I have simply to say that I [believe] my first note sufficiently explicit," was how Grimes responded on January 16. The war of words continued to escalate when Grimes received a reply that same evening: "I demand of you a retraction of the insulting threat you made against me, quoted in a former note, and an apology for the same or the satisfaction usual among gentlemen."[42]

Unwilling to yield, Grimes replied, "Your note of this evening having in effect answered my first note to you, [when he had queried Blount as to what his intentions were] I will immediately tender my resignation. When it is accepted will promptly notify you of the fact."[43] His anger aroused and honor attacked, Grime wrote his resignation that same evening to Asst. Adj. Col. Thomas Jordan. "I have the honor most respectfully to request the acceptance of the resignation of my command as Major of the 4th N.C. State Troops to take effect immediately."[44]

The escalating exchange of vitriolic letter writing continued unabated. Around 11:00 p.m. that night Blount sarcastically responded to Grimes first note of that day: "Your note—I do not deem it sufficiently explicit," wrote Blount. "I demand to know distinctly whether my call upon you for a retraction of your language and an apology for it, or in default of these, the satisfaction usual among gentlemen, will be granted by you."[45]

Predictably, Grimes wasted no time replying. "Your note of last night was handed to me this morning by Capt. Carter," he penned on January 17.

"The tender of my resignation sufficiently indicates my course of action." It is interesting to note that Blount was still using Carter as his courier.[46]

That same day Grimes learned that his resignation would not be accepted until it was forwarded to headquarters for approval. Lt. Col. John A. Young asked Grimes to do nothing until such word arrived. Ever the obliging soldier, Grimes informed Young that he would resist acting. "I pledge you my word as a gentlemen that the difficulty existing between myself and Capt. Blount shall not on my part be prosecuted while restrained by my present military position."[47]

The situation with Blount troubled Grimes more than he admitted publically. The same day he tendered his resignation he posted a letter to his brother. "I need both advice and friendship from any military man who is cognizant of the fact of a challenge or duel pending," he wrote. "Will he be dismissed form the Army? I am in doubt as to how to act and wish some friend in whom to confide and consult with." Fearing the worse, Grimes sought his brother's personal assistance. "If possible I should like for you to pay me a visit at this time. Please mention the fact to either Satterthwaite or Singletary and procure their services in case it results in a hostile meeting." "Guns with buckshot" was Grimes' personal choice of weapons. "I will write you again on this point and if I conclude to risk military law will telegraph you. I wish to God it was Carter instead of Blount, the satisfaction would be heartfelt." Grimes' letter reveals much about both his confusion surrounding the legal consequences of his possible actions as well as his strong dislike for Carter.[48]

A new wrinkle in the hostile affair took place the following day when Lt. Col. Young made a determined effort to quash the dissension among the regiment's officers. Young pledged to have them each "Court Martialed if we did not promise to put an end to this difficulty and sign an agreement drawn up by him," Grimes wrote William, "and at the same time inform[ed] us that our resignations had not been forwarded to Headquarters."[49]

Young's intervention was successful. The matter was "settled" for the present, explained Grimes, but his distrust of Captain Carter continued to burn within him. "I wish to God I could have a fair chance at him," Grimes wrote in a letter home. "I will forward you a copy of the correspondence and the whole transaction so that you can judge how I came out of the difficulty."[50]

Perhaps fearing the worst, on January 21 William wired his younger brother a telegram: "Let me hear from you. Satterthwaite and I will join you if necessary. Do not make it necessary." Although he agreed to come to Grimes' aid, William was trying to cool his hot tempered brother and avoid the duel.

A calmer Grimes wrote back three days later that his resignation had gone to Headquarters "and [I] have not the least idea under the circumstances that it will be accepted and have concluded to postpone the matter until some more fitting time."[51] General Beauregard, however, refused to accept the resignation, and there the matter stood. "I have heard nothing from the other parties," Grimes wrote William on February 2, "and suppose I shall not until Carter returns to urge it on."[52]

In fact Grimes "heard nothing" more on the subject and Blount was released and returned to military duty. The obstreperous captain does not again appear in Grimes' letters until shortly after the Battle of Seven Pines, which was fought on May 31–June 1, 1862. "Captain Blount after the battle asked to make up old differences to which I consented." Grimes would later inform his brother.[53]

There was but little time left to soothe ruffled emotions, though, for Thomas M. Blount was killed at Gaines' Mill on June 27, 1862. It is unknown whether the scar between he and Grimes healed without hard feelings. Even Capt. David Carter ceased to be a thorn in the side of Grimes, for he would be wounded in the Seven Pines fighting seriously enough to cause him to resign his commission in December of 1862.[54]

Thus after only some six months of service the young major had been forced to deal with a serious insubordination episode. The manner in which he handled this difficult situation reveals something of the intrepid character of the young officer, a trait that would emerge with greater clarity in the coming months.

While the Blount-Carter controversy simmered during the fall of 1861, another issue of regimental leadership had to be dealt with. The promotion of Colonel Anderson to brigadier general left a void at the top of the regiment, and the issue of who would fill it caused some concern amongst its members. "Col. Anderson has been Brigadiered," Grimes penned to William, "and I learn that a civilian, Rodman, for instance is to be his successor which by no measure of means comports with our idea of what is our due in the matter." To Grimes the solution was a simple one: appoint someone from within the ranks of the unit. "After having suffered camp diseases and exposure and taken the brunt, we can see no justice in others being placed over our heads in our regiment. Particularly, when we know that we are fully competent to the task of taking charge of our regiment."[55]

Although he offered a suggestion as to what should be done—and what he and Lieutenant Colonel Young were prepared to do should the decision go against them—Grimes' motives may have been induced by the possibility of personal advancement:

> [Please] press upon Governor Clark our desires upon the position. Col. Young, now Lt. Col. Young, is entitled to the colonelcy, and I think I am sufficiently qualified to fill with credit to myself [and] safely to the service, the post of Lieutenant Colonel. At any rate, if the authorities put an outsider over our heads, we both intend resigning which is very far from our wish. Influences, combined with the justice of the request, may secure the appointment.[56]

Grimes' agitation over the issue was for naught, however, for Anderson was not promoted until June 1862. Nevertheless, Grimes received some satisfaction when a letter arrived from Pulaski Cowper, an aide to North Carolina's governor and Grimes' brother-in-law, claiming that the governor was inclined to promote officers from within the ranks. Rodman, wrote Cowper on behalf of the governor, was not qualified "mentally or physically" for the position. "I don't think you need give yourself any uneasiness about the matter."[57]

The months of service in 1861 and early 1862 proved to be a period of rapid and sharp transformation for Grimes. The North Carolina civilian, with no formal military training and certainly no awareness of what constituted a good military officer, had evolved into an apprentice soldier with the rank of major with more than a rudimentary understanding of an officer's role. He learned quickly under Col. George Anderson's mentoring. Indeed, with hindsight it is evident that the type of officer he would ultimately become was already beginning to emerge: stern but capable, one that demonstrated leadership by example and followed a strict allegiance to duty, supported by personal courage.

# Yorktown and Seven Pines

## "Forward! Forward!"

The 4th North Carolina remained at Manassas Junction throughout the first winter of the war. Important events, however, including a massive Federal amphibious thrust up the Virginia peninsula, spelled the end of the Confederate occupation of Manassas. Orders arrived on March 8, 1862, to break camp and evacuate the vicinity, and after a march of several days, the regiment was halted at Clark's Mountain, near Orange Court House, about three miles from the Rapidan River. There it remained with a large segment of Joe Johnston's army until April 8, when it was ordered to continue its journey to Yorktown, a strategically important point on the tip of the peninsula formed by the York and James rivers. The months of drilling and instruction at Manassas had instilled in the regiment a feeling of pride and accomplishment. As Capt Edwin A. Osborne of Company H later wrote, the Carolinians left the plains of north central Virginia "with the bearing and spirit of regular troops." Only time would tell whether that "bearing" would hold up on the field of battle.[1]

Prior to the transfer—and after the distracting Blount-Carter fiasco—Grimes had taken the opportunity to write Bettie, his daughter, several warm and informative letters. The correspondence showed Grimes to be a loving and protective father. His close relationship with his daughter would continue to manifest itself in this manner throughout the long years of war. "My Dear Little Darling," he began in February 1862, "Are you so taken with city life that you have forgotten me? And with such a nice new writing desk, I would think you would wish to write most all the time," he softly chided. Grimes had sent his daughter to live with her uncle William and his wife, Bettie, in Raleigh, where he had bought her a writing desk while getting her settled into "city life." He continued by showing concern about her dental health, writing words that he might well have spoken had he enjoyed the luxury of holding his child in his lap. "Do not fail to have those old snaggle teeth pulled out so good ones can come in their place. I neglected to buy you a tooth brush after you lost yours, [so] ask Aunt Bettie to buy one for you and brush your teeth every morning." Behave yourself "prettily," he added, "and when you see a nice pretty lady that you want me to marry, tell her so and write me about who it is."[2]

Other family-related matters in addition to his daughter's welfare concerned the young officer during this period. Now that he had fully recovered from his prior illness, the idleness of camp life grew more irksome as the days passed. "How provoking to be forced here idle and inactive when our services are so much needed at home," he lamented. Apparently William deemed it possible that some of Bryan's slaves would attempt a break for freedom. "You inquire which of my Negroes would be most likely to run away. Shannon, Aaron, Richmond, Edmund, Elliott, George and Romeo in that order," he answered, "and perhaps Anthony and Mack might be induced to leave. Is Faithful still in the neighborhood? There is danger to my property and [much] to be feared from him."[3]

Soon after Col. George Anderson's Manassas garrison command arrived at its destination on the Virginia peninsula, its command structure and make-up were rearranged. The 49th Virginia, the 27th and 28th Georgia, and the 4th North Carolina were pulled together into a brigade and placed under the command of Brig. Gen. Winfield Scott Featherston. A stranger to the North Carolinians, Featherston was a native of Tennessee and resident of Mississippi. He had carved out a respectable political and legal career in the Magnolia State. Whether he was capable of handling a combat brigade remained to be seen. Featherston's promotion to brigadier general resulted in Anderson's resumption of command of the 4th North Carolina, although it appears that for a time Major Grimes temporarily led the unit during this period. The brigade was assigned to Maj. Gen. Daniel H. Hill's Division.[4]

With the regiment camped near the Rapidan River, Grimes provided a realistic glimpse of the difficulties of campaigning in the field. "Very few tents were moved with the army and for the first eight nights my best covering has been a few branches of pine thrown up to cover myself from the rain," he wrote William. "Last night for the first time, I procured a couple of planks and thought myself particularly fortunate." The movement heralded the start of the campaigning season, and Grimes knew it. "I now begin to experience the rougher phases of soldier life," he wrote, "but which has the effect of making me more desirous of encountering the d——Yan-kees." Despite these hardships, Grimes vowed he would "never complain no matter what deprivation I may have to endure for since I have embarked on this course, my whole heart and soul is in its final success which from the present aspect of affairs, appears gloomy at present."[5]

And indeed, Grimes had reason to be concerned. The war since the Southern victory at Manassas had not been going well for the Confederacy. Two critical back-to-back defeats in Tennessee at Forts Henry and Donelson in February 1862 had opened a pair of important rivers into the Confederate heartland and disrupted the entire Southern defensive strategy west of the Appalachian Mountains. While authorities in Richmond were still scram-bling to repair the  damage, another crippling blow was dealt the South at Shiloh. Despite the delivery of a devastating surprise attack by Gen. Albert S. Johnston's Confederates on April 6, Federal Maj. Gen. U. S. Grant's army survived the daylong onslaught and drove the Southerners from the field on April 7. Johnston's death the first day made the lost that much more costly for the South. Another critical loss was sustained less than three weeks later when New Orleans surrendered to Admiral David Farraugut.

As the Confederacy was being chipped away in the west, Federal Maj. Gen. George B. McClellan was gathering, equipping and training an army of over 100,000 soldiers to land at Fort Monroe, on the tip of the Virginia peninsula near Yorktown. McClellan hoped to move quickly, capture the historic city and drive on Richmond before Joe Johnston's army in northern Virginia could appreciate and respond to the threat. The Federal army began pouring ashore on March 17 and arrived before Yorktown's circle of en-trenchments on April 5.

To defend against this massive invasion, at least initially, the Southern-ers pinned their hopes on the several thousand men led by Maj. Gen. John Bankhead Magruder, whose defensive line stretched from Yorktown across the peninsula behind the Warwick River toward the James River. Magruder played a bold game of bluff by marching his men back and forth to create the illusion of strength. His charade, coupled with a stout string of earth-works and a trickle of reinforcements, conspired with the geography and poor weather to cool McClellan's ardor for a fast thrust up the peninsula. In addition, the Warwick, contrary to McClellan's information, was a formida-ble stream, and the Federal navy was unable to proceed up the James River beyond the Southern right flank because of the dominating presence of the ironclad *CSS Virginia*. On April 6, several brisk skirmishes flared along the lines as Federal probing actions felt the defenses in search of weaknesses. The unexpected defense of the lower peninsula, coupled with the heavy rains, convinced the Federal commander that the line could not be broken by direct assault.[6]

While advance elements from Johnston's army began to arrive at York-town on April 7, Grimes' regiment did reach the front until three days later. The North Carolinians filed into the trenches near the York River—described by one astute observer as "mere ditches with dirt thrown out in front"—on the left flank of the long and meandering Confederate line. "Here for the first time, I became acquainted with the fire of the enemy, and was assigned the post of commander of the picket line," Grimes wrote. "I was appointed officer of the day and had to go out picketing and give the yankees a chance to plant a minie ball in some indigestible spot."

McClellan's reliance on siege tactics created a tense atmosphere for those stationed near the front, and the steady shelling and zipping minie balls took a toll on the psyches of the soldiers defending Yorktown. "What will you think when I tell you that only one night since the 8th day of March have I taken off any of my clothing to go to sleep," Grimes rhetorically asked Bettie in a letter dated April 18, "and that now I sleep with boots and half the time with sword and pistol attached to my person to be prepared to meet the foe at any minute." He also described for his daughter in some detail the more unpleasant aspects of war. The Yankees were close by, "within one half mile and shooting at us upon all occasion whenever we show ourselves," he wrote. "Not since my arrival here on the 10th of April has there been two consecutive hours without their firing into our camp and sometimes at the rate of fifty shells a minute. But Sunday night at about 2 oclock we all thought the battle was opened, such a hail storm of iron and lead I had never conceived of." No doubt reflecting the thoughts of other comrades similarly seeking shelter behind their breastworks, Grimes observed that "Every man in less than five minutes was at his post behind the breastworks that serve not only to shoot from, but to prevent the shots of the enemy from hitting us. Our poor men were nearly worked to death to erect them, but it will be their preservation, if they stand." The artillery shells impressed Grimes. "If you wish to imagine how a bomb or shot sounds as it comes whizzing through the air, get Spilman to make you a Whirl-a-Gig that children often play with, and whirl it around a few times and the noise that it makes somewhat resembles the sound, except that you can hear the ball that is the larger one [from] a half mile [away] and have to drop behind the breastworks for protection."[7]

The ongoing quasi-siege and shelling dampened Grimes' inexperienced fervor for battle. "Not since the commencement of hostilities, have I felt so despondent as at present," he confessed to his brother William. "Everything assumes a somber hue and war in all its horrors and realities begin to present themselves to me, and the number of large bombs that are now fired at us does not at all alter the sensation." The 4th North Carolina's exposed position near the York River, which was completely dominated by the Federal navy, allowed enemy gunboats to add their metal to the land based artillery firing from the east. The effect of this gunfire was very disheartening. "A gun boat is lying off in the stream and firing 18 lb. bombs at us every two minutes, and two have fallen within sixty yards of where I am now writing, but I have schooled myself to think one position is as safe as another." Indeed, he described his regiment's predicament as "most critical, perhaps more so than of any other hereabouts, being subjected to fire from the left flank, (that is the river) as well as from the front." The enemy in front of us "we do not fear," he told William, "but the river bombardment is dreaded by us." The gunboats, concluded Grimes, "force an enfilading fire upon us from the effects of which we can neither defend ourselves [and] is rather calculated to demoralize our troops." As if to prove his last point, Grimes concluded his letter to William with an up-to-the-minute observation: "a 18 pounder fell in a tent not 75 yards from this spot a moment ago in which a sick man was lying and completely buried him."[8]

Private James C. Steele, a member of the 4th North Carolina's regimental band, also remembered the large shells that streaked with some regularity toward their position. The musician stood on the breastworks and "timed the 8x19 shells which usually went over our heads." Writing long after the war, Steele recalled that the boats were "four miles down the [York] river and from the time we would see the flash until we could hear the shell was twenty-two seconds."[9]

While exposure to the shelling was bad enough, the 4th North Carolina's location in the lengthy line, which faced southeast below Yorktown, was also cause for concern. As Grimes some came to realize, "Our position is just outside the fortification of the tavern and in case of the defeat of our army, those of us that are situated upon the left wing, will necessarily fall into the hands of the enemy because the road by which we will have to make our retreat, is much nearer to the Yankees than to us."[10]

The steady siege-like situation continued unabated for some time, and the mood in camp became more somber as the shelling continued. "[We] begin to hear a gloomy aspect, but of the final success of our course, I have not the least doubt, if the people will only be true to themselves, though many a poor fellow will bite the dust in the achievement of our independence." The waiting made the men restless and rumors of imminent battle spread quickly through the ranks. "Gen. Hill's opinion is that tomorrow the fight will commence," Grimes wrote William on the 27th of April. "Our force is estimated by those who have an opportunity of knowing, at about fifty thousand men while that of the enemy is supposed to be fully two hundred thousand and well entrenched behind breastworks which if we were to repulse them would have to be stormed and taken before we could claim a victory."[11]

For Grimes and members of the 4th, picket duty and the attendant sharpshooting brought about by the close proximity of the opposing lines, had become a way of life. "Our pickets are shooting at each other most of the time and occasionally wound each other," he noted. In a letter to his daughter he reiterated the dangers of the picket line, noting that he often visited the front, although "very few officers do so, as it is exceedingly dangerous in the daytime to move about." His presence attracted serious attention, for he was "shot at by the sharpshooters of the enemy at least forty times in my rounds and some of the balls, I feel confident, did not miss my head by more than three inches. I had five men wounded by them, some of them seriously." Grimes himself engaged in the deadly pastime. "I, while Officer of the Day, shot at them several times, but with what effect [I] cant say. Edward Porter Alexander, an artillerist with James Longstreet who would later rise to prominence within the army, wrote about the deadly exchange of rifle fire on the lower peninsula. "The sharpshooting between the two armies was exceedingly vicious wherever pickets or line could see each other. It was the first time they were ever located near enough to each other for this & both sides went at it with vim, and the artillery too often took part."[12]

Despite the danger, Grimes found humor in his precarious situation. "A rather amusing conversation took place across the lines a day or two since, " he informed his brother near the end of April. "Yankee says to one of our boys, 'do you have plenty to eat?' 'Yes.' Yankee says, 'Do you get any coffee?' 'Yes and sugar too.' Yankee says, 'What's that corporal and four men digging up sassafras for then?'" Grimes wryly added, "Being Southerners that question was unanswerable and rather insulting to a man who was drinking sassafras tea, which has been our beverage part of the time since our arrival here."[13]

Fortunately for Grimes, the sporadic pitched fighting that symbolized the drawn-out affair before Yorktown did not seriously involve the 4th North Carolina. In fact, the heaviest fighting of the siege took place on April 16 near the Warwick River at the opposite end of the line. There, at Dam Number 1 near Lee's Mill, William F. Smith's Federal division moved out with orders to stop the Confederates from strengthening their works. The tepid assault-style reconnaissance—McClellan admonished Smith to avoid a general engagement—resulted in little other than the waste of artillery ammunition and the killing and maiming of 165 Federals. Southern losses were negligible. The probing action, commented one Federal engaged in the fiasco, "took place at Dam No. 1. . .and was a Dam failure."[14]

By the time the April-long siege stretched into early May, Joe Johnston determined that he had squeezed as much benefit as possible by holding the line at Yorktown. McClellan had spent weeks emplacing heavy guns in order to pry the Rebels from their lines with a massive artillery and mortar bombardment. How much longer would it be before he opened fire? Johnston knew that when that day arrived his army could not stand long under such a barrage. In the hopes of finding a location from which to more favorably oppose McClellan, Johnston quietly slipped his divisions out of the line on the night of May 3 and marched them up the peninsula toward the Confederate capital. Although some criticized this withdrawal, he did not leave too soon. McClellan later reported that he was ready to open fire with his heavy artillery on May 6.

The retreat order that filtered down to the troops in the trenches included instructions for the 4th North Carolina and other regiments of D.H.

Hill's command to keep firing throughout the night and "retire about dawn." The evacuation was both arduous and dangerous. The heavy rains and hundreds of wagons had turned the roads over which the army marched into ribbons of mud, and "torpedoes had been planted on all the roads and streets leading into Yorktown."[15]

By the afternoon of May 4, much of the retreating army was camped near Williamsburg, a small hamlet about eleven miles northwest of Yorktown. Months earlier Maj. Gen. Magruder had erected a series of crude field works a couple miles east of the town, including a powerful earthwork near the center of the line named in his honor. James Longstreet's Division, which composed the rear guard of Johnston's army, filed into this line on the evening of May 4, while the balance of Johnston's force continued moving up the peninsula with the bulk of his slow-moving trains. Bryan Grimes held the picket line as directed and eventually caught up with his command late that afternoon near Williamsburg, where it had camped for the night. Early the next morning he asked for and received permission to visit William and Mary, the historic college in Williamsburg. Given the serious state of affairs, Grimes' request seems somewhat out of character. His visit, however, was abruptly terminated when an explosion of rifle and artillery fire broke out. "I followed the sounds of the strife until in the midst of the battle," he later wrote, "and never realized my danger until I saw several officers and couriers of General Johnston killed." Grimes may have come upon General Johnston at about time. According to a private in Company C, 4th North Carolina, the general said "Colonel Grimes, [turn] rightabout and we will go back and give them a little brush, and this was the first fight of the war for our Regiment."[16]

The fighting that Grimes heard began when the Federal vanguard of two divisions under Joseph Hooker and William F. Smith struck Longstreet's line. Hooker's initial attack was beaten back and Longstreet launched a counterattack with some success. By the time, however, Longstreet's left flank was seriously in danger of being crushed, and he sought assistance from D. H. Hill's Division in Williamsburg. Johnston himself rode upon the scene shortly thereafter. As elements of Hill's Division aligned themselves and moved out to engage the Federals, Grimes trotted into the area after his brief visit to William and Mary. Seeing the 4th North Carolina's regimental flag flying, he hurriedly rode up to join the unit. His horse carried him near the brigade commander, Col. George Anderson, who was guiding his regiments toward the action over difficult terrain. "I hope you have not required my services," Grimes stated. Anderson's terse reply carried a strong bite. "In the only severe and abrupt manner used towards me before or after," Grimes related with some candor, "I was informed that my conduct was unmilitary, and my proper position was with my regiment." Either Anderson forgot or he did not know that Grimes had been given permission to leave his regiment earlier that day.[17]

Grimes later recalled his ride through the town to rejoin the 4th Regiment when he described the scene in a letter to Bettie. ". . .what a spectacle presented itself to my sight," he exclaimed. "Wounded brought in by ambulances, some in wagons, others in blankets and litters, some in front of their friends on horses and one poor officer, I saw, brought in in the arms of his servant." The effect of the fighting on the area's civilians was not lost on the lieutenant colonel. "Women rush[ed] half frantic over the streets, children distracted and crying."[18]

As it turned out, Grimes' participation in the battle was negligible. The counterattack launched by Hill was delivered piecemeal and the fighting grew more confused and bloody as the hours wore on. Nightfall brought about an end to the brisk action without the 4th North Carolina firing a shot. The cost in killed and wounded was about 2,000 Federals and 1,600 Southerners. As far as rear-guard actions went, the fight at Williamsburg was a moderate Confederate success. It bloodied McClellan's vanguard and allowed Johnston to continue his retreat up the peninsula.

The march from the field was "one of the most disagreeable of my army experience," Grimes related. The weather had turned cold, "a heavy, penetrating mist, nearly freezing the men to the bone. . .all would huddle together for the natural warmth of their bodies, and when my horse became the centre for the regiment, around which they collected, the first few attracted by the animal heat from the horses body, until they formed a complete mass of men." The men "literally waded almost knee deep in mud," was how Grimes described the journey to his daughter Bettie. With their rations exhausted, "each man received an ear of hard corn for his supper."[19]

The skies cleared about midnight as the difficult trek continued toward Richmond. The weather on May 7 was substantially better, the warmth and sunshine cheering up somewhat the exhausted soldiers on both sides. After struggling for several days, the 4th North Carolina went into camp on May 13 near the Chickahominy River. The waterway was a slow moving swampy morass that ran north from the James River for some miles before meandering in a generally northwest direction toward Richmond. The river bisected the peninsula and was its dominant geographic feature below the Southern capital. Within three days Johnston had shifted his army south of the stream, which was also the last major natural obstacle before McClellan's army reached Richmond.

While Johnston's forces had been withdrawing up the narrow land neck, McClellan slowly followed, marching his large ponderous army up the same narrow quagmires that doubled for roads. Progress was slow as heavy rain continued to saturate the axle-deep mud. By May 21 Federal troops in a driving rainstorm began crossing to the south side of the Chickahominy. The movement continued the following day, although McClellan retained three of his corps north of the stream to both protect the Richmond and York River Railroad, a vital supply line that was used to feed and outfit his men. The force north of the Chickahominy also served to establish a link with a Federal force supposed to be moving in McClellan's direction from Fredericksburg. It was a potentially dangerous alignment, for McClellan had divided his army in the face of the enemy, leaving but two corps—the III under Samuel Heintzelman and the IV under Erasmus Keyes—below or south of the Chickahominy. Much as he had at Yorktown, McClellan's strategy to capture Richmond centered around his big siege guns, which he planned utilize in the reduction of the Confederate defenses.[20]

In Richmond, meanwhile, President Jefferson Davis was worried. The general of his leading field army had retreated to the very gates of the city without fighting a major battle, and the reticent officer was want to share his plans, if he had any, with anyone. At a meeting on May 15, Johnston informed Davis that he would have to rely on unforeseeable circumstances or Federal mistakes to seek an opportunity to strike a blow against McClellan. That opportunity arrived sooner than even Johnston expected. The steady rain was slowly spilling the Chickahominy River over its banks and effectively separating McClellan's army into two unequal segments. By the 22nd of the month, Confederate cavalry reported on the divided Army of the Potomac, presenting Johnston with a remarkable opportunity to destroy his enemy in detail.[21]

On the evening of May 30 McClellan's army, separated by a widening river and only six miles from Richmond, was dealt a severe blow without the firing of a shot. That Friday night a violent rain and thunderstorm saturated the region, transforming the normally sluggish Chickahominy into a rushing torrent of muddy water. Heintzelman and Keyes were now stranded below the stream, isolated from support because the raging water had either washed away the bridges or made them particularly unsafe for passage. To his credit Johnston seized the opportunity and devised a complicated plan of attack for the following day. The plan committed two-thirds of his army to the offensive, three separate commands ordered to attack from three separate directions on different roads. While it looked workable on a map table, it was a recipe for disaster for the green soldiers and officers who were called upon to execute it.[22]

The two Federal corps Johnston planned to fall upon had established a string of fortified positions near the vital road hub of Seven Pines. Others were thrown up at Fair Oaks, about one mile north of Seven Pines on the Richmond and York River Railroad. Johnston's plan called for James Longstreet, the commander of Johnston's "right wing," to attack the center and flank of Keyes' IV Corps, deployed between Seven Pines and Fair Oaks, while the left wing under Maj. Gen. Gustavus W. Smith was to supply troops as needed and prevent Federal reinforcements from crossing below the Chickahominy. The first prong of Longstreet's attack called for the divisions of Maj. Gen. William H. C. Whiting and John Magruder to march west along the Nine Mile Road and strike the Federals along their right flank. The offensive's pivotal role was delegated to Maj. Gen. Benjamin Huger's Division. Huger, whose earlier controversial performance in defense of Roanoke Island had created quite a controversy, was ordered to march his division down the Charles City Road southeast from Richmond to White's Tavern. There, Huger would turn north, deploy, and sweep through the woods, catching the Federals south of Seven Pines on their left flank and rear. Daniel Harvey Hill's Division, of which the 4th North Carolina was a component, was positioned a few miles east of Seven Pines on the Williamsburg Road. Hill's orders were simple: move his brigades east directly down the Williamsburg Road and attack once Huger's assault was underway. The chance for a successful attack deteriorated almost immediately when Johnston's aide, Lt. J. B. Washington, was captured by Federal pickets in a fruitless search for Longstreet. The Federals correctly guessed that if Johnston's staff officer was this close to the front, an attack was imminent.[23]

Although the battle was to have begun early on the morning of May 31, D. H. Hill sat with his division under arms from 8:00 a.m. to almost 1:00 p.m. without hearing a shot. Where was Huger? Unbeknownst to Hill, a dispute between Longstreet and Huger over seniority and marching routes (Johnston had foolishly relied on verbal rather than written orders) strangled the initial attack and delayed it for hours. Fearing that a further delay would doom the plan, Hill decided to attack anyway and ordered his men to advance against the Federals in their front.

Hill's divisional front that afternoon was divided by the Williamsburg Road. Deployed left of the road and in front was Samuel Garland's Brigade, which was supported by Winfield Featherston's Brigade about one-quarter of a mile in its rear. The right half of Hill's line was held by the brigades of Robert Rodes and Gabriel Rains.[24]

Since Featherston was absent with an undefined illness, the brigade marched into battle behind Garland about 1:30 p.m. that afternoon with Col. George B. Anderson in command. Lieutenant Colonel Bryan Grimes' 4th North Carolina held the brigade's right front and moved well in advance of its sister regiments. Grimes went into his first action as a major, although his May 31st promotion to lieutenant colonel was dated back to May 1. The other three regiments of the brigade, the 49th Virginia, 28th Georgia and 27th Georgia extending the line to the left. The movement forward was executed with some dash, reported Anderson, even though "the whole advance. . .[was] over ground exceedingly boggy and much of it covered with a very thick growth of trees." Grimes' assessment of the terrain was even more graphic. "The woods were very thick and water deep in ponds from recent rains, in places waist deep." The green regiment, about to encounter the enemy in a pitched fight for the first time, "was in fine condition," reminisced one of its officers after the war. "[Its] twenty five commissioned officers and five hundred twenty men and non-commissioned officers. . .presented a splendid picture of manhood, energy and courage."[25]

Within a short time this "splendid picture of manhood" began to suffer from the effects of an enfilading Federal fire "from a battery stationed on the road, concealed by the woods." Unbeknownst to Grimes, the artillery was positioned in a powerful redoubt behind a strong line of abatis held by Silas Casey's Federal division. In an attempt to shield his men from this fire, Grimes shifted his line to the left and continued advancing, "the enemy. . .playing on us with canister and shell." The heavy terrain and sharp fire "made it impossible to keep an accurate alignment," and Grimes halted his regiment inside the belt of timber to straighten its line before "uncovering my men." At the same time, remembered one of the regiment's officers, "heavy musketry on the right indicated that the battle was raging there with terrible fury."

The men of the 4th North Carolina were the first of Anderson's Brigade to come within sight of the artillery-studded Federal redoubt, about one-half mile to their right front. The earthwork, which stood out as the center strong point of Casey's front, was "supported by a mass of infantry" and flanked on both sides by extensive earthworks and protected in front felled trees. As soon as the North Carolinians stepped from the woods they were met by a withering fire of shot, shell, and canister, which tore through the trees and plowed up the ground around them. Grimes right-obliqued his regiment and made for the thundering guns, determined to capture the work and silence the battery. To his dismay, another section (two guns) of artillery opened on his line, "dealing destruction to my left wing, while my center and right wing were being mowed down by grape and canister from the redoubt." Even though the regiment began suffering heavy losses, "the men steadily advanced in admirable order."[26]

The North Carolinians had little opportunity to return the fire because of their difficulty in climbing over the abatis, which Grimes described as "thick and entangled." Passing through the obstruction was both arduous and dangerous, and casualties continued to reduce his numbers. By this time the enemy had abandoned the irksome section of guns which had been blasting away at the left front of Grimes' regiment, "and we then concentrated our whole attention to the redoubt." The terrain beyond the felled trees, a muddy plowed field "in which the men would mire ankle deep at every step," proved only marginally easier to pass over—and further exposed the troops to the enemy fire. Grimes' solitary regimental attack was finally joined by two other regiments, which began to emerge from the wooded obstructions on both sides of his advance. Seizing the moment—and still well in advance of his supports—Grimes ordered his North Carolinians forward. "I gave the

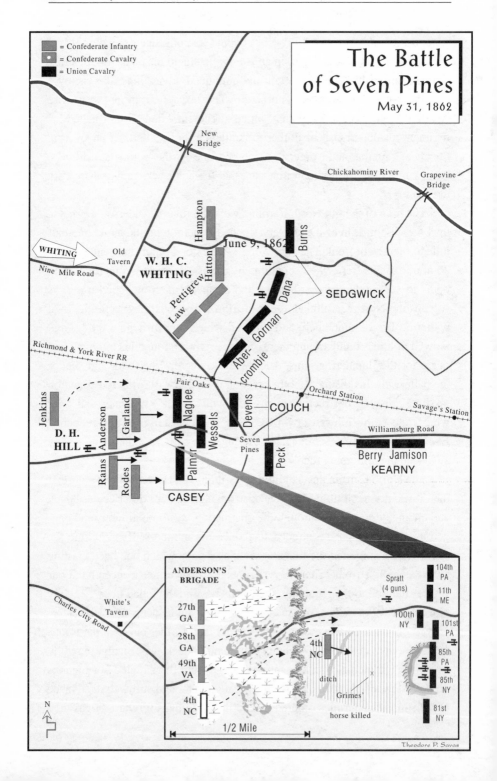

**The Battle of Seven Pines**
May 31, 1862

= Confederate Infantry
= Confederate Cavalry
= Union Cavalry

New Bridge

Chickahominy River

Grapevine Bridge

Hampton

Burns

WHITING

Old Tavern

W. H. C. WHITING

June 9, 1862

SEDGWICK

Nine Mile Road

Hatton

Pettigrew

Law

Dana

Gorman

Aber-crombie

Richmond & York River RR

Jenkins

Fair Oaks

Naglee

Devens

COUCH

Orchard Station

Savage's Station

D. H. HILL

Anderson

Garland

Wessels

Seven Pines

Williamsburg Road

Berry   Jamison

KEARNY

Rains

Rodes

Palmer

Peck

CASEY

Charles City Road

White's Tavern

ANDERSON'S BRIGADE

Spratt (4 guns)

104th PA

11th ME

27th GA

100th NY

101st PA

28th GA

4th NC

85th PA

49th VA

85th NY

ditch

Grimes'

4th NC

horse killed

81st NY

N

1/2 Mile

Theodore P. Savas

order to charge," he later remembered, "which was done by my men in gallant style." It was also the first time the men had a good opportunity to return the fire of the Federals, and they took up the task with great relish. "[We] opened fire upon the enemy with such deadly effect as to cause a momentary lull in the storm of deadly mssiles that were assailing us," remembered Captain Osborne of Company H, "but again the enemy renewed his fire with redoubled fury."[27]

In spite of the rain of lead and iron spraying about, the gray wave continued it advance, halting temporarily near a "zigzag fence to await support on the right, which had failed to come up." The position was an exposed one, however, and according to Captain Osborne, "it was evident that the regiment could not remain there without being utterly destroyed." Seeking a field officer, Osborne observed "Grimes. . .sitting calmly on his iron-gray horse, with one leg thrown over the saddle bow, as afterwards so often seen on the battlefield." According to Osborne's post-war account, he seized Grimes' leg and urged him to order a charge. "Charge them! Charge them!" Grimes' replied, his shouted words sending Osborne over the fence with sword in hand. The North Carolinians swept to within 100 yards of the flaming walls of the redoubt when both Grimes and his horse crashed to the ground, the latter killed by a Federal missile which tore off the animal's head. As Grimes later described the episode, his horse fell "so suddenly as to catch my foot and leg under him," pinning him beneath the dead beast. "The regiment seeing me fall," he remembered, "supposed I was killed or wounded, and began to falter and waver." Stuck fast "I. . .waved my sword and shouted Forward! Forward!" As the regiment swept by the prone officer, "some of my men came to my assistance and pulled the horse off."[28]

The uninjured and probably somewhat dazed commander now watched as the attack moved past him and crested about 30 or 40 yards from the front of the redoubt. Unable to advance further in the face of an intense fire and unsupported on either flank—"we were 200 yards in advance of any other regiment"—Grimes wisely ordered his men to fall back. The objective of his timely withdrawal was "a ditch midway between the redoubt and entangled woods." The Carolinians retired "in good order," but Grimes' directive was misconstrued by the regiment's colorbearer, who fell back all the way to the obstructions. The mistake probably incensed Grimes, who watched with no little dismay as the men in the ditch followed the flag to the rear. Retiring with them, Grimes ordered his entire line to lie down and hold their position, which was now about 250 yards from the smoke-filled Federal line. The brief attack before the redoubt had shredded the regiment, as Grimes grimly noted in his report of the battle: "As an evidence of the severity of the fire of the enemy while in front of the battery[,] 46 of my men were found killed within an area of one acre."[29]

The attack and repulse had almost completely enervated the 4th North Carolina. Colonel Anderson, who had spent most of his time behind the left-front of his brigade line, rode to the right at about this time and found Grimes' regiment "under fire, but completely exhausted and very badly cut to pieces." A battery of Southern artillery rode up and unlimbered nearby, adding its metal to the storm that had  engulfed the usually quiet Virginia countryside. The thundering guns may have helped steady Grimes' soldiers. "After allowing my men time to recover from their fatigue," Grimes recalled, he watched in dismay as his third color bearer was shot and killed. A dramatic moment on the field ensued when Captain A. K. Simonton of Company A raced Grimes for the fallen banner. "Captain Simonton and myself rushed to raise the colors," recalled Grimes in his report of the affair. "Captain Simonton, reaching them first, placed them in my hands, and I raising them aloft, called upon my men to rally around their standard." The height of the action was at hand for the North Carolinians, and they responded to the challenge "with alacrity." "On we rushed," wrote the regiment's historian, "with such impetuosity and determination that the enemy abandoned everything and retired." The 4th Regiment, "together with several other regiments. . .reached the redoubt, the enemy fleeing."[30]

After capturing the works, which contained six abandoned artillery pieces to boot, the North Carolinians withdrew a short distance back to the now-broken "zigzag" fence to regroup. The Federals, meanwhile, began to rally in the rear of their tents, about 300 yards to the left of the redoubt. "I saw two regiments of the enemy drawn up in line of battle, protected and partially concealed by woods," remembered Grimes. With Colonel Anderson nowhere to be found, Grimes made for Brig. Gen. Samuel Garland, whose brigade had gone into action ahead of Anderson's. When informed of the gathering enemy, Garland ordered Grimes to take possession of the woods and fire into them. "I faced my men to the left and double-quicked them through the open field to reach a cover of the same woods." By this time the regiment was but a shadow of its former strength. "It was appalling to see how much the line had been reduced in numbers," wrote one officer. "The heavy, compact, orderly line of half an hour previous was no scarcely more than a line of skirmishers." As he drove his men to the left, however, Grimes noticed Federal troops fleeing a breastworks on his right. Appreciating the protection the overturned dirt would offer his soldiers, Grimes ordered his men "to move by the right flank and get behind their breastworks, firing upon them during the while. . ." The North Carolinians continued to load and discharge their weapons into the enemy's ranks until Grimes spotted "a regiment of ours marching to the left to attack them." Fearful that his men would fire into their supports, Grimes ordered his troops to cease fire.[31]

Before long the 4th North Carolina was ordered forward to support other regiments. As its members advanced, two of the four officers "who had followed the flag through the day" were shot. Captain Simonton, who had earlier played an instrumental role in rallying the men, was killed instantly, while Capt. James H. Wood of Company B was seriously wounded. With darkness almost upon them, Colonel Anderson—who latter described the condition of his brigade at this time as "exhausted and cut up and to some extent scattered"—collected his bloodied regiments into a clearing near the Williamsburg Road. In an effort to determine the extent of his losses, Grimes ordered an on-the-spot head count which revealed only 54 men present for duty of the 678 he had carried into action. Thoroughly exhausted, Grimes' men stretched out on the ground, "surrounded. . .by dead and wounded men and animals, while the air was filled with cries and groans of the wounded and dying." Grimes himself "slept between General Garland and Colonel Anderson on one horse-blanket and covered by another. . . ."[32]

The bloody seesaw battle experienced by Grimes and the 4th North Carolina was repeated up and down the line that afternoon. In a little over two hours, D. H. Hill's Division had managed to capture the first line of the Federal defenses and bend back much of Keyes' IV Corps toward Fair Oaks. The piecemeal attacks, largely the result of difficult terrain and inexperienced officers, resulted in heavy Southern casualties. The near-rout suffered by Casey's Federal division, which had offered a spirited though short-lived defense of its front, was alleviated to a large degree when Samuel Heintzelman brought up his III Corps divisions and fed reinforcements into the fight. Heintzelman, too, felt the sting of Hill's attacks, although by that time much of their weight had been spent against the first line of works. Limited Federal counterattacks sealed some of the breaches and forced portions of Hill's line rearward. By 6:00 p.m. the serious fighting at Seven Pines had ended.[33]

The story to the north near Fair Oaks was also marked with delay and missed opportunities. By the time Longstreet managed to deliver his attacks, about 4:00 p.m., elements of the Federal II Corps under Edwin V. Sumner had managed to cross south of the Chickahominy and absorb the crippling blow intended to destroy Keyes' Corps. It was here, near Fair Oaks, that the most important result of the battle took place. In an effort to observe Longstreet's attack, General Johnston rode too near the front in the gathering twilight and was struck in the shoulder by a bullet. Within seconds an artillery shell exploded in front of him and whizzing pieces of shrapnel struck him in the chest and thigh, unseating him from his mount. The crippling wounds also unseated him from army command, for the injuries proved serious and kept him from the field for six months. Major General Gustavus Smith, who was about to provide ample evidence of his mental and physical unfitness for the top slot, temporarily succeeded Johnston. Smith ordered a resumption of the attacks at dawn the following day.[34]

Sunday, June 1 opened with the Anderson's Brigade in the rear and under arms. Somehow Grimes' managed to telegraph his brother William that he had passed through the first day's fight unscathed, losing only his horse in the process. A second message followed the next day in which he exhibited sadness at the carnage he had witnessed: "I now feel as if I was a part of them. You cannot image how painful and harrowing to a commanding officer's sensibilities to see his men fall. The flag was shot 32 times."

As Gen. Gustavus Smith had directed, the battle resumed on June 1. Longstreet opened the Southern assaults, which were delivered primarily between the Williamsburg Road and the railroad, with little result. Fresh Federal reinforcements and the heavy terrain quickly bogged down the attacks, which lacked the spirit of the previous day. Thankfully for the North Carolinians, the battle passed them by and they were not actively engaged.[35]

The Battle of Seven Pines-Fair Oaks witnessed the end of Johnston's tenure with the Army of Northern Virginia and the beginning of another that would last through Appomattox Courthouse. President Davis, who had

quickly grasped that General
Smith was not suited to command (and indeed, Smith
asked to be relieved), appointed his military advisor,

Gen. Robert E. Lee.
*Generals in Gray*

Gen. Robert E. Lee, com-
mander of the army on the afternoon of June 1, 1862. Lee
immediately ordered a general withdrawal to the original
position held by the army be-
fore the battle opened. Although Federal losses were heavy (around 5,000),
they had prevented the destruction of the pair of isolated corps and had
beaten back the Confederates, whose casualties exceeded 6,100. In addition
to General Johnston's wounding, Grimes' boyhood friend and Chapel Hill
classmate, Johnston Pettigrew, was wounded and captured by the enemy.
Although severely injured, Pettigrew survived and was later exchanged.[36]

Colonel George Anderson was duly impressed with both the performance of his brigade and the actions of his subordinates—especially the
young and previously untested Bryan Grimes. The freshly-minted lieutenant
colonel had displayed sustained courage under fire and capable leadership
qualities that marked him for higher command. According to Colonel Anderson,

> Maj.[sic] Grimes, commanding the Fourth North Carolina State Troops, led
> his regiment in the thickest of the fight. His horse was shot under him not
> more than 100 yards directly in front of the enemy's redoubt. After three
> color-bearers of his regiment had been killed he bore in his hands and
> brought out of action its tattered but honored flag.[37]

While it was common for a superior to extoll the virtues of subordinates in their after-action reports, Anderson's commentary was indeed deserved. In addition to generally handling his men well, Grimes had demonstrated a calmness under fire and an innate ability to grasp the ebb and flow of combat. Writing after the war, D. H. Hill, known more for his sharp tongue and salty opinions than his willingness to heap undeserved praise upon others, wrote that:

> Major Grimes showed in this, his first serious battle, those instinctive qualities of soldiership that led to his promotion through successive grades to major-general. He was endowed with a cool courage that even in the hurried fury of battle enabled him to see unperturbed and with an inflexible will that rendered instant decision and persistent action natural to him. His mind was disciplined by education and thought, and his disposition just, even to the point of severity. Naturally, then, with these qualities, he learned rapidly to become a soldier whom his men admired and on whom his official superiors leaned in confidence.[38]

The fighting of May 31 shattered the 4th North Carolina. According to Grimes' postwar account, the regiment entered the battle with 25 officers and 520 non-commissioned officers and men. Every officer except Grimes was killed or wounded, and the regiment suffered 462 killed and wounded—a staggering 89% of those engaged. Only six men were officially listed as missing. If Grimes' figures are accurate, the 4th North Carolina suffered the highest percentage loss in a single battle of any regiment in the war on either side. These staggering statistics earned the regiment the grim sobriquet "Bloody Fourth." Anderson's Brigade as a whole also suffered heavily, taking 1,865 bayonets in the fight and emerging with just 999.[39]

The Battle of Seven Pines–Fair Oaks was a valuable—and expensive—baptism of fire.

4

# The Seven Days Through Fredericksburg

## "I have no prospect for going home until this war concludes."

Grimes and the 4th North Carolina spent the several weeks following the costly battle of Seven Pines recovering and recruiting new soldiers. These weeks were filled with organizational concerns, as the army under Robert E. Lee underwent a number of command modifications. Largely as a result of the heroism and leadership skills he had demonstrated at Seven Pines, and because there was a vacancy at the regimental command level, Grimes was promoted to full colonel on June 19. His former regimental commander, George B. Anderson, had thirteen days earlier been promoted to brigadier general and given command of a newly-formed North Carolina brigade. In addition to Grimes' 4th Infantry, Anderson's Brigade also contained the 2nd, 14th and 30th regiments.[1]

On June 21, a frustrated Grimes wrote to his brother William about Capt. David M. Carter, the officer with whom he had quarreled during the fall of 1861. Carter, Grimes learned to his dismay, was to be promoted to lieutenant colonel. "I should like to prevent his appointment, and I learned that the officers intend petitioning to the appointing powers not to force him upon them," he wrote, requesting that William use his influence to "have Cowper mention privately to the Governor to try to stop it. His appointment would be very objectionable to the Regiment and I as well." Despite his best efforts, however, Grimes was unsuccessful in stopping Carter's promotion.[2]

The fighting at Seven Pines had not noticeably altered the strategic picture outside of Richmond. The wounding of Joe Johnston, however, turned the tide of the fighting in Virginia in favor of the Confederates with the elevation of Lee to the command of the army. As his men dug in east of Richmond, Lee sought to devise a means of wresting the initiative away from his opponent by taking the offensive. The Seven Pines fighting had caused McClellan to move the bulk of his army south of the Chickahominy River, leaving but a single corps under Fitz John Porter north of the stream. On June 12 Lee probed McClellan's right to determine its exact alignment. The daring Jeb Stuart boldly encircled the Army of the Potomac and returned with news that the Federal right wing was subject to a flanking operation. When McClellan failed to withdraw his exposed right, Lee decided to crush the lone Federal corps. His bold plan was daring and complex. Almost 50,000 men from the divisions of Thomas Jackson (who was recalled from the Shenandoah Valley with 18,000 men), A. P. Hill, James Longstreet and D. H. Hill were ordered to mass against Porter's corps. Thus Lee planned to attack with about two-thirds of his 75,000-man army, leaving only about 25,000 men behind in the entrenchments to protect Richmond.

The plan went awry almost immediately. Jackson, who was to have placed his men in a position to flank Porter, failed to arrive on the 26th as scheduled and did not communicate this information sufficiently to A. P. Hill, who was to coordinate his attack with Jackson's. The impatient Hill threw his "Light Division" against a strong Federal position at Mechanicsville late in the afternoon and was chopped to pieces by the Federal artillery and small arms fire. D. H. Hill, whose division also suffered losses in the attack across swampy Beaver Dam Creek, called the fighting "a disastrous and bloody repulse." Fortunately for Colonel Grimes, he and the men of the 4th North Carolina spent much of June 26 near Mechanicsville in a supporting role "under a terrific infantry fire," but were not actively engaged in the battle. The Army of Northern Virginia suffered about 1,500 casualties and gained nothing in return, losing valuable officers and men in the process. Federal losses amounted to less than 400.[3]

The Confederate assault forced Porter's retreat to a prepared position behind Boatswain's Swamp at Gaines' Mill, where the armies clashed for much of June 27. D. H. Hill's Division found the way to Cold Harbor blocked early that morning by a battery of Federal artillery. Hill, who had been ordered to cooperate with Jackson, determined to drive off the guns with infantry. "Near daylight. . .we were ordered off to report to General Hill, by his special orders," explained Grimes. The general "directed me to 'charge that battery,' which was the only obstacle on the road to Cold Harbor." He inquired of Hill "if he was aware that I had no officers, and only about sixty men." This information seems to have altered Hill's decision, who directed Grimes to hold his men "in readiness to charge if others who were ordered forward a second time, failed to take it." Grimes deployed his men into line and directed them "to fire upon any of these troops who failed to move forward to the charge." This rather pointed command reveals once again Grimes' fervent fighting attitude. Ultimately Hill determined to "accomplish his purpose without further sacrifice of life, by a circuitous route," Grimes reported, which "caused them to abandon their position."[4]

As Hill's Division approached Cold Harbor, A. P. Hill's Division had again found Porter's Federals, this time firmly positioned at Gaines' Mill. Hill spearheaded a series of attacks, supported by Longstreet's Division on his right, that were unsuccessful. As the headlong assaults continued, D. H. Hill's route to the battlefield was again hampered when he ran into yet another battery of artillery deployed in his front. "Here General Hill, seeing a battery and not being positive whether they were Jackson's men, expected at that point, or the enemy," wrote Grimes, "ordered a flag forward to be waved." Grimes seized the standard of his 4th Regiment and "galloped [his] horse towards the battery. . ." This action drew the attention of the gunners, who opened "with the whole battery on the line in column in my rear," explained Grimes, who while again demonstrating to his men his willingness to risk death somehow managed to avoid becoming a casualty. John A. Stikeleather, the 4th Regiment's color bearer, appreciated Grimes' heroics. "Col., afterwards Gen. Grimes," he remembered long after the war, "by a chivalrous act on the battlefield endeared himself to me in such a manner as to make me a life long admirer and friend of his."[5]

D. H. Hill's brigades had marched directly into Brig. Gen. George Sykes' Federal division, which manned the right wing of Porter's embattled front. "I was on the extreme left of the long continuous line of battle and kept the enemy in check," reported Grimes. According to the historian of the 4th North Carolina, the fighting across Hill's swampy front was "very heavy and incessant." After shifting further to the left to take advantage of the cover provided by a piece of woods, the North Carolinians waited while the intense fighting raged on their front and right. Stikeleather again had an opportunity to hear and observe Grimes as he prepared his men for battle. While the soldiers were loading their guns in preparation for an advance, Grimes "poked along down the line of his regiment, halting in front of each company and with a face expressive of the extreme gravity of the situation, simply said, 'do your duty men.'"[6] Grimes, concluded Stikeleather, was "not a man of many words, but decidedly a man of action."[7]

Flanked by the brigades of Samuel Garland on the left and Robert Rodes on the right, George Anderson's North Carolina regiments were ordered forward in line of battle across an open field and into a stand of timber. "Suddenly we encounted a line of battle concealed in the underwood in front of us," wrote one Confederate officer. The Federals opened fire on Southerners, who "halted and poured a volley into their ranks." The advanced line of Federals grudgingly fell back, allowing Grimes the opportunity to rest and briefly reform his men. A new round of heavy firing opened in front and to the right. This time Grimes thrust his soldiers across an open field to the top of a ridge running parallel with his line. From that point the Federals were observed, as one officer put it, "lying in an old road, seeking shelter behind its banks and other objects that afforded him protection." The order to charge was given and the soldiers responded with a shout and rushed across a field into "the face of a furious fire." The scene was "terrific beyond description," recounted Capt. Edwin A. Osborne of the 4th North Carolina. "The yells of men, the roar of musketry, the thunder of artillery, the shrieks of the wounded and dying, the screaming of shells, with the loud commands of the officers, all combined to excite and stimulate the men, who rushed across the field, closing up their ranks as their comrades fell, cut down by the enemy's fire . . ." The deadly fusillade was coming from Col. Robert C. Buchanan's Regulars, who "held their ground stubbornly until we were almost near enough to cross bayonets with him," recalled Captain Osborne. The pressure of the determined North Carolinians, however, proved too much and the Federals "gave way in confusion."[8]

The steady fire of the Federal Regulars had almost killed Grimes, who again lost another horse beneath him. "I continued on foot," he recounted, "driving the enemy from his breastworks, through his camps, taking his artillery and supplying myself with another horse." "Fortunately I was unhurt," he later informed his brother William, "a ball passing through my overcoat and a grape shot carrying away my knapsack which left me minus a supper that night."[9]

In addition to a tactical victory, Grimes' other "prize" of the day was the capture of a Saint Bernard dog. The animal, recalled Grimes, "was protecting the corpse of a colonel of a Pennsylvania regiment, who, upon inspec-

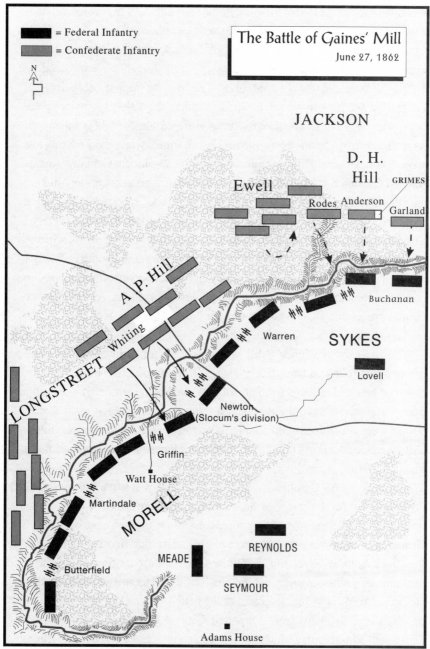

The Battle of Gaines' Mill
June 27, 1862

= Federal Infantry
= Confederate Infantry

N

JACKSON

D. H. Hill     GRIMES

Ewell     Rodes   Anderson   Garland

A. P. Hill

Whiting     Buchanan

Warren     SYKES

LONGSTREET     Lovell

Newton
(Slocum's division)

Griffin

Watt House

Martindale

MORELL

REYNOLDS

MEADE

Butterfield

SEYMOUR

Adams House

Theodore P. Savas

tion, was found to have on steel breast-plates, which had protected him so long as his face was to the fire, but upon retreating, had received a mortal wound in the rear." He sent the plate home to William. "I expect to keep it as a memento of the battlefield and of Yankee cowardice."[10]

The fighting at Gaines' Mill raged for much of the day and finally ended in a Confederate victory when two fresh brigades spearheaded an assault and pierced the Federal lines. The rupture caused the exhausted Federals to fall back in retreat, essentially ending the action. Casualties were heavy on both sides. The Confederates suffered almost 9,000 killed and wounded, surpassing the bloodshed of Seven Pines, while the Federals lost some 6,800. General Hill took special pains to compliment Generals Anderson and Garland for "their skill in discovering the weak point of the Yankees and their boldness in attacking it. Their brigades," reported Hill, "being more exposed than the others of my command, suffered more severely." Casualties in the 4th North Carolina bore out Hill's assertion, for Grimes went into action with less than 150 men and lost eleven killed and fifty four wounded. He was pleased with the way his men had performed, noting in particular the bravery of the regiment's color bearer, John A. Stikeleather. Grimes' regiment, together with the 5th North Carolina, was detailed the unpleasant duty of burying the dead.[11]

The victory at Gaines' Mill was enhanced for Grimes by a chance meeting that followed later than evening. "Here, for the first time, I had the honor of being introduced to the great Jackson," he remembered with some pride, "and I now have the mess-chest upon which he joined us at dinner, dining from the contents of a sutler's wagon captured the day previous." Grimes made no further mention of Stonewall Jackson or his impressions of him in his letters home.[12]

Grimes' North Carolinians enjoyed two days of relative quiet on June 28-29 while other elements of the Army of Northern Virginia took up the pursuit of McClellan's retreating forces. Early on the morning of June 30 Grimes, in conjunction with the rest of Hill's Division, led his men across the Chickahominy River toward White Oak Swamp via Savage's Station, the scene of a bitter engagement the previous day. The advancing Confederates streamed directly into the wake of the battle. "We picked up about 1,000 prisoners and so many arms," reported General Hill, "that I detached the Fourth and Fifth North Carolina Regiments to take charge of both." Grimes also recalled his detachment, adding that "the captured stores and prisoners" were to be taken to Richmond. General Anderson protested Hill's decision in vain while complimenting Grimes, arguing that "although small in numbers, Colonel Grimes' regiment is the key-stone of my brigade." While near the Savage's Station field Grimes observed again the horrors of battle, including "a man perfectly rigid in death, with his musket up to his face, and in the act of taking aim. . .[and] a pile of metallic coffins. . . ."[13]

Hill's order detaching the 4th and 5th North Carolina regiments ended Grimes' participation in the bloody Seven Days' Battles. The week long series of engagements concluded with the doomed assault against Malvern Hill on July 1, in which Anderson's Brigade again suffered heavy losses. Anderson himself endured a severe hand wound during the attack.

Grimes remained in Richmond until the middle of July, when he suffered from an attack of typhoid fever that forced him to return to Raleigh to regain his health. Momentous events transpired during his absence. As the Southerners rested and reorganized early that month, the Army of Virginia was gathering near Washington under Maj. Gen. John Pope. Unwilling to be caught between the pincers of two large enemy armies, Lee eventually moved north to deal with this new threat. He left troops behind near the capital, including D. H. Hill's Division, to protect Richmond from a possible thrust from McClellan, whose army was camped at Harrison's Landing on the James River. When it became clear

Maj. Gen.
Thomas "Stonewall" Jackson

*Generals in Gray*

that McClellan was evacuating his troops and reinforcing Pope, Hill's Division was released from its position near the capital and dispatched to the Army of Northern Virginia. Grimes had by this time recovered from the fever that had stricken him a month earlier and rejoined his regiment about this time. He was too late, however, to participate in the stunning battlefield success at Second Manassas on August 29-30. A few days earlier during the journey north, a member of the 4th North Carolina again confirmed the regiment's faith in Grimes' abilities as a battlefield commander. "They all love him since the fights that he has led them in," wrote Walter Battle in an August 23 letter to his mother.[14]

The victory on the plains of Manassas convinced General Lee of the necessity to seek a similar success north of the Potomac River, and Grimes found himself on their way to Maryland. On September 5 while crossing the Potomac River at White's Point, near Edward's Ferry, he suffered a serious leg injury from the kick of a horse. The blow was so severe that it caused a permanent indentation of the bone. The injury "incapacitated me for active duty," he wrote, "not being able to walk or ride, but had myself carried in an ambulance, in anticipation and hopes of a speedy recovery."[15]

As Grimes dealt with this new setback, the Army of North Virginia concentrated about Frederick on September 7, where General Lee formulated the details of a bold offensive that dangerously divided his army. In order to remove a Federal garrison in his rear at Harpers Ferry, three separate columns were dispatched under Stonewall Jackson. Longstreet and the balance of the army, including D. H. Hill's Division, remained near Boonsboro on the western edge of South Mountain. One of Hill's tasks was to guard the crucial gaps in the mountain range in order to prevent the Federals from moving through them against Lee's dispersed legions. Unfortunately, although Lee had wrecked Pope's army, he underestimated the time it would take to ready it once again for field operations. With McClellan again in command, the revitalized Army of the Potomac moved west in search of Lee. Fortunately for McClellan, a copy of Lee's operational orders (No. 191) fell into Federal hands, and the Federal commander set off toward South Mountain in an attempt to catch the Army of Northern Virginia, which was strung out and ill-prepared for battle.[16]

At 3:30 a.m. on the morning of September 14, the 4th North Carolina—with Grimes still accompanying his men, probably in a wagon—was marching down the National Turnpike toward Boonsboro with the other regiments of Anderson's Brigade and a portion of Hill's Division. Anderson's brigade that morning numbered 1,174 officers and men, while Grimes' regiment fielded less than 200 bayonets. Two of Hill's brigades, those of Alfred Colquitt and Samuel Garland, had already moved forward through Turner's Gap to take up defensive positions on the eastern slope of the wooded range. By 9:00 a.m, Garland's men were in contact with the enemy, who in large numbers were ascending the mountainside. Hill dispatched Anderson's Brigade to its assistance. "Seeing an engagement with the enemy was inevitable," wrote Grimes, who was barely able to walk, "I had myself placed upon my horse and took the command of my regiment."

The North Carolinians double-quicked to the summit of the mountain, and "[we] filed on a left-hand road, which overlooked the enemy's approach." At this point General Hill ordered Anderson to align his right flank against Garland's left. Anderson soon discovered that the order asked an impossibility, for Federal troops were already between the two brigades. The fire emanating from the right distance against Garland's thin regiments was heavy, and Anderson knew he had to act promptly. He dispatched two regiments, Grimes' 4th North Carolina and Col. Charles C. Tew's 2nd North Carolina, to try and reach Garland. "In advancing," reported Grimes, "[we] met. . .the corpse of that gallant officer [Garland] being brought off the field." Garland, one of the army's promising brigadiers, had been felled by enemy rifle fire. The pair of regiments—under Tew's command as senior colonel—somehow managed to reach Garland's left rear and formed on the left of the 13th North Carolina. Grimes remembered the desperate nature of the developing battle for Fox's Gap as a regiment of Ohioans pushed forward against him. The Federal thrust exposed the weakness of the North Carolinian's position. "Upon joining on to General Garland's left wing, Colonel Tew saw the necessity for re-enforcements to our left, and requested Captain Grimes to return and report the fact to General Anderson or General Hill." The courier, Grimes' half-brother Capt. John G. Blount Grimes, never reached his objective.[17]

Positioned on the brow of a ridge behind a low stone wall, the 4th North Carolina opened on the advancing Federals. Grimes held this point "for perhaps half an hour," he recalled in one of his few extant battle reports, "the enemy in front, from 100 to 200 yards distant. . ." He detailed his "best marksmen" to "[shoot] them whenver they appeared," adding that "I have reason to believe they killed several." Although it is impossible to determine exactly when it transpired, Grimes' third horse was killed under him on the slope of South Mountain. "To my own and the surprise of my men," explained the crippled officer, "I commanded my troops in the battle [on foot] until nightfall. . ." As the intensity of the fighting contained to escalate, Anderson dispatched an order for Tew to move his two regiments to the left, away from Garland's men. Under fire, Grimes sidled his men along the ridgeline, "joining on to the right of the regiments of our own brigade." The move, however, caused Grimes some concern, for it left an "interval of from 300 to 400 yards unoccupied between our right and General Garland's left wing," a critical circumstance which the astute Grimes "reported immediately." Before the gap could be filled, however, the 30th Ohio Infantry poured into the opening, flanking both the 4th North Carolina and Garland's exposed left. Unruffled by this desperate turn of events, the confident and capable young colonel "formed in line of battle at right angles with our former position," and continued to hold the ridge.[18]

As the battle flowed through the woods past his position, Grimes moved his regiment "in line of battle. . .up the mountain." The movement was slow and difficult, recalled one of the regiment's officers, for "the woods were very dense and the ground very rugged and mountainous." According to Grimes, when his men reached "the summit [they] discovered a battery of the enemy in a corn field and supported by infantry." The Federals moved in line against them and "opened upon us a heavy fire," wrote Captain Osborne. The North Carolinians "received them firmly, returning their fire with spirit." Displaying his aggressive streak, Grimes attempted to capture the artillery. "We made a charge on the battery, but were repulsed," was his terse explanation of the event. The colonel pulled back his sparse line of battle and reformed it yet again. By this time shadows were beginning to descend on the field, he noted, "and it was too dark to proceed." The regiment was withdrawn to the main road, ending "one of the most trying and, in some respects, one of the most splendid days of the war," believed Osborne. Grimes had once again handled his regiment firmly and confidently under very difficult circumstances. Osborne agreed, adding that "the men bore themselves with much coolness and courage throughout the entire day." While the defenders of South Mountain had fought well, the large Federal force had almost wiped D. H. Hill from the wooded slopes. Unable to hold the position, the Southerners relinquished the critical passes.[19]

The engagement over, Grimes dropped beside General Anderson to rest. The action on South Mountain was harder on Grimes than he later reported, and Anderson immediately recognized its impact on the officer. "Seeing me so exhausted after the excitement of the day," wrote Grimes, the brigade commander "insisted upon me going to the rear, and called upon four litter-bearers and had me carried to the hospital." The 4th North Carolinas "was now under command of Captain W. T. Marsh," wrote Captain Osborne, "Colonel Grimes having been compelled to retire." The exact losses for the 4th North Carolina at South Mountain are unknown. Osborne, the regiment's postwar historian, described them as ". . .small, but among them some of our best men." Anderson's entire brigade lost seven killed, fifty-four wounded and twenty-nine missing, about 7% of its total engaged.[20]

A new danger awaited Grimes when he reached the field hospital, "as the enemy were threatening the wagon trains, and in consequence, as a matter of safety, the wounded who were able to be moved without danger were ordered to be transported across the Potomac at Williamsport. . ." Roaming enemy cavalry intercepted a portion of the train and guided them down a wrong road. They had, wrote Grimes, "by this means secured very many of our wagons and ambulances, before the trick was discovered." The disabled officer was fortunate the ruse was discovered when it was, for "there were not more than half a dozen wagons intervening between the wagon carrying me and the road which led into the enemy's lines." With some assistance from other wounded soldiers, Grimes "drove the enemy off" and successfully crossed the river. For him, at least, the Maryland Campaign was over.[21]

Grimes spent the next two days with the wagons and was carried to Shepherdstown. There I remained, he later wrote, "being unable to report to my regiment, which was then engaged in battle at [Sharpsburg]." Lee's decision to stand and fight along Antietam Creek near the small town of Sharpsburg, Maryland, had important ramifications not only for the army, which suffered horrendous casualties, but for Grimes himself, who lost several close comrades in the engagement. One of these, "my friend and messmate, General G. B. Anderson," he lamented after the war, " received the wound from which he subsequently died after returning home." Anderson, whose regiments were defending the infamous "Bloody Lane" position, was struck in the foot, near the ankle joint, by a minie ball. The wound, while severe, was not considered life-threatening, and he was sent home to Raleigh to recover. Infection set in and the foot was finally amputated. Anderson died shortly after the surgery on October 16, 1862. Grimes lost both a friend and mentor with Anderson's passing.

Many other regimental officers fell that day. Captain Marsh, who led the regiment into the battle, was mortally wounded and carried from the field. Command of the 4th fell to Captain Osborne, who also was wounded and carried off to the rear. One by one the officers fell until the regiment was led by Company H's 2nd Lt. F. H. Weaver, who "was killed bearing the colors of the regiment in his hand." The regiment entered the fight with about 150 men and "was left without a commissioned officer," recalled Osborne. By the end of the fighting it was led by Orderly Sergeant Thomas W. Stephenson, Company C. General D. H. Hill formed the remnants of Anderson's Brigade the following day and commended them for their courage, calling them "the faithful few." Hill paid special attention to the 4th North Carolina and her disabled commander in his official report of the Maryland Campaign. "This gallant regiment," he wrote, ". . .has never been surpassed by any troops in the world for gallantry, subordination, and propriety. . ." Colonel Grimes, he continued, "was disabled, by the kick of a horse, from being with his regiment at Sharpsburg, and unfit for duty for months afterward. The Fourth thus lost his valuable services."[22]

In retrospect, while the regiment may have lost his "valuable services," Grimes' leg injury may have saved his life by preventing his participation in the slaughter at Sharpsburg. Given the appalling causalities suffered by the 4th North Carolina and Anderson's Brigade as a whole, it seems likely that Grimes, with his tendency to lead by example, would have been one of the casualties at the Sunken Road. Although he passed through numerous battles unscathed during the war, to have survived the Sharpsburg slaughter without a crippling or fatal wound would have been perhaps Grimes' most remarkable achievement.

While Grimes recuperated in a hospital in Winchester, Virginia, his bloodied regiment went into camp along the Opequon River. His leg wound suffered almost two weeks earlier from the kick of his horse continued to plague him, and "amputation began seriously to be talked of." Fortunately, his health slowly improved and the severe remedy discussed by his doctors was not necessary. Grimes remained in Winchester and in camp at Martinsburg, Virginia, until November. "[I] would have asked for a furlough but for the ride, &c.," he later wrote.[23]

Shortly after the South Mountain engagement Grimes wrote William that their half-brother, John Grimes, had disappeared during the battle and was probably captured by the Federals. Later in the month he wrote William again, informing him that his leg was recoverering "very slowly." He finally had good news to share with William on October 16, when he happily informed his brother that he had learned that their half-brother, John, had indeed been captured, sent to Ft. Delaware and eventually exchanged. He arrived safely in Raleigh thereafter and "doubtless has a horrid experience of which to narrate." Grimes, optimistically expecting to return to duty, asked William to have a tailor in Raleigh make him a new "suit" (uniform) with the proper insignia for the rank of colonel. "[Put] the gold bar on the sleeve and stars on the collar," he instructed, "but avoid anything that is gaudy and showy." As if as an afterthought, he mentioned near the end of the letter that his men "now only draw 6 ounces of flour as a day's rationing."[24]

While recovering from his leg injury Grimes had time to contemplate his position within the brigade's hierarchy. On October 22, following the unexpected death of General Anderson, Grimes revealed some of his ambition for higher command when he asked William to have his friends in Raleigh mention his name for promotion to brigadier and command of the brigade.[25] Although his promotion to brigadier was not yet forthcoming, a major organization was sweeping the army. On November 6 it was formally announced that the army's two unofficial "wings" would be formally divided into the First and Second Corps headed, respectively, by James Longstreet and Thomas Jackson. Thus when Grimes reported to D. H. Hill for duty later that month—"though not recovered (and still have an indentation in the bone from the injury)"—he found the division now a part of Jackson's II Corps. Hill, glad to have Grimes back with his men, "relieved Colonel [Daniel H.] Christie," who had been assigned to the command of Anderson's Brigade, and put me in charge," wrote Grimes. His first chore in that role was the task of destroying the Baltimore and Ohio Railroad from Charleston, West Virginia. "The work was done effectually at night," he reported, "by tearing up the cross-ties and putting them in large piles of twenty to thirty and then crossing the iron rails over them and piling them a few ties on top of each end of the rails and just before daylight setting fire to them—the whole at once—the fire so warping the rails as to unfit them for use."[26]

During the last week of November Jackson's Corps left Winchester and moved north down the Shenandoah Valley. His divisions, detached from Lee and on a semi-independent status, reached New Market on the 24th before marching east over Massanutton toward the Shenandoah River. On this march Robert E. Rodes, described by Grimes as "one of the bravest and best officers of the Confederate Army," took temporary charge of D. H. Hill's Division during that officer's brief abscence. The expedition developed a minor but sharp feud between the two men that Grimes described as "a misunderstanding. . .that continued until the spring of 1864, and then ended by a gentlemanly and chivalrous action on the part of General Rodes."[27]

This "misunderstanding" sprang from Rodes' order that the men could not remove their pants or shoes while crossing the Shenandoah River. Grimes thought the directive otherwise, "so as to enable the men to be dry after crossing, when the exercise would in a short time warm them up." Not knowing that Rodes had issued the order, Grimes expressed his opinion to him. "General Rodes said in a sharp tone he saw nothing hard in the order," recalled Grimes, "and that I had better go to the river and see it obeyed." Much to his chagrin, Grimes also learned that Rodes "was in command of the division," and that the directive was his. "The order was reluctantly obeyed," Grimes wrote. Once the crossing was completed, Colonel Grimes halted the brigade, "to enable the troops of my command to close up and recover their proper position in line." Rodes, apparently still miffed by Grimes' innocent remark, demanded to know why the men had not stacked their arms after halting, as General Jackson had ordered. Observing Rodes' grim mood, Grimes explained that it was only a temporary halt to allow the men to close up ranks and form the proper line. He exercised the good sense, however, to order his men to stack their weapons. Still irritated, Rodes ordered him to remain stationary while an artillery unit passed. The obediant Grimes waited for hours, as instructed, but not a single cannon rolled past. Disturbed by Grimes' absence from the front, Rodes dispatched a courier to fetch him. "I sent word to him that I was waiting for the artillery," explained Grimes. By the time the colonel reached Paris, Virginia, with his brigade, "General Rodes was standing on the piazza of the hotel, and enquired in a very cross manner, 'What has kept you so long?'"

"Obeying your order," was Grimes' reply.

"What was that order?" demanded Rodes.

"To let the artillery pass me."

Grimes' terse answer seems to have increased his superior's anger. "When you saw that no artillery came up," he chastised, "you should have have come on, as the enemy are advancing."

"You had just reproved me for not obeying General Order No. —," Grimes retorted, "and if you had not countermanded your order to await the arrival of the artillery, I should have remained there until General Hill resumed command."

The not-so-subtle reference to the division's official commander only served to heighten the tensions between the two men. Rodes descended to the street level and directed Grimes on where to place his men. "When I gave the command 'Order arms,' preparatory to stacking arms" Rodes retorted, "you need not stack arms."

"It is General Jackson's order," Grimes replied, standing his ground, "and you have just reproved me for its violation, and I shall do it."[28]

Clearly Grimes and Rodes got off on the wrong foot, and the "misunderstanding" spiraled into an exchange of sharp words over nothing of serious consequence. As earlier noted, the lingering strain between these two capable and dedicated officers "continued until the spring of 1864." After this incident Jackson's men engaged in several light skirmishes with Federal cavalry before moving through Fisher's Gap and on to Orange Court House.

The weather had turned cold by mid-November. "There are thousands of barefooted men in Virginia," wrote a soldier of the 4th North Carolina home to his mother, ". . .and we have a good many in our Brigade stark barefooted, and have not had a shoe on since we left Richmond some months ago."[29] Camped near Gordonsville two weeks later on November 27, Grimes substantiated the soldier's description in a moving letter to his daughter Bettie:

It would make your little heart ache to see the suffering and hardships that our poor soldiers have to endure. Think how a thinly clad and barefooted man must suffer in these cold windy nights and frosty mornings. Many poor fellows, with frostbitten and bleeding feet, are forced to drag their weary limbs along over hard frozen ground and crying from pain. In the mountains the water would freeze in the mens canteens.[30]

In the same letter Grimes expressed frustration over not being picked to permanantly command Anderson's brigade. "Colonel [Stephen] Ramseur has been forwarded and assigned to this brigade, but he has not reported as yet for duty. A man who has never been present but in one engagement, and then entered the fight after night, and happened to be one among a dozen who was wounded in his regiment, and having been very polite to Mrs. President Davis, has been advanced for his attention," he wrote. "Such is the reward of men who stay in the field and perform their duties faithfully to be over looked by one who has seen no service."[31] Some of Grimes' troops felt the same way as their commander. "I like Col. Grimes very much," wrote Walter Battle of the 4th North Carolina, "and I think he is more entitled to the promotion of Brigadier than Ramseur, who was only a Captain of Artil-

lery, though they say he is a West Pointer, and a very good officer."[32]

General Lee's selection of Col. Stephen D. Ramseur to command the four North Carolina regiments (4th, 2nd, 14th and the 30th) was not intended in any way as a slight against Grimes, who

Brig. Gen.
Stephen Dodson Ramseur

*Generals in Gray*

had performed with courage and ability on several fields. While he had been in temporary command of the brigade only a short time, Grimes' deep ties to the unit and its members convinced him that he deserved the promotion. Certainly he had the ability to do so. Capable West Point graduates, like Ramseur, however, were desired to lead brigades. Ramseur had demonstrated courage and steady leadership qualities at Malvern Hill and a strong ability to train both infantry and artillery units for combat. His absence from the field for much of November and December—alluded to by Grimes in his letter home to Bettie—was the result of a severe arm wound that had left the limb with some residual paralysis and intense pain that required the employment of morphine. Ramseur had some doubts about accepting the responsibility, and voiced as much directly to President Davis, who urged him to accept the command—but only when he was strong enough to rejoin the army. Ramseur's promotion to brigadier general was formally announced on November 6, although he was unable to return to the field to assume his new duties until January 1863. It was during his recuperation in North Carolina that Ramseur visited and fell in love with his cousin, Ellen "Nellie" Richmond, who soon thereafter became his fiance.[33]

It is clear from his letters and actions that Grimes was ambitious and sought higher rank. The obvious sarcasm in his letter home in late November, however, must not be construed as a personal attack against Ramseur. Instead, it should be read in its proper context. Grimes had not yet met Ramseur. Although he had no way of knowing it, Grimes' life and that of his future wife, Charlotte, would become entwined with those of Stephen and Nellie Ramseur. The two young officers would become fast friends and their wives would travel together to join them at winter quarters. They would share the joys of the birth of their children, and finally in a climatic and sad irony, Grimes would succeed Ramseur in command of a division when that officer fell at the Battle of Cedar Creek.

On December 3, Thomas Jackson's Corps marched into Port Royal, Virginia, about twenty miles from Fredericksburg, where it remained until December 12. During this time Grimes, still in temporary command of the brigade, reconnoitered the terrain to familiarize himself with the surroundings and roads of the area in which he believed the next battle would be fought. On December 5, he wrote William that he had witnessed "four of the enemy's gunboats anchored in the stream not exceeding 250 yards from the shore where I watered my horse." The occupants of the vessels on the Rappahannock River "had out their spy glasses trying to discern what sort of man I might be, but no effort was made to molest me. We are anxious for them to land and advance," he added, "for we feel very secure of a convincing victory."[34] Three days later Grimes wrote again to his brother, informing him that the Seven Pines wound suffered by Col. David Carter, the officer with whom he had earlier squabbled, had rendered him unfit for field duty. Carter's resignation from the army, coupled with Capt. Thomas M. Blount's earlier death at Gaines' Mill, brought an end to the previous year's lingering dispute that had almost resulted in a duel.

The sojourn at Port Royal, "where we had the first snow of any depth of the winter," ended on December 12 when elements of the Army of the Potomac forced a crossing of the Rappahannock River at Fredericksburg. Jackson's entire corps marched all night and near daybreak reached Hamilton's Crossing, a few miles southeast of the city. Grimes' North Carolina brigade—Ramseur had not yet taken command—was placed in reserve on the extreme right of Jackson's line near Prospect Hill.

The Federal army that faced the Confederates had a new commander. Concern over George McClellan's failure to aggressively pursue Lee after the Maryland Campaign had prompted President Lincoln to replace him on November 7 with Maj. Gen. Ambrose E. Burnside, the former commander of the IX Corps. Burnside's strategy was to interpose his army between Lee (whose own divisions were scattered in the lower Shenandoah Valley and in the Piedmont region) and Richmond at Fredericksburg. Burnside calculated that it would be relatively easy to cross the Rappahannock on pontoon bridges, take the historic city, and then weigh the tactical and strategic advantages such a position might offer.

Although the bulk of Burnside's army had arrived opposite Fredericksburg on November 17, his pontoons did not make an appearance for several weeks, and any opportunity for a speedy strategic victory vanished. By the time the Federals crossed on December 12, Lee had his army well in hand. By the morning of December 13, his strong defensive line west of the city stretched for several miles, with James Longstreet's Corps holding the left on Marye's Heights, and Jackson's divisions the right in the Prospect Hill sector. Burnside's plan of attack called for a strong assault against Jackson's front, with another against the Mayre's Height's position, both of which were preceded by a heavy artillery bombardment. Although his brigade was held well in the rear behind the army's right flank, it "suffered considerably from the artillery of the enemy," wrote Grimes.

Except for a brief success in the center of Jackson's line—which was quickly plugged with reserves—the numerous Federal assaults were a bloody failure. "The brigade was moved forward to support the troops in the trenches, and took the front line" after the initial breakthrough, recalled Grimes. "The cries of the wounded in the hedged old field in our front where the enemy had charged was heart-rendering and sickening—pleading prayers to the Almighty for mercy, and begging for water to quench their thirst, which was continued all night."[35]

"Anxious to meet the enemy" on such good terms, explained Grimes, "the officers of the command petitioned General D. H. Hill to allow us to remain in the front line until the enemy did advance." Although Hill granted the request, "the expected charge of the next day was deferred," lamented Grimes. While the new position in the front line did not bring combat, it did result in an arduous and unpleasant chore. "[We were given] the task of burying the horses belonging to the artillery that had been killed, to prevent the awful stench, not knowing how many days we would have to keep in the line of battle. We found it a difficult task and not easily accomplished."[36]

On the night of December 15, Grimes observed a "commotion among the enemy, and could see light in the distance among the enemy, and could see a light in the distance flash up and then again be darkened." The strange circumstance, he reasoned, was "the enemy. . .moving to their right, and that the light was obscured as the troops passed, and flashed out at the interval between the passage of one regiment and the head of another." Although he believed the information important, his superior did not. General Hill told him "not [to] be uneasy, they were not going to retreat until after another effort, and to be ready for their charge in the morning."[37]

"By the next morning we were up," wrote Grimes, "every man at his post, awaiting the expected charge." The morning broke with a heavy mist along the ground. "The fog hung low, and we waited impatiently for it to rise and show us the plain below." When he "saw the enemy were not in sight," Grimes, characteristically, "went forward some few hundred yards to reconnoitre and in the meantime sent word to General Hill that the enemy had disappeared from my front." Grimes' discovery was forwarded through

Hill to Stonewall Jackson. Hill had only "been there a few minutes," re-membered Grimes, "when General Jackson, accompanied by General Lee, rode up to this spot, the highest eminence on that part of the field and asked, 'who says the enemy have gone?'"

General Hill replied, "Colonel Grimes." Jackson turned to face the colo-nel.

"How do you know?" asked Jackson.

"I have been down as far as their picket line of the day previous," explained Grimes, "and can see nothing of them."

"Move your skirmish line as far as the line, and see where they are," directed Jackson. As Grimes later described it, both Jackson and Lee dis-played "a look of deep chagrin and mortification, very apparent to the observer. . .though nothing of the sort was expressed in words." Grimes was indeed correct. The Army of the Potomac had abandoned the offensive and had withdrawn over the Rappahannock River during a noisy storm on the night of December 15-16. The battle had cost the Federals some 13,000 casualties, compared to Confederate losses of less than 5,000.[38]

The defensive victory along the Rappahannock River brought about the end of another year of soldiering for Bryan Grimes. Throughout he had shown courage, a propensity for action, and good judgment on and off the field. Although disappointed about his failure to be promoted to replace George B. Anderson, his merits as an officer had not gone unnoticed. "Un-der tried veterans as brigade commanders, Rodes, Colquitt, Iverson, Doles and Grimes," reported D. H. Hill in his report of the fighting at Fredericksburg, "I feel confident that they [the men] will do well whenever called upon to meet the infernal Yankees."[39]

On December 18, a few days after the Fredericksburg fighting, Grimes found the time to sit down and write William. "All our causalities [were] caused by shell, grape and canister, which at one time was most terrific. Capt. Carter, a brother of Col. Carter, was killed being struck by a shell taking off the lower part of his face and carrying away the upper part of his chest." In the same letter, Grimes displayed his open disgust for the editor of the Raleigh *North Carolina Standard*, W. W. Holden. Many believed that Holden's proclivity to constantly criticize the policies of the Davis admini-stration and Governor Zebulon Vance was detrimental to the Southern cause. "Why don't you all down there kill Holden?" inquired Grimes.[40]

Meanwhile, the North Carolina Brigade moved to winter quarters on the Rapidan River near Orange Court House late in December. Now that the campaigning season had effectively drawn to a close, Grimes found himself spending a lonely Christmas in cold Virginia. He used some of his time to write his little daughter, Bettie, on Christmas day 1862. "My dear little darling," was how he began a letter both vividly descriptive and often inappropriate for young eyes. "This is Christmas morning, and as I am unable to be with you all in person, the next best thing to it is thinking of you and your enjoyment on this day." Grimes described for his daughter many of the sights he had witnessed at Fredericksburg. "In riding over the field [I] saw many things that would have pleased you. Articles stolen by the Yankees out of the houses in Fredericksburg and many fine dresses were seen upon the battlefield, piled up by the dead bodies of their dead comrades. [They] piled them one upon another and [hid] behind them [so as] to shoot at us."

Then, with a grim detail that must have terrified the little girl, he went on to describe the horrors of the field:

In one place there was a house filled up with dead bodies that they had thrown head foremost not taking the time to bury them, and several graves had at least five hundred in each. Some were buried so shallow that the dogs were scratching them up and gnawing their limbs for two days after the battle before the enemy returned for their wounded men [who were] laying upon the field without any attention. Moaning, crying and begging for water, their cries could be heard throughout the night and day. In one house that I entered, near the city, was the children's playhouse in which a bomb shell had exploded and scattered all the toys and dolls and play things all about the rooms. Here was a head, there a leg, and now the body of a doll baby with their little dresses all about, and a baby's cradle had been made as a trough out of which they fed their horses. Many dead Yankees were lying about showing that we had repaid them for their vandalism.[41]

Finally with some degree of melancholy, but framed in the stark truthfulness that always marked his communications, he confirmed her earlier suspicions that he would not be with her that holiday season. "You guessed correctly when you feared I would not come home this Christmas, and what is worse, I have no prospect for going home until this war concludes. Be a good girl and give my love to all the folks."[42]

Bryan Grimes' frock coat. Note the belt plate, which was damaged by a minie ball during the Battle of Chancellorsville. *The Museum of the Confederacy (photograph by Katherine Wetzel), Richmond , VA.*

## Chancellorsville and Gettysburg

"I put my foot on the back and head of an officer of high rank
and ground his face in the earth"

fter Fredericksburg, Colonel Grimes and his brigade—he was still in
temporary command pending Stephen D. Ramseur's arrival—moved
into winter quarters on the Rapidan near Orange Court House. The new year
passed quietly. In January 1863, the recently promoted Ramseur felt well
enough to return to Virginia and assume command of the North Carolina
Brigade, which was now in Robert Rodes' Division. While the men of the
brigade might have greeted the new brigadier general rather coolly, they did
not. According to one of brigade's colonels, Ramseur "at once disarmed
criticism by his high professional attainment and great amiability of character, inspiring his men, by his own enthusiastic nature, with those lofty martial qualities which distinguish the true Southern soldier." Ramseur,
likewise, was impressed with his new command, although he believed that
its lengthy service without a brigadier had left it somewhat disorganized.[1]

On January 30, while his Carolinians were on picket duty along the
Rappahannock River, Grimes requested a thirty-day furlough to return to his
home state. After a brief visit he returned and, once again at the head of the
4th North Carolina, participated in drilling and disciplining the regiment.
The 4th, he wrote at this time, was "noted for its *esprit de corps*." Although
Grimes had not selected to command the brigade on a permanent basis, his
bravery and leadership skills, demonstrated on several fields of battle, were
not going unnoticed. Appreciation of his abilities came in the form of a
recommendation for promotion to brigadier general from Maj. Gen. D. H.
Hill, who wrote on March 10, 1863:

> Colonel Grimes led the Fourth with most distinguished gallantry at Seven
> Pines, and in all the subsequent battles of the year 1862, except for

Sharpsburg, when he was ill. He has been in many pitched battles, and has behaved most gallantly in them all. I think that he has seen more service than any colonel from North Carolina. His gallantry, ripe experience, admirable training, intelligence and moral worth, constitute strong claims for promotion.[2]

Although his promotion to brigadier was still a year away, Hill's acknowledgment of the 35-year-old colonel served notice of both Grimes' abilities and the force of his personality. If he survived, he would eventually be recognized and rewarded by the Confederate high command.

The drilling and conditioning of the 4th North Carolina abruptly ended for Grimes on March 15, when he received word that his little six-year-old boy, Bryan, had died of scarlet fever at the home of his great aunt in Warren County, North Carolina. Shouldering this crushing news Grimes returned to his home state to bury his son. Despite this personal tragedy, the grieving colonel took the opportunity to call once again on, Charlotte Emily Bryan, a young woman in Raleigh. He had first met with Charlotte during his furlough in February; his second visit with her would change his life forever. "At home the ladies had sewing societies, where they made sheets and all garments necessary for the soldiers," Charlotte remembered. "My mother, and all of us knitted many socks and gloves for the soldiers." I recall "knitting a nice pair of gloves for Col. Grimes, afterwards my husband," she wrote. Grimes was:

> calling one evening and saw me knitting gloves for the soldiers and asked me to knit him a pair. I told him I did not know whether I could or not, as they would be troublesome to knit with all the fingers; those we knitted for the soldiers had only the thumb and fore-finger so they could load their guns, the other fingers with all in one. I decided however, that it was my duty as well as a pleasure to knit the gloves and sent them to him. He said they were a great comfort and kept them until after the war and packed them in camphor to prevent moths from eating them.[3]

Charlotte remembered Bryan's visit with her in April 1863, when the death of his son had called him home. "He always said I was engaged to him from that time," she later wrote, "though I did not so consider it."[4] The couple had initially become acquainted in a more formal setting before the war, when Charlotte "attended [her] first Commencement at the University

Charlotte Emily Bryan, the wife of Bryan Grimes, in an undated image. *The North Carolina Division of Archives and History, Raleigh, NC.*

of North Carolina," in June 1859. The Chapel Hill commencement was quite an event, especially for "the girls of the state." Charlotte remembered that commencement in particular, for "President Buchanan and Jacob Thompson of his cabinet attended. . . On his staff was Lieutenant Stuart, afterwards the famous Confederate General, J. E. B. Stuart." President Buchanan and his entourage paid a visit to Charlotte's home after the close of the ceremonies. "I met my husband for the first time at Chapel Hill," was how she described it.[5]

There is nothing in the written record suggesting that Grimes and Charlotte kept in touch or corresponded after their first formal encounter, although he had must have made an impression on her, for she remembered meeting him at the 1859 UNC Commencement. Despite the tragic loss of his son, the meeting and courting of young Charlotte—he was thirty-five and she was twenty-three—must have helped ease his pain and lift his spirits, and the romance blossomed during the late winter months of 1863.

Soon after returning to his regiment, still camped in the vicinity of Fredericksburg, Grimes wrote "Miss Charlotte" the first of many affectionate letters. "In return for the sweet songs with which you favored me on my visit, I hope you will accept this music and forgive my presumption which requires that you will add this to your list [so] that I may enjoy later pleasure if hearing them sung under more favorable circumstances than now surrounds me." He added, "If they are not as sweet and affectionate as I could wish, you at least will appreciate the motive which induces me to forward them [to you]." Grimes also enclosed what he described as "a sort of medley taken from a dead Yankee's knapsack after the battle of Fredericksburg. Doubtless he had pilfered it from some Southern fireside." He closed by thanking her for the gloves she had knitted him: "Perhaps you are too ultra Southern to admit such influences among your treasures and keepsakes. Are you?. . . .but allow me to extend my thanks again for your gloves. I learn day by day to appreciate their comfort more highly as the winter has been severe the whole of March and several days of April." He closed the missive with "very sincerely and truly yours, Bryan Grimes."[6]

The time Grimes spent in camp with his regiment that April passed quickly enough, consumed as he was with matters both personal and professional. Despite the cold weather and short but difficult marches they endured that winter, the rank and file of Stephen D. Ramseur's Brigade were confident that the new round of campaigning awaiting them would result in more victories. They "hailed the dawn of the campaign with beautiful confidence in the future," wrote a soldier in the 14th North Carolina. On April 24, from near Fredericksburg, Grimes found time in his busy schedule to write to his daughter Bettie about picket duty, a dreary task his regiment had been performing for some weeks. "We are preparing this morning to go down on picket," he informed her. "You don't know what picketing is do you? It is to stand in front of the whole army and wait to see what the enemy is doing and report to the generals, and if they advance, fight them."[7] The coming of spring in Virginia and the drying of the roads brought with it another season of campaigning, and Grimes and the 4th North Carolina would shortly be involved in more than just picket duty.

After his disastrous performance at Fredericksburg, which was followed by the woefully inept "Mud March" a few weeks later, Ambrose Burnside was replaced as the commander of the Army of the Potomac by the politically connected Joseph Hooker. As he planned his spring campaign, Hooker took steps to improve the army's morale and ready it for combat. Wisely unwilling to attack Lee's army on the heights behind Fredericksburg, Hooker planned to cross his several corps over the Rappahannock far upstream, thus turning the Army of Northern Virginia out of its daunting position behind the river. By mid-April the Federal army began to come to life, and the pickets watching the banks of the Rappahannock withdrew. By the 27th large portions of Hooker's army were moving upstream, and before long crossed U. S. Ford and Kelly's Ford. Joe Hooker had stolen a march on Lee and was now beyond his left flank.

The dim sounds of scattered musketry and artillery fire greeted the men of Ramseur's Brigade on the foggy morning of April 29. The North Carolinians, together with the rest of Rodes' Division, were camped near Grace Church southeast of Fredericksburg. Grimes withdrew his men from picket duty and the division marched to the vicinity of Hamilton's Crossing, five miles from town. Ramseur deployed his brigade along the southern bank of Massaponax Creek. There, wrote Ramseur, his men were "occasionally annoyed by their artillery (by which I lost a few men)." The North Carolinians remained in that position, on the army's right wing, until the following evening, when they were marched to Hamilton's Crossing.[8]

Confederate reports had confirmed the presence of several Federal corps below the river 25 miles upstream, all of which seemed to be converging toward Chancellorsville, a small hamlet and important crossroads about a dozen miles west of Fredericksburg. The roads from that point fed into the rear of Lee's army. In addition to this ominous threat, other Federals had crossed the river on pontoons at Fredericksburg and were poised to strike there as well. Once he had a firm grasp of the developing strategic situation, Lee ordered his cavalry, under Maj. Gen. Jeb Stuart, to harass and slow the progress of Hooker's marching columns while a division of infantry under Richard Anderson hurried toward Chancellorsville. With another division under Lafayette McLaws set to support Anderson, Lee held Stonewall Jackson's Corps in place behind the Rappahannock River to await developments.

He could not afford to remain idle long. With James Longstreet and most of his First Corps on a foraging mission below Richmond, the Army of Northern Virginia numbered less than 60,000 men—only about one-half of Hooker's total. Once he determined that the enemy marching beyond his left posed the real threat to his army, Lee moved to counter it as quickly as possible. He left one of Jackson's divisions under Jubal Early and an additional brigade, about 10,000 men, to hold the high ground behind Fredericksburg, dispatching McLaws and Jackson's remaining men west to assist Anderson.[9]

Early the next morning on May 1, Ramseur's Brigade marched in the vanguard of Rodes' Division as Jackson's Corps trudged west at first light. The column wound its way on the military road to the Plank Road, which connected Fredericksburg with Chancellorsville. As the 4th North Carolina marched along, Colonel Grimes caught a glimpse of Stonewall Jackson. "For the first time General Jackson appeared in full military costume," he recalled, "and conveyed by his personal appearance an idea of the great military hero he was." The march continued as the sun climbed in the sky, warming up the morning. Ramseur's Brigade turned left on the Plank Road and made its way to Tabernacle Church, on the eastern fringe of a heavily wooded area called the Wilderness. The region was bisected by few roads of any significance and even fewer farms, and was choked with second growth timber, dense underbrush and thick vines. Lee knew what he was up to. If he could force Hooker to give battle within the depths of the woods, he could nullify the enemy's advantage in both manpower and artillery.[10]

As Grimes and his men marched west, Richard Anderson's Division assumed an entrenched line overlooking the Plank Road and Old Turnpike, just west of Tabernacle Church. The head of the North Carolina brigade arrived there about 8:00 a.m. Jackson, unwilling to turn over the initiative to Hooker, decided to advance along both roads against the approaching enemy. With Anderson's brigades moving west on the Plank Road, and McLaw's brigades moving on the Turnpike, Jackson pressed the troops forward, with his corps moving behind Anderson. The advance began an hour before noon and almost immediately ran into approaching Federals on both thoroughfares. Grimes' men could hear musketry fire in the thickets as opposing skirmishers settled into their deadly business. At 2:30 p.m. the aggressive Jackson directed Rodes to dispatch a brigade to assist Anderson's developing engagement on the Plank Road. "At a distance of 7 miles from Fredericksburg," reported Ramseur, "we were detached from our own division and ordered to report to Major General Anderson, when we advanced upon the enemy."

Jackson had directed Ramseur to deploy his regiments between the brigades of Ambrose Wright and Carnot Posey, which the young brigadier did with some skill. As Grimes' recalled the early stages of the battle, his 4th North Carolina, with skirmishers deployed, was ordered to "feel" for the enemy and upon encountering them were "to drive them in when found." Jackson's men had run into Henry Slocum's Federal XII Corps, and as the intensity of the fighting grew, Stonewall remained near the front, admiring the developing action. "General Jackson rode down the turnpike with the artillery," Grimes remembered, "and whenever necessary, would then ride along my line, and upon much resistance being shown by the enemy, would say in suppressed tones, 'Press them, Colonel.'"[11]

Although the resistance was fierce, Ramseur's regiments steadily moved west, slowly driving the enemy before them. One North Carolina officer, in an article published in a Raleigh newspaper, compared the advance to a fox hunt and commented on how artfully the brigade was handled that afternoon. The enemy "fell back in confusion for several miles," reported Ramseur, "strewing the way with their arms and baggage." Grimes supported Ramseur's observations by noting that "several of their regiments [left] their knapsacks piled up where they had been thrown off when called out to oppose our onward march." The heavy terrain began to wear on the

North Carolinians, who continued on in a "wet, tattered and torn" condition. As Grimes ushered the 4th North Carolina over the brow of a hill at about 6:30 p.m., "the whole line of the main army opened fire upon us." Grimes later concluded that " if they had reserved their fire until we had gained the summit, my command would have been annihilated." As it was, he continued, my men "were so astounded by the suddenness of this alarming fire, that they began to fall back in confusion." Grimes coolly rallied the men and "ordered them to lie down, as we were protected by the eminence upon the hill above." When his line was firmly reestablished, Grimes went forward to reconnoiter in person. ". . .I saw that we had come upon a large force entrenched," he later explained. "[I] made a report of these facts of General Jackson, and was ordered to hold my position until relieved, which was done about 12 o'clock that night." Ramseur's Brigade, including Grimes' 4th North Carolina, had driven within about one mile of Hooker's headquarters at the Chancellor house crossroads. Taken aback by the sudden and sharp Southern assault, the Federal commander had called off his advance and concentrated his legions around Chancellorsville. The initiative was now in Confederate hands.[12]

Sleep was hard to come by that night. The opposing lines were so close together that the North Carolinians could hear the work of ax-wielding Federals strengthening their positions for the renewal of the contest the following morning. For the first time in the war the North Carolinians utilized a sign and countersign to distinguish friend and foe in the inky-black tangles of the Wilderness. While the men pondered their situation, Generals Lee and Jackson met to ponder their options. Although Stonewall believed Hooker would withdraw that night, Lee believed otherwise and favored a renewal of the offensive. This issue was where the blow should be aimed. Cavalry intelligence reported that the extreme right wing of the Federal army was "up in the air," unanchored to any position of strength and vulnerable to a flank attack. The balance of the Federal army was either entrenched or unapproachable because of the thick terrain. It was thus decided that Jackson, with three divisions, would attempt the dangerous flanking operation with about 28,000 men, leaving Lee and but two divisions, some 14,000 men, to hold Hooker in position. It was a bold plan that divided Lee's army into three widely-separated segments.

The flanking operation began early on the morning of May 2. "About 8 o'clock, after noticing Generals Lee and Jackson in close conference for some time," wrote Grimes, "we took up that long march for the flank movement. . ." Rodes' Division, with Ramseur's Brigade near the head of the line, was the first to depart, followed by the divisions of Raleigh Colston and A. P. Hill. The pace of the march was deliberate, and although the day was warm and dry, the moist roadbed alleviated the clouds of dust that usually accompany thousands of marching feet. To Grimes, the march was "long, tedious and circuitous." By 4:00 p.m. Rodes had his division facing east and aligned for battle. He deployed the brigades of George Doles and Alfred Colquitt south of the Old Turnpike, and placed Alfred Iverson and Edward O'Neal north of it. Ramseur's Brigade was deployed behind Rodes' right flank in order to support Colquitt and secure the right flank of the attacking line. An hour later Jackson's second division under Colston had taken up a position behind Rodes, extending the line north beyond Ramseur's left flank. Two of A. P. Hill's brigades were filing into place north of the road as part of a third line north when the momentous hour struck.

"Are you ready, General Rodes?" inquired Jackson.

"Yes, sir!" came the division commander's reply.

"You can go forward then," order Jackson. It was 5:15 p.m.

Bugles and shouted commanders launched the attack, which was preceded by thick clouds of skirmishers breaking their way through the brush several hundred yards in advance of the main line. The unsuspecting Eleventh Corps Federals under Oliver Howard, facing generally south with their flank gaping wide, did not stand a chance against such unequal odds.[13]

"The sweet, wild rebel yell," wrote John A. Stikeleather, color bearer for Grimes' 4th North Carolina, ". . .rolled in volume over the hills and vales, [and] carried dismay into the enemy's ranks."[14] The brief pockets of resistance offered by the Federals quickly collapsed and they fell back in wild confusion, strewing the ground with objects of every description. The first objective of the attack, the clearing around the Talley farm a mile down the turnpike, was soon buried under an irrepressible wave of onrushing Confederates. The second objective, another clearing another half-mile beyond at the Melzi Chancellor house, also fell after a determined defensive effort behind hastily prepared works failed to hold back Rodes' division.

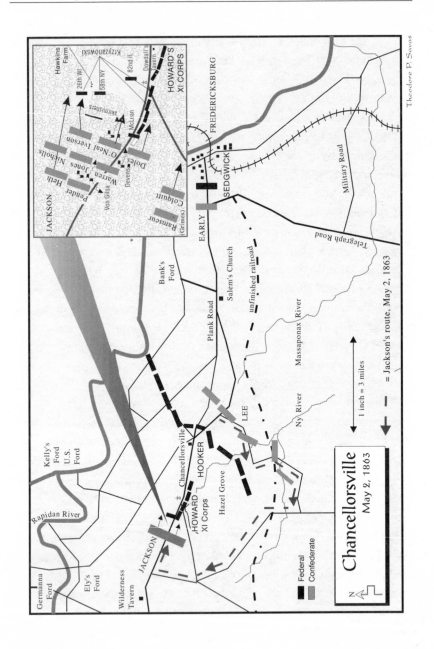

Chancellorsville
May 2, 1863

As part of Ramseur's North Carolina Brigade, Colonel Grimes' role in the attack is best described as fitful and exasperating. All of Ramseur's regiments were impeded by the timid and hesitant handling of Alfred Colquitt's Brigade, which he claimed was threatened by nonexistent Federals lurking beyond his flank. As a result, Grimes spent an inordinate amount of time and covered half a mile tramping through the thorny underbrush with his regiment while other portions of Rodes' attacking line experienced unqualified success against the retreating enemy. Grimes omitted mention of his irksome side journey in his postwar recollection on the subject, writing simply that they "drove them back for miles upon their lines behind the entrenchments, attacked them and carried the line of earth-works." The earthworks Grimes mentions were near the turnpike near the Chancellor farm clearing, which the exhausted North Carolinians reached about 7:15 p.m. "[We] took the enemy's camp baggage, the meals and coffee, then boiling hot on the fire, which we found very refreshing," remembered Grimes. They spent the night in the line of abandoned Federal entrenchments.[15]

Grimes and his men had scarcely settled down to a late supper when a renewed round of firing opened across their front. "When we supposed the fighting over, and was in the act of eating my supper," recalled the colonel, ". . .very unexpectedly a brisk fire commenced, and in a few minutes cannonading, the enemy raking the woods and plank road with grape and canister." Assuming a charge was imminent, Grimes ordered his men behind the breastworks and prepared for an attack. "I went up the road to see if I could hear anything to account for the sudden firing," he explained, "when I met a party bearing a litter off the field." The curious officer asked the identity of the unfortunate occupant, and "some one said 'Lieutenant Sumter,' and upon going a step or two further," he remembered, "I encountered General Rodes." The litter's occupant, murmured the division commander, was not a lieutenant but a lieutenant general: Stonewall Jackson. "[Rodes] thought it advisable that it should be concealed from the troops," Grimes later wrote, "for fear of disheartening them."

The aggressive commander of Lee's Second Corps had been wounded by his own men when he rode east in the darkness to survey the terrain for a possible night attack. The volleys of small arms fire had struck Jackson in the arm and hand, while the artillery barrage triggered by the firing wounded

A. P. Hill shortly thereafter. For a short while Rodes was in command of the corps (and consequently Ramseur assumed the reins of Rodes' Division, with the brigade command mantle falling on Grimes as senior colonel) until cavalryman Jeb Stuart appeared and assumed Jackson's place.[16]

The Federals spent the night of May 2-3 entrenching and consolidating their lines, which opposite Grimes' position ran from the dominating terrain at Hazel Grove southwest of the Chancellorsville crossroads over the Plank Road and north toward the Rappahannock River. Grimes roused his men before sunrise on the Sunday morning of May 3 "to hold ourselves in readiness to support other troops when needed." General Stuart had re-aligned the infantry divisions, placing Rodes' bloodied brigades in the third line about three-fourths of a mile behind the new front. This was done ". . .in consideration of our having borne the brunt of the fights for the two pre-vious days," explained Grimes, and "others were to take the advance." All three divisions spanned the Plank Road, with A. P. Hill's (now under Harry Heth) holding the front rank, and Raleigh Colston's next in line.

General Stuart opened the day's assaults shortly before 6:00 a.m. He drove his new command steadily east and quickly seized Hazel Grove, which he reinforced with numerous artillery pieces. While Heth was moving forward, Grimes and his 4th North Carolina rested in rear of the Stonewall Brigade preparing breakfast. The North Carolinians listened to the raging battle for about two hours, during which time the attack ground to a halt deep in the woods and thickets bounding the Plank Road. Sometime before 8:00 a.m. Grimes and Ramseur rode in advance of their line up the road to observe the progress of the battle. According to the former officer, a staff officer galloped upon them "and directed, by command of General J. E B. Stuart (who had assumed command after General Jackson was wounded), the officer in command of [the Stonewall] brigade to advance and charge the enemy." Both Grimes and Ramseur witnessed the delivery of the order, but the "brigade commander declined to move forward his command except by order of his division commander." The combative Ramseur turned to the staffer and said, "Give me the order and I will charge." Grimes, somewhat uncharacteristically, remonstrated against Ramseur's suggestion. "As we had done the fighting of the two previous days," he urged, "let this brigade move forward and we will support them." Ramseur turned aside Grimes' sugges-tion and repeated his offer to advance. "Then you make the charge, General

Ramseur," directed the staff officer. "General Ramseur then turned to me," wrote Grimes, "saying, 'Let us hurry back. Call your men to attention!' which I did upon reaching the command."

Ramseur ordered three regiments of his brigade to advance south of the Plank Road, detaching the 30th North Carolina to protect his right flank and the 40 blazing guns firing from Hazel Grove. The command "Forward!" was given and Grimes and his men moved up to a line of earthworks occupied by another brigade jammed in three or four deep behind them. Despite several requests for them to advance, these men would not budge from behind the freshly overturned reddish earth. A frustrated Ramseur received permission to drive his own men over the cowering soldiers milling across his front, and he again gave the command to advance. "We had to climb over these men now lying down behind it for protection, and over the breast-works and again form in line of battle," remembered Grimes, who noted that his own soldiers "were entirely disgusted at their cowardly conduct." Grimes displayed his own lack of respect for the embarrassing performance when he put his "foot on the back and head of an officer of high rank, in mounting the work, and, through very spite, ground his face in the earth." One of the members of the prone brigade was heard to exclaim, "You may double-quick, but you will come back faster than you go." The prediction would soon prove wildly inaccurate. Douglas Southall Freeman, historian of the Army of Northern Virginia, was closer to the truth when he later wrote that for the next hour "the battle was to be Ramseur's."[17]

Grimes drove his men forward through a thick undergrowth into the face of what one officer described as a very "destructive fire," which emanated from behind the log and earth entrenchments held by Alpheus Williams' division of Federals. "The Fourth Regiment and three companies of the Second Regiment never halted or fired until we had taken the enemy's works in our front," wrote Grimes, "bayoneting Federal soldiers on the opposite side of the earth-work." The smoky foliage made it doubly difficult to determine what, exactly was transpiring. Soon Grimes' men found themselves next to a swampy ravine, above and to the east of which was the firing Federal artillery at Fairview. "The hill across the ravine was covered by many batteries of artillery, from forty to fifty guns, which had been scouring the woods through which we had just passed with grape and canister," explained Grimes. "Seeing their infantry driven from their works, they abandoned this artillery."[18] The 4th North Carolina had rushed ahead of most of the rest of Ramseur's Brigade and was taking fire from both its front and flank. Hunkering down behind the abandoned mounds of dirt, Grimes' men lowered their rifles and sent sheets of lead into the advancing enemy soldiers, who were attempting to recapture the position. "The enemy made three distinct attempts to retake this work," Grimes wrote, "forming their men in column by taking advantage of a ravine just beyond the turnpike." The assaults were turned away each time, "driven back with severe loss, our men acting with great courage, enthusiasm and determination."[19]

The situation, however, was growing more desperate by the minute. The Federals artillerists rallied to their guns and renewed their fire against Ramseur's Brigade. As the shell and canister poured down upon them, Grimes took notice of the changing circumstances beyond his vulnerable right flank. "My attention was called to my right and rear," Grimes remembered, "where I saw large numbers of the enemy fast closing up our line for retreat (the right of Ramseur's Brigade having halted to deliver their fire upon encountering the enemy where they were engaged, while we had taken the breastwork.)" Ramseur noticed his dangling right flank as well. The general personally rode to the rear on a pair of occasions to prod Brig. Gen. John R. Jones to move his brigade forward to plug the gap between his men and the artillery at Hazel Grove. Jones, however, refused Ramseur's pleadings and remained immobile. Even the dashing Robert Rodes could not get Jones' men to move forward. Meanwhile, Grimes and his embattled soldiers were running low on ammunition, scrounging cartridges from the dead and wounded while holding their position amidst a scattered collection of brush fires. Fortuitously for the Confederates Jeb Stuart managed to prod the Stonewall Brigade into action. The Virginians moved out from their position in the rear and swept past Hazel Grove together with the previously detached 30th North Carolina, shoring up Ramseur's imperiled right wing and driving the enemy back, capturing hundreds of prisoners in the process. The attack allowed Grimes to safely withdraw from his advanced position to the line of works from which he had earlier launched his attack. Grimes, perhaps not realizing that the Stonewall Brigade had finally, albeit belatedly, attacked, scathingly wrote that his men fell back to the "protection of the earth-work still occupied by this [Stonewall] brigade, through whose cowardice we had suffered so severely."[20]

The assault and subsequent retrograde action had been costly in both blood and energy. Scores of men had fallen in the attempt to get to the guns at Fairview. Grimes himself, although not seriously wounded, barely managed to escape the inferno. "In this charge my sword was severed by a ball," he observed, "my clothes perforated in many places, and a ball embedded in my sword-belt and the scabbard." A whizzing piece of metal had struck him in the lower leg, leaving "a very severe contusion on the foot." He was so fatigued he "had only sufficient strength to get over" the earth works before he "lost consciousness from exhaustion and pain."[21]

The prone colonel was revived when an ambulance corps member, "seeing my condition, came to my relief, and from a canteen [poured] water over my head. . ." As Grimes regained consciousness—or as he describes it, was "recalled to my senses"—he heard the bellowing voice of General Rodes, his division commander, questioning another officer.

"What troops are these?" demanded Rodes.

The officer to whom the question was directed, the same one "who had refused to advance when ordered by General Stuart's staff officer," noted Grimes, replied, "the [Stonewall] Brigade."

"Why have you not joined in the charge?" asked Rodes.

"We have had no orders to advance," came the reply. The answer enraged Grimes.

"Under the stimulus of this falsehood," the North Carolinian later wrote, "I full aroused and pronounced it a *base lie;* that I had heard the order given myself."

Grimes' pronouncement satisfied Rodes, who was in a similar state of mind as his subordinate. The division commander, related Grimes, "took out his pistol, rode up to this officer, presented the muzzle to his head, and, with an epithet of odium, told him to forward his men, or he would blow his brains out."[22]

The brigade, noted Grimes with some measure of satisfaction, "moved forward, and, without firing a gun, reached the breastworks that we had taken, and found the Federal forces had evacuated the hill, and safely carried off all their artillery." Grimes' frustration with the Stonewall Brigade's refusal to charge is evident in his subsequent observation: "If these troops had moved forward in obedience to orders, and encountered the enemy, we would have advanced quickly to their support and captured the principal part of Hooker's artillery. As it was, we met with terrific slaughter in my command, and failed to take the artillery."[23]

The fighting prowess of the North Carolina Brigade and its component regiments impressed everyone who witnessed the engagement, especially Jeb Stuart, who ordered cheers for the victorious soldiers. The adrenalin of battle ebbed soon enough, however, when the men took stock of the thin lines of survivors. "On beholding the shattered remnants of the. . .brigade," wrote an officer from the 2nd North Carolina, its commander "wept like a child." Realigned for battle, the North Carolinians marched north across the Plank Road to protect that sector against an expected Federal assault. When the attack failed to materialize, the brigade was shifted just below the road, with Grimes' 4th North Carolina holding the extreme left flank. There the brigade remained while General Lee prodded Hooker's divisions into a tight concentric front and fought off another threat to his rear from the direction of Fredericksburg. The battle drew to a close on the evening of May 5-6 when Hooker withdrew across the Rappahannock River.[24]

The casualties suffered by both sides at Chancellorsville were horrific. The Army of Northern Virginia suffered 1,665 killed, 9,100 wounded and 2,000 missing, in addition to the loss of Stonewall Jackson, who succumbed to his wounds and the subsequent amputation of his arm on May 10. The Army of the Potomac also suffered grave losses which included 1,606 killed, 9,762 wounded and some 6,000 missing. Ramseur's North Carolina Brigade contributed significantly to casualty lists by suffering higher losses than any other Confederate brigade at Chancellorsville. The unit carried 1,509 men into battle and lost 788 of them. Federal metal exacted a heavy toll on Grimes' 4th North Carolina. Of the 327 bayonets mustered for the battle, 46 were killed, 157 wounded and 58 taken prisoner, or about 80% of its fighting force. The 2nd North Carolina, which also carpeted the woods with corpses, left behind almost 75% of its strength in a quarter hour of fighting.[25]

Following the battle Grimes was taken by litter to the hospital, where his severely bruised foot was treated. The following day he rode across the wooded ground through which his men had made their gallant charge. "[I] examined the works we had taken," he observed, "and found scores upon scores of the enemy's dead, around and in front of the work, doubtless killed

by my command and the three companies of the 2nd Regiment." Grimes'
dead were "buried near this breastwork the next day."

Deeply moved by the somber scene, Grimes reflected on the courage of
his men at Chancellorsville: "This charge was as gallant, noble and self-sac-
rificing as the world-renowned charge at Balaklava of the 'immortal six
hundred.'" General Lee recognized the contribution of the North Carolina
Brigade to the significant battlefield victory in a letter to the state's governor, Zebulon Vance. "I consider its [Ramseur] brigade and regimental commanders as among the best of their respective grades in the army." The 4th
North Carolina's historian, Captain Osborne, observed that nothing could
surpass the "dashing skill and courage of the brilliant and accomplished
Ramseur," while the "intrepid Grimes shone with magnificent splendor by
his side."

Dodson Ramseur, writing in his official report of the action, took pains
to mention the courage displayed by his regimental commanders, including
"the gallant Grimes of the Fourth [North Carolina] whose conduct on other
fields gave promise of what was fully realized on this." He had every right
to boast. In his first battle as a brigadier Ramseur had handled his brigade
masterfully. His attack had blocked a Federal thrust and driven it back with
heavy loss at a critical juncture in the fighting. Perhaps as important was his
splendid coordination with his subordinate officers. The duel performance
of Grimes and Ramseur forged the initial link in the chain of respect and
friendship that would develop between them over the coming months and
battles that lay ahead.[26]

Rumors that Grimes had been killed at Chancellorsville reached Charlotte Bryan in Raleigh. "I went into the sitting room to speak to my father
and mother," she remembered in her memoir:

> Mr. Winder was in there and was telling the news from the battle. He said,
> among others, Col. Grimes was killed. He said I turned white as a sheet. I
> was standing in the door so I went out into the dining room. My mother came
> in saying there was a letter for me. It was from a gentleman who had courted
> me from my first season, saying he would come to Raleigh and visit me. I
> remember thinking why was it he was alive and Col. Grimes killed. I threw
> the letter in the fire, realizing I cared more for Col. Grimes than anyone
> else.[27]

Although the Chancellorsville Campaign was over, the saga of the brigade that wouldn't charge, was not. The Stonewall Brigade's commander, Col. John Henry Stover Funk of the 5th Virginia, was outraged when he learned that General Ramseur was claiming that the Virginians refused to advance and were overrun by Ramseur's regiments. Funk, who had taken charge during the fighting on May 3 after Brig. Gen. Elisha Paxton was killed, wrote to Ramseur that he had wrongly impugned his men, and that he did not recall any troops passing over them. Ramseur replied shortly thereafter on May 22 that during the course of the action several of the men milling behind the works claimed to be part of the Stonewall Brigade. "Therefore I ordered my Brig[ade] forward over those of Gen. Jones and over those who told me that they were of the Stonewall Brig[ade]," he wrote Funk. Ramseur offered to correct the mistake by reading or posting Funk's letter for his men to see. Despite this exchange, Ramseur's official report, dated the following day, referred to the men as "a small portion of Paxton's [Stonewall] Brigade." It is possible the malingering men lied and said they were from the Stonewall Brigade; in all probability some of them were. Certainly Grimes and Ramseur believed that at least some of the troops they climbed over were from Funk's command. Writing after the war on this subject, Grimes identified them in his original manuscript. Colonel E. A. Osborne, in his history of the 4th North Carolina, also identified the reluctant brigade as that of Paxton's.[28]

Following Chancellorsville, Grimes and the 4th North Carolina, with the balance of Ramseur's Brigade, returned to the vicinity of Hamilton's Crossing near Fredericksburg, where the men spent the next three weeks recovering from the battle, on picket duty, drilling, and regrouping for the next campaign. With Ramseur absent until May 20 seeking treatment for his leg wound, Grimes was probably once again in temporary command of the brigade. The foot contusion he suffered was slow to heal. "My foot in which I was wounded has not quite gotten well so that I could put on my boot," he wrote his daughter Bettie later that month.[29]

Although the armies were not actively engaged at this time, the opposing pickets were often in close contact. "My regiment is down on picket duty with the enemy not more than 150 yards from us," Grimes wrote his daughter near the end of May. "They are very anxious to communicate, but we forbid our soldiers to reply to them when they wish to talk as we do not wish to have anything to do with them except at the point of the bayonet." Despite his crippling foot wound, which provided a ready means of obtaining a medical furlough, Grimes would have none of it. "I would have liked very much to have visited home, but my conscience would not permit me to leave the Regiment."[30]

The days of relative peace between the two main field armies in the Eastern Theater were rapidly drawing to a close. Lee, who had long believed that his pair of infantry corps were too large for a single general to effectively handle, reorganized the Army of Northern Virginia into three corps following the death of Stonewall Jackson. General Longstreet, who rejoined the army immediately following Chancellorsville from his sojourn around Suffolk, retained the First Corps. Richard S. Ewell was promoted to head Jackson's former organization, while A. P. Hill was called upon to lead the newly-created Third Corps. Robert Rodes' Division, with Ramseur's Brigade still within its ranks and Grimes at the head of the 4th North Carolina, remained with the Second Corps.

By the first of June the Army of Northern Virginia was again prepared for active campaigning. Should Lee seize the initiative? Virginia had been denuded of supplies and horses by almost two years of hard war, and Lee was confident he could relieve his state by marching his army north into Maryland and Pennsylvania. Perhaps a stunning victory on Northern soil, comparable to Second Manassas or Chancellorsville, would relieve the growing pressure against Vicksburg, Mississippi, and prompt the North to seek terms of peace. Almost certainly a thrust north of the Potomac River would force the withdrawal of Joe Hooker's Army of the Potomac from central Virginia.

Following a review of the Second Corps by Lee at the end of May, the army received its marching orders. Few knew Lee's intent or destination. Rodes' Division left its encampment on June 4 and tramped its way north through Spotsylvania Court House, over the Rapidan River and north of Culpepper. The weather was been warm and dry, although brief showers on the second day of the march helped settle the choking dust along the dirt roads. The ninth day of June saw at least the prospects of action when Ramseur's Brigade was dispatched to Brandy Station, just east of Culpepper, to assist the army's embattled cavalry arm. A surprise thrust by Federal horsemen threatened to overwhelm Jeb Stuart's troopers, and the action escalated into the war's largest cavalry battle. Fortunately for the North Carolinians, their participation was not necessary. "Though under fire," wrote Captain Osborne of the 4th North Carolina, "we were not actively engaged." Grimes marched his regiment back to Culpepper late in the day, where it arrived with the balance of the brigade, exhausted but intact. The march north was resumed the following afternoon toward the Blue Ridge Mountains, which were reached and crossed at Chester Gap two days later. At Cedarville the Second Corps' new commander, General Ewell, divided his divisions into two wings. Rodes' Division of some 8,000 men was dispatched toward Berryville to drive back its Federal occupants, while the remaining divisions under Jubal Early and Edward Johnson drove forward against the enemy holding Winchester.

The movement was crowned with relatively easy success. Ewell's pincer against General Robert Milroy at Winchester was a small but stunning victory that cleared the lower Shenandoah of Federals. Rodes, meanwhile, faced a retreating enemy who evacuated Berryville in face of the advancing Confederates and fell back to Martinsburg. Rodes' men made a demanding twenty mile march the following day "not including the wide detours [with] the brigades of Daniel, Doles, Ramseur, and Iverson, in the effort to surround the enemy." Rodes found the Federals, a brigade under Daniel Tyler, drawn up in line of battle "on the right of the town." Sending his mounted men forward toward Martinsburg to reconnoiter, Rodes quickly formed his several brigades for an attack as they arrived on the field. Ramseur's regiments were deployed on the left of the line four-brigade front (with one in reserve). Fearing the Federals were about to fall back, Rodes ordered Ramseur to launch his assault, to be taken up in echelon from left to right.

"Notwithstanding their fatiguing march," wrote Rodes after the campaign had ended, "the troops exhibited great enthusiasm, and rapidly occupied the town and the enemy's position." The "battle" quickly became little more than a footrace, as Colonel Grimes and his fellow regimental commanders "pursued the enemy at almost a run for 2 miles beyond the town." Rodes, lamenting the pyrrhic nature of his victory, mourned the fact that he had not been able to get his division to the town "an hour or two earlier." Had that happened, he explained, "I would have captured the whole force." As it was he ended up with several pieces of artillery and a couple hundred prisoners.[31]

The division got a late start the following day, June 15, when Rodes allowed his men to rest before pushing on toward the Potomac River. He made up for the delay by setting a punishing pace on the road to Williamsport. Grimes' 4th North Carolina was one of Rodes' first units to cross the Potomac when Ramseur's Brigade splashed across the wide river in advance of the other four brigades. It is likely that Grimes crossed the river in an ambulance, for his badly contused foot wound suffered at Chancellorsville was still bothering him. "I rode in an ambulance all the time," he later scribbled in some postwar marginalia, "except when expecting an engagement, owing to the injury on my foot." Even though the campaign was just beginning, the cohesion of the veteran regiments was starting to wear thin under the intense summer sun, the men exhibiting "unmistakable signs of exhaustion," observed Rodes.

The next forty-eight hours were spent resting and recuperating. "We are on the move in Maryland, and I trust and believe our success will be better and greater than during our visit of last year," wrote an optimistic Grimes to his young daughter Bettie. The local citizenry, he noted, hoped otherwise. "The women and children at this town [Williamsport] look very grim and severely at us, but I made my band play Dixie and the Bonnie Blue Flag for them." Writing less as a soldier and more of a father, he informed the young girl that he had "captured as part of the spoils of the Yankee camp, a dog and a tame squirrel. I wish you could see him. He is very tame and gentle. You would be amused at his pranks." Perhaps to lessen the child's fears about his safety, he closed his letter by informing her that the "enemy are badly frightened at our approach and flee before us like frightened deer."[32]

Rodes set his division in motion again on June 19, leaving Williamsport for Hagerstown Maryland. His infantry crossed into Pennsylvania, or as Rodes put it, "penetrated into the enemy's country," on June 22. While in Hagerstown Grimes wrote to his cousin Mollie about his activities during the exhausting advance. "I was appointed to act as Provost Marshall of the city, and only had I time, [I] would have had a good time with the ladies who are great sympathizers with our cause." Grimes' perception of the sympathies of these women from western Maryland differs considerably from his earlier letter to Bettie. If he really believed the local population supported the raiding Confederate army, he and other Confederates were disappointed, for little of substance was offered them. As one officer from the 4th North Carolina concluded, "Maryland has not the sympathy for the South that we had been made to believe she had."[33]

The division left Hagerstown and marched through Greencastle and Chambersburg on its way to Carlisle, which was reached on June 27. Carlisle was but eight miles from Harrisburg, the Pennsylvania state capital, and the area had thus far been spared the chronic presence of rampaging armies. Foodstuffs and animals abounded. "The war had not hurt them like it had us," commented one of Grimes' North Carolinians. While the rest of Ramseur's Brigade took possession of the former United States Barracks in Carlisle, Grimes and his 4th North Carolina were dispatched on picket duty. The assignment offered Grimes a unique opportunity to ambush some green Pennsylvania militia. "Saw the. . .militia coming out with their high sugar-loaf hats," he later wrote, "[and] put a portion of my picket in ambush, allowing militia to pass." The enemy cooperated by tramping blissfully unaware past Grimes' position. "[We] surpris[ed] them in front" and shot into their rear, he explained. The unpleasant experience threw the unsuspecting Pennsylvanians into a panic and they bolted for Harrisburg as fast as they could run. "Supplied my men with their hats, which fell off in their confusion," Grimes recorded with some amusement. "We stampeded all of them, about five hundred. Killed and wounded many." By the time the affair ended, "[we] were nearer Harrisburg than perhaps any troops except cavalry scouts."[34]

Rodes' Division spent a trio of relaxing days in and around Carlisle before receiving orders on the last day of the month to move out for Cashtown. After a dusty march of more than twenty miles the division reached Heidlersburg, where they camped for the night. At some point during the advance through Pennsylvania (probably during the sojourn around Carlisle), an incident took place that once again demonstrated the strict military attitude and moral character of Bryan Grimes. The colonel casually passed over the event in his memoirs, describing it as "insidious talk of man of Company A; turned him over to his own men for punishment." Thankfully another witness, the 4th's color bearer John A. Stikeleather, left a more thorough accounting. Stikeleather, who served in his dangerous capacity throughout the war, received his promotion to Ensign (First Lieutenant) for gallant action on the battlefield. In his memoir he noted with pride that just before the Seven Days' Battles "Col. Grimes told me to take good care of the flag. With some misgivings, I assumed the grave responsibility."

The "insidious talk" mentioned by Grimes and recorded in detail by Stikeleather emanated from a member of the regiment's Company A, "quite a character in his way, Hugh H. [Hall]." Hugh was with a foraging party "that left camp soon after we stopped, and in a short time returned well supplied with the best the country could afford," recalled Stikeleather. "Knowing we were in the enemy's country," explained the color bearer,

> [he] seemed to think when he was out foraging that he would be more successful if he would in speech and manner show himself just a little disloyal to southern interest. In a farm house near our camp, in the presence of several other soldiers from different regiments in our Brigade, he remarked to the lady of the house, that at Chancellorsville, two months back, several of our officers fell, shot by our own men, and if get into another fight soon, more of them will go the same way.[35]

Stikeleather, who claimed the reference to shooting officers was "a falsehood out of the whole cloth," observed "a soldier from the 14th Regiment feeling indignant at what he overheard." Upon inquiry it was discovered that the culprit, according to his own words, belonged to "Co. A, 4th." The soldier returned to camp and reported the incident to Grimes, who promptly demanded to know the speaker's name. While the soldier from the 14th North Carolina could not provide his identification, he informed Grimes that he would recognize him should he see him again. Grimes, no doubt incensed at both the lie about killing officers as well as the inappropriate behavior, ordered the captain of company A to report with his men to his headquarters immediately. After the company assembled Grimes turned to the soldier from the 14th North Carolina and directed him to "point out the man you heard using that insidious language." The soldier "ran his eye along the line till it revealed Hugh, when he said, 'there he is.'" In describing Grimes' anger, Stikeleather observed that,

> those acquainted with the noble Grimes can well imagine what his feelings were at this juncture of affairs. His face turned livid and for a few moments he could scarcely articulate coherently at all so great was his anger and indignation that one of his men should demean himself in the enemy's coun-

try. Col. Grimes told Hugh that his want of sense was all that saved his life, that, but for that fact, he would have him shot right off. [36]

According to Stikeleather, Grimes turned to Capt. William F. McRorie, Co. A. "Captain, have two men detailed to dunk this fellow in the creek one dozen times, and see that he double-quicks for two hours around a ring with a sentinel inside of it, immediately after his dunking." The captain promptly complied with his superior's directive, "detail[ing] Pink Smith and Bill Carter to go with Hugh down into the creek to do the dunking." As one might imagine, the bulk of the 4th North Carolina, together with knots of men from other regiments of the brigade, "at once repaired to the banks of the creek to witness the scene." Grimes was not among them, choosing instead to remain at his quarters. "Smith and Carter waded in with Hugh to where the water was waist deep and ducked him one dozen times in due and ancient form," Stikeleather recalled. Despite the dunking Hall remained belligerent: "[He] stood it pretty well, but as he came up out of the creek, he looked up towards the Col.'s quarters saying, 'by George, you brought me into Pennsylvania, but you will never take me out again.'"

This first phase of the punishment ended and "Hugh was taken up the Col.'s quarters," wrote Stikeleather. "Had he shown any signs of penitence, he would have been released at once without further punishment, the Col. having cooled off very considerably in the mean time. But Hugh was still incorrigible as was shown by his answers to the Col." When Grimes asked the private "if he thought he was cured, the answer to which was in a half defiant tone, 'Well, I don't know whether I am or not.'" Without much hesitation Grimes ordered the rest of the punishment—two hours of quick time drill. The insubordinate Southerner was right about one thing: Grimes would not be taking him out of Pennsylvania. "We saw no more of him till after the war," recalled the regiment's color bearer, "when he came back to North Carolina wearing a suit of blue." Hall deserted the army and eventually reached Washington, D. C., where he took the Oath of Allegiance on July 7 in 1863.[37]

Colonel Grimes, though by now an experienced officer and a veteran of several fields, still possessed both a hot and extemporaneous temper and the willingness to mete out hasty but fair punishment upon any man who violated his strong sense of morality and military discipline. He had displayed similar behavior in the charges of insubordination brought against Captain Blount in 1861. Grimes was a strict, no nonsense commander, as Stikeleather clearly implies in his discussion of the Hall incident. Although the chosen chastisement was quickly delivered, it is important to note that Grimes did not watch the punishment, which suggests that he did not receive any sadistic joy or pleasure in the administration of his disciplinary orders.

Although Grimes did not know it, important events to which he was not privy had positioned the armies on a collision course. Major General George Gordon Meade had replaced Joe Hooker as the commander of the Army of the Potomac on June 28. On that day General Lee discovered that the Federal army was pursuing him and was north of the Potomac River. This was disturbing news as Lee's strategic situation was somewhat precarious since Jeb Stuart's cavalry had been absent on a reconnaissance raid for several days. As a result, the separate pieces of the Army of Northern Virginia had been feeling their way blindly through Pennsylvania without the benefit of important intelligence information. Lee used the knowledge of Meade's ascension and pursuit as a basis for ordering a concentration of his scattered infantry corps at Cashtown, about eight miles west of a small town called Gettysburg, where nine separate roads converged.

On the morning of July 1, Robert Rodes led his division out of Heidlersburg toward Middletown, where he learned that A. P. Hill's Third Corps was moving from Cashtown to Gettysburg. Ordered to concentrate, Rodes dutifully marched his division south with Ramseur's Brigade bringing up the rear of the column. Distant rumblings reminiscent of summer thunder reached the division as it approached Gettysburg from the north. The developing battle, which involved one of Hill's divisions and the First Corps of the Army of the Potomac, had been ongoing since early morning when some of Hill's men stumbled into Federal cavalry west of town. Both sides fed troops into the spreading battle. While Hill's men had suffered heavy losses, by the time Rodes came up on his left flank, the Confederates were beginning to take control of the fight.[38]

Bryan Grimes and his 4th North Carolina (and the balance of Ramseur's Brigade) arrived near the battlefield about 2:30 p.m. on the afternoon of July 1. Strategically, the Confederates could not have planned Rodes' appearance better. His march led him up to Oak Ridge, a commanding eminence squarely on the right flank of the force confronting A. P. Hill's Corps. The wooded hill dominated that part of the field. "I found that by keeping along the wooded ridge," explained Rodes after the battle, "I could strike the force of the enemy with which General Hill's troops were engaged upon the flank, and that. . .whenever we struck the enemy we could engage him with the advantage in ground." Rodes grasped the importance of the situation immediately. He deployed his division in two lines of battle, the brigades of Iverson, O'Neal and Doles, from right to left, in the front, and his remaining brigades of Daniel and Ramseur in reserve. Grimes' 4th North Carolina held the far left of Ramseur's front line. Concern for his own left flank caused Rodes to dispatch Doles to watch that sector while Iverson and O'Neal advanced alone against the Federals. The move was an unmitigated disaster.

Unfortunately, only three-fifths of Col. Edward O'Neal's Brigade advanced down the eastern slope of Oak Hill, and none of it with its commander. The regiments began suffering from the fire of the enemy and quickly lost their cohesion and fled back up the hill. O'Neal's quick repulse exposed the left flank of Iverson's advancing brigade, which suffered an even worse fate than O'Neal's because its commander failed to deploy skirmishers. The marching men walked obliquely into an ambush, and Federals stood from behind a stone wall and slaughtered them by the score.

The swift repulse of two brigades threatened to cripple Rodes' thrust, and he called on Ramseur to rescue the deteriorating situation. Mounted atop a large gray mare, Ramseur directed his brigade of 1,027 men forward down the slope of Oak Ridge. His two left-most regiments, the 4th and 2nd North Carolina, advanced to support O'Neal's retiring troops, while the 14th and 30th North Carolina regiments assaulted the stone wall.

"After waiting a few minutes," wrote Grimes, "[we] were ordered to advance in line of battle, which was soon countermanded, and we then moved by the right flank." Ramseur, however, continued forward with the brigade's two remaining regiments and a third from O'Neal's battered brigade, losing his mare in the process. Grimes' men and the 2nd North Carolina, meanwhile, shifted "a few hundred yards" before being "recalled by Major-General Rodes and fronted on a hill to repel any attack from that quarter, as at that time there were indications of an advance on the part of the enemy." An attack was the last thing that Gabriel Paul's hard-pressed Federal brigade was contemplating. Paul's position was desperate and deadly. He was unenviably situated in a wide "V" formation behind the

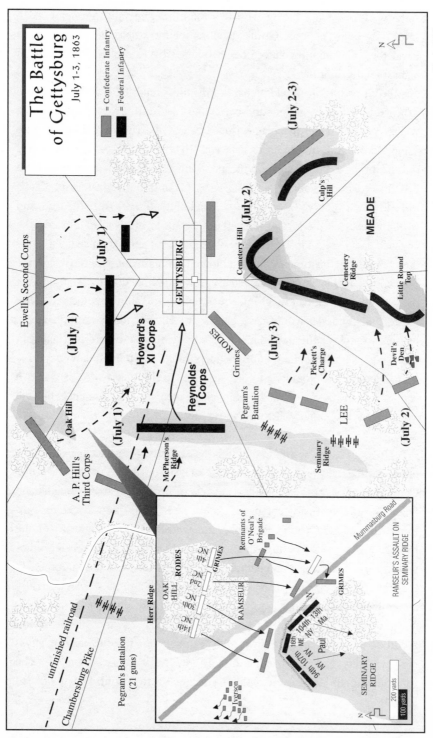

The Battle
of Gettysburg
July 1-3, 1863

= Confederate Infantry
= Federal Infantry

Theodore P. Savas

N

Ewell's Second Corps

(July 1)

(July 1)

Oak Hill

(July 1)

A. P. Hill's
Third Corps

unfinished railroad

Chambersburg Pike

Pegram's Battalion
(21 guns)

Herr Ridge

McPherson's
Ridge

Howard's
XI Corps

Reynolds'
I Corps

GETTYSBURG

RODES

Grimes

Pegram's Battalion

(July 3)

Pickett's
Charge

LEE

Seminary
Ridge

Cemetery Hill (July 2)

(July 2-3)

Culp's
Hill

MEADE

Cemetery
Ridge

Little Round
Top

Devil's
Den

(July 2)

RAMSEUR'S ASSAULT ON SEMINARY RIDGE

Remnants of
O'Neal's Brigade

OAK HILL RODES

GRIMES
4th
NC

2nd
NC

RAMSEUR

30th
NC

14th
NC

Iverson

Herr Ridge

Mummasburg Road

GRIMES

16th 104th 13th
ME NY Ma

Paul

94th 107th
NY NY

SEMINARY
RIDGE

200 yards
100 yards

stone wall, one wing facing west and the other generally northeast. Both sides were being pressed. Grimes held his regiment near the Mummasburg Road for some minutes before being ordered by Rodes to move forward against Paul's right flank.[39]

"After getting from under cover of the hill," reported Grimes, "we were exposed to a severe, galling and enfilading fire from a woods to our right, which compelled me to change front towards the right." This heavy fire came from the 13th Massachusetts and 104th New York, part of Paul's refused brigade line facing north and northeast. The 4th and 2nd North Carolina regiments continued to advance against the right-rear of Paul's brigade. The Federals, faced with overwhelming pressure from the front and with a sizeable force turning their flank, began to break in confusion. The advance of George Doles' Brigade well behind Paul's right-rear hastened their retreat. By this time Grimes had joined his regiment with the rest of the brigade line and swept after the enemy toward town, "driving them in great confusion." Unfortunately, Grimes was unable to follow up the retreating foe as quickly as he would have preferred. "But for the fatiguing and exhausting march of the day," he explained, "[we] would have succeeded in capturing a very large number of prisoners." Fatigued though they may have been, the North Carolinians turned in a fine performance. "As it was, we captured more by far than the number of men in our command, but the troops were too exhausted to move rapidly, as they otherwise would have done."[40]

The climax of the first day's fighting at Gettysburg was at hand. With other Confederate brigades joining the attack from north of the town, the Confederates swept the remaining pockets of opposition from the hills and fields toward the already congested streets. A. P. Hill's Corps drove forward from west of Gettysburg. Ramseur and Doles held the vanguard of the pursuit. "We were the first to enter the town of Gettysburg," boasted Grimes with some satisfaction, "and halted to rest on the road leading to Tomsfield [Fairfield]." Stikeleather, carrying the 4th North Carolina's colors, vividly remembered the advance into Gettysburg. "We swept right on the field, never stopping till the left of our Brigade, which was the 4th Regiment, rested on the main street of town." The panic among the citizens of Gettysburg was very great the evening of July 1st," Stikeleather continued. "The panic among the women and children was pitiable to behold. They imagined us to be no better than semi-barbarians. . . .our officers used their utmost endeavors to prevent violence of any kind to them in person or property."[41]

The inexorable advance drove through Gettysburg and netted Lee's army a large cache of captives. "In the pursuit," explained Rodes, "the division captured about 2,500 prisoners—so many as to embarrass its movements materially." Rodes was correct. The stunning victory had disorganized the Confederates almost as much as the routed Federals, who were streaming southeast out of town and up the slopes of Cemetery Hill. The rising heights below Gettysburg offered a powerful position for a defensive line, and Federal officers of every rank were endeavoring to organize a coherent front to meet the expected onslaught. As the Federals worked to strengthen their position, Rodes sought to organize his division and "prepared for further action." While he, Ramseur, and others believed an attempt should be made to drive the enemy from the high terrain, the commander of the Second Corps, Lt. Gen. Richard Ewell, did not issue the order to do so. Rodes deployed his division for the night within Gettysburg, prepared to meet an attack from the enemy should such a thing be attempted.[42]

Whether an attack that evening would have been successful will never be known, but we do know that the Federals put the respite to good use. General Meade ordered his army to coalesce on the high ground below the city. Before too many hours had passed he had the bulk of his army deployed in a powerful "J" or "fishhook" alignment. His right flank was anchored southeast of town on Power's Hill and Culp's Hill (the tip of the fishhook), which bent back toward the south across Cemetery Hill and down the shank of the hook along Cemetery Ridge. The position offered several advantages, including interior lines and wide open fields of fire for the Federal batteries that studded the line. By the morning of July 2, the position was virtually impregnable.

Although the second and third days of July are etched in Civil War history as two of the bloodiest of the war, Grimes' North Carolinians played virtually no role on either day. The morning of July 2 found Ramseur's Brigade in line of battle along West Middle Street on the western outskirts of town, its right flank near the bottom of Seminary Ridge. It was a good position from which to resist an assault, but a poor place from which to launch one. Heavy skirmishing punctuated by sporadic artillery fire occupied much of the day across the brigade front. Late that afternoon, James

Longstreet's First Corps launched a massive assault against Meade's left flank in the hope of driving it back and seizing Little Round Top. Several hours of heavy fighting ensued before darkness effectively ended the unsuccessful effort. On the opposite end of the line Ewell attacked Culp's Hill and East Cemetery Hill. He, too, was unsuccessful.[43]

Throughout the late afternoon and early evening hours of July 2 Robert Rodes had standing orders to "co-operate with the attacking force as soon as any opportunity of doing so with good effect was offered." When artillery and infantry in his front appeared to be withdrawing—Rodes' referred to the movement as a "stir" in his battle report—he sought out Maj. Gen. Jubal Early and the two prepared to attack Cemetery Hill in concert with their divisions. Rodes' orders for the attack, passed through Ramseur and down to Grimes, were to move out of town by the right flank, advance, and strike the northwest face of Cemetery Hill.

"About dusk," reported Grimes, "we advanced to make a night attack upon the enemy's works." The coordinated move with Early's Division was more difficult than anyone could have imagined. The left portion of the division's advance was obstructed by the town itself, which meant that Rodes' brigades had to shift far to the right to clear Gettysburg. Ramseur led the way, guiding his regiments by the right flank until George Doles' Brigade finally cleared the town. We were then "to advance in line of battle on the enemy's position on the Cemetery Hill," wrote Ramseur, whose brigade spearheaded the maneuver from the right front of the line, which was extended toward town by the brigades of Iverson and Doles; Daniel's and O'Neal's brigades were deployed behind in a supporting role. "[I] was told that the remaining brigades of the division would be governed by my movements," recalled Ramseur, which effectively meant he was in command of the division during the assault. Jubal Early's Division, however, with whom Rodes was to have cooperated, was already assaulting the enemy lines on East Cemetery Hill. Rodes later explained his failure of coordination by pointing out that "General Early had to move only half [the] distance without change of front, the result was that, before I drove the enemy's skirmishers in, General Early had attacked and had been compelled to withdraw." Why he did not prepare his men sooner is a mystery.[44]

Despite the lack of coordination, Rodes' five brigades continued advancing. It was at this time that Grimes and his men learned that they were to carry Cemetery Hill at the point of the bayonet if necessary, and that they would probably be unable to distinguish friend from enemy once they reached the crest of their objective. If there was a question as to one's identify, they were to shout "North Carolina to the rescue!" The men continued on, over a dirt road and through the thin shield of pickets. "We. . .approached to within a few hundred yards, and [drew] the fire of their pickets," recalled Grimes, "which wounded several of my men." Ordered to stop, the North Carolinians lay down and waited for the command to charge. Instead of charging, wrote Grimes, "we were recalled."

They were "recalled" for good reason: Ramseur's own personal advance made it clear that a slaughter was awaiting them. "Batteries were discovered in position to pour upon our lines direct, cross, and enfilade fires," he reported to Rodes. In addition, the guns were supported by "two lines of infantry behind stone walls and breastworks. . ." Ramseur prudently halted his command and conferred with fellow brigadiers Alfred Iverson and George Doles. Both concurred with Ramseur: an attack would be folly. Rodes, when informed of the circumstances awaiting his troops in the darkness ahead, and having been "officially informed" of Early's repulse, ordered Ramseur to "retire quietly." The men fell back to the dirt lane (known today as Long Lane), and piled up fence rails and dirt in an effort to strengthen the position.[45]

The third day at Gettysburg proved to be a disastrous one for Confederate arms. Lee, believing he was out of other viable options, decided to launch a heavy infantry assault against the right-center of Meade's line, a naturally powerful position perched atop Cemetery Ridge. The attack was to be preceded by a massive artillery bombardment intended to soften the defenders. The strike force was a patchwork of brigades pulled from the divisions of George Pickett, Henry Heth (under Johnston Pettigrew, Grimes' friend), and Dorsey Pender (under Isaac Trimble). According to one of the officers in the North Carolina Brigade, "The position we had enabled us to see the whole affair." The horror of the situation did not escape him. "Oh what an awful sight it is to see an army marching upon another!" The assault, known popularly (but incorrectly) as Pickett's Charge was, as one historian describes it, "reminiscent of Malvern Hill. . . .Pickett's Charge was high drama, but it was doomed from the start." The broken remnants of the attacking force streamed back to Seminary Ridge and the battle of Gettysburg drew to a close. Although Lee held the field the next day (like he had at Antietam), Meade did not attack him. This interlude allowed Lee the time he needed to send off some of his wagons of wounded and other supplies in preparation for the long and grueling retreat that awaited his army, which began withdrawing on the evening of July 4.[46]

Grimes' regiment, together with the rest of Rodes' Division, formed the army's rear guard during the withdrawal toward the Potomac River. Late on the afternoon of July 14 Ramseur's men easily brushed aside a Federal probing action and that night waded across a deep section of the river. The bloody campaign was officially over. The three-day battle cost George Meade's Federals 3,155 killed, 14,500 wounded and 5,350 missing. General Lee's losses were substantially larger with almost 4,000 killed, 18,700 wounded and 5,400 missing. Bryan Grimes' 4th North Carolina accumulated the highest losses of any regiment in Ramseur's Brigade, suffering eight killed, 24 wounded and 23 missing or captured. The brigade as a whole lost 23 killed, 122 wounded, and 32 missing, or about 17% of its effective force. While the campaign had been costly to both armies, it was especially so for the Army of Northern Virginia, which could not as readily make up its losses.

The devastating setback north of the Potomac does not appear to have had any lingering negative effects on Grimes or his men, at least initially. "The regiment behaved splendidly," wrote one officer. "In fact, the men had become so much accustomed to marching and fighting that we never thought of their doing otherwise." Even the retreat did not bother the men as severely as it might have. "The men bore the hardships and privations of his most trying campaign with remarkable cheerfulness and fortitude," wrote Captain Osborne. Similarly, Grimes wrote his brother from Maryland in early July that the troops "are by no means disheartened and only wish to go at them in an open field." By late July, however, Grimes had time to reflect on the army's defeat, and his letters began echoing views held by many Confederates concerning offensive operations. "Our invading campaigns have both been attended with such unfortunate results," he informed his cousin Mollie on July 26, "and I hope our authorities will ponder long and deeply before we again advance upon their territory. Ill luck appears to overtake our Army whenever we assume the offensive. In my opinion, it is advisable to act hereafter on the defensive entirely."[47]

By the first week of August the Army of Northern Virginia was camped near Orange Court House. The respite from marching and fighting was a welcome one, and Grimes' North Carolinians remained there for about six weeks. Morale remained strong throughout the brigade, which had lost almost 1,000 men in its last two engagements. Its *esprit de corps* was a direct result of the quality of the brigade commander and his regimental leaders. Ramseur, Grimes, and the other officers of the North Carolina Brigade were a cut above most in the army, a fact aptly demonstrated on and off the field of battle. Even on the parade ground the regiments stood out. A writer for one of the Richmond newspapers opined positively about the brigade's prowess in late August, observing that the "perfection of Ramseur's men in drill is truly astonishing, and reflects the highest credit upon the proficiency and skill of that officer."[48]

Grimes and the 4th Regiment spent most of their time in camp engaged in picket duty, drilling, and matters of administrative import. One important issue outside the confines of army life which engulfed Grimes' energies in August 1863 was the North Carolina peace movement of August 1863. The stimuli for this mini-rebellion hatched from the opposition to the growing centralization and power of the Confederate government. This aversion to centralized power escalated into contempt for the conscript laws and an intense displeasure with the Confederacy's practice of placing North Carolina soldiers under the command of officers from other states. Some North Carolinians used the expression "too many Virginians" to underscore their resentment and explanation as to why North Carolina army officers were not promoted quickly enough, if at all, by the military powers in Richmond.

W. W. Holden, editor of the Raleigh *Standard*, was the leading proponent of the peace faction. Early in July 1863 Holden called upon the people of North Carolina to assemble and express their opinions. In an editorial a week later he called for "Peace! When shall we have peace?" Much of the movement was spearheaded by the Heroes of America, a strong Union faction later called the Union League. During that hot summer of 1863, the Heroes of America held more than one hundred peace meetings throughout the state. Holden's *Standard* reported on sixty of them. President Davis had been warned of the meetings and many feared they would lead to open resistance to the Confederacy. The publication of the proceedings of these meetings touched off bitter resentment in the army. Over thirty regiments passed resolutions denouncing Holden and the meetings. Such prominent North Carolina officers as generals Ramseur and Dorsey Pender had condemned Holden. Pender, prior to his mortal wounding at Gettysburg, expressed his strong resentment in a letter to his wife in April 1863: "I am very much worried of late about desertions. Our N.C. soldiers are deserting very rapidly. I have had about 30 in the last 20 days and all due to those arch traitors Holden and Pearson and Co. I cannot bear to think about those rascally 'conservatives' as they term themselves. Next to a Yankee a 'conservative' is the most loathsome sight." Ramseur, too, attacked Holden and his methods, labeling him a traitor who tarnished the name of North Carolina.[49]

Despite the lull in the shooting war, at least in Virginia, the growing peace movement in North Carolina reached such a level of intensity and inflammatory anti-Confederate rhetoric that many North Carolinians within the army felt they had to make an effort to extinguish it. Colonel Grimes moved to the forefront of this effort by calling the first of many North Carolina regimental meetings on August 4, 1863, "for the purpose of consulting as to the best means of suppressing the disloyalty and toryism at home."

The meeting was attended by virtually the entire regiment and was chaired by Grimes and a committee of five sergeants, one corporal and four privates, who were appointed to draft a resolution expressive of the sense of the gathering. Captains J. F. Stansill and S. A. Kelly served as secretaries. The men passed a resolution which unanimously approved "that we have witnessed with profound indignation the course pursued by the Raleigh *Standard* and a few other papers, and that the sentiments enunciated by those journals are in the highest degree treasonable." In addition to this strong statement, the resolution recommended "the appointment by election of two officers from each regiment to a general convention of North Carolina Troops." The resolution also sought to have the proceedings published "in all the papers in North Carolina favorable to the object in view."[50]

The resolution's call was heeded, and every North Carolina regiment sent two delegates to a general convention at Orange Court House, Virginia, on August 12, 1863. Bryan Grimes, who was appointed President of the convention, together with nine secretaries from the various brigades were selected to conduct the proceedings. A committee presented eight resolutions and these were approved unanimously. Following this action a committee of seven, including Grimes, was appointed to prepare an address to the people of North Carolina. The meeting adjourned after a speech by Capt. Richard W. York, 6th North Carolina, Company I, in which the *Standard's* editor, W. W. Holden, was denounced as a "son of Hell." The Wilmington *Journal* reported that the resolution in reference to the *Standard* was passed "amidst great applause."[51]

We are especially "appealing to the good and the patriotic to rise in their might and put down the small (as we believe) but treasonable faction in their midst," proclaimed Grimes' address to the people of the state of North Carolina, "whose machinations we have more trouble to resist than the power of our enemies." The lengthy address, signed by Grimes and others, made a patriotic appeal to North Carolinians to denounce the sentiments of the peace faction, and "for all good and patriotic men in the State to put down and destroy, and to silence forever, the voice of a faction. . .which is daily growing bolder in the expression of treasonable and mischievous sentiments . . .and whose machinations are directed towards poisoning the minds and hearts of our soldiers and people." The address clearly and singularly identified editor Holden and his paper: "the sentiments of the parties referred to find utterance principally through the columns of the Raleigh *Standard*." The address noted that those at the forefront of the peace movement "say our soldiers do not procure a fair share of military honors in the shape of promotions," to which came the caustic response: "the soldiers of North Carolina do not feel so poor in fame as to find it necessary to rely upon ephemeral puffs of ignorant newspaper correspondents for the maintenance of their claims to a just share of reputation." A grave warning followed: "It is possible that the conduct of these men may bring on us a calamity to be deplored even by themselves. It is not impossible that these men should succeed in lighting the blaze of intestine Civil War in our own State. The fate of Maryland, Kentucky and Missouri is before us for solemn warning."[52]

Not surprisingly, Holden refused to remain silent. On August 28 the Raleigh *Standard* identified Colonel Grimes as the leader "of a group of army officers who are grossly defamatory of the Editor of the *Standard*." Holden claimed that all the convention's delegates were army officers, and that the army's privates were sympathetic to him. On this point Holden was incorrect. In fact, many of the delegates were privates. Although Grimes did indeed preside over the first meeting on August 4, the committee appointed to draft the resolution was composed entirely of non-commissioned officers and privates. Holden never publicly acknowledged the presence or sentiments of these soldiers.[53]

Grimes' efforts were not in vain. Opposition meetings were organized in several counties and Holden was burned in effigy in a number of places as bitter feelings against him grew both outside and inside the state. Virtually every newspaper in the state except the *Progress*, a shrill anti-Confederate paper, condemned him. Holden continued to protest and fill his own paper with anti-Davis administration rhetoric, and the factionists somehow managed to gain the majority in the state legislature. Still, the positive effects of Grimes' labors were noticeable. "By his wisdom, prudence and candor," notes one historian of this event, "he exerted a most happy and beneficial influence in arresting the progress of disloyal sentiments at home, and securing renewed efforts to maintain Confederate armies in the field."[54]

Somehow, in addition to the serious work in opposition to the peace movement, Grimes found the time and energy to marry Charlotte Emily Bryan on September 15, 1863. Charlotte was twenty-three when she married the thirty-five-year-old colonel. She was the daughter of prominent Raleigh lawyer John H. Bryan, who had also been a member of the Federal House of Representatives. He was "a union man as long as we could remain there in honor," she wrote of her father, "but after Lincoln's proclamation called for troops to subdue the South, he became one of the strongest and most earnest supporters of the Confederacy."

The young bride was born in Raleigh, January 27, 1840. Unlike many women in her day, she received an excellent education, first at St. Mary's School in Raleigh, and later (in 1857) at Madame Carpenter's School of Philadelphia, where she studied music and languages. "I took piano lessons from Carl Wolfsohn and singing lessons from Parelli," recalled Charlotte, "the two foremost teachers of the day." She observed with some pride and humor that "Parelli always tried the voices of his pupils and would not take any girls unless their voices justified the expense and trouble of cultivating them." He was "Italian and rather a unique character," she added. This love of music was a common interest shared by both Charlotte and Bryan, a theme evidenced in their early letters.

In the summer of 1859 Charlotte traveled extensively, first to St. Louis, then Baltimore, New York, Buffalo and Cincinnati. She had seriously considered remaining in St. Louis, but eventually returned to Raleigh in June 1860. When the legislature met that winter she observed that "the times were quite exciting with much talk of secession and many parties. Most of our friends, among the gentlemen, were secessionists, though some were for the Union." In May 1861, the Secession Convention met in Raleigh and passed an ordinance of Secession. One of the signers, Bryan Grimes, she wrote in her memoir, "was a secessionist and kept and treasured the pen with which he signed the ordinance."

The romance between the colonel and Charlotte had blossomed over several months, although "he did not come home until September, 1863 (though I heard from him between times and he sent me music and other things), when he urged me so strongly to marry him at once, and I did not have the heart to refuse." The night before we were married, explained Charlotte years later, revealing Bryan's romantic side in the process, "my husband gave me the loveliest watch and chain I ever saw. I was overcome with surprise, as I had not expected a wedding gift during such hard times. It was a blue enameled heart set with diamonds. The chain was long and of beautiful workmanship. He had seen it in Paris [1860] and bought it, thinking he might sometime have a use for it." Bryan's hope for a future bride and an appropriate gift had been well conceived. After the couple married at Christ Church in Raleigh they took the train for Warrenton, North Carolina, where Grimes had relatives and friends. After a honeymoon lasting little more than one week they returned to Raleigh. Soon thereafter Grimes said his goodbyes to his new bride, his furlough expired.[55]

Colonel Grimes returned to his regiment at Orange Court House. The men of the 4th North Carolina took some interest in the union between their colonel and Charlotte. John Stikeleather, the regiment's color bearer, wrote that "it was gratifying to the Col's friends and admirers in the Regiment that he took this step. We felt that so true and excellent a man as Col. Grimes needed the sunshine thrown into his life, that marriage, under such circumstances, was sure to bring." Perhaps Stikeleather, writing after the war, is referring to the tragic deaths that had so permeated Grimes' life. His father had died suddenly in 1860, his mother while he was a young boy, and his first wife, Elizabeth, after a few years of marriage. Heaped upon these tragedies was the passing of his young son, Bryan, just a year earlier in 1862. This immense mountain of personal sorrow, in addition to the horrors of war and responsibilities of command, weighed heavily on Grimes. Stikeleather was right; the marriage was bound to throw some "sunshine into his life."

The newly-married colonel also made another momentous decision that fall of 1863 by deciding to run for a Congressional seat in his home (Second) district. "I saw your name rumored in the papers this morning as a candidate for Congress," she wrote her new husband on September 29. "I hope you will be elected and get out of reach of Yankee bullets."[56]

Oddly enough, it appears as though Charlotte first learned of his possible candidacy from Raleigh newspapers rather than from him directly. Grimes, as the evidence suggests, was asked to run for the office and did not initiate his candidacy himself. His name was being mentioned months earlier. In a letter to his brother William in June 1863, he concluded that he was "rather inclined under the circumstances to decline it." By the fall, however, with the Peace movement within the state at full swing and a marriage just behind him, he penned a letter to the voters in his district announcing his decision:

> Having been repeatedly solicited, both through the public channels of communication as well as by private letters from numerous and influential gentlemen from the different counties composing the district, [and] also from troops in the field, urging me to announce myself as a candidate to represent the Second District in our next Congress. . . I shall esteem it a high honor to become their representative.

Grimes made it clear that if he was elected he would remain "a staunch secessionist. . .no terms should be considered for our interest that do not recognize our complete and eternal separation from the North, and acknowledgment of our independence."[57]

Running for public office seemed out of character for Bryan Grimes. He had returned to Pitt County, North Carolina, following his graduation from UNC and for more than a decade assumed the quiet role of gentleman-farmer. Although educated and from a wealthy, prominent family, he never sought public office. Not surprisingly, prior to the November election he wrote a letter to the voters of the Second Congressional District announcing his withdrawal from the race. "[I prefer] to remain in active service in the field until peace and our independence is secured," explained the veteran soldier. ". . .I can render more effective aid in attaining that end in my present position, [and] I have, under the circumstances, concluded to withdraw my name." He ended his first brush with political office by voicing his concern that "my friends will appreciate the motives which induce me to this step," assuring them that "at some future time I will cheerfully assume any trust or responsibility that they may see fit to require at my hands." Early warning signs of his indifference to the demands of political life had crept into an October 6 letter to Charlotte. "This is the ninth letter I have forwarded today," he complained. "So much for allowing myself to be persuaded into being a candidate—and these letters in addition to my unending regimental duties." Grimes never sought public office again.[58]

Unable to be together as often as they would like, the newlyweds began a regular correspondence. "You cannot know how lonesome I was at times," Grimes revealed to Charlotte on October 3. A recurring refrain in Bryan's letters to his wife was his strong desire that she write him often. Three days later, on October 6, he expressed his yearning by telling his new wife that her "letters can never be as frequent as I could wish. For one each night would be a source of great comfort to me. [You haven't] any idea how despondent I become when the mail fails to bring a letter from you," he added, directing her to "write often, at least daily." Charlotte would write him, and often, but not daily as he requested.[59]

Grimes' letters of late September and early October were written from his camp south of the Rapidan River, where General Lee had withdrawn the Army of Northern Virginia from its position behind the Rappahannock River in mid-September. The move was necessitated by the transfer of James Longstreet and a large part of his corps to Georgia to bolster General Braxton Bragg's Army of Tennessee. "Our Army is in Morton's Ford except for our brigade [which is] left down here to do picket duty for a while longer," Grimes informed Charlotte on October 6. "Whether the object be to get nearer the road to have transportation nearer at hand, or for the purpose of a general forward movement, we don't know. But the war will develop itself in a day or two, and then I will write to you in our camp. I shall expect to see you, [but] weeks or months may elapse before I enjoy that pleasure." A concerned Charlotte responded, "please do take care of yourself for heaven's sake [and] don't let those Yankees shoot you. [I] do so long to see you." In an expression of strong feelings she continued, "my own darling husband, I would give anything I possess in this world if this war was over, but I suppose I must make the best of it."[60]

Indeed a forward movement was underway, and on October 8 the entire brigade was ordered to head for Orange Court House. Shortly thereafter Lee executed a flanking operation that ended in a small disaster in the Battle of Bristoe Station, where elements of Meade's Army of the Potomac roughly handled an imprudent and unsupported attack by A. P. Hill. Grimes, who spent some of the operation tearing up railroad track and destroying bridges, was not involved in the one-sided and bloody affair. When Meade withdrew, Lee followed suit, and it looked as though the campaigning season in Virginia had drawn to a close.[61]

In the midst of the Bristoe Station Campaign Grimes offered Charlotte a revealing glimpse into his life as a soldier and his attitude toward the hardships and dangers of battle. We have endured "a long and fatiguing march in pursuit of the enemy who refuses to give us battle," he wrote on October 13, the day before Bristoe Station. ". . .Every time we overtake them they show fight for a little while and then break and flee; one day [we] were marching upwards of thirty miles and expecting each hour to fight. Much to my surprise, I feel no more hesitation [to risk] my life in the chances of battle than heretofore." Reflecting on the physical hardships Confederate soldiers had to endure, he vowed, "I am willing to sacrifice all selfish considerations to pursue the call of duty. I have not, since last Thursday slept under a tent, but taken it under the broad canopy, and on one cold night had no covering except a cloudy sky." Grimes' sacrifice included poor rations which affected his generally robust health. "The gratification of my appetite. . .I have not had an opportunity of doing since leaving home," he lamented, "and part of the time living upon short rations, and all the time upon [illegible word] which has caused me to have sick nervous headaches that appear almost impossible for me to relieve myself of. But still I manage to stay with my regiment."[62]

The marches, sacrifices and responsibilities steeled the colonel, who enjoyed the challenges of military life. "Yesterday we had a most exciting chase after the enemy," he informed Charlotte, describing a deadly military operation as though recounting a fox hunt in North Carolina.

[We ran]. . .them to the Rappahannock where they disputed our word until the arrival of the artillery, when after a few discharges the infantry was ordered to charge, and you would have enjoyed the sport of seeing them break and run. [A. P.]Hill's Corps, who was sent around by Murphy's Junction to cut off their retreat. . .and [we] will overtake Meade's Army and see if he intends giving battle at all. We have not the slightest idea of what Gen. Lee's intentions may be except that we have three days rations with orders to be prepared at once to march. [63]

After the Bristoe Campaign ended and Lee's army was again safely below the Rappahannock River, Grimes applied for leave and returned to Raleigh on October 20 to make the necessary arrangements for withdrawing his name as a candidate for Congress. By all accounts his sojourn home was a pleasant one, and by November 17 he was back with his regiment. With General Ramseur still away in North Carolina on his own honeymoon, Grimes assumed command of the brigade until his return on November 23. Grimes' return to the army was greeted with disturbing news. On November 7 two regiments of the brigade, the 2nd and 30th, had suffered significant causalities in a brisk action at Kelly's Ford when a large Union force poured across the Rappahannock. While the former unit had offered a stout defense, the latter, in the words of division commander Robert Rodes, "did not sustain its reputation." Some 300 members of the 30th North Carolina—nearly one-quarter of the brigade—simply surrendered to the advancing enemy. This "affair was rather badly managed by the officers in command," was how Ramseur worded his understated censure upon his return to the army. The brigade's cohesion and morale had suffered during the duel absence of Ramseur and Grimes, and it took several weeks to pull the regiments together into their old fighting trim.[64]

The absence of active operations, coupled with shorter days and colder nights, cast Charlotte back into the forefront of Grimes' thoughts. In a November 21 letter he chided her for not writing him. "It was a great disappointment this morning not to receive a letter from you." With an outpouring of emotion, he confided to her that "the inclemency of the weather has kept me in a state of semi-somnolence dreaming of you, and indulging in fond hopes of the happy future that I pray is in store for us when this cursed war is over and our independence from Yankee thralldom achieved."[65]

The contemplation of peace and all of its implications gripped Grimes. ". . .I can return to the pleasures of domestic bliss," he informed Charlotte, "with the [knowledge] that my full duty to my country has been performed and has [been] exhibited to my enemies that I have fulfilled [it] in the hour of danger." I pledged "on the [stump] and have never hesitated to jeopardize my life in vindication of the principles that I advocated before the commencement of hostilities," he continued, and "if this vandal foe would only leave unmolested what now remains of our substance."[66]

Thinking of their future together, he asked Charlotte whether life at Grimesland would make her happy: "Could you make Pitt [county] your ideal of a home? Would you be content to live [away] from all other society and live for me alone? Or do you recoil at the thought of a lonely, dull home on the banks of the Tar River?"[67]

His question is revealing, for it demonstrates how little time the couple had actually been able to spend together discussing their future. Bryan had to return to duty shortly after their marriage, and the constant threat of battle and separation from one another made it difficult for the young married couple to seriously ponder their future. With a lull in the fighting Grimes seriously pondered the issue. Would such a sociable young woman, educated and raised in Raleigh, be happy living on a working planation in rural eastern North Carolina? He hoped so but could not know for certain. Only the end of the war would bring about such a thing. "Pray my dear darling for the success of our peace, for a speedy termination to this terrible, unprovoked invasion of our soil, and that the foe may be hurled back and our rights vindicated." He closed the letter somewhat poetically, by adding, "[May] the white winged messenger of peace. . .once again alight among our [illegible word] people. Pray for it my child."[68]

Writing somewhat facetiously, while at the same time underscoring their poor diet, Grimes wrote Charlotte that "the luxury [of our dinner] simply consists in our bunch of greens or cabbage and in consequence of that addition, we will dine at the fashionable hour of 4 p.m." Typically the men had to get by on daily rations of very little meat (usually salt pork or bacon as beef was rare) and some flour. It is no wonder, then, why Grimes described greens as a "luxury" consumed during the late afternoon hours: they were hungry. Food shortages over the coming months would cause severe health problems for the army as the men suffered from scurvy and other more deadly diseases.[69]

Few events broke the monotony and boredom of a soldier's life. Some relief was found on November 23 when the brigade "carry[ied] into execution the sentence of court martial upon a fellow of the 14th Regiment by having his head shaved in presence of the command and then drummed out of the service to the tune of the Caissons March and Yankee Doodle, which was done amid the mirth and derision of the men." Similarly, his spirits brightened at the prospects of a grand review of the army. "We are to have a grand gala day as we are to be reviewed by President Davis and Gen. Lee," Bryan wrote to Charlotte on the 23rd of the month. "I wish that you could be present to witness the display for it certainly will be interesting and imposing. You would be able to see all the magnates and potentates of the Confederacy, both civil and military, and have something to talk about in years after, when you are surrounded by your descendants, say fifty years hence."[70]

His thoughts about the event took a pensive turn when he ruminated about the coming prospect of battle. "Some predict a fight shortly, thinking the President's purpose in visiting the army at this time is to confer with Gen. Lee about the expediency of attacking the enemy," he explained to his wife. "I have no idea of such a course, and if we have an engagement it must be of the enemy's seeking, for at present we are heavily and actively engaged in entrenching ourselves in a most formidable position from which," he added, "without us flanked, numbers alone cannot drive us from it."[71]

Grimes' perception of warfare had shifted in a not-so-subtle manner. While he was a seasoned veteran of many of the army's largest and bloodiest offensive battles, by the end of 1863 he acknowledged the wisdom of fighting behind a fortified barrier. The colonel had learned much from his two years of active campaigning. The methods of waging war had changed, and it was obvious, at least to him, that the army's tactics had to change with it. One apt description of perhaps what Grimes had experienced puts it thus: ". . .fresh troops enter a campaign with plenty of enthusiasm but little skill. Then as they mature their skill improves until they reach a peak of efficiency. . .their skills continue but their enthusiasm and energy fade away. They get to know too much about the terrible risks which combat entails. . .

They stand appalled at the memory of their own lack of caution in earlier battles, while they were still green."[72]

Grimes again expressed his desire to see Charlotte, revealing the effects of being away separated from her: "My anxiety and desire to see you increases daily, but it appears that fate has deemed otherwise for a while longer." It seems the soldier's concerns haunted him even while he slept. "Last night I had a very troubled dream that we had to be married over again," he revealed, "and that you took up your lodging for the night elsewhere than with me which caused me to awake in great distress. Captain Giles," he noted, closing his letter along a familiar theme, "with whom I am acquainted at present, receives letters from his wife almost daily, and I always envy him that is—when I have none."[73]

Worried other than the martial variety also concerned Grimes. In a letter to his daughter Bettie on November 25 he advised her "to study your books and try to be at the head of your class," interesting advice from one who was an average student in college. Within twenty-four hours, however, he was preoccupied with matters of greater, or at least more immediate, consequence: The Federals were crossing the Rapidan River in large numbers beyond their flank.[74]

Late that night Grimes received orders to march his regiment, together with the balance of Ramseur's Brigade and Rodes' Division, from near Morton's Ford to Zoar Church just southwest of a small crossroads known as Locust Grove. The North Carolinians took up the cold march in the middle of the night and fell into line near the church the next morning with the rest of the division. With the enemy already holding good ground around Locust Grove and skirmishing with Harry Hays' Division, Rodes advanced his brigades with Ramseur's deployed on the right. By the time the divisions linked, heavy skirmishing had spread across the entire divisional front. Although Grimes may have never known it, Rodes' third division under Edward Johnson saved the entire Second Corps from serious embarrassment. Marching on a different road, Johnson's men stumbled into a powerful Federal effort aimed at getting into the left rear of the Confederates. The erupting late afternoon battle at Payne's Farm on November 27—the only serious fighting of the Mine Run Campaign—pitted Johnson against a well-supported Federal corps. Only the rough and wooded terrain and Johnson's bold assault saved the heavily-outnumbered Southerners from disaster. The action and the general deployment of the contending armies convinced Lee he was in a precarious position and he withdrew behind Mine Run creek, with Ramseur's men acting as a rear guard. There Grimes' North Carolinians entrenched and awaited the enemy's attack.

On December 1, with the armies still glaring at one another across a landscape scarred with entrenchments, Grimes hastily penned a letter to Charlotte detailing his desire to "strive harder [to] whip the Yankee vandals."[75] In his own way Grimes explained how inadequately the Southern army was provisioned: "Should I tell you of the blue coated people in our front who have such nice new overcoats and overburdened knapsacks, their contents consisting of coffee, sugar and many other luxuries to which we rebels are unaccustomed?"[76] The sharp weather and lack of food made conditions along Mine Run especially difficult. "Our men are constantly expressing the hope that they will attack us soon for they are anxious to have a supply of provisions by way of change from fasting, and a new overcoat would not be objectionable for this is a terrible winter." It is "freezing cold both day and night," he added, claiming that "today, it has not thawed even to the teens, and since last Wednesday night, I, together with all the command, have not had a tent, but taken it out with the sky alone to protect us from the weather." With the enemy in close vicinity even the small luxury of a campfire was difficult to obtain. "Part of the time, the near proximity of the enemy prevent[s] us from having fires for fear of exposing us to the enemy and thereby showing our embankments." The Federals have delayed attacking for so long, he explained, "we don't know what to expect." Even during active campaigning Grimes was thinking ahead of the possibility of Charlotte joining him during winter quarters, and he reminded her not to "forget to bring the ladies saddle with you." Several sleepless nights surrounded by overturned dirt and bitter cold engulfed both armies before General Meade called off the operation and retreated over the Rapidan, effectively ending the campaign.[77]

The Army of Northern Virginia returned to its familiar lines behind the Rapidan River and went into winter quarters. On a cold December 6 near Morton's Ford, Grimes wrote John A. Young, a former lieutenant colonel of the 4th Regiment and now a member of the North Carolina Legislature, about Federal prisoners. We are "taking up a goodly number of stragglers—the meanest in appearance that we have ever encountered yet," he explained to the former soldier. They were "the lowest scum of the Yankee foreign population." Grimes viewed the captives as inferior soldier stock. "It was really a source of congratulation and encouragement to see that they were reduced to such straits for filling their ranks," he wrote somewhat optimistically.[78]

Much to Grimes' delight, Charlotte joined him there on Christmas Eve, 1863. "Just before Christmas, I had a letter from Col. Grimes saying he had procured a comfortable boarding house near camp," she wrote after the war, "so I went as far as Richmond. . .[and] from there I went to Orange Court House, reaching there the night before Christmas, 1863." Charlotte and Bryan enjoyed the company of another couple on the train ride: "General Ramseur and his wife boarded at the same place with us, and we found them very pleasant and agreeable." Obviously planned in advance, the 4th North Carolina band turned out "shortly after [we] reach[ed] the army." During her winter stay Charlotte recalled that "Governor Vance made a visit to the army that winter, made speeches and reviewed the North Carolina troops." Thankfully little fighting ensued during her visit, although she remembered "there was a small fight on the Rapidan River while we were there. The Yankees attempted to cross and of course our husbands had to go and left very miserable, anxious wives."

Charlotte returned to Raleigh in April and within a short time the full fury of the 1864 campaigning season opened with a vengeance. The colonel's wife would "pass many long days consumed in misery and anxiety as my husband was in a battle almost every day."[79]

# The Battle of the Wilderness

## "We Whipped Them Badly"

**T**he close of the Mine Run operations and cold winter weather brought about a lull in active campaigning. With his 4th North Carolina settled into winter quarters south of the Rapidan, Bryan and Charlotte took advantage of the solitude by obtaining comfortable accommodations in a boarding house. For the newlyweds the blissful respite of several months passed far too quickly. When early April arrived, Grimes, well aware that fighting would soon begin, sent Charlotte back to the safety of Raleigh.

During a cold January 1864, while Charlotte was still with him, Grimes allowed himself to once again become embroiled in a war of words and bad feelings with a subordinate officer reminiscent of his dispute earlier in the war with Captains David Carter and Thomas Blount. This round of pettiness escalated from a misunderstanding of an order between Grimes his regimental surgeon, John F. Shaffner, and ultimately resulted in formal charges being levied against the doctor. On the morning of January 10, Grimes issued orders for Dr. Shaffner to "examine Capt. McRine [William F. McRorie, Company A] and report his condition to these Hd. Quarters." Shaffner was not happy with the orders but performed the exam nonetheless. "This is the second time I have been ordered to examine Capt. McRine," he complained, "and it is getting unpleasant. Last Wednesday I did so under orders." The results of the exam, which were forwarded to Grimes, found the captain "complaining with Lumbago—Dyspepsia & Diarrhoea; of the latter there are symptoms—the former must be aggravated to be distinguished." Shaffner closed his report with a gentle admonishment: "I hope this will be the last time I shall be required to examine this Captain."[1]

Grimes, however, who believed Captain McRine was a malingerer attempting to avoid picket duty, was not about to let the matter rest. Later that evening, Shaffner received additional orders that "either you or your Asst. Surgeon must examine Capt. Wm. F. McRine [sic] (3) three times each day and report in writing to this office." In addition, Shaffner was to display a Special Order issued that day (January 10) by Grimes which proclaimed: "Hereafter Company Officers when sick, will report to the Surgeon in person or through their orderlies, or they will be considered for duty." Shaffner set forth early details of the event to his fiancee, Carrie L. Fries, a few days later on January 14. "A captain of this Regiment did not go on picket and had not reported sick, to me, but did so to the adjutant's office," he explained. "Col. Grimes finding out that this captain had not been examined by me, ordered me to examine him and report in writing. I reported him as sick." According to Shaffner's diary entry of January 12, Grimes inquired as to whether he had obeyed the order to examine the captain three times a day. He had been in his tent all day, the doctor replied tartly, and "was prepared to examine Capt. McRine [McRorie] whenever he presented himself." Since the captain "failed to do so—I had no report to make." Shaffner obviously resented Grimes' interference with his official duties.[2]

Grimes, in turn, immediately ordered Shaffner to visit the captain in his "tent immediately and report his condition in writing by 12 o'clock M. today." Shaffner dutifully if reluctantly performed the examination and reported McRorie showing symptoms of "dyspepsia and diarrhoea," and possibly "rheumatism." A note from Grimes asked if Shaffner had obeyed the orders of the 10th and if not, to state "your reasons for disobeying the order." Your report, wrote Grimes, convinced me "this officer was not too sick to attend to his duties." Shaffner had already made it clear that he did not visit McRorie three times on January 10, either because he did not understand the order, which is unlikely, or he thought McRorie was well enough to come to his surgeon's tent for the examinations; either way, he did not specifically obey Grimes' directive. Unwilling to overlook what was obviously a minor infraction, Grimes preferred formal charges against Shaffner for disobeying his orders, and added a second charge alleging that the doctor had been drawing forage for two horses when he only possessed one.[3]

Days passed without the setting of a formal trial date. "To be 'in arrest' and 'court-martialed' is not an unusual occurrence in this army or regiment," was Shaffner's caustic observation to his fiancee in an obvious reference to Grimes' strict observance of military protocol. "Even now he [Grimes] professes respect and esteem for me (to others) and told his adjutant [W. S. Barnes] that he never did prefer charges with more reluctance," he continued. "Of course this is all bosh." On January 17, Grimes responded to a request from Shaffner that he not be confined to his tent: "There exists no necessity for Surgeon Shaffner to confine himself closely to his quarters," wrote the colonel. "He can have the limits of the Camp and its near vicinity."[4]

Despite his anger, Shaffner downplayed the significance of his arrest. "Let me assure you that to be 'arrested' is not [a] disgrace." he wrote Carrie. "It is simply an order with no particular effect. Many of our most popular leaders have frequently been 'in arrest.' Among others I will mention Generals A. P. Hill, D. H. Hill and Rodes." In his diary on January 29, however, Shaffner notes that he "received a severe lecture for my difficulty with Col. Grimes—a source to me of considerable pain." While he did not identify who lectured him, the "difficulty" with Grimes bothered the surgeon more than he was willing to admit publicly. On January 31, a cloudy and cold Sunday morning, Shaffner wrote a letter to Grimes trying to explain the situation. "The alleged disobedience of orders," he opined, "should better be termed a misunderstanding of orders. If you fail making reply to this—I shall presume that nothing but a Military investigation will suffice." Shaffner believed that Grimes' "personal feelings had become involved; in relieving me from going on picquet with the Regt. I have understood otherwise hence this letter." Grimes replied to Shaffner's letter the same day. "The motives which led me to prefer charges against you," arose from a "stern sense of military duty," said the colonel. "I will extend to you the privilege of resuming your duties until the day of the trial, suspending your arrest for that purpose, and in the meantime, if there be any personal favor, not inconsistent with my duty in a military point of view, you have but to make it known to have it granted." Shaffner requested a suspension of his arrest, and Grimes granted it.[5]

In early March, Shaffner obtained some measure of satisfaction in a most unexpected manner. "About 8 o'clock Gen'l Lee and staff ride by," he penned in his diary on March 2, "& seeing the bridge burned at several places—inquired for the commanding Officer. Col. Grimes was soon found & informed that charges would be preferred against him. An order was served upon him through Gen'ls Rodes and Ramseur, ordering him to consider himself in arrest. The biter at last is bitten!" Grimes never mentioned the incident in any of his correspondence, and other than Shaffner's journal account, no other tangible evidence of the incident exists. It is doubtful, though, that someone would pen an outright lie in his own diary.[6]

The original matter between Grimes and Shaffner dragged on until the cool and partially cloudy morning of March 17, when a formal military trial was finally convened. Grimes, Shaffner recorded in his diary, "testified in a violent and passionate manner, endeavoring to leave the impression with the Court that I am a scoundrel of the darkest dye. I made him however admit many things in my favor, and upon the whole I do not think his testimony has damaged me any." Satisfaction for both parties was delayed for time, however, when the president of the court became ill and the proceeding was postponed until March 21. The matter concluded, weeks passed without word from the court. On April 3, Shaffner wrote Carrie that he had been "requested by Col. Avery to return to the 33rd Regiment as Surgeon. I have declined and here I can manage very well to get along with Col. Grimes in an official manner." Finally, on April 4, a resolution was forthcoming. Shaffner was right, Grimes' testimony had not "damaged" him, and the surgeon was acquitted of the charges and restored to duty.[7]

This unfortunate waste of time and energy, which was little more than a clash of egos and wills, revealed something about the character and person-ality of each man. Before he had transferred as surgeon to the 4th North Carolina, Shaffner had clashed with a superior officer in his former 33rd North Carolina. "Lt. Col. and I have been at dagger points for more than 12 months," he recorded in a letter to Carrie. Almost a year earlier in May 1863, just a short time after joining the 4th, Shaffner thought highly of his new colonel. The men of the 4th are less disposed to grunt and 'play off' than those of the 33rd," he remarked. "The colonel [Grimes] prefers me and is endeavoring to have me retained. This is very gratifying to me indeed. . . . he treats me very kindly. . .and is well pleased with my conduct during the recent battle [Chancellorsville]." Colonel Grimes, continued Shaffner, "is a gentleman and treats me with consideration." If Shaffner's letters are an honest indication of the their relationship, both men respected one another until the "incident" came between them. Of the few photos that exist of Grimes, one pictures him seated between Capt. E. A. Osborne on his right and John F. Shaffner on his left. Had they disliked one another at that time, it is hardly possible they would have sat for such a photograph. Grimes "has

One of the few wartime photos of Bryan Grimes. Since he is wearing a colonel's uniform, he probably sat for this image before May 1864. *North Carolina Collection, University of North Carolina at Chapel Hill.*

heretofore treated me with uniform kindness and been more of companion than a superior officer," wrote Shaffner in a January 1864 letter. Following his trial and acquittal, Shaffner wrote an interesting (and perhaps revealing) statement to Carrie: "In regard to my trial, I rather am of the opinion that you thought 'oversensitivness' had gotten me into trouble." The acquitted Shaffner returned to duty as the regiment's surgeon.[8]

With Charlotte gone and the Shaffner affair behind him, Colonel Grimes turned his full attention once again to a variety of problems plaguing the regiment, desertion in particular. The growing number of men absent without leave had to be stemmed. As a result, Grimes and other high ranking officers carried out official Confederate policy by administering harsh but, to them, necessary punishments. "This afternoon at their request I visited three men of my regiment in the dungeon at division headquarters, under a sentence of death for desertion," Grimes wrote Charlotte in late April. "It was heart-rending to listen to their appeals for mercy and soliciting interference on their behalf—if not for a pardon [then] at least a suspension of their executions for a while which will take place next Thursday." Despite his personal emotions, the colonel believed he had an unavoidable duty to carry out. "It was with heavy heart that I informed them that I would not make application for a [pardon] of their sentence for I conscientiously believe that the good of the service absolutely demands the infliction of the severest penalty of the law to prevent desertion," he explained to Charlotte, "though it is trying to the stoutest heart and strictest principles to turn a deaf ear to the pleadings of nature and the solicitations of their dear ones at home." A few days later Grimes wrote Charlotte just before the three were to be shot, "It makes my heart break to think of shooting a man in cold blood, [but] for the good of the service it should be carried out. I have decided to remain in camp, and I avoid the exhibitions whenever it is possible."[9]

Grimes had already experienced the trauma of a firing squad. Earlier in January, one of his privates, James King of Company E, was court martialed for desertion and summarily shot. J. M. Goff, a lieutenant with the 6th Alabama attached to the Provost Marshal's office, wrote Grimes concerning this incident. Goff's letter was eventually published in the *Wilmington Journal* (N. C.) on March 10, 1864:

Colonel, I deem it my duty to make known to you the last words of private James King of your regiment, who was executed for desertion. After bandaging his eyes I told him that he had but two more minutes to live, and asked if he had any message he desired to send to his relations or friends. He replied, "I have no message. I only wish that my body may be sent to my friends, but I wish to say to you, Lieutenant, though others persuaded me to do what I did, the reading of Holden's paper has brought me to this, but I shall soon be at peace."

The reference to W. W. Holden no doubt hardened the attitude Grimes held toward the newspaper editor and his anti-war advocacy. "The [Goff] letter affords a melancholy example of the effect of bad teaching," commented the *Wilmington Journal* with an editorial slap at Holden. "We hope such examples will be rare."[10]

The official attitude toward Confederate deserters is reflected in the published observations of John Parris, a chaplain with 54th North Carolina. Commenting on the eventual hanging of twenty-two deserters at Kinston, North Carolina in March 1864, Parris wrote:

I made my first visit to them as chaplain on Sunday morning. Some of them were comparatively young men. But they had made the fatal mistake. They had only twenty-four hours to live, and but little preparation had been made for death. Here was a wife to say farewell to a husband forever. Here a mother to take the last look at her ruined son; and then a sister who had come to embrace for the last time the brother who had brought disgrace upon the very name she bore by his treason to his country. I told them they had sinned against their country and that country would not forgive; but they had also sinned against God, yet God would forgive.

Parris continued detailing the grim events. "The thirteen marched to the gallows with apparent resignation. On the scaffold they were all arranged in one row. At a given signal the trap fell, and they were in eternity in a few moments. The scene was truly appalling. But it was as truly the deserter's doom. Many of them said I never expected to come to such an end as this. But yet they were deserters, and as such they ought to have expected such a doom."[11]

Late in the spring on April 25, Grimes wrote Col. W. H. Taylor that he believed one of the conventional means of punishing deserters, labor and confinement, was not working because many of them preferred this to the dangers of battle. "[I] judge the ill effects of sentencing deserters to labor on the fortifications at Richmond (unless laborers are very much needed)," wrote Grimes. "By the execution of this sentence the object of many deserters in many instances is accomplished by being exempted from the dangers of the battle field. Labor and confinement," he explained, "is no punishment to a coward or to a man so devoid of principle as to desert. Any disgrace and punishment short of taking life is to him preferable to encountering the perils of battle." Grimes offered a remedy: "In my opinion, from what I hear among the men, it would be much better to inflict all punishments in camp requiring the offender at the same time to participate in all fights in which his regiment is engaged."[12]

As Grimes and the other officers of the army grappled with the problem of desertion, others maneuvered and politicked for promotion. Colonel William R. Cox of the 2nd North Carolina was a "sly one," Grimes wrote Charlotte in April, referencing Cox's efforts to get himself promoted to brigadier general of a new brigade about to be formed. Grimes believed Cox was "taking underhanded means" to accomplish his ends. The officer was

networking through his friends and connections in Richmond to lobby President Davis for his promotion, an action Grimes found distasteful. With his strict interpretation of military ethics and procedures, Grimes objected to Cox going over the head of his

William R. Cox,
as a brigadier general

*Generals in Gray*

commanding officer to seek the promotion, since army colonels were usually promoted on the recommendation of their superior officer. Such was not always the case. "Ambitious officers," writes one modern historian, "were never shy in pressing their claims for promotion directly upon President Davis and enlisting their congressman to press their claims, even though such conduct. . .was considered a breach of military discipline."[13]

Part of Grimes' distaste for Cox's method was probably grounded in the fact that he was in competition with the officer. Like most of the colonels in the army, Grimes wanted and at times sought promotion. While Generals Dodson Ramseur and Junius Daniel recommended both Grimes and Cox for a brigadier's wreath, Grimes was clearly their preferred choice. Not only was his name submitted ahead of Cox's, but his substantial accomplishments were meticulously noted.

"We feel it to be our duty as North Carolina officers, and with a high sense of the good of the service," wrote Ramseur and Daniel in their April 24th recommendation, "to recommend Colonel Bryan Grimes, Fourth North Carolina Troops, for promotion to the command of the brigade about to be formed of the First, Third, Fifty-fifth and another North Carolina regiment." Almost as an afterthought, the generals added: "We do also recommend for this position Colonel W. R. Cox, Second North Carolina."

Then Ramseur and Daniel turned specifically to Grimes:

Colonel Grimes is among the senior colonels from our State. He has commanded his regiment from the battle of "Seven Pines" through all the battles in which the Army of Northern Virginia has participated, except "Sharpsburg" when he was disabled, and "First Fredericksburg," when he commanded the brigade of which he was senior colonel. In the official reports of all their actions, Colonel Grimes' conduct is highly spoken of by his senior officers. In battle, Colonel Grimes is conspicuous for skill and gallantry. He commanded for several months (from Maryland to Fredericksburg) the brigade now commanded by Brigadier-General Ramseur.

As a disciplinarian, Colonel Grimes has few superiors. He is ever zealous in the performance of military duty and in providing for and taking care of his men.

We believe the claims of Colonel Grimes and Colonel Cox to be very strong: by the appointment of either, the good of the service will be secured. We, therefore, earnestly recommend their claims to His Excellency the President for promotion.[14]

Three days later, Maj. Gen. Robert Rodes heartily endorsed the duel recommendation. "I take pleasure in endorsing Colonel Grimes' claims to promotion," wrote the division commander. "He has served with me in this division since its formation at Yorktown, and shown himself, under all circumstances, to be a good and reliable officer. He is a thorough gentlemen, brave to a fault, invaluable in an action, and his habits are worthy of imitation." Rodes' strong and warm endorsement belies the tension that had existed between he and Grimes since their falling out in the Shenandoah Valley in November 1862. When Grimes later wrote about the bad blood between the two, he reported it ended with a "gentlemanly and chivalrous action on the part of General Rodes" in the spring of 1864. Perhaps his division commander's recommendation was this action.[15]

On the last day of April, Grimes wrote Charlotte of the recommendation and enclosed Rodes' endorsement, adding, "You may show this to brother, he would understand, [but] your family might think it vanity in me to report it." In the same letter he engaged in a little gossip. "I inferred from what Ramseur said today that his wife is in a similar situation as yourself." He meant (correctly) that Nellie Ramseur was pregnant like Charlotte. Grimes also added that he thought Mrs. Davis was "developing," and that Ramseur had remarked on it also.

As the calendar eased toward warmer weather and the inevitable resumption of active campaigning, no one knew what the future held. Morale in Lee's Army of Northern Virginia was high, James Longstreet's First Corps had recently rejoined the army, and the two major Confederate field armies were led by the South's two most popular generals: Lee in the east, and Joseph E. Johnston in North Georgia at the head of the Army of Tennessee. George G. Meade remained at the head of the Army of the Potomac. Ulysses S. Grant, however, recently promoted to lieutenant general and commander of all the Federal armies, transferred east and decided to hitch his headquarters to Meade's army. That rather awkward arrangement (for Meade, especially) meant Lee and his men would essentially be facing yet another commander in the field. Since Charlotte was with Grimes during most of this period, any thoughts on the subject were likely spoken to his wife instead of recorded for posterity; certainly he was not aware of the relentless campaign Grant would wage against his new opponent.

Grant's blueprint for victory was simple: he would wage a war of attrition against Lee's army and supplies. Unlike his predecessors, he was far less concerned about holding a piece of territory or seizing the Confederate capital. Instead, his single-minded focus was to engage Lee's army and defeat it in combat—over and over again. The first years of the war demonstrated the difficulty of defeating an enemy army in the field. While both sides were able to trade bloody and occasionally temporarily crippling blows, neither was able to wage and win a battle of annihilation. While this was largely due to the increased power of the defensive brought about by the rifled musket, it was also because each campaign consisted of only one or two sizeable battles, after which one side or the other would withdraw, reorganize, and move out to fight once again. Grant realized this fact and appreciated the North's massive abundance of manpower and war materials relative to his opponent's. By making Lee's army the objective, he would seek to engage the enemy until he was so weak and broken the war would inevitably draw to a close. Lee, contrarily, with the offensive power of his army limited by prior setbacks, knew his best chance for ultimate victory was to prolong the war as long as possible to persuade a war-weary North to seek peace or a change of administrations in the 1864 presidential elections.

As a result of his strategy, Grant's campaign plans were simple and direct. He would move the Army of the Potomac southeast over the Rapidan River into the Wilderness area, where the army had come to grief a year earlier at Chancellorsville, pass through the wooded terrain and turn Lee's right flank. Such a move, if successful, would place his army between Lee and Richmond. The Federals opposing Lee numbered about 118,000 men and 316 guns, and was organized into three infantry (four counting the unattached IX Corps) and one cavalry corps: the II Corps under Winfield S. Hancock; the V under Gouverneur K. Warren; the VI under John Sedgwick; the unattached IX under Ambrose Burnside; and the troopers under Philip H. Sheridan. Opposing the Federals, Lee fielded about 224 guns and some 65,000 men, composed of James Longstreet's First Corps, Richard Ewell's Second Corps, A. P. Hill's Third Corps, and Jeb Stuart's cavalry.[16]

The campaign opened on May 4 before daybreak, when Grant began crossing the Rapidan at Germanna and Ely's fords. A few hours later he wired Gen. Halleck at Washington: "The crossing of the Rapidan effected. Forty-eight hours now will demonstrate whether the enemy intends giving battle this side of Richmond." Lee, of course, had no serious intention of either falling back or relinquishing the initiative to his opponent. Grant's decision to plunge into the Wilderness could be used against him to nullify his overwhelming strength in both infantry and artillery. Lee, therefore, ordered Ewell to advance east on the Orange Turnpike and catch the Federal army in motion, while A. P. Hill marched his corps in the same direction on the Orange Plank Road to the south. Longstreet, who had been stationed miles to the rear at Gordonsville with his divisions, was ordered to follow Hill on the Plank Road. Ewell prudently left several units, including Ramseur's Brigade (and thus Grimes' 4th North Carolina) deployed along the Rapidan at Raccoon Ford until he was sure no sizeable Federal force was planning to approach from the direction of Culpeper Court House. The next morning, Ramseur's Brigade crossed the Rapidan and probed toward Culpeper in search of a non-existent enemy. The Army of the Potomac was no longer there. With that information in hand, Ramseur's regiments spent much of the rest of the day marching south to catch up with the balance of Ewell's Corps.[17]

While Grimes and Ramseur were reconnoitering north of the river, Ewell's Corps ran into Warren's V Corps in the Wilderness on the Orange Turnpike. The heavy presence of the enemy caught Grant somewhat by surprise, and the veteran commander stopped his army and immediately attacked Ewell's line, which straddled the turnpike and faced generally east. A. P. Hill's Third Corps, moving east on the Orange Plank Road, also found the enemy, veterans from Winfield Hancock's II Corps. The fighting, eerily reminiscent of the savagery of Chancellorsville a year earlier, raged with unrelenting ferocity throughout the day until darkness brought it to a close. Neither side gained any substantial advantage, although Lee had committed virtually every brigade on hand, and Longstreet's First Corps was still marching to the field and would not be available until early the next morning. Grimes and his men could hear the muffled strains of thousands of small arms roaring in the distance as they hurriedly stepped toward their embattled comrades. The brigade reached the front late that evening, "taking position in echelon on the extreme left to protect Major-General Johnson's left flank," wrote Ramseur. The North Carolina brigade was the Second Corps' sole reserve. After a fitful night, Grimes's 4th, which numbered about 325 officers and men, together with the balance of Ramseur's regiments were shifted south through the thick underbrush below the turnpike "in rear of our center as a reserve to Major-Generals Johnson or Rodes."[18]

The widespread and confused May 5 fighting had effectively cleaved Lee's army into two sections, leaving a gap a mile wide between Ewell's right flank and Hill's left. Nothing but the brushy terrain concealed the extent of Lee's strategic dilemma from Grant. Aggressive and nonplussed by the bloody encounter thus far, the Federal commander ordered a resumption of the offensive at 5:00 a.m. on May 6. Part of Grant's plan entailed sending Ambrose Burnside's IX Corps toward the Chewing Farm, one of the battlefield's few clearings just beyond Ewell's right and directly into the gap Lee was so painfully aware of and unable to satisfactorily fill.[19]

As the battle unfolded with the coming dawn, the Federal corps of Warren and Sedgwick pounded Ewell's line, and Hancock's divisions thrust against Hill's shaky and unorganized front a mile to the south. Lee's entire position immediately became unstable when two of A. P. Hill's divisions began to collapse before the onslaught. His men, tired and fought out from the previous day's fighting, had been expecting Longstreet's veterans hours earlier, and thus little had been done to reform the line and prepare for battle. Just as Hill's front collapsed, Longstreet's divisions arrived on the field, marching through the chaos to stem the surging and victorious Federals. Several hours of seesaw action finally stabilized the front. While "old Pete" and his legions were saving Lee's right flank, elements from Burnside's IX corps made their appearance north of the William Chewning farm, beyond Ewell's right flank. The Chewning land was a cleared plateau and would be strategically beneficial to whomever could hold it in strength.

Luckily for the Confederates, Burnside was late getting into position, and Ramseur's Brigade was ordered to block the potentially decisive advance. "General Rodes ordered me to form on Brigadier-General Daniel's right and to push back Burnside's advance," remembered Ramseur. Daniel's organization, another full North Carolina brigade, comprised the far right of Ewell's line, and his flank was wide open to the developing Federal turning movement. Ramseur's soldiers threaded their way behind Ewell's battling brigades and across the newly-planted fields of Jones's farm. Deploying quickly for the attack, Ramseur and his regiments threw themselves against the IX Corps troops and stopped the Federal advance. "Moving at a double-quick," Ramseur later reported, "I arrived just in time to check a large flanking party of the enemy." Knowing he was unsupported on his right, Ramseur stretched out in that direction in an attempt to cover as much ground as possible and hopefully gain a tactical advantage over his opponent, whose strength and composition he had no way of knowing.

Musketry popped and crackled along the lines as the opposing soldiers came into contact. The nature of the terrain—open cropland in places and full of choking vegetation elsewhere—effectively shielded Ramseur's small numbers. Documentation on this small but decisive portion of the battle, while scarce, suggests that Grimes' 4th North Carolina held the right end of Ramseur's tenuously extended front, which by this time consisted of little more than thinly-spread skirmishers. Before long the line lapped against and around Burnside's left flank. "By strengthening and extending my skirmish line half a mile to the right of my line I turned the enemy's line," Ramseur reported proudly. As luck would have it, the 4th North Carolina played the decisive role in the action. ". . .A dashing charge. . .by the gallant Major [Edward] Osborne, of the Fourth North Carolina," wrote Ramseur, "drove not only the enemy's skirmishers, but his line of battle, back fully half a mile." The deft move netted "prisoners and the knapsacks and shelter-tents of an entire regiment."

It is not clear what role Grimes himself played in the event. Part of the captured booty consisted of bibles written in the Indian language Ojibwa and thrown down in haste by members of a unit of Indian sharpshooters. One North Carolinian claimed the Indians had stood and fought "bravely in the woods," but when forced into an open area, "did not again fire on us, but ran like deer." Ramseur's small but important victory, generally overlooked in most histories of the battle, prevented Burnside from driving an all but certain wedge between Ewell and Hill, protected both of their respective flanks, and linked the two corps, albeit thinly so, together. Had the North Carolinians not attacked when they did and in the manner described, the battle in the Wilderness could easily have turned out very differently. With his own casualties at a minimum, Ramseur staked out his new line and nothing but skirmishing occupied his front until darkness put an end to the fighting.[20]

At the end of the day on May 6, a weary Grimes wrote Charlotte a letter describing the battle. "After a most laborious day of marching and fighting, I have thrown myself down to write you a few lines," he said, "and to inform you of my continued good fortune in escaping the bullets of the enemy." We "whipped them badly," he boasted, "Burnside's Corps, particularly, they stampeded like sheep. . . .helter skelter." Our brigade," he continued, "has suffered but slightly. We charged at Burnside's Corps who broke and ran before we could get a good chance to execute harder punishment upon them." I am "so broken down and worn out that I cannot write much at present," penned the spent colonel. "Perhaps in the morning I may add a little to this. Good-by my precious darling until tomorrow night when I will, if possible, write you again. God grant that this victory will envision the North of the utter futility of further efforts to subdue us. God protect and preserve us my dearest darling and make us continue to love each other."[21]

His isolated and limited perspective of the field of battle on May 6 convinced Grimes that the Confederates had won a major victory in their first encounter with Grant. "The enemy has been active, but has accomplished nothing at all," he informed Charlotte the next day, refreshed somewhat after a few hours' sleep. "They are regarded as badly whipped." Letters picked up on the field led Grimes to conclude the enemy was "greatly demoralized. . .from the tenor of their correspondence between wives, sweethearts and husbands." Some of these materials may have been semi-pornographic in nature. "No people could be more demoralized in general character [than] themselves for the most obscene prints and letters exploring ideas that the modest would blush upon [reading it] and their utterances ought to shame any female let alone committing such lewdness to paper. No modest wife would have such ideas." Grimes was too much of a gentleman to explicitly relate to Charlotte the exact nature of his discoveries. "I trust the campaign will soon terminate, and I'm able to return to you," " he wrote optimistically, "and if the present indications are any criteria to judge by, it will soon be done." Grimes could not have been more wrong in his assessment.[22]

While Lee had managed to tie up and pummel Grant's larger and better equipped army in the neutralizing terrain of the Wilderness, the fighting effectively ended in a tactical draw. Neither side had gained any decided advantage. To make matters worse, James Longstreet, Lee's best corps commander, had been critically wounded by his own men at the height of a devastating counterattack against Hancock's exposed left flank, which was being rolled up "like a wet towel" when "Old Pete" fell. By the close of the

battle, the Federals had suffered almost 18,000 casualties, while best estimates place Confederate losses around 11,000.[23]

Neither combatant was anxious to renew the bloodshed on the morning
of May 7, and both Lee and Grant pondered their next moves. Would Grant
attack again—he had exhibited unusual tenacity by fiercely attacking on two
consecutive days—or withdraw across the river as had previous Federal
commanders? Unbeknownst to the Confederate leader, Grant had no intention of recrossing the Rapidan. In fact, he sent word through a war correspondent to Lincoln that "there would be no turning back."

Hours passed that hot and sticky Saturday morning before the Confederates realized no assault would be forthcoming. Probes on Ewell's front
revealed empty Federal lines and abandoned corpses. Lee was unsure
whether Grant was moving east toward Fredericksburg or south to Spotsylvania Court House, which was in the direction of Richmond. Cavalry reports suggested that Union wagon trains were moving in the latter direction,
and Lee correctly anticipated that Grant was on the move to Spotsylvania.
Longstreet's Corps, which was now commanded by Richard Anderson, was
ordered to move early the next morning, and the rest of the army prepared to
sidle southeast in its wake. In a fortuitous set a circumstances for the Southerners, Anderson left hours earlier than ordered and could not find a suitable
place to rest him divisions on the march because of the poor road and
numerous fires that burned from the previous fighting.

These conditions, and nothing else, won the race to Spotsylvania for
Lee and his army.[24]

# Spotsylvania, North Anna, and Beyond

## "We have good breastworks and will slay them worse than ever"

s Richard Anderson's [Longstreet's] First Corps prepared to move toward Spotsylvania, General Ewell's Second Corps brigades pulled out of line and marched south, with Rodes' Division leading the way. The weather was unusually hot for early May, and the burning sun conspired with the rotting corpses of men and horses, smoldering fires, and choking smoke to add hellish hues to the march. Ramseur's Brigade, one of the few in Lee's army to emerge comparatively unscathed from the Wilderness, faced a difficult march of some fifteen miles through a suffocating atmosphere that sapped the soldiers' strength. Ewell later described the effort as "a very distressing march through intense heat and thick dust and smoke from burning woods." Many fell out from exhaustion and heat strokes.

As exhaustion dropped some Confederates, others were being felled by iron and lead a few miles ahead, where by the narrowest of margins Anderson's infantry and Jeb Stuart's cavalry had managed to beat the Federals to the critical crossroads at Spotsylvania. Their position, however, was precarious and Anderson sought reinforcements as quickly as possible. Ramseur received a plea for help and entreated his soldiers to double their efforts to help their embattled comrades. The weary troops, some "so tired they could hardly haloo," picked up the pace to the strains of battle emanating yet again on another distant field. One of the leading regiments, Grimes' 4th, reached Block House Bridge on the Po River, about three miles west of Spotsylvania, around 6:00 p.m.[1]

The fight for Laurel Hill northwest of Spotsylvania was reaching a crescendo just as Ewell's troops reached the field. Rodes' Division led the advance by turning north at the Block House on Old Court House Road and then tramping across country, over the Brock Road and behind Anderson's exposed right flank in the direction of the McCoull house. A recent historian of the battle called Ewell's arrival "a breathtaking appearance seemingly orchestrated by fate itself." Rodes' leading brigade under Cullen Battle deployed and attacked, driving back advancing Unionists from Warren's V Corps. Some of John Sedgwick's VI Corps troops had taken position on Warren's left and were also pushing forward, but Ramseur's Brigade was pouring into position to stop them. The North Carolinians trotted to the line and ran head-on to meet the tired and somewhat disorganized Federal brigades of Col. Emory Upton and Brig. Gen. Henry Eustis. Major Osborne of the 4th North Carolina recalled that Ramseur rode his mount to the front and "with a shout, the men pushed forward, and the enemy's line gave way." "By a wonderfully rapid march," wrote Ramseur, "[we] arrived just in time to prevent, by a vigorous charge, the Fifth Corps [sic] from turning" Anderson's flank. Grimes led his 4th North Carolina forward with the balance of the brigade, and together they "drove the enemy back half a mile into his intrenchments." As the colonel was driving his men forward, a ball "struck on the left foot in the instep," temporarily crippling him. Although the wound "smarts a good deal," he later wrote his wife, "I expect to remain on duty."

Unable to carry the works, Ramseur's soldiers retired a short distance and continued the musketry action. Cullen Battle, whose Alabamians had actually taken a portion of the line before being driven back, exhorted his men to attack again, to no avail. Ramseur joined him in the effort to get the brigades moving forward, but the men were too worn out to accomplish more than they had. With darkness falling, Rodes' ordered his division to fall back and entrench itself. Losses for Ramseur's Brigade as a whole and Grimes own regiment, specifically, are not known, but they probably were not severe.[2]

"I am well and safe, but so exhausted," Grimes wrote Charlotte after the action had ended. "[We] are getting the best of the fights," was his optimistic assessment of the actions thus far. As Grimes was penning these words, much of Lee's army was digging entrenchments. Eventually the line of fortifications would stretch for three miles around Spotsylvania Court House, much of it formed into the shape of a jagged inverted "V," with a large angle jutting out northward where the line followed the high and generally open ground of a low ridge which overlooked the Ny River running to the east. Many Southerners were not pleased with the bulging mile and one-half wide salient, which its defenders called the "Mule Shoe" in deference to its shape. A different configuration, however, would have surrendered the higher ground to powerful Federal artillery. Lee's engineers believed that, with the construction of traverses, abatis (entanglements strewn in front of the lines), and well placed artillery, the line could be defended.

Rodes' Division occupied the western face of the bulging Mule Shoe on the immediate right flank of Anderson's First Corps, its entire front covered by a heavy woods. Ramseur's Brigade formed the left center of Rodes' line, with Battle's men on his left and Junius Daniel's North Carolinians on his right. Johnson's Division aligned itself on Rodes' right, extending the line around the top of the Mule Shoe. While some Confederate officers were concerned that the salient was indefensible, Brig. Gen. James Walker apparently was not. The commander of the Stonewall Brigade described his sector as "one of the best lines of temporary field works I ever saw. It was apparently impregnable."

Walker's Virginians, who held the center position in the salient, would soon get to test their commander's judgment. With A. P. Hill again disabled from an unspecified illness, Lee tapped Jubal Early to command Hill's Third Corps. Early brought his new command up on May 9 and deployed it on Ewell's right, extending the line south toward Spotsylvania Court House. Early's temporary promotion opened a similar temporary division command within Ewell's Corps which was filled by John B. Gordon, who had displayed both aggression and intelligence in the Wilderness. Gordon's Division deployed in reserve facing north and stretching across the interior of the Mule Shoe.[3]

May 9 found the men reinforcing their lines amidst heavy skirmishing. "Our sharpshooters were actively engaged, day and night," wrote Major Osborne, "and the regiment kept in line of battle most of the time." The most important event of the day went unnoticed by almost everyone on both sides: the death of Federal Maj. Gen. John Sedgwick, commander of the VI Corps, who was felled by a Confederate sharpshooter. With a major battle looming and the skirmishers making life uncomfortable all along the lines, Grimes took a few moments to write Charlotte. He "enclosed a good Yankee letter, the only one to have been written by an educated human and the only one that has not contained some vulgar illusion."

Most of May 10 passed quietly until late in the afternoon, when Grimes and his men listened as the woods on their left exploded with artillery and small arms fire. Warren's V Corps was attacking the western flank of Mule Shoe on the same ground it had fought over on May 8. The fighting was fierce and the Federals were repulsed with heavy loss. Shortly after 6:00 p.m., a second and heavier attack erupted directly against the western face of the Mule Shoe. A dozen hand-picked regiments numbering 5,000 men and led by Col. Emory Upton massed in regimental columns and covered the narrow distance to the works within minutes. The sudden rupture occurred on the narrow front held by Brig. Gen. George P. Doles' Georgians. One of them recalled the force of the assault: "They came at us with a yell and never made any halt. . . .We were simply overwhelmed and forced to retire, every man for himself." The Federal wave soon carried deep inside the lines and smashed the 32nd North Carolina of Daniel's Brigade, which was attacked from the rear and lost 225 men and 6 officers captured. The attack also pried loose at least two of Walker's Stonewall regiments as well, and threatened to unhinge Lee's line of battle. Contrary to Walker's earlier assumption, the salient was vulnerable to a determined attack.

The fighting had reached a critical phase. Fortunately for the stunned defenders, the Federals fumbled the valiant effort and reinforcements to exploit the breach were not forthcoming. Daniel's Brigade advanced upon Upton's troops, as did others from Gordon's reserve line. The counter-attack was well handled, with Ewell playing a large role in the final result. Upton's men were forced to relinquish their gains and retreat, but the attack had demonstrated the salient was vulnerable and relatively easy to overrun.[4]

The role played by Ramseur's Brigade and how well it performed in this effort is a small mystery. Ewell's report, which goes into some detail as to the troops involved, does not mention Ramseur's participation. Similarly, Ramseur's own report—admittedly written weeks later and relatively skimpy—says only that the day was filled with "constant and sometimes heavy skirmishing. . ." First Corps artillerist E. P. Alexander, however, reported that "Ramseur's Brigade did especially good work this afternoon [May 10th]." Similarly, Major Osborne, in his history of the 4th North Carolina, offers strong evidence that Grimes and balance of the brigade joined in the effort to throw back Upton. "On the evening of the 11th [actually the 10th] an attack was made upon our right, breaking the line," Osborne recorded. "General Battle's (Alabama) Brigade rushed in and supported the line that had been driven back, and with the aid of our brigade, which charged the enemy's right flank, they were driven back and the line was restored after a most stubborn and determined resistance on the part of the foe." Grimes, in a letter the following day to Charlotte, makes vague and incomplete references to the fighting but leaves no doubt that the action was more substantial than simply heavy skirmishing. "By the grace of God I am still spared and hope that the fighting for the present is about over," he wrote Charlotte. "The Yankees have been punished very severely. There is this morning brisk picket firing along the lines, but now we have good breastworks and will slay them worse than ever." One source claims that near the end of the fighting, when the Federals were milling about outside the Confederate works, Ewell asked Ramseur to drive them across the field. The North Carolinians, claims a Southern gunner, "behaved badly" and refused to attack across the open terrain. With his sword drawn and exhorting his men to follow, Ramseur leaped atop the works but was unable to organize his men sufficiently to attack.

Unfortunately, the paucity of Southern after-action reports makes it impossible to determine Grimes' losses or reconcile the differing accounts as to the brigade's effectiveness. Overall Southern losses are also problematic. Although early Southern accounts reported about 600 killed, wounded and missing, the results of a recent examination of the rosters of the regiments involved more than doubles that figure. Indeed, Federal provost marshal Marsena Patrick estimated that 913 enlisted men and 37 officers were herded through the ranks as prisoners by Upton, who placed his own losses at about 1,000 men.[5]

The same May 11 letter home to Charlotte containing information of the enemy repulse also contained news of a more distressing nature. "Poor Major Iredell was killed yesterday evening about sundown," explained Grimes, "shot through the head while rallying his regiment, the ball striking a little to the rear of the left temple and coming out the back of the head." James Johnston Iredell was Grimes' longtime friend and former classmate from their college days at the University of North Carolina. Both had graduated in 1848, and had been active participants in the Philanthropic Society.

When his good friend and classmate Johnston Pettigrew had died shortly after Gettysburg, Grimes was not saddled with the painful responsibility of burying him. At Spotsylvania, this duty fell on Grimes' shoulders. When I heard of his death immediately after dark, he remembered,

> I got a candle and blanket for his body. I took him to the house of a Mr. Norman Harrison which was the headquarters of Gen. Ewell, on the road heading south. Under an apple tree had him buried after wrapping his body in two blankets and an Indian cloth. . . .Col. Cox and Capt. Giles accompanied me to the grave when I went to bury him which was done between 12 and 1 o'clock by lantern light. . . .The Indian cloth had been cut in the center, and I had it tucked with thread for this purpose. He has on high army boots, and in the apple tree, in the direction of the house, I have had his name, rank and regiment inscribed. I have described this place in order that his family may recognize it without difficulty, if they should wish to view it. I forgot to mention that I drove down stakes at both ends and near the boards is a bayonet.

Iredell's death touched Grimes in a very personal way. "It was the last and melancholy duty of friendship," he grieved to Charlotte. "No more perfect gentlemen has fallen during this unnatural war. Extend my sympathy and condolences to his family for the blow to them must be terrible." Thinking again of Iredell's family, he reminded Charlotte that, "All articles about his person and his effects are in the possession of Col. Owens. . . .Now my dear darling, keep in good heart and trust to the Lord to protect me. I shall write you in a few days a long letter."[6]

The eleventh of May provided a respite of sorts to both armies, who suffered through more heavy skirmishing and pouring rain, but no serious combat. Grant spent the day attempting to discover "the weakest points in the line with a view to breaking through," while Lee sifted through conflicting reconnaissance reports suggesting his opponent was retreating toward Fredericksburg. Desiring to move as early as possible, Lee ordered Ewell to withdraw his twenty-two guns from the salient and send them to the rear. The roads leading into the Mule Shoe were poor and with darkness compounding the problem, Lee wanted to get a head start on removing the artillery. That night, however, pickets reported the sounds of massing Federals in the woods opposite the apex of the angle in the Mule Shoe, which was manned by Edward Johnson's Division of Ewell's Corps. The urgent appeals of George H. "Maryland" Steuart, one of Johnson's brigadiers, finally convinced his superiors to return the guns. The men in the ranks knew something was up. A member of the 45th North Carolina, Daniel's Brigade, recalled that "we sat with guns in hand the entire night, with a man to each company whose business it was to see that the men kept awake." The lines were so close, he added, that the men "heard them knocking open cracker boxes." As the night wore on, another Confederate observed, "We could hear, during the night, the sound of axes. They were evidently engaged in clearing away the pine bushes near the toe of the horse shoe to unmask their batteries."[7]

Between midnight and until 3:00 a.m. Grant moved large segments of his army into position to launch a massive assault against the tip of the Mule Shoe. The column slated for the task was composed of Winfield Hancock's II Corps and elements from the VI and IX Corps. Hancock had taken up a position less than a mile from the northern tip of the mule shoe, from which point he prepared to hurl about 19,000 men at the Confederate position. By 4:00 a.m. the rain had stopped and was replaced with a misty fog that blanketed the area. Though nothing could be seen in the damp and heavy darkness, the Confederates sensed a battle was looming. Ramseur and Grimes were up long before dawn getting their men ready for action. "In anticipation of an attack on my front," wrote Ramseur, ". . I had my brigade under arms at early dawn." The North Carolinians were barely ready when at 4:35 a.m., the order was given and the mass of Hancock's Federals lurched forward, spilling out of the woods and into the apex of the Mule Shoe.[8]

"Very soon I heard a terrible assault on my right," remembered Ramseur. The general, like Grimes and the rest of their men, spent several anxious minutes listening as the growing roar of battle crept slowly toward their rear. "From the direction of the fire," wrote Ramseur, "I soon discovered the enemy was gaining ground." Indeed they were. Hancock's avalanche of men had charged up and over the fortifications and widened the breach immediately on either side, spilling over traverses and capturing Confederates by the hundreds. The Southern artillery recalled only a short time earlier arrived just in time to be captured by the charging Federals. Other than a few pockets of resistance, Johnson's Division, for all intents and purposes, ceased to exist. The depth of the assaulting column, coupled with the sheer speed of the Confederate collapse, spread the chaos up and down the line of trenches.[9]

While Colonel Grimes' immediate reaction to the developing disaster are unknown, Ramseur left enough of an account to piece together his gallant and judicious response. The veteran commander pulled the 2nd North Carolina from its reserve position and formed it "on the right perpendicular to my line of battle." General Rodes also experienced one of his best days as a field commander. The division leader searched out Ramseur and ordered him "to check the enemy's advance and drive him back." Ramseur withdrew his brigade rearward and formed it under a heavy fire on Junius Daniel's right flank "in a line parallel to the two lines of works (which the enemy had taken and were holding)," he noted in his report. The regiments were aligned, from right to left, as follows: 13th, 2nd, 4th (Grimes), and 14th. Knowing that the circumstances were grave, Ramseur cautioned his men "to keep the alignment, not to fire, to move slowly until the command 'Charge,' and not to pause until both lines of works were ours." With the light of dawn just beginning to filter through the gray skies, the North Carolinians could make out the captured works in their front and knew they were in for hard work. "Ramseur, on his fiery steed," remembered Grimes' subordinate, Major Osborne, "looked like an Angel of war." Grimes likewise impressed Osborne. "Grimes, too, was on his horse, the very picture of coolness, grim determination and undaunted courage."[10]

As Ramseur's men aligned themselves for the advance, so too did Junius Daniel's Brigade on their left. Daniel changed from west to north, swinging his right regiment, the 45th North Carolina, perpendicular to the rest of his line to attack the Federals in the captured works and support Ramseur's exposed left flank. "We were exposed to a cross fire all day," wrote a member of the 45th, "and it was the hardest fight we have ever had." The advance was difficult and bloody. "We dropped upon our knees and opened fire upon the enemy, every man loading and firing as rapidly as possible." Ramseur's veterans impressed a sergeant with the 45th, who later marveled that his brigade "always seemed to be in the right place at the right time." Ramseur's men "sprang up and dashed forward into the horse shoe. For a moment it seemed to me our brigade [Daniel's] ceased firing and held its breath as these men went forward, apparently into the very jaws of death." The advance was against the secondary line of works, where Ram-

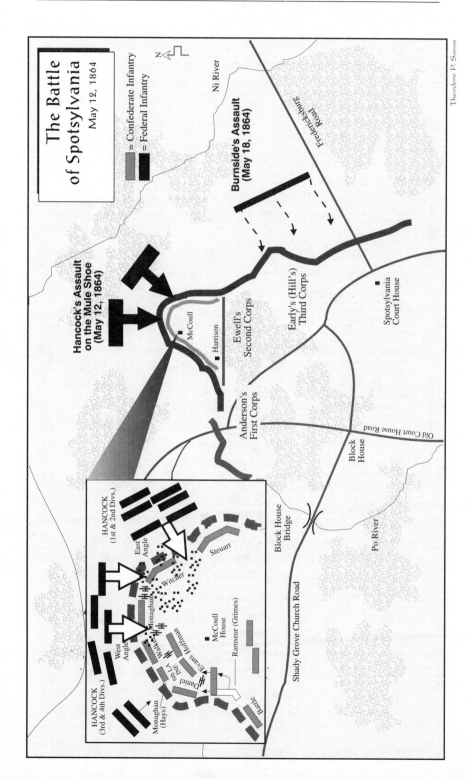

The Battle
of Spotsylvania
May 12, 1864

= Confederate Infantry
= Federal Infantry

N

Ni River

Fredericksburg Road

Burnside's Assault
(May 18, 1864)

Hancock's Assault
on the Mule Shoe
(May 12, 1864)

McCoull

Harrison

Ewell's
Second Corps

Early's (Hill's)
Third Corps

Spotsylvania
Court House

Anderson's
First Corps

Old Court House Road

Block
House

HANCOCK
(1st & 2nd Divs.)

East
Angle

Steuart

Witcher

Block House
Bridge

Po River

West
Angle

Walker

Monaghan

Daniel

6th LA

Evans Hoffman

McCoull
House

Ramseur (Grimes)

Battle

HANCOCK
(3rd & 4th Divs.)

Monaghan
(Hays)

Shady Grove Church Road

Theodore P. Savas

seur's horse was killed beneath him; two more would suffer a similar fate before the close of the day. Another bullet ripped through Ramseur's right arm below the elbow. The wound was painful and it was difficult for Ramseur to keep up with his advancing men. Before long Federals abandoned the interior line and fled rearward. Ramseur's advance was supported on his right by John B. Gordon, who led his division in a magnificent counterattack from a secondary line behind the McCoull house directly into the northern and eastern sectors of the Mule Shoe. His three brigades plowed forward and broke off the tip of Hancock's penetrating spearhead, stemming the tide and throwing the attacking ranks back toward the original line in serious confusion.[11]

Colonel Grimes and his 4th North Carolina had reached the line of works but had become badly entangled with the 14th North Carolina, a mere handful of yards separating their respective banners. The jumble of men, general confusion, and wounding of Ramseur threatened the effectiveness of the counterattack, which was degenerating into a slug fest of musketry. Luckily, Grimes had seen Ramseur fall and, as the brigade's senior colonel, he realized he was now in command. Grimes surveyed the situation and determined on a course of action. As he did so, the lone voice of Tisdale Stepp, of the 14th North Carolina, was heard above the din singing "The Bonnie Blue Flag." Others picked up the melody, and the strange chorus of voices floated above the cacophony of death for a short time until Stepp's head was blown apart accidentally by a soldier standing behind him.[12]

The aggressive Grimes knew that decisive action was needed, and he was not about to hesitate with so much at stake. The main line of works was but 50 yards in advance, clustered thick with men from Hancock's II Corps. "Seeing no one to apply to," he later recalled, "and seeing the necessity for speedy action, I ordered a second charge, myself leading them." Ramseur, his right arm crippled and bleeding, tried to keep up with the brigade as it hugged the western face of the Mule Shoe and headed for the northern portion of the overrun salient. The attack grimly ground forward through choking smoke and misty rain, traverse by traverse, sweeping the ground inside the works free of the enemy. Bayonets and swinging rifles were freely used, and although the North Carolinians were steadily gaining ground, their losses were heavy. "So close was the fighting there. . . ," recorded a Southern correspondent, "that the fire of friend and foe rose up rattling in one common roar. Ramseur's North Carolinians dropped in the ranks thick and fast, but still he continued, with glorious constancy, to gain ground, foot by foot." "By the very boldness of the move," recalled Grimes, "[we] recovered the entire works and all the guns, capturing many prisoners and killing more Yankees than the brigade numbered men. The field was perfectly blue with them." The ground, low and soggy, remembered an officer with the 4th North Carolina, was covered with "many dead and wounded from both sides. . . .The water was red with human gore." Major Osborne received a "painful contusion," at these works when a musket ball "passed through a heavy canteen of water" and struck him in the body. Grimes's resolute leadership had guided the brigade forward and against the interior side of the outer works just to the left of the former position held by the Stonewall Brigade, much of which, for all intents and purposes, no longer existed.[13]

Third corps commander General Ewell later called the Grimes' counter-attack, "a charge of unsurpassed gallantry," and Ramseur praised Grimes for charging at "exactly at the right time."[14] While the attack was indeed effective, the brigade was now in a perilous position. Just yards away on the other side of the works were masses of the enemy, and the Federals holding the trenches on Grimes' right were smothering his flank with a devastating small arms fire. Once again the bayonet was employed with telling effect. Somehow amidst the carnage the 14th North Carolina managed to overwhelm several traverses jammed with the enemy and force them back. Grimes problems were far from over. The works held by the brigade were situated on low ground and subject to a deadly plunging fire from Hancock's soldiers manning the top of the Mule Shoe.

"Yankees held a position on our right, upon a hill," explained one Confederate, "which enabled them to keep up an incessant enfilading fire upon us." The plummeting fire was so deadly that "two thirds of the men which we lost were done that way."[15]

Grimes had seen enough combat to know that he had to push his men along the works and drive the Federals away from the west angle at the top of the Mule Shoe. Ordering his men onward, Grimes led them forward into the blistering fire. The North Carolinians clawed and scratched their way along the works, overrunning one traverse at a time. "It was here for the first time I ever knew the enemy to run upon our bayonets," wrote a North Carolinian, "but they came down with such fury that we pitched many of them with the bayonet right over into the ditch." The Southern advance continued until it reached a small muddy lane leading from the McCoull house and bisected by the works. Offensively, the brigade was fought out and could go no further. The success of Grimes' slow but steady advance, however, prompted General Hancock at about 6:00 a.m. to issue an urgent fall for reinforcements, which arrived soon thereafter in the form of Brig. Gen. Thomas Neill's division of Horatio Wright's [formerly Sedgwick's] VI Corps. New Yorkers from Col. Daniel Bidwell's brigade and a Massachusetts regiment from Brig. Gen. Henry Eustis' brigade poured out of the woods on Hancock's right flank and struck the main line of works held by Grimes' men, where the battle intensified and spread out along the trenches.[16] According to Ramseur's biographer, Gary Gallagher, the fighting at Spotsylvania was the only instance during the war in which any sizeable number of his men used the bayonet in action.[17]

At this point the battle degenerated into a senseless savagery that shocked the hardened veterans of both sides. Men were physically pulled over the works and stabbed to death, while rifles were hoisted high into the air to shoot over the bloody mounds of earth into the seething masses of men huddled and fighting on both sides. Pressed hard in front and still taking a heavy fire from his right, Ramseur—who was probably back in charge of the brigade again by this time—sought out General Rodes for assistance. Long minutes passed until about 9:00 a.m., when one of Rodes' staffers guided Nathaniel Harris' Mississippi Brigade past the McCoull house and into position on Ramseur's right flank. The move cost the Mississippians about one third of their number, but it forced the Federals back toward the angle and relieved the building pressure against Ramseur's exposed flank.[18]

A bloody and protracted stalemate ensued throughout the balance of the day during which neither side could gain the upper hand. The Confederates had grimly driven back the initial attack and sealed the breakthrough, but could not force the enemy to relinquish their bulldog grip on the Mule Shoe salient, while the Federals—men from Hancock's, Wright's, and Burnside's corps—fought just yards away on the other side of the works with equal ferocity and tenacity. Both sides fed troops into the grinding action, and the fighting degenerated into nothing more than a large-scale hand-to-hand killing fest, a battle of attrition that the Southerners could not hope to win.

As Ewell, Rodes, Ramseur, Gordon, Grimes and others worked to turn the tide of battle, General Lee oversaw the construction of a partially-completed defensive line across the base of the salient. His warriors could not withdraw until the line was ready, and if they broke before it could be occupied, the army was doomed. Because of the proximity of the opposing forces, the setting of the sun and the arrival of nightfall only enhanced "the awful terror of the scene," remembered a participant to the action. "The pitiful groans of the wounded could be heard above the gunfire, and desperate cries for water went unheeded because neither side could stop fighting to attend to the poor souls. Spurting flames from the barrels of muskets lit up the night, [an] illuminated Dante's hell on earth." Ramseur's men held the line until the following morning, when the order to retreat finally arrived. Grimes withdrew his soldiers, described by one as "black and muddy as hogs," to the new line of works across the base of the Mule Shoe, which they reached around 3:00 a.m.[19]

Without food and with little water, they had fought continuously for over twenty hours. Lucky to be alive, completely exhausted, and numbed by the horror of what they had endured, the men looked for solace, and perhaps found it, in knowing that they had done their duty as soldiers. The fighting performed that day, wrote a captain in the 2nd North Carolina, was the "crowning glory of the career of Ramseur's Brigade." Another soldier, a member of Grimes' own 4th regiment, marveled at "what our brigade did actually accomplish that day." General Lee "rode down in person to thank the brigade for its gallantry, saying 'we deserved the thanks of the country; we had saved his army," wrote Grimes proudly.[20] "In all the bloody fighting of the two armies," wrote Douglas Southall Freeman, the Army of Northern Virginia's best-known historian, "there never had been such a struggle as this." Lee's soldiers thought as much also, for thereafter the Mule Shoe was always known as the "Bloody Angle."

Lee's losses at Spotsylvania through May 12 were around 12,000 men, and when losses in the Wilderness are added total 23,000. Ewell's Corps was hardest hit, beginning the campaign with 17,000 men and now barely able to field a third of that number. Losses in Ramseur's Brigade were staggering, although no specific numbers seem to exist. Grimes did not leave a battle report, nor did any of the other regimental commanders in the brigade. Among the fallen from the ranks of the 4th North Carolina was

Capt. William F. McRorie of Company A, the officer who had caused such grief a few months earlier between the 4th North Carolina's regimental surgeon, John F. Shaffner, and Colonel Grimes.[21]

The dreadful casualties had ripped apart the command structure of Lee's brigades and necessitated an immediate field reorganization in order to preserve the army's ability to continue fighting. The casualty that had an immediate effect on Grimes' future was the costly loss of Brig. Gen. Junius Daniel, who had fallen mortally wounded with a shot to the abdomen at the height of the fighting in the Mule Shoe. Carried to the rear, the officer suffered greatly and expired the following day. "Gen. Daniel, who was engaged on our left, was wounded through the bowels and yesterday I was assigned to the command of Daniel's Brigade," Grimes wrote Charlotte on May 14. "The poor fellow died last night from his wounds. [He] was decidedly the best general officer from our state. Although in all probability I gain a brigadier at his death, I would for the sake of the country always remained in status quo than the country should have lost his services. North Carolina has suffered very much indeed in killed and wounded."[22]

Daniel's death weighed heavily on Grimes, who wrote of it again three days later. "The loss to North Carolina in soldiers has been very great indeed," he informed Charlotte, "and many of her most gallant and valuable officers have fallen. Gen. Daniel had been recommended by Gen. Lee for a major general at the time of his death. Poor fellow, I regret his death very much and regarded him as decidedly the best general officer from our state."[23] Grimes thought so much of the fallen general that after the war he named a son Junius Daniel Grimes. To no one's surprise, General Rodes honored Daniel's dying request and appointed Grimes on May 13 as the temporary commander of Daniel's Brigade, which was composed of the 32nd, 43rd, 45th and 53rd regiments. Virtually nothing is known as to how Grimes was initially received by his new command.[24]

The vicious and unprecedented close-quarter fighting on May 12 sapped the strength of both armies. As the rains continued to fall, the soldiers rested, regrouped, wrote letters, and buried the dead. As the skirmishers kept up their deadly business, Grant shifted men from his right to his left flank, and Lee did likewise. The move left Ewell's weakened corps holding the army's left flank. Grimes and his men, however, remained in place, and the stagnant living arrangements in the open trenches wore on them. "If this continues much longer," Grimes told Charlotte, "[I] expect to be covered with vermin [lice] as mingling with the men in such close proximity." Many in the army considered Grimes' "escapes. . .as miraculous, when account is taken of number killed," he wrote his wife on May 16, "particularly as I never order my men to perform any duty attended with danger without sharing it with them."[25]

Warm and dry weather on May 17 led to a renewed effort by Grant on the following day against the new Southern line drawn along the base of the old Mule Shoe. The Federals had little chance against the strong fortifications and the clear lines of fire enjoyed by the Confederate infantry and artillery. Grant's decision to test Lee's left was a miserable failure. "The Yankees charged us in front today but were repulsed with considerable slaughter," explained Grimes in a letter home, "but Grant continues to send them against us. They certainly cannot hold out much longer for it will be beyond the power of human endurance." Wounded Yankees, he continued, "are within a stone's throw and paying the penalties of their tenacity. The continuous fighting and sight of dead men is truly heart sickening and the stench is awful, but all is endured cheerfully on account of the interests at stake." The new brigade commander continued to ponder his good fortune at having avoided death or serious injury. "I have been spared, [but] many better men have fallen, and I am truly grateful for this continued kindness, and my health, considering the trying circumstances, continues very good."

While his general health remained good, the continuous fighting was taking its toll on Grimes and his men, who were surely suffering from what we would today call 'battle fatigue." I am "nearly all fagged out and need rest," he admitted, before closing with a rather curious observation: "A very strange fact in connection with the dead is that the Yankees always turn black and drawn, rapidly becoming very offensive, but our soldiers retain for days their natural appearance and never dry up. A great many of the dead Yankees [are] now most ghastly objects. Their skulls in many instances look as if they had been dead ten years instead of as many days."[26]

Following the ineffective assault on May 18, Grant decided to end operations on the Spotsylvania front and sidle once again southeast around Lee's right flank. Assaulting Confederate entrenchments was too costly and it was time to catch Lee out in the open. With information that Grant was moving, Lee ordered Ewell to probe beyond his front against the Federal right and determine the enemy's strength and intentions. Ramseur's Brigade moved out first over roads so muddy that artillery was left behind. Bryan Grimes and Cullen Battle followed with their brigades. John Gordon's three brigades also advanced well to the left of Rodes' Division. The reconnaissance column crossed the Ny River late that afternoon. Ramseur's men ran into a strong force of the enemy near the Harris farm and was forced to fall back some distance to save his brigade, which was being overlapped on both flanks. Grimes' regiments soon arrived and took position on his left, while Battle's Alabamians deployed on Ramseur's right. Neither side had the benefit of entrenchments. With an aggressiveness that probably surprised the Confederates, the Federals attacked Ewell's men and caved in Gordon's left flank, which in turn caused his division to fall back in disorder. Gordon's tactical defeat exposed Grimes' own left flank and in turn threatened the entire corps with defeat. Ramseur, Grimes, Battle, and John Pegram—whose brigade came up at this time—stood their ground and held back the enemy until nightfall. "We made a flank movement and had a hard, very hard fight with the enemy," Grimes wrote his wife the next day. "The old Fourth had 65 killed and wounded. Daniel's Brigade behaved most gallantly, conducting itself most excellently. The bullets fell thick and heavy around me and amidst it all has my life been spared. Haven't yet counted the number of casualties in this Brigade, but it was very large."[27]

So little is known about the Harris Farm engagement it is difficult to gauge Grimes' first complete combat performance at the head of a brigade. Every indication is that he was more than equal to the task, for his division commander, General Rodes, sought out Grimes soon after the battle. Shaking his hand, Rodes said, "You have saved Ewell's Corps and shall be promoted, and your commission shall bear the date from this day." The probe discovered the enemy in force and cost the Confederates about 1,000 men—one-sixth of Ewell's effective strength. The Federals lost around 1,500 men.[28]

Ewell's probe did not alter Grant's plan, but it did mark the end of the Spotsylvania Campaign. The Federal II, V and IX Corps pulled out of their lines and moved toward Guinea Station on the night of May 20-21. On the 21st, when he was sure Grant was moving, Lee ordered Ewell south to Hanover Junction, where he could construct a new defensive position near the North Anna River, protect the Virginia Central Railroad, and block a direct thrust against Richmond. "We reached here [Hanover Junction] today after a most fatiguing jaunt," remembered Grimes, who commented that "the enemy [was] attempting to flank us as we moved down." By the time his army was in place, Lee's line below the North Anna was powerful and brilliantly arranged. The line was a large inverted "V" with the point resting against the river at Ox Ford. Ewell's Second Corps was deployed on the army's right, angling away from the river and astride the rail line, while Anderson's First Corps held the center, and Hill's Third Corps the left. This disposition gave Lee the advantage of interior lines, which would allow him to reinforce either flank easily, while Grant would have cross and recross the river to accomplish the same thing.[29]

The maneuvering and fighting along the North Anna River, just 24 miles north of Richmond and two miles from the vital Virginia Central Railroad, is best described as a series of lost opportunities for the Confederates. Although the army was reinforced by the divisions of George Pickett and John C. Breckinridge, as well as another North Carolina brigade under Robert Hoke, the decisive blow Lee wished to deliver did not materialize. Late on the afternoon of May 24, Winfield Hancock's Second Federal corps advanced south of the river below the Chesterfield Bridge. Leery of what lay before him, Hancock advanced a brigade under Thomas Smyth to reconnoiter. The Federals were moving against a hinge in the Southern front formed by the junction of the right end of Anderson's line and the left flank of Ewell's line. At this point Anderson's line ran east and west along a road below the Miller farm, while Ewell's men occupied works that turned sharply at an almost ninety degree angle south, or parallel to the Richmond, Fredericksburg, and Potomac Railroad. Grimes' Brigade faced west, flanked by the brigades of Ramseur on his left (Ewell's far-left brigade) and George Doles on his right. Thus the front against which Hancock advanced was an inverted "L." The main line of Southern works was shielded by a thick screen of skirmishers in rifle pits deployed on a line running east and west, parallel with Anderson's line and perpendicular to Grimes'. As Smyth's regiments moved within range, four companies of skirmishers from Ramseur's 14th North Carolina opened on the advancing enemy, and a heated exchange developed. Before long Grimes' skirmishers from the 43rd regiment, together with a pair of companies from the 53rd, joined the spreading engagement. More skirmishers from Doles' Georgia brigade and Battles' Alabama brigade moved up to assist.[30]

The weight of numbers began to tell, however, and the Southern pickets fell back and abandoned the advanced line of rifle pits. Believing they had captured the main Confederate line, the Federals poured more men into the heated firefight to hold it. The sharp action, known as the fight at the Doswell House, was fought through difficult underbrush and heavily wooded terrain, all of which shielded the small number of Confederates actually engaged. The North Carolinians launched a sharp counterattack to retake the works about 5:30 p.m., and the fighting raged across the front. Before long, John Gibbon had committed his entire division to the action, not knowing (or believing) he was facing nothing more than a well-handled veteran screen of skirmishers. At one point, some of Grimes' men from the 43rd North Carolina believed a group of the enemy was trying to surrender and advanced to accept them as prisoners. The Federals, men from the 170th New York, mistakenly believed the Southerners were surrendering and moved forward to meet them. The confusion erupted into a close-quarters hand-to-hand combat until the New Yorkers broke and ran for cover. The action ended with nightfall, with the Federals holding the rifle pits and the Southern line intact.

Grimes' role in the battle is unknown, as are his exact losses, which were small. "The Yankees still continue to be obstinate and still continue to rush on to their doom, as more of them did yesterday when they came on my line," he wrote Charlotte the next morning. "We drove them with considerable slaughter, losing but few in Daniel's Brigade, [which] bore the brunt of the fighting." The non-stop nature of the fighting below the Rapidan continued. "Have now been in line of battle forty-eight hours," he observed.[31]

Grant, suddenly realizing the perilous situation he faced and how vulnerable he was to a sudden and heavy attack, withdrew to the southeast once again, sidling to his left toward Cold Harbor. Since early May Lee had successfully maneuvered his army to counter Grant's moves. Unlike in the past, his men now constructed formidable defensive entrenchments from which they could inflict heavy loses on the aggressive "obstinate" Federals. Outnumbered and with several of his key subordinates either wounded or ill, Lee was forced to use the region's geography, especially the wooded terrain and waterways, to thwart, slow, and obstruct enemy movements. Unable to resort to the wide-ranging strategic maneuvers he had employed which such brilliance in 1862-1863, Lee was forced onto the defensive in a chess-like game where a wrong move could spell mortal disaster to both his army and the Southern capital below him. Despite laboring under several significant handicaps, including his own ill-health, the general's campaign from the Wilderness to Hanover Junction refected his outstanding grasp of field leadership and command.

On the same day the Federals abandoned the North Anna front, Grimes wrote Charlotte from Hanover Junction: "We are expecting from the preparations that Grant has made that he will await an attack, or move down the north side of the Pamunkey [River]." Grimes again complained of the fatigue under which he was laboring, admitting to his wife that he was "suffering a great deal from exhaustion." "You are present to my mind no matter how busily engaged," he noted, "except in the excitement of battle when I am glad to forget for a while lest my love should make a coward of me." His prediction of Grant's operations along the Pamunkey proved essentially correct. The Northern general followed the east bank of the Pamunkey River in the hope of turning Lee's right flank. By now Grant was feeling supremely confident: "Lee's army is really whipped," he wrote, a perception generated perhaps in part by his opponent's failure to attempt a major offensive action along the North Anna.[33]

The heavy losses sustained in the non-stop campaign necessitated another reorganization within the Second Corps on May 27. Richard Ewell, ill and thoroughly exhausted, no longer commanded the confidence of either his subordinates or Lee, who replaced the gallant old warrior with Jubal Early. Early's vacancy at the head of the division was filled by Ramseur, whose brigade was in turn taken over by the 2nd North Carolina's colonel, William Cox. Although they would fight together on other fields, Ramseur's promotion and transfer to another division severed temporarily the tight field relationship that had developed between he and Bryan Grimes, who continued to lead Daniel's Brigade in Robert Rodes' Division.

By noon of May 28, Grant had his army across the Pamunkey, and the Second Corps under Early established a defensive line in the marshes behind Totopotomoy Creek. "I think that we ought to pounce down upon them and fight whenever they can be found," Grimes wrote home the following day, revealing once again his proclivity for offensive action. He did not have to wait long before Lee decided to go over to the attack. On Monday, May 30, Lee ordered General Early to move the Second Corps forward to block the Federal advance toward the Chickahominy River. His goal was to strike the advance elements of Grant's army that had crossed Totopotomoy Creek before they could strongly entrench. The aggressive Early found the enemy near the crossing of Bethesda Church. Rodes' Division, with Grimes' North Carolinians, "came down the Mechanicsville Pike at a run. . ." wrote an enemy officer, and easily rolled back beyond the crossroads a brigade-sized line of the enemy under Martin Hardin. "We came across the enemy," wrote a soldier in the 43rd regiment. "They were posted in a slender breastworks, [and] we saw them out of this and they fled. . .in confusion." Rodes' pushed forward and struck another pair of brigades from Warren's V Corps.[34]

For reasons that are not completely clear, Rodes stopped to consolidate his gains and did not continue pressing the enemy. Still, the engagement, as far as Grimes was concerned, was a significant one. "Yesterday [was] a hard day, the exertion I made and the fatigue undergone almost superhuman," he wrote Charlotte. "Again this division was called upon to make a flank movement. Whipped them, but at considerable loss to Daniel's Brigade. At least three-fourths of the killed and wounded were from this brigade. There is no doubt of it being a fine body of men and will do credit to my command." Early, meanwhile, brought up Ramseur's Division and the initiative passed to the Federals, who had time to regroup and collect themselves for another expected assault.

Ramseur, in his inaugural performance at the head of Early's former division, persuaded Early to let him attack the Federals. The thrust was led by John Pegram's Brigade and was conducted without proper reconnaissance. As the Confederates crossed into an open field, a line of artillery opened on them and shredded Pegram's Virginians. The fire from the entrenched enemy stopped Ramseur dead in his tracks and quickly forced him back with heavy losses. In the eyes of many soldiers, the blame for the bloody fiasco was Ramseur's, whom they believed was out to prove himself as a new division commander. "A murder for ambition's sake," was how one soldier described it. Another, Virginian George Peyton, was even more forthright in his assessment: "Ramseur was to blame for the whole thing and ought to have been shot for the part he played in it." Jubal Early made no mention of Ramseur in his report, and neither did Grimes in his letters to Charlotte. The operation did confirm that Grant was still moving toward the Chickahominy, and Lee positioned his army accordingly.[35]

As the Army of North Virginia took up a line running north from the Chickahominy to Totopotomoy Creek, and Grant's men aligned themselves opposite it, Grimes took the time to jot a quick note to Charlotte with news of Ramseur's expected promotion. "Ramseur is about to be promoted to Major General and Rodes has recommended Cox for the command of that brigade. Genl. Lee telegraphed for my commission the other day," he continued, "but so far it has not been received, but suppose it will come in good time." Grimes was worried that the 4th Regiment would not be part of his new command: "I prefer this command, but am anxious to get my regiment in here with me, but Rodes has said that it will spoil that brigade to take them out, but as I made them what they are, think that they ought to follow my fortunes." While he clearly did not know it, General Lee had already promoted Grimes to brigadier general and had sent an order to him on June 1, 1864 to: "Report for duty to Genl. R. E. Lee to command Daniel's Brigade, Rodes Division, 2nd. Army Corps." As much as that must have pleased Grimes, much to his disappointment the 4th Regiment remained with Cox's new brigade.[36]

"I have heard that Genl. Longstreet's Corps, consisting of about 20,000 men are now moving out to attack the enemy on their left flank," he wrote his wife in the same June 1 letter. "It is a real treat to have a sort of respite from the flanking expeditions for it appears to me that all of the hazardous undertakings have fallen almost entirely upon Ewell's Corps, and we wish now to gladly share the honors with some other command." The armies continued to face each other in close proximity at Cold Harbor on June 2, and the daily grind of constant contact and sudden death was wearing on the North Carolinian. "Since yesterday morning, we have been in [range] of the sharpshooters of the Yankees [who] are shooting at our men whenever they expose themselves," he wrote Charlotte from his camp near Mechanicsville on Thursday, June 2. "Last evening just before dark we were sent forward and immediately [encountered] a strong line of skirmishers and drove the enemy back, but Hill's Division on our left did not do [much]. Then Yankees fired enfilading fire on us and caused our men to keep their heads down. Occasionally, a fellow gets killed." To Grimes' surprise, Federal captives were not nearly as well-supplied or fed as he probably had been led to believe. "The prisoners we take complain very much of hunger and eat most voraciously when it is given to them," he informed Charlotte. "So far as my own experience goes and from what the men say we are better supplied."[37]

Lee's defensive line was one of the most powerful he had ever occupied, a well-entrenched front stretching from Totopotomoy Creek to the Chickahominy River. His moves had continually thwarted Grant's efforts to either catch him in the open or steal a march on the Southern capital. Grant, however, believed that if he could break Lee's lines one more time, his army might well collapse. As a result, he decided to launch a massive frontal assault on the morning of June 3. A thundering rumble shook Richmond's population, most of which was sleeping about twelve miles away, wide awake just as dawn was spilling over the landscape. Grant's infamous effort dissolved almost immediately in the face of one of the heaviest and sustained defensive exhibitions of firepower ever offered by the Army of Northern Virginia. Within 30 minutes it was over, and some 7,000 Union dead littered the Virginia soil. One Yankee captain described it best when he wrote, "we were simply slaughtered." A Confederate officer, Col. Pickney Bowles of 4th Alabama, remembered that, "Our artillery was cutting wide swaths through their lines. . .Heads, arms, legs and muskets were seen flying high in the air at every discharge." As a South Carolinian in Joseph Kershaw's Brigade described it: "Men lay in places like hogs in a pen, some side by side, across each other, some two deep, while others with their legs lying across the head and body of their dead comrades." Confederate casualties are not specifically known, but were probably less than 1,000 killed and wounded.[38]

With the battle over, Grimes penned a note to Charlotte describing the continuous fighting. He also took time to criticize the former colonel of the 2nd North Carolina, William R. Cox. That Grimes harbored something personal against the officer is clear from the amount of ink he expended privately disparaging him. "[Cox] has been at the hospital for days and has avoided the fights," reported Grimes, implying Cox was a coward. This oblique accusation appears completely groundless. Grimes' fellow North Carolinian had thus far in the war suffered at least seven wounds, and his record was replete with acts of bravery and competence. Cox had been assigned to lead Ramseur's Brigade on May 27, and was promoted to brigadier general on June 2, to rank from May 31. While the record does not evidence that Cox suffered any additional wounds during the May-June fighting, it is impossible to say that his old ones were not bothering him, or that he simply reached a level of exhaustion that required rest.[39]

A brief—and welcomed—lull in the fighting engulfed both armies, allowing Grimes time to write Charlotte a long letter. He began with news about Charlotte's younger brother, George, who "came by yesterday and took breakfast with me and I gave him the opportunity to wash his face. He said it was the first time in three weeks that he washed his face on a towel." Perhaps in a somewhat playful mood and proud of his new rank, he boasted that:

> five hundred dismounted cavalry are under the temporary command of Brig. Genl. Grimes. I don't know their commanding officer, Maj. Fowling, [who] appears to be an arrogant fool, and I take pleasure in bringing him down. I send you for safe keeping my commission as Brig Genl. It was dated the 19th of May by request of Genl Rodes. At which time while on the flank movements near Fredericksburg, I handled this brigade so efficiently as to save Ewell's Corps from a rout. So he requested that the commission should be from that date and the request was granted. So you are Mrs. Genl Grimes. Do you feel at all elevated by one additional star? My rank is permanent.

Grimes also commented on his two contemporaries, noting "Cox was temporarily assigned to duty with Ramseur's Brigade with same rank, but perhaps may have to come down to plain 'Colonel' again." His friend Ramseur, he explained, "has temporary rank of Major Genl but may have to come down again. [My] promotion has been a long time in coming." Charlotte at this time was not well, although the nature of her illness is unknown. "I regret very much that you continue to suffer," lamented her husband, "but hope that the time has about gone away for such sickness and that you will regain your usual robust health." Although General Grant "continues to butt up against our works as he may have done lately," he said, ". . .we will thin out his army so much that he will have to quit."[40]

Promotion to brigadier general meant Grimes' uniform needed some refurbishment Transform it, he instructed Charlotte, "into a brigadier uniform and have the buttons rearranged, two by two, right on the side, have the stars fixed and the braid on the sleeves, but I do not wish any buff on the collar nor on the sleeves for it becomes easily soiled, and the plainer (so it denotes rank) the better I shall like it, and when completed please send it on."[41]

While Lee's army was being bled north of Richmond, Southern setbacks in the Shenandoah Valley, as well as Joseph E. Johnston's inability to stop or even slow down William T. Sherman's armies in North Georgia, weighed heavily on the Confederate high command. The Valley, still a major source of supply for the Army of Northern Virginia, had to be retained. Where would the men to hold it come from? As Lee contemplated options with President Davis, a brief truce of two hours duration was observed on June 7 for each army to gather its wounded and bury its dead, which had been suffering and deteriorating between the lines for days. As this was being accomplished, John C. Breckinridge's thinned division was shipped west for the Shenandoah to reinforce that theater.

The next day, a Wednesday, was rather quiet on the Cold Harbor front. When Lee learned that Phil Sheridan and his Federal cavalry had been detached to destroy the Virginia Central Railroad and then head toward the Valley, he had little choice but to counter it by dispatching two of his own horse divisions (more than half of his cavalry) to counter the move. That evening, as the bands of the opposing armies played to everyone within earshot Grimes again poked fun at William Cox. "It is amusing to see how important Col. Cox [thinks he] is by his new appointment and the airs he assumes," he wrote Charlotte, refusing to use Cox's appropriate rank of brigadier general. "I wish you could see him." Lamenting Ramseur's absence via promotion, Grimes observed that "he [Ramseur] had rendered himself very unpopular in his brigade before leaving." Exactly how or why he did not discuss. "My Regiment is very anxious to be transferred to my Brigade, and I much appreciate this effort which I trust will be granted for I have an affection for them having been with them for so long."[42]

June 9 was another miserable day in the Cold Harbor trenches. "I promise to do the fighting. . ." he wrote Charlotte with some frustration, "if they will only do me the pleasure of forwarding my letters regularly. I do get unreasonably angry when the mail comes and no letter for me. It makes me right nervous and I wish that I had the delinquent under my military control, and he would mend his ways." Although the Confederate postal system left much to be desired, it typically took but five or six days for Charlotte's Raleigh-posted letters to reach him. Speculation as to Grant's next move dominated Grimes thoughts, and his conclusion may have surprised Charlotte. "It is believed that Grant's intention is to put himself on the south side of the James and try that route," he explained, "but I secretly think he will succeed no matter what route he takes." Grimes, who for so long was convinced of victory, was perhaps beginning to entertain second thoughts. Reflection and some nostalgia crept into his June 10 letter home. As the armies glared at one another across no-man's-land, Grimes "visited the old Cold Harbor battlefield as well as the spot where I first saw my dog, General [in 1862]." Adding a bit of financial advice, Grimes noted that "Confederate money is beginning to be very scarce in Richmond and elsewhere, better postpone any purchasing."[43]

Grant had been mulling over plans for some time to shift his army yet again, this time south of the James River for a strike against Petersburg, a critical railroad and logistical center thirty miles south of Richmond. Lee expected Grant would move, but where would he go? "We were up at 3 a.m. with orders to march to Petersburg to meet the enemy down there," wrote Grimes on June 10, "but it was countermanded before we got off." Grant's move below the James, one of the few times he managed to steal a march on Lee—the move caught the Confederate leader completely off guard—began on the evening of the 12th. Grimes's Brigade, however, would not be following. Mounting concerns of the growing Federal threat in the Shenandoah prompted Lee to dispatch Jubal Early's Second Corps away from the bloody battlefields of the previous six weeks to the beautiful valley. Lee hoped Early would deal with the Federal threats in the Valley and divert men and resources away from Grant and Meade. From near the South Anna River, Grimes informed Charlotte that he and his men left Cold Harbor at 2:00 a.m. that morning and "marched over thirty miles to-day over [a] sandy road. Everything and everybody exhausted." Although he did not know for sure since he was not privy to Lee's strategic plans, Grimes speculated that they were "going to the Valley of Virginia. Are now on the Charlottesville road. Must either be after [Maj. Gen. David] Hunter or going into Maryland." On the prospects of the latter, he prayed "to God that it will end more successfully than the other invasion."[44]

I "rode in an ambulance much of the time and found it very comfortable," he wrote Charlotte as the column wound its way toward Gordonsville. "The stench of dead horses affects my olfactories to such an extent that I may never find my stomach."[45] The men reached that place on June 15, where it began to become clear to almost everyone that "we will be moving up the Valley." Three days later, the exhausted general was probably pleased to note that he and his men would "in morning. . .take the cars for Lynchburg, after a most fatiguing and oppressive march. You need not be astonished if you hear of us on our way to East Tennessee." With Robert Rodes away on leave, Grimes as senior brigadier assumed the reins of leadership on the march, affording the recently-minted general a small taste of divisional command.[46]

The columns' brisk pace continued. "Have been pursuing Yankees at such a rapid gait, haven't had time to write," Grimes scribbled on June 21 from atop the Blue Ridge Mountain. "Been almost without rations; hard marching, and nothing to eat. Start before day, not stop till dark, except to rest for ten minutes. We move immediately." Exhausted and hungry, Grimes wrote home the next day from Salem, Virginia, on June 22. "My brigade did not have a mouth full of bread and but little flesh, but there was little straggling and not much complaining," he boasted, obviously proud of his men. "Occasionally, when either Genls. Rodes or Early passed the lines the cry was 'bread, bread, bread' and each would take it up from the others." When an opportunity presented itself to strike a blow, the Second Corps veterans "made a forced march for the last day, and arrived two hours too late to inflict much damage on the enemy, which was very annoying, as we expected to get supplies from them, but instead found empty wagons and worthless provisions."[47]

Jubal Early's early days in command of the corps did not overly impress Grimes, who penned one of his angriest letters home on June 22:

All this inefficiency and coordination of [John] Imboden and his cavalry and perhaps just a [criticism] of Genl Early who in every instance has been a little too late. Which to us after undergoing such fatigue and hardships is not only annoying, but a good deal mystifying for the men are anxious for supplies from the Yankee wagons and expected some good edibles. But instead we found only a few cannons and empty wagons and their crews; their worthless provisions against whom I feel so bitterly that my heart quickens in pulsation when we pass them. I universally feel a longing to kill them. Really blood-thirsty. Everyday since leaving Lynchburg we have been overtaking a few.[48]

Lynchburg proved a welcomed respite for the Confederates, where "ladies forwarded to us a supply of good edibles for the general officers." Grimes' place in the marching column, however, caused him to miss out on the best Lynchburg had to offer: "As Ramseur and Gordon had first pull at them they secured the portions that would have been the most palatable to us. You know that Ramseur always had a hankering after the best of everything and in this instance, appropriated all the sweetmeats and everything that was good, and left to us the substantials." After eating a more substantial breakfast at Liberty, Grimes complained that there was nothing to drink but "an abundance of sulphur water. "We are packing two days rations and expect to leave here tomorrow morning."[49]

The toll of active campaigning finally overwhelmed even Bryan Grimes' abundantly robust constitution. Suffering from exhaustion and ill with rheumatism and "disordered bowels," he was admitted to the hospital in Lynchburg in July. He was so sick he could not continue the march with Jubal Early's army into Maryland, and was given a medical furlough to return to Raleigh in order to regain his health. A surgeon's certificate explained that the new brigadier general was unfit for duty. The spring of 1864 had been a defining period for Grimes. Like virtually everyone else in the army's ranks, he had been in almost constant combat for almost seven weeks, from the Wilderness Campaign through the fighting at Cold Harbor. The continuous campaign had highlighted his abilities for higher command, and his promotion to brigadier general was overdue and warranted by years of dedicated service. Although they were already close, the day-to-day fighting through some of the war's bloodiest battles had cemented permanently his friendship with the equally fiery Dodson Ramseur. They were, in many respects, the Castor and Pollux of the Army of Northern Virginia. The two officers and friends were experiencing a remarkably parallel path through the war's tribulations. Both North Carolinians were expectant fathers, both had been recently married, and both faced the burdens of higher command with promotions during a critical phase of the conflict. Although neither could have known it, they had little time left together.

The other and dominant mainstay in his life remained Charlotte. The fervent warrior and hotheaded officer continued to express his love and devotion to her through his almost daily letters home, which continued despite nearly constant combat and his chronic level of fatigue. There is no small level of irony in his personal situation, for with men being killed around him on a daily basis, Grimes concerned himself with his wife's delicate condition and developing pregnancy: the general who ordered men to their deaths was awaiting the arrival of a new life. His correspondence made it clear that he had reached (and exceeded) the limits of human endurance, yet one perceives that he may not have persevered for so long had it not been for the inherent therapeutic value of writing and receiving the letters.

Despite his fatigue and the unexpected trip to his home state, the new brigadier knew more fighting lay ahead.

# Third Winchester and Fisher's Hill

"Our troops did not behave with their usual valor."

**W**eary and sick from exhaustion, Grimes returned to Raleigh in July 1864 to recover his health. Little is known of his sojourn home, for his letters to Charlotte were no longer necessary. No matter how ill he was, it would have been difficult for a soldier like Grimes to passively sit home while the war went on without him. Resigning to his desire to rejoin his command—and against Charlotte's protestations to remain in North Carolina—he returned to the front before fully regaining his health, disregarding his surgeon's certificate declaring him "unfit for duty."

Grimes reached Richmond in early August and took a room at the Spotswood Hotel. There he learned that joining Jubal Early's small army, which was maneuvering in the Lower Shenandoah Valley and occasionally foraying north of the Potomac River, would be a more difficult proposition than he had originally assumed. "Our troops moved on into Maryland, and I fear that it will be some time now before I can overtake them for the route is attended with some danger in following our troops as there has been some bushwhacking done in the rear of our army," he informed Charlotte on August 6. "I should dislike very much to have my career ended in such an inglorious manner."

Still, he could not remain in Richmond with the army on the move, and Grimes dutifully packed his bags and headed toward the Shenandoah. On his way there, he learned that it had been reported to his brigade that he had died of typhoid while at home. "I will show them how my ghost can make himself heard and felt too if necessity requires it when I again return," was his playful response to the news. The handful of weeks home with Charlotte had made it difficult to leave her. "I had a most terrible headache which usually happens upon my separation from you. My head must be in sympathy with my heart or else it would not always have that effect. I do miss your loving kindness so much," he added, "that I feel terrible and more angry with the Yankees than ever for by their actions alone, I am disjoined from the enjoyment of my darling society." The proper and loving husband ended his note to Charlotte with a remark completely out of character for him: "If I had been so [inclined] and could have forgotten your precious self, would have had quite a pleasant adventure at the Spotswood Hotel last night." Grimes' remark was probably in reference to the prostitutes that frequented Richmond's streets and hotels. Charlotte's response to his reference to his suggestion of passing up a "pleasant adventure" is not recorded, but given her temperament it was likely spirited. Since Grimes liked to tease Charlotte and enjoyed arousing her not inconsiderable temper, he may have simply been trying to provoke her. If so, he likely succeeded.[1]

The military situation had substantially changed during the few weeks Grimes had spent recuperating at home. After Cold Harbor, General Grant stole a march on Lee and slipped his army across the James River. His goal was the critical railroad logistical center of Petersburg, thirty miles below Richmond. Only desperate fighting by a motley collection of defenders, the timely arrival of advance elements from the Army of Northern Virginia, and Federal timidity saved the city for the Confederacy. Unbeknownst to everyone, the army of maneuver in the East was all but over, and trench lines cropped up from Richmond to below Petersburg. Although months of fighting lay ahead for Lee and his veterans, he knew it was only a matter of time before the massive Federal army squeezed his own divisions into submission. In June, Lee had prophetically told Jubal Early: "We must destroy this Army of Grant's before he gets to the James River. If he gets there it will become a siege, and then it will be a mere question of time."

Matters were not much better in North Georgia, where Joe Johnston's Army of Tennessee had fallen back steadily before Willliam T. Sherman's trio of armies. Out of patience with the retreating and reticent Johnston, President Davis removed him from command and John Bell Hood took over on July 18. Three bloody battles followed in little more than one week on the outskirts of Atlanta, and when they ended the city looked doomed to fall. Many soldiers, Grimes included, understood that the outcome of these two major campaigns would have a substantial impact on the upcoming November presidential elections.

As these events were playing out, Jubal Early's small Army of the Valley—sent by Lee into the Shenandoah to protect the region, threaten

Lt. Gen. Jubal A. Early

*Generals in Gray*

Washington, and hopefully convince Grant to weaken his army to counter the move—was enjoying some success. Throughout the war the Army of Northern Virginia had relied heavily on the abundant food supplies from this region. With the siege at Petersburg beginning to choke off the railroad lines bringing food from the south to Richmond, Lee was more dependent on the Shenandoah Valley than ever. Without it, his army would probably starve.

Early's initial objective of repelling the repulsive David Hunter from the vital farming region suceeded when Hunter, fearful of an engagement with the Confederates, removed his larger army westward to Lewisburg and out of the area altogether for several crucial weeks. Operating with a great deal of discretion and desiring to carry the war into the North, Early moved down the Shenandoah and cleared the Lower Valley of the enemy before fording the Potomac River on July 6. Three days later he waged a sharp engagement outside Frederick, Maryland at Monacacy with General Lew Wallace's Federals, who were attempting to slow down Early's advance toward Washington. By noon on July 11, Early was gazing at the outer defenses of the capital. His army was strung out and exhausted from the intense heat and hard marching, and any opportunity he may have had of actually moving on Washington vanished when troops from Grant's army filed into the defenses with little if any time to spare. By the evening of July 14, the Southerners were back across the Potomac and more than a month of steady campaigning came to and end.[2]

Grimes reached New Market on August 8 and promptly informed Charlotte of his progress and a humerous incident:

> Last night was spent near Harrisonburg, Va at the home of a Dr. Kaufman who put me to sleep in a remarkably superb, fresh bedstead, and I was anticipating a delicious night's rest, but about the time the drowsy god had overcome me something began to bite, bite, bite. I began to fear that I might have caught a creeper from the soldiers in the camp, but fortunately I caught one of the animals, and upon testing them with the only sense, besides feeling in the dark, my olfactories confirmed the fact they were chinches. They really became so annoying that I arose and laid my comfort on the floor and spent the night down there. It took nearly all the soap that your thoughtfulness had provided me with to wash the bed bugs off.[3]

The early effects of the Union army pillaging of foodstuffs in the Shenandoah Valley, coupled with the spiraling costs of everything from food to clothing became evident to Grimes when he sat down to dinner on the night of August 9. "I got my dinner yesterday at a house," he wrote, "and the only dish upon the table was one of Apple dumplings for which we were charged the merchant sum of two dollars a pair."[4]

He finally caught up with his command camped at Bunker Hill on the night of August 10. After listening to a serenade by the 4th North Carolina's band, he passed along news from the front to Charlotte: "The raid of the cavalry who burnt Chambersburg [PA] has resulted in disaster to our army, having upon their return been surprised at night and severely handled, losing upwards of a thousand men. All of Col. Bradley Johnson's staff was captured—he alone escaping by taking his heels to the woods." Grimes was glad to be back with the army and his friend Dodson Ramseur who, he wrote Charlotte, "had two wagon loads of dry goods which he had brought from Maryland, both of which were captured by the Yankees when he so unfortunately was surprised by the enemy. What will Nellie say?" "While bathing I found a strand of your hair on my person," waxed Grimes somewhat nostalgically, " and I was romantic enough to put it in your daguerreotype. This is the performance of a real lover ain't it?"[5]

Jubal Early's overall success in the Valley was causing some concern in within the Union high command. He had throttled a 10,000-man Federal force at the Second Battle of Kernstown on July 24. This victory, coupled with his continuing threat to Washington and the importance of the Valley itself, finally prompted Grant to dispatch his cavalry commander, Maj. Gen. Philip H. Sheridan, to deal with the irascable Confederate. Sheridan, who had graduated an undistinguished 34th in a West Point class of 52 cadets in 1853, had proven his abilities on battlefields from Tennessee to Virginia. The fiery Irishman formed an emotional bond with the men under him and they believed in his abiltiy to lead them to ultimate victory. The fact that he heavily outnumbered his opponent did not hurt, either. His Army of the Shenandoah was composed of the veteran VI Corps, XIX Corps, and VIII Corps (also called the Army of West Virginia), as well as three divisions of cavalry, some 40,000 troops with which to assail his opponent.[6]

In contrast, Early's army fielded five infantry divisions and two cavalry divisions. The Southern infantry, veteran warriors largely from Richard Ewell's Second Corps, were commanded by Maj. Gens. John Breckinridge, John Gordon, Joseph Kershaw, Dodson Ramseur and Robert Rodes. While Early had justifiable faith in his foot soldiers, his confidence did not extend to his mounted arm, which consisted of a pair of divisions under Fitz Lee and Lunsford L. Lomax. Early did not believe the commanders were up to the task at hand, and he viewed horsemen in general with distain. Early's Army of the Valley was also supported by forty guns under the capable command of Col. Thomas H. Carter. In total, the small force mustered some 13,000 men, giving Sheridan a numerical advantage of about three to one.[7]

As matters of grand strategy played out, Grimes took the time to write Charlotte about various matters on August 15. "I have seen Ramseur only for a few moments since his return," he explained. "He appeared to be in very good spirits and anxious to do something about his fight which up here is called the 'Hasty Affair.'" Grimes reference to his friend's "fight" was in reference to an engagement at Stephenson's Depot on July 20, where Ramseur had deployed his division to confront what he had erroneously been led to believe was but a small enemy force. Before Ramseur could act, his flanks were overlapped by the enemy and, regiment by regiment, his division broke and ran from the field. The humiliating exhibition cost Ramseur 73 killed, 130 wounded and 267 captured. Although he was taken to task by the Southern press, General Early (as well as General Lee) still had confidence in Ramseur, who had not taken "proper precautions" in advancing.

Grimes was also disgusted by the setback, although for different reasons. "Genl. Bob Johnston," he informed Charotte, "is backbiting him all the while he too is aspiring to Ramseur's position." Johnston commanded a brigade in Ramseur's Division at Stephenson's Depot. "He is in my opinion, a mean, low sneaking puppy," continued Grimes, "for Ramseur to my knowledge assented in signing his appointment before the [N.C.] Senate where an effort was being made not to have it confirmed. And Ramseur promoted its passage by his signature, and now he is making every effort to have it appear that Ramseur is [to blame] in permitting the surprise, but Ramseur cannot be held responsible for Johnston not having his guns loaded which was the case, and he was in line of battle at that."[8] The criticism mounted as the days passed. "On the march two or three days ago his command passed the ambulances with Ramseur's name written upon them," explained Grimes to Charlotte. "One soldier inquired, 'who is Ramseur?' Another replied, 'he is a Major General.' And another says, 'No, he is a dog,' and then another calls out, 'No, he ain't a dog, but we would like to swap him for a dog.'" The insults did nothing to alter Grimes' opinion of Ramseur. "All such remarks culimated to show their disrespect for him," was his explanation, "which makes me like him all the more than I did."[9]

With an odd summer lull between the warring parties Grimes, camped with his brigade at Strasburg in mid-August, informed Charlotte of the peace and quiet he was enjoying in the lovely and verdant valley. The army was sending grain and cattle on the hoof back to Lee's embattled men around Richmond and Petersburg, as well as tying up a large number of the enemy. Early's almost constant marching and maneuvering, intended to confuse the enemy and obfuscate his paltry numbers, did not appear to dampen morale in the ranks. On the evening of August 15, members from Grimes' old 4th regiment sought him out, he wrote with some pride, and delivered "a delightful serenade." The army prepared for yet another move the following day, and Early's army spent most of the hot 17th on the march. Outside of Winchester, Grimes reported home that the enemy was "still falling back and not showing much fight [although] their numbers are double ours." Few could fathom Early's plans, and he shared them with no one. "General Early outgenerals all of us," Grimes had written several days earlier. "No one can guess when he is going to move, or where he will next bring up. The Yankees begin to think him ubiquitous." Nothing had changed by August 19. "What is General Early's intention, I can't say."[10]

Many in the army believed August 20 would see a serious encounter with Sheridan's Federals when Grimes received orders to meet and block an advancing body of Federals. I was directed to "make a big show of fight and bluff them off, if possible," he told Charlotte that evening in yet another letter home, "but if they came in force, to hold them a little while, to give the others time to retreat, and then fall back." Although light skirmishing erupted near Berryville and Opequon Creek, nothing of consequence developed. Turning his thoughts homeward, Grimes dwelt on the forthcoming arrival of his new child. Charlotte, he wrote, must "trust in God [for] your safe delivery from the perils attendant upon childbirth." "If you take a meal out of camp," he wrote on a more playful note, "you have to encounter such ugly women that the pleasure of eating is greatly lessened for you. Remember I have a horror of ugly women." The troops were also in a playful mood, he reported, and "some fellow set fire to a horse's tail by tying straw to it and drove him through the cavalry corps, causing quite a stampede and frightening them out of their wits."[11]

Fighting of a more serious nature broke out the next day at Charlestown, western Virgina, where Grimes' Brigade led the advance against elements of Sheridan's command. "I have had today a good many killed and wounded," he reported. "The enemy have a large force between us and Harper's Ferry, which Early is demonstrating upon, and is contesting the ground most stubbornly." Still, Grimes did not believe a major battle was in the offing. "This is a mere feint to frighten them and cover some important move on our part," he explained. "I have no idea we will fight here, for the enemy outnumbers us three to one, and Early knows [too] well the importance of preserving his army."[12] The next day Early demonstrated in the direction of Harpers Ferry, and "drove them through Charlestown to their position on Bolivar Heights, where they are watching us and occasionally throwing a shell at us," reported Grimes. In reality, Sheridan was not prepared to wage a pitched engagement and had withdrawn when Early displayed an aggressive posture. Grimes had a close call on the front line of the demonstration, which he commanded, when "their artillery opened on us," a shell passing "within a few feet of my horse." The inhabitants of the beautifual valley who lived below the confluence of the Shenandoah and Potomac rivers impressed Grimes, who described them as "loyal to the backbone."[13]

Most of the last ten days of August were consumed with skirmishing and marching, as Early probed the fords over the Potomac and kept up a threatening posture before Sheridan's larger army. Sheridan's cautiousness and reluctance to engage in battle did not garner Early's respect, and indeed made him less cautious than he should have been. In fact, the exact opposite was the case. Sheridan, a naturally aggressive leader, was following Grant's orders. He was simply biding his time, measuring up his enemy, making his maps, and looking for the right time to strike. From the perspective of a brigade command (or an enlisted man in the ranks), the strategic situation was a confusing one. "Genl. Early's movements are still kept in mystery. No one understands what his intentions are," wrote Grimes in a letter home. "[Before] the privates have always been able to grasp what was the intention of commanding generals, but now they are completely [confused] as to military movements."[14]

The prospects for battle brightened when Federal cavalry struck John C. Breckinridge's command on the 25th. Rodes' Division, with Grimes' Brigade marching in the van, "formed line of battle. . .and advanced upon them, driving them before us." The nearly bloodless warfare they had been conducting especially excited Grimes, who explained that "whenever we are able to get them in a run, I feel really boy-like and enjoy the sport very much indeed."[15] After chasing the Yankees through Martinsburg, Grimes observed that "the citizens of Martinsburg are Dutch and all union with the exception of a few good families who are very enthusiastic."[16]

Grimes was quickly reminded that not all the fighting was bloodless when he received especially sad news from Charlotte that George, her younger brother, had been killed in battle. Being so far from home, Grimes responded to the terrible news the only way he could, by expressing his sympathy in a letter. "George, I fear was rash and exposed himself more than the proper discharge of his duties required," he explained after offering words of consolation, "but that is always the case with the brave and magnanimous. I trust my darling and feel that I will be spared to you until this war is over."[17]

The light skirmishing and marching in northern Virginia allowed the soldiers time to speculate on the upcoming 1864 Presidential election. Many in the army believed that the end of the war was in sight. General Rodes predicted a termination of hostilities by year's end, and President Lincoln was considered a weak incumbent. "[I] was informed by a citizen from Fredericksburg," Grimes wrote Charlotte, "that McClellan was the nominee for the Yankee presidency on a sort of ambiguous peace platform and the prospects of peace brighten daily." Grimes was not alone in the army, for many viewed the nomination of "Little Mac" as a sure indication that Northern resolve to continue the bloodshed was weakening.[18]

Presidents and procreation continued to occupy Grimes' thoughts. "You must keep me informed as you get on and if you should be confined before you anticipate, make sure some of your sisters write me daily for I shall be anxious indeed about you. God grant that you may have a safe delivery and that you and your infant may prosper well. I shall be mighty anxious to see your offspring."[19] Although Grimes professed not to care about the gender of the child, writing, "I fear my darling from the manner in which you heard me express myself that you may suffer if your offspring should be a female," he wrote Charlotte on September 13. "Lest my foolish remark may give you some unnecessary pain, let me assure you that I shall be pleased whatever may be the sex. True, I had somewhat rather that it was a boy, but if it should turn out otherwise, I shall be thankful for your safe delivery and shall love a girl fully, as it is my own flesh and blood. Let it be what it may."[20]

Although the August and early September marching and skirmishing did not extract much of a toll in terms of casualties, the hot and humid weather and constant exercise quickly wore out uniforms and footwear. "We are now very much in need of clothes and shoes," lamented Grimes, "there being at least two hundred barefooted and half-naked men in my command." Still, the North Carolinians were hardened veterans and had experienced much worse in both weather and battle. "But with all our rags and nakedness," he boasted, "[my men] can put up a most beautiful fight. The men go into action with spirit." As for his own attitude after more than three years of war, he claimed that he felt "twenty years younger after being in a fight for a few minutes . . .and think only of killing the detested, hated Yankees and driving them off our soil."[21] From camp once again in Bunker Hill, Virginia, Grimes contemplated the army's situation: "I scarcely think it possible that we will enter Maryland again unless we receive larger reinforcements, and I suppose Genl Lee has his hands full to keep Grant at bay and can spare no more troops."[22]

While the Valley's farmers sowed their fields with winter wheat, Grimes quietly celebrated his wedding anniversary by writing to Charlotte from Stephenson' Depot on September 15. "This day twelve months since we were united in the holy bond of wedlock," he recalled fondly. "Marriage at best is but a lottery and a step which people should be careful of taking without great consideration, but my dearest darling in this lottery, I have drawn the highest prize." While deeply pleased with his choice of martial partners, Grimes was anything but satisfied with the state of affairs in Raleigh, where once again Davis Administration critics were hard at work. "And so the people of Raleigh are becoming despondent again," he lamented. "I wish that I had a few of the croakers to put in front of my Brigade. They would learn to appreciate our efforts more highly and be of some service if they think the Confederacy is about to fail." His anger up, Grimes continued, "How can they reconcile it to their consciences [to sit] quietly at home, hugging their dollars and cents and not raising a finger to assist the cause?" With mounting frustration, he closed by noting the complainers were "unworthy of the air they breathe and should be put in [illegible word] or emasculated for they only have the resemblance of men and not their spirit."[23]

Although the 'mimic war," as one observer called it, continued between Early and Sheridan, Grimes drilled his soldiers to keep them ready for action. "I am beginning to draw the reins pretty tight upon my brigade, because the discipline was becoming rather lax," he wrote Charlotte. "I can see the improvement. If we could have a [lull] in fighting for about three months this would render them very efficient. But as they now are there is no better Brigade in this army and will compare favorably with all in any respect." The evening of September 16 passed pleasantly for the general, and he shared his experience with his wife: "Had a serenade last night, given by the band of the 'old Fourth Regiment,'" he penned. "I appreciate [this] as a mark of respect and esteem which all men who have ever served under me retain, even if my reputation is one for severity and rigid discipline for they are well aware that it was just." After the band had finished playing Grimes, who loved music all his life, exclaimed, "[If] I could only hear our band about every other night. [I] would live twenty years." Unbeknownst to

Grimes or any other Confederate, music of a different sort was about to be heard in the Shenandoah Valley.[24]

Phil Sheridan's policy of cautiousness reaped dividends. His new Army of the Shenandoah was well organized, his men rested and, best of all, Jubal Early had grown overconfident by Sheridan's reluctance to engage in a pitched battle. By the 11th of September, however, "Little Phil's" patience, like his superior's, was wearing thin, for he had always been on the lookout for an opening. "It is exceedingly difficult to attack [Early] in this position," Sheridan explained from the east side of the Opequon Creek, for the water-way ". . .is a very formidable barrier; there are various crossings, but all difficult; the banks are formidable." Outlining his plan, Sheridan informed Grant that he intended "to remain on the defensive until [Early] detaches, unless the chances are in my favor. The troops here are in fine spirits." Sheridan's hopes that Early would separate his army were realized within a few days. Unable to get along with the prickly Early, First Corps leader Richard Anderson finagled a return to Lee's army. For a reason that is still difficult to comprehend—overconfidence is the perhaps the best explanation—Early voluntarily dispatched Joseph Kershaw's First Corps division and a battalion of artillery with Anderson—even though he probably could have kept them had he wished to do so. By the morning of September 15, these veteran troops and officers were marching out of Winchester. When Sheridan received news of the transfer he held a brief meeting with Grant at Charlestown, where the decision was reached to take the offensive. Although no one knew it at the time, the apparent Confederate dominance of the Lower Shenandoah Valley was over.[25]

Just before daylight on September 19, a division of Federal horsemen trotted their mounts across Opequon Creek east of Winchester. The troopers were the vanguard of almost 35,000 infantry and artillerymen, who tramped behind them in search of Early's Confederates. Unfortunately for Early, his own under strength divisions were scattered. Two days earlier, Rodes and Gordon had been sent by Early north to Bunker Hill, and then to Martinsburg to search for work crews on the Baltimore and Ohio Railroad—more than twenty miles from Winchester. When "Old Jube" learned the ominous news that Sheridan and Grant had met, he realized something was afoot and that his army needed to reassemble. Winchester was not the best place to fight a defensive battle, but Early had no choice: he had to

cobble his army back together and hold the town or face piecemeal destruction. Marching hard, Rodes' Division, with Grimes' Brigade in the ranks,
reached Stephenson's Depot on the evening of the 18th; Gordon's men
reached Bunker Hill. Early's far-flung command was still strung out and
vulnerable. Luckily for Early, as his two errant divisions were marching to
Ramseur's support early on the 19th, Sheridan's column got bogged down in
Berryville Canyon, a narrow and wooded two-mile gorge that choked his
advance to a crawl for hours.[26]

Dodson Ramseur's Division, fewer than 2,000 men, faced the first Federal thrust of the day by Horatio Wright's VI Corps while deployed about a
mile east of Winchester on the Berryville Pike. As Sheridan's advance was
pinning Ramseur in place, Bryan Grimes' Brigade marched past Winchester
on the east and deployed in open fields with the rest of Rodes' Division
several hundred yards north and west of Ramseur's left flank. Grimes' men
comprised the far right front of Rodes' divisional line. As he did so, artillery
fire erupted as the opposing guns supporting Ramseur's and Wright's men
pounded each other. Gordon's Division, part of John C. Breckinridge's unofficial "corps," followed Rodes onto the field and extended the line to the left
toward Red Bud Run and the Hackwood estate. The balance of Breckinridge's command, a small division under Gabriel Wharton, had remained in
the rear to watch the army's left flank. Early himself positioned much of the
artillery, and his untrustworthy cavalry was stationed on his flanks. With the
preliminary maneuvering over, about 11:40 a.m. Sheridan launched a direct
attack with three Federal divisions against Ramseur's front, driving him
slowly rearward. The fighting grew heavier, and within the hour much of
Ramseur's division was falling back. Gordon's Division, too, was struck
when a pair of brigades from Brig. Gen. Cuvier Grover's division (XIX
Corps) advanced through a pair of woodlots below Red Bud Run. When
Grover's attack stalled, Gordon launched a furious counterattack that shoved
back the XIX Corps Federals.

Up until now, Grimes' men had suffered little, positioned as they were
on the right center of Early's line. The time for Rodes to attack had arrived,
however, for Sheridan's own center was vulnerable and Gordon's assault
was inching east. While guiding his division forward with all four of his
brigades in line, the gallant Rodes was struck in the head with a piece of
shrapnel and knocked from his horse. He lived perhaps for a few moments

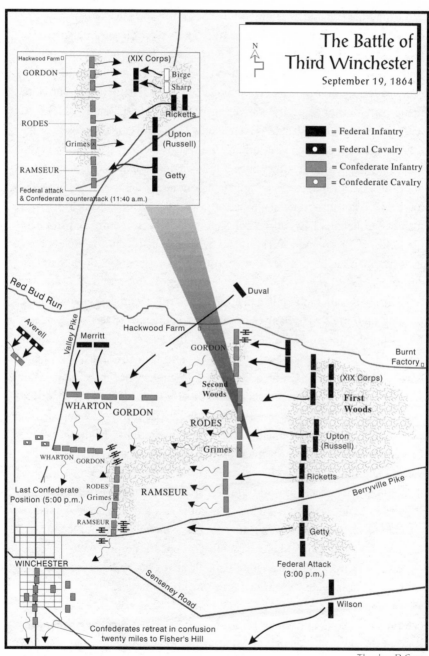

The Battle of
Third Winchester
September 19, 1864

■ = Federal Infantry
● = Federal Cavalry
▨ = Confederate Infantry
◉ = Confederate Cavalry

**Inset (upper left):**

Hackwood Farm

(XIX Corps)

GORDON

Birge

Sharp

Ricketts

RODES

Upton
(Russell)

Grimes

RAMSEUR

Getty

Federal attack
& Confederate counterattack (11:40 a.m.)

**Main map:**

Red Bud Run

Averell

Valley Pike

Merritt

Duval

Hackwood Farm

GORDON

Burnt
Factory

(XIX Corps)

Second
Woods

First
Woods

WHARTON
GORDON

RODES

Upton
(Russell)

Grimes

WHARTON GORDON

Ricketts

Berryville Pike

Last Confederate
Position (5:00 p.m.)

RODES
Grimes

RAMSEUR

RAMSEUR

Getty

WINCHESTER

Senseney Road

Federal Attack
(3:00 p.m.)

Wilson

Confederates retreat in confusion
twenty miles to Fisher's Hill

Theodore P. Savas

and expired, a stunning loss for both Early's army and the Confederacy. The division swept forward, for the men "did not observe [Rodes' death] at that time," wrote Major Osborne, and for about an hour engaged in a bitter stand-up fight. There is some question as to who took command of Rodes' now leaderless division. Its senior brigadier was Cullen Battle, and command by virtue of seniority was his to wield, and he probably did so. At least one modern historian, however, claims Grimes eventually took over the division and effectively led it through the rest of the day. Grimes, however, makes no mention of having done so in his letters home to Charlotte. With both sides exhausted, the fighting petered out along the front. Although his losses were not insubstantial—especially with the death of Rodes—Early's men had crippled a large portion of Sheridan's powerful army and still held the field. While some in the army believed they had won a relatively easy victory, Sheridan's other shoe was waiting to fall on the tired Southern defenders.[27]

During the afternoon lull, a pair of Breckinridge's brigades initially took position on Early's right flank (they later moved up next to Rodes' [Battles'] line, while his remaining brigade moved to the left. It was from that direction—Early's left flank—that disaster struck. Two divisions of Federal horsemen with George Crook's VIII Corps of infantry had marched past the Confederate left and were bearing down on Gordon's left from beyond Red Bud Run. By now someone—either Battle or Grimes, had assumed firm control of Rodes' Division and it, together with Gordon's Division, battled Crook's advance. Sheridan's main body below the swampy creek also advanced and pinned the Southerners in place. Slowly crushed, Gordon's soldiers finally fell back toward Winchester, reforming on Rodes' left and Wharton's right, where the vicious musketry and artillery battle continued unabated. According to one Vermont soldier, men under Grimes' command let loose "a most murderous volley" that stopped a portion of the Federal advance in its tracks. The weight of Crook's attack had molded the Southern battle line into a wide "V" northeast of town, with Grimes' North Carolinians holding the center of Early's front north of the Berryville Pike. Continued pressure all along the lines forced the Confederates gradually back, with Ramseur's and Rodes' divisions withdrawing westward and facing east, and Gordon's and Wharton's divisions falling back south and west and facing north. Artillery was piled into the angle formed by the two wings of Early's army. There was now no where else to pull back to without relinquishing the entire field.[28]

About 5:00 p.m., Grimes and his men could hear the roar of battle behind them as well as in front. The ominous thunder was the result of two divisions of Federal cavalry bearing down on Winchester from the north, sweeping aside light opposition mainly in the form of Confederate troopers. The infantry line on Grimes' right evaporated within minutes. Jubal Early rode upon the scene and ordered Grimes to refuse, or pull back, his left. As he attempted this difficult maneuver, Grimes rode in the direction of the mounting danger and was astonished by what he beheld. "Upon coming into the open field, I perceived everything to be inextricable confusion, " he wrote Charlotte after the battle. "Horses dashing over the field, cannon being run to the rear at the top of the horses' speed, men leaving their command, and scattering in confusion." Veteran that he was, no one needed to tell Grimes what was happening: Early's army was melting away. Within a few moments, his brigade (and the division) followed suit.

"My men seeing this state of things," he wrote home a week later, "began also to show symptoms of alarm, which I in a great measure checked, threatening to blow the brains out of the first man who left ranks." By sheer force of will and character, Grimes "succeeded in quieting them down and keeping them under control. Then [I] directed my attention to arresting the flight of others," he continued, "and many a fellow felt the full weight of my best blows from my sword." Somehow, in spite of the crumbling tactical situation, Grimes managed to swing enough of his line to the north to offer some credence of a defense. "During this time the Yankee cavalry was dashing among them, cutting and hewing right and left. We then attempted to fall back slowly, confronting them and fighting every inch of the ground."

It was when the fighting reached such close quarters that Grimes' horse shuddered and fell dead beneath him; three of his staff officers also fell in rapid succession with serious wounds. One of them, Captain W. L. London, "poor fellow, was shot, and caught by me as he fell." Despite his gallant stand, Grimes could not hold his men in position against overwhelming odds, and they were swept by the Federal wave into town. "The ladies of Winchester came out into the streets when the stampede first began and formed across the streets and entreated the stragglers to return, but without success," he later lamented. "Our troops did not behave with their usual valor." Driven from the field, Early's soldiers streamed south twenty miles to Fisher's Hill, which he thought "was the only place where a stand could be made." As darkness fell, we "marched until about 2 o'clock," recalled Grimes, when we lay down and slept until about 4, at which time we were again on the road. . . ."[29]

Third Winchester was an unmitigated disaster. Of the 12,000 men Early had available to him, about 2,000 were killed or wounded and another 1,800 were missing or captured. Overall, his losses approached one-third of his army. Rodes' Division suffered 686 killed, wounded, and missing—more than any of Early's four divisional organizations. Sheridan's losses, which were much higher because he was on the tactical offensive, totaled about 5,000 men. Since he had an army of about 40,000, however, his comparative loss was small (about 12 percent). Sheridan could withstand such bloodlettings; Early could not.[30]

In a letter difficult to pen, Grimes broke the news of the stunning defeat to Charlotte the next day and again in a letter a week later. "Yesterday we had a terrible fight at Winchester and were very roughly handled by the enemy," he explained. "We lost a great many men. . .With great exertion on my part and that of my staff, mine did better than any other, but that was not as well as I desired." The battle "up to 4 o'clock in the afternoon looked bright and promised well for a complete victory," he continued, ". . .Then their cavalry charged our cavalry, which was on the left of our line. . ." General Rodes "was killed." The general's place, Grimes added, "cannot be supplied. He is a serious loss to the Confederacy."[31]

Sheer exhaustion brought about by the long marches for the two days leading up to the battle, coupled with the day-long fight east of Winchester, might have been the culprit for some of his reticence immediately after the action. "For nine hours was under heavy fire, men falling around me almost every instant," he explained. "Have been as near exhausted as a man could well be, not slept ten hours in forty-eight. It was to me the most trying day of the war, when after what I supposed was a victory." Reflecting on the ferocity of the battle, during which he lost his fourth horse in action, Grimes concluded that his "escapes from death on that day appeared marvelous, for from ten o'clock in the morning until after eight at night, I was in the thickest of the fight. . . . Am truly thankful for my safety. . . .I have never

A faded letter written in pencil by Bryan Grimes to his wife Charlotte on September 20, 1864, informing her of the defeat at Third Winchester and the death of General Robert Rodes. *North Carolina Division of Archives and History, Raleigh, NC* exerted myself so much in my life and my voice was completely gone; could scarcely speak above a whisper." So sore he could hardly move, Grimes had "Polk," his body servant, "rub me over with liniment."[32]

As his dejected army gathered in its old line of trenches below Strasburg at Fisher's Hill, Early decided to stand firm and offer a fight there. To fall back further would open the upper Shenandoah Valley to Sheridan's army. The Army of the Valley, however, had to be reorganized before it could effectively fight again. Although Cullen Battle had performed well at Third Winchester, he was not considered sufficiently seasoned to lead a division. The solution was to have Dodson Ramseur transferred from his own division to lead Rodes' old organization, leaving Battle to revert back to his brigade command. Ramseur's vacancy was filled by the elevation of John Pegram, who had led a brigade under Ramseur and earlier in the war a division in the Western Theater. John Gordon remained at the head of his brigades.

With his command assignments at least temporarily cobbled together, Early set about preparing for battle. The series of hills parallel to the Valley Pike was flanked by Massanutten Mountain to the east and Little North Mountain to the west. The Fisher's Hill position spanned the Valley at its narrowest point, and if properly manned, was virtually impregnable. But it was not properly manned. With his divisions thinned by the Winchester fighting, Early now had to deal with the loss of John C. Breckinridge, who were called back to the Department of Southwest Virginia. The First Corps troops under Joseph Kershaw, however, were turned around and marched back to Early, offsetting to some degree his Third Winchester losses.

Reorganized or not, Early's command was simply too small to occupy the entire four-mile front he wanted to defend, from the North Fork of the Shenandoah River west along Tumbling Run to Little North Mountain. Since the Valley Pike had to be held, Early defended it (his right) with his seasoned infantry, which he stretched westward. His front was aligned right to left as follows: Wharton, Gordon, Pegram, and Ramseur. Grimes' Brigade occupied the far left of Ramseur's line, and was thus the far left infantry unit. On Ramseur's left Early deployed the dismounted cavalry of Maj. Gen. Lunsford Lomax's Division on a low wooded ridge, which restricted Early's view to the west. While there were many brave soldiers fighting under Lomax, who was himself a capable leader, Early had nothing but disdain for the horsemen. These troopers were undermanned and poorly-armed, which compounded problems of poor discipline and low morale. They also missed the able Maj. Gen. Fitz Lee, who was seriously wounded at Third Winchester. Early compounded his problems with an ill-chosen defensive alignment: his strongest flank (right) was manned with his best men, while his weakest flank (left) was held by little more than a strong skirmish line of cavalry he did not trust to put up a good fight. As events would soon bear out, Early's deployment would prove fatal.[33]

As the army drew itself up at Fisher's Hill, Grimes sat down to write Charlotte a few lines. Somewhat refreshed from a brief rest, he expressed fatherly concern (and more than a bit of realism) over an earlier letter he had sent his daughter Bettie. "I wrote Bettie a scolding letter about not writing me," he explained. "I wish you would get the letter from her and destroy it for if any accident was to happen to me that letter would be a reminder to her that would always sting her conscience." Other matters of more direct concern also occupied his thoughts. "Genl Ramseur is assigned to the command of the Division, and Battle was our senior officer, but he was totally unqualified for the position," he editorialized. "[I was] glad when Ramseur was sent over." The army's "firm position at Strasburg" provided Grimes with some comfort, "and [we] can in all probability hold our on against an advance of the enemy."[34]

If Early was hoping Sheridan would revert to his prior cautious ways, he was quickly disappointed. On the evening of September 21, Federal skirmishers began probing the Fisher's Hill line. Large formations of infantry could easily be seen behind them. Nothing developed that night, however, and both sides settled down to an uneasy sleep. Morning, however, opened again with the crackling of musketry as the skirmishers renewed their deadly engagement, and the firing continued throughout the morning and into the afternoon. As the minutes ticked by on that clear and warm fall day, Grimes began to worry about his exposed left flank and the weakly-manned far left near Little North Mountain. If the Federals attacked there, he had little confidence the cavalry would hold out for long. Compounding the problem was a lack of ammunition in Ramseur's Division, which limited for some hours the rate of return fire on a large segment of Early's line. By 1:00 p.m., a heavy force of infantry and artillery moved forward and within the hour was driving in Grimes' skirmishers.

As if history was quickly repeating itself, Grimes saw trouble to the west. About 3:00 p.m., as he remembered it, "We perceived two columns moving up the side of the mountain to our left, when the cavalry was again fronted." Just as at Third Winchester, it appeared as though Sheridan was pinning Early's infantry in front and moving to turn his left. In response, Grimes "urged Ramseur to send a brigade or two over to their assistance," since he believed "the cavalry would run if attacked." To his dismay, Ramseur "declined to do so until he could communicate with General Early." Sensing that help would not arrive in time, Grimes grew despondent. "During that hour," he lamented, "I suffered more than I've ever done in my life. My anxiety for the fate of the army was intolerable." The crushing and still fresh defeat at Third Winchester played heavily on his mind, and the specter of a left flank assault haunted the North Carolinian. Acting apparently on his own authority, Grimes refused his left two regiments, the 32nd and 45th, together with the 2nd North Carolina Battalion, to protect his flank while the 43rd and 53rd regiments kept up their fire to the front against the advancing Federal skirmishers. With the enemy clearly visible in strength on the left, no one of sufficient authority took control of the situation. As historian Jeffery Wert notes in his fine study of this action, "A storm was brewing on Little North Mountain. . . .and, somewhere along the line, the Confederate chain of command failed."[35] A private soldier in a Southern artillery outfit supports Grimes post-battle account of seeing Federals climbing Little North Mountain, and scribbled as much in his diary as it was transpiring. "We will have to get from this position, and very quickly," was his on-the-spot and correct conclusion.[36]

About 4:30 p.m., Sheridan's army made a determined move forward, followed shortly thereafter by the explosion of musketry from Little North Mountain. The failed "chain of command" problem became obvious to Ramseur, who pulled General Cox's Brigade out of line and to support Lomax's dismounted troopers. It was too little too late, and within minutes the cavalry was streaming in panic to the rear. The wave of Federals enveloped Grimes and his men from the left, front, and rear. While the North Carolinians attempted to hold their works, Ramseur shifted units about in an attempt to form a coherent defensive line. The heavy Federal assault from the front, however, spun his efforts into confusion. Grimes, who later described the swirling attack as an "avalanche," only attempted a withdrawal

when "Ramseur came up and told me to save my brigade if possible."[37] It
was a difficult order, for his men were "firing to the right, left and rear," and
the "colors of the United States troops were less than a hundred yards from
me." Grimes was in perhaps his most dangerous predicament of the war.
Almost surrounded by the advancing Yankees, his only chance was to fight
his way out, and he intended to do so. Shouting out his orders, he directed
his men to move by the right flank, "firing to the front and left as I
marched." Grimes' problems were compounded by an odd set of circumstances: "Thinking that we were going to fight in the trenches, [I] had sent
my horse to a hollow for protection. A while before this time I had fallen
and sprained my ankle and was able to hobble along, but very slowly.
Through a mistake, my horse had been carried from the place where I left
him, and I found myself a foot." At one point he attempted to form his men
into line, but he "found it almost an impossibility, on account of the nearness
of the enemy." For the first time in the war, Grimes faced the likely possibility that he would "fall into the hands of the Yankees."

Thundering weapons mingled with the screams of terrified horses and
wounded men to fill the once-quiet valley with a cacophony of noise. As
Grimes sidled and fought his way east, an artillery round "cut down two
horses in a caisson, and the drivers were engaged in getting the others loose
from their harness," he remembered. It was a critical moment for the crippled general officer:

Two were loosened, and the drivers had mounted them before I could get up,
and others were cutting out the two which remained. To procure one of these
horses was a matter of life and death with me, and, while one of these
artillerymen was cutting away, I vaulted into the saddle and told him to hurry
up—that I must have that horse. He didn't take time to parley with me, but
ran off, leaving the horse still fastened by one trace to the horse that had been
killed; I [pulled] out. . .my knife and began to cut away, when another driver,
who had by this time disentangled his horse, loosened this trace for me, and I
put spurs to my horse. The Yankees were then not over fifty yards from me,
and I had an open field of two hundred yards to run the gauntlet through,
with but few other objects in view for them to shoot at.

As the bullets buzzed around him, Grimes, riding low in the saddle,
urged his horse on through the hail of musketry to the relative safety beyond. "My escape," he added, "was almost miraculous." As he rode on,

Grimes came across "Colonel Winston, broken down, and took him behind me" on the horse. Keeping his head in the midst of utter disaster, Grimes formed his men into line several times and conducted a fighting retreat from the field as best he could. "The troops on all sides were too much demoralized to make a successful fight," he lamented, "and it was fall back all the time." Chaos ruled the field. "I was carried along in the current only by order, when I found no support," he added, as if to emphasize that matters had spiraled out of everyone's control.[38]

# Cedar Creek

"...The hardest day's work I
ever engaged in—trying to rally the men."

Jubal Early's army was in full retreat, swept from the field as if by a
giant broom. Ramseur had charge of the rear guard, and with some
well-handled artillery kept the enemy at bay long enough to allow the bulk
of the Confederates to stream southward to safety. By the morning of September 23, the Southerners congregated at Mount Jackson before moving
south to Rude's Hill. Pressed by Sheridan, Grimes' Brigade, with the rest of
Early's men, fell back in line of battle south of New Market. "Our troops,"
Grimes wrote Charlotte in a quick note to let her know he was well, "have
not behaved well at all."

The army marched toward Port Republic on the 25th. The historical
significance of the area was not lost on Grimes, who remembered it as "the
place of one of Jackson's greatest victories." The army had finally "reached
a point of safety after one of the most harassing weeks of anxiety ever spent
by me," he informed his wife. "It has been fight and run all night."[1] Joseph
Kershaw's footsore and ill-used division of some 2,000 men met up with
Early near Port Republic. Although Kershaw's arrival raised the spirits of
the army, everyone realized the significance of their dire situation. The
seventy-five mile retreat finally reached Waynesboro west of Rockfish Gap
near the Blue Ridge. The Confederates left behind at Fisher's Hill more than
a dozen guns and a thousand prisoners, losing only about 250 killed and
wounded in the lopsided fighting. Sheridan's losses numbered a few hundred at most. My cavalry, complained Early when sending news of the
defeat to General Lee, "has been the cause of all my disasters." Old Jube
could not bring it upon himself to admit any responsibility for the setbacks.[2]

With the army regrouped, Grimes found the time during the last few
days of September to write about matters of a more personal nature to

Charlotte. Part of a letter of the 28th dealt with his good friend Ramseur, who continued to impress Grimes. "It was right amazing during the fight at Strasburg to have Ramseur say that his wife was about to be confined and he feared the effects of the disorder upon her," he told his wife.[3] The next day he wrote again, his optimism about the army's fortunes rising. "Our troops are beginning to recover from the effects of last week's misfortune," was how he described the drubbing at Fisher's Hill, "and are now in a tolerable fighting trim and anxious for an opportunity to retain their lost reputation." On the last day of the month, cracks in Grimes' hardened belief of victory began to appear when he admitted to Charlotte that the "stampede" at Fisher's Hill had caused him to believe "for the first time that we would not establish the Confederacy. . . .I have been selfish in asking you to link your fate with me." The defeats at Third Winchester and Fisher's Hill had taken their toll on Bryan Grimes.[4]

Jubal Early's October 9 report to Robert Lee sustained Grimes' assessment of army's morale. "My infantry," wrote Early, "is now in good heart and condition." The Valley commander's ink was not even dry by the time he learned that on the same day, his cavalry had suffered another humiliating defeat at Tom's Brook at the hands of Sheridan's mounted arm. Ramseur expressed it best, declaring himself "sick at heart from these repeated disasters—but I hope this is the last." It wasn't. In the weeks following Fisher's Hill, Sheridan sent his legions far and wide across the Shenandoah in what John B. Gordon later called "a season of burning." Barns, corncribs, houses, haystacks, and winter wheat fields went up in smoke as Grant's former cavalry commander destroyed the region so that Lee's men could never feast from it again.[5]

With little to do but remain alert and drill, Grimes confessed to Charlotte that he had "relapsed into one of my old habits, that of chewing tobacco and feel already the nervous effects upon my system, but when all becomes quiet again [I] will try and break myself of the habit." He also reminded her that "if anything happens to me you will hear of it soon for ill news flies rapidly."[6] After Sheridan moved to Harrisonburg a quiet time prevailed and Grimes expressed some deep emotional feelings to Charlotte in one of his most poetic letters of the war: "This afternoon I watched the sun set and the star view which you remember we promised to watch and think of each other and image what the other was about. And then again the idea presented itself to my mind that perhaps you were suffering pain and agony, and I, far distant, am unable even to express a word of sympathy, let alone, assist in administering to you comfort and alleviating your pains."[7]

Subtle doubts about the success of the war again crept into a letter home: "Sometimes the thought haunts me that if we are unsuccessful in this contest for freedom then I have doomed you to a life of poverty and misery." In closing, he expressed a rare, although mild, criticism of Jubal Early:

> He was circumspect in his movements, but our great danger lies in the fact that since our recent reverses, the troops do not have that unbounded confidence in his judgment which is necessary for a successful military leader, for without that he can hardly expect his men to act well their part. When they think he is deficient in judgment then each one will be considering his individual safety instead of relying upon him and their command to take care of the whole. But I hope for the best."[8]

Grimes was not alone in his criticism of Early. Ramseur expressed misgivings about the defensive line taken by Early at Fisher's Hill, and ex-Virginia governor and Confederate general William "Extra Billy" Smith chastised Old Jube in a long and caustic letter to Lee. "What was left of our army now lost all confidence in General Early as a leader," wrote yet another soldier in the Valley army, "and they were therefore much demoralized." Even Surgeon John F. Shaffner had an opinion, writing his fiancee Carrie L. Fries on October 3, 1864 that: "our men have lost confidence in Gen. Early. Soldiers will not fight well when led by a man for whom they have no respect. It is said that Early drinks freely." On the same day Shaffner was spreading gossip about Early's drinking habits to his fiancee, Grimes, perhaps unwittingly, revealed the almost impossible odds facing the crumbling Confederacy when he wrote to Charlotte that all would be well if "the mails will only confirm the report of the enemy defeat at Richmond and that Hood has succeeded in whipping Sherman, the horizon of the Confederate sky will brighten."[9]

With the beaten remnants of Early's army camped at Mount Sydney on October 6, Grimes continued to drill his brigade. According to returns for the end of September, his brigade numbered just 795 present "for duty," with an effective strength of just 763, smaller than an early war regiment. He appreciated the benefits of order and morale whatever its strength, saying, "I know the necessity of drilling and discipline to make good soldiers." The ill-will between William Cox and Grimes continued to fester. Cox, the latter claimed correctly in a letter to Charlotte, was late in joining the battle at Fisher's Hill. The North Carolinian's brigade had been pulled out of line by Ramseur to confront the flanking attack pouring forth from Little North Mountain, but Cox lost his way and ended up in the rear and out of the battle. Cox's wife, however, in a conversation on the subject with Charlotte, apparently knew nothing of the affair. "By all means do not undeceive his wife for if she thinks he accomplished wonders let her believe it so," cautioned Grimes. "I am glad that you had too much good sense and modesty to contradict her or to praise your husband; leave that to others for further events will show the extent to which the services of each are held in this army."[10]

Sheridan's soldiers continued to loot and burn the Valley. "They destroyed everything in their retreat," related Grimes on October 9. "We have not the wherewithal to subsist our army on. Country [is] a perfect desolation. All stock and provisions destroyed." Grimes would have been even more disheartened had he learned, as Jubal Early had after penning his report to Lee, the outcome of a cavalry fight that day. At Sheridan's urging, his horsemen sought out the enemy and scored a sharp victory at Tom's Brook near Fisher's Hill. Led by George Custer and Wesley Merritt, the Federals attacked and routed Thomas Rosser's and Lunsford Lomax's Southerners, chasing them for miles in yet another humiliating exhibition by Early's mounted arm. Rosser's cavalry brigade (about 600 men) had joined Early a few days earlier, just in time to be routed from the field. Grimes learned of the affair soon enough. "Yesterday we had another of those unaccountable stampedes among the cavalry," he wrote with some anguish. "I had hoped that when Genl. Rosser came up here that he would encourage a change, but he also appears to have become demoralized. There must be something contagious in this atmosphere, or in this valley cavalry for they cause everything to stampede that comes in association with them. If I had a dictum in the matter at least one hundred of them would have been suspended this morning as a warning to others."[11]

Another subject widely debated within the ranks—other than the pathetic Confederate cavalry—was Jubal Early's diminishing capacity for command. While Early's strategy and tactics—particularly his use of cavalry—were roundly criticized, so too was his personality and treatment of others. "Old Jube's" sarcastic tongue and criticism of fellow officers did not endear himself to his subordinates, and there was a reason why many in the army referred to the arthritic general as "Lee's bad old man." Grimes, a stickler for military protocol took issue with Early's harsh style in dealing with others. "Only yesterday is an instance of his severity," he wrote Charlotte on October 10, "[when] he ordered charges to be preferred against Adj. —Lindsay for anticipating his time (furlough) five days which he was inclined to do so by the sudden and serious illness of his mother, who requested that he stay until she was better or died. This appears hard and is in my opinion unnecessary. If [Early] would only be more rigid with delinquents from the battlefield and less so in minor details, it would certainly raise the discipline of his command."[12]

Believing Early was no longer a serious threat, Sheridan began withdrawing down the valley on October 6. He moved his army to Strasburg on October 9 and then east and just north of Cedar Creek, a major tributary of the North Fork of the Shenandoah River, where he went into camp. The Federal general burned or destroyed the bridges in his wake, which made subsequent move southward against Early less of a possibility. "The question now is, what he intends doing," Early wrote Lee on the 9th of October. The devastated Shenandoah was no longer capable of feeding his small army for a sustained period. Without waiting for an answer from Lee, Early decided to probe north and ascertain Sheridan's intentions. On the morning of October 12, the Confederates broke camp and tramped north. By mid-morning on the 13th, they were aligned for battle on Hupp's Hill a short distance below Cedar Creek. Early announced his presence by opening with his artillery on the unsuspecting soldiers of the XIX Federal Corps. Advancing enemy infantry was dealt with sharply on the Stickley farm by a brigade of South Carolinians and retreated in some haste. The presence of heavy forces of Federals behind Cedar Creek ended the action, and the Confederates withdrew to their old line of works at Fisher's Hill. The engagement at Stickley Farm, though minor, proved strategically significant. The probe demonstrated to Early that any further advance would be contested by Sheridan, who had only hours earlier recalled Horatio Wright's recently detached VI Corps veterans. Even if the fight did not result in Wright's recall, Early's presence opposite Sheridan probably would have had the same effect. One of Early's objectives, after all, was to keep Union troops operating in the Valley and away from Lee's front around Richmond and Petersburg.[13]

Settled in camp and with the immediate threat of battle having receded, Grimes turned his attention once again to Charlotte and her pending delivery. "Any day I am expecting to hear of your delivery," he wrote. "Please have me written to daily for I shall be very uneasy about you."[14] The next day he wrote again to share the latest news: "The Yankee brigade commander who has been burning all the barns and houses was wounded and captured. What," he inquired, "do you think ought to be his penitence—fire?"[15] Unfortunately Charlotte's reply is not recorded.

On a lighter note the following day, Grimes returned to the issue of chewing tobacco—a habit he had apparently begun while in the army. "You seem to think the use of tobacco something horrible and when I hear of something else to compensate for the relinquishment of such a pleasure and comfort, and if you will not kiss me with a quid of tobacco in my mouth, then perhaps I will forgo its use," he teased Charlotte. "The habit I know to the non-user appears disgusting, but it is of great comfort to me. How I ever abstained from its use for so long I cannot imagine and the only way to break me will be to refuse to kiss me and until that is the case I expect it will not be broken." Grimes finished his letter by revealing a mild level of discord he and Charlotte were experiencing (perhaps she more than he) over the naming of their forthcoming baby, which was due any day. "What is the question you have asked," he inquired in reply to her most recent letter, "to which I have made no reply?"[16]

The only one of any importance that I remember is relative to a name for your unborn and thought that I had left that for you to decide for yourself, but if you want an expression of preference from me; if a girl suppose you call it for yourself. Now I don't think Charlotte such an ugly name as I once did and prefer that to anything else, but if you prefer to call it after your sister, Mary Speight, or let your mother name it. If a boy, I expect it would be gratifying to you and your family to call him after your brother George. Which do by all means if you wish, or as I suggested sometime since, call him Alston after my Warren friends, or let your father and mother name him. Any name that you may select will meet with my approval. Please yourself my darling and in doing so you will please me.[17]

The clear and warm morning of October 16 brought with it a most unusual assignment for Grimes when Early hatched a plan to capture one of George Custer's cavalry brigades, which was thought to be camped near Turkey Run, northwest of Cedar Creek. Late that afternoon around 5:00 p.m. under orders from Early, General Rosser saddled up his Laurel Brigade to begin a night march over the eastern side of Little North Mountain to surprise the Federals from the rear the following morning. The ambushing force was augmented by Grimes' infantrymen, who climbed behind the troopers to add their firepower to the effort. All night the cavalry horses, carrying double and stumbling often, worked their way toward the Federal camp. It was a miserable journey. Grimes remembered that the march was conducted "over the most rugged roads I ever traveled." One of those unlucky enough to have made the trip, Pvt. William Ball, remembered that "Sometimes I would feel as if my horse were standing on his head, so steep was the descent; next moment, that I would fall off behind, so steep the ascent." Grimes's men dismounted about 3:00 a.m. and prepared to advance on the sleeping enemy from one direction while Rosser's troopers approached from another. The North Carolinians rushed forward and captured the Federals without firing a shot. Much to their surprise and chagrin however, they did not capture a Yankee cavalry brigade, but only a picket (a single squadron) from the 1st Connecticut Cavalry; the brigade had withdrawn. "[We] found only forty men," Grimes recalled, and "every one of whom we captured with their horses."[18]

Rosser's men approached several minutes later and the confused Confederates opened fire on each other, although the mistake was quickly rectified. Once Rosser realized the situation, he ordered a speedy withdrawal to extricate his command from behind enemy lines. Although the raid was difficult and potentially dangerous—and disappointing—Grimes found it a rather welcomed break from the tedium he and his men had been experiencing. It was, he wrote, "a pleasant time." His men must have thought so as well, for some of them spent the return journey, according to Rosser, "robbing [the cavalry] of socks, shoes, food, etc., and other things from the saddle pockets." The expedition was Grimes' first and last mounted foray of the war.[19]

While Rosser and Grimes spent the night fruitlessly riding across Little North Mountain, Jubal Early contemplated the results of the Stickley Farm engagement and recent intelligence. His options were severely limited. He could attack Sheridan's powerful army with his outnumbered command, retreat to another location, or stay put and lure Sheridan into attacking him. Lee wanted Early to press Sheridan with his whole force, either to defeat him or at the least to prevent him from sending troops to Grant. Lee's objective for Early, of course, meant that retreat was not a viable option. Neither, apparently, was remaining at Fisher's Hill in his fortified lines, for Sheridan did not seem inclined to attack him there, and Early did not have sufficient supplies to remain motionless for a prolonged period of time. Sheridan's army, however, held a strong defensive position behind Cedar Creek, outnumbered Early's force two to one, and had a string of victories to its credit. Desertion was beginning to plague the Army of the Valley, and Early had to act soon and decisively. Lee's words from late September, "The enemy must be defeated and I rely upon you to do it," likely haunted him. There was no choice: he would attack.[20]

But how could he take the offensive against Sheridan with a only prayer of success? Sheridan had deployed his veterans behind Cedar Creek, a meandering stream with sharp banks which made it a naturally formidable obstacle. His left was anchored on the North Fork of the Shenandoah River and the slopes of Massanutten Mountain and patrolled by a heavy column of cavalry, while his center was strongly manned, partially entrenched, and studded with artillery batteries. The Federal right flank, which appeared the most open to attack, was manned by two divisions of cavalry whose numbers alone approached Early's entire command. Early turned his attention again to the Union left flank, where Sheridan surely would not expect an attack. Success there seemed unlikely. His troops would have to climb over the steep heights of Massanutten Mountain, wade the Shenandoah River, and hit the enemy before being seen or attacked by Federal cavalry in the area, which could quickly be reinforced by the nearby VIII Corps. The best plan seemed to be a move on the Union right flank, where there was room to maneuver. And this is precisely what Union generals Horatio Wright and Phil Sheridan expected Early to do.

Confederate prospects for a successful attack against Sheridan brightened on October 17 when Early sent Maj. Gen. John B. Gordon to reconnoiter the Union left flank. Map maker Jed Hotchkiss and Brig. Gen. Clement Evans accompanied Gordon, and together they climbed to the signal station on Signal Knob atop Three Top Mountain (near the summit of Massanutten). From there, virtually the entire Federal line of battle could be discerned. The left flank, Gordon later informed Early, was indeed vulnerable to an attack. So confident of victory was Evans that he exclaimed, "we can literally rout them." A daring but ingenious plan developed from the reconnaissance. In essence, the Second Corps would undertake a night march around the Union left, along the steep face northern face of Massanutten and across the North Fork of the Shenandoah River. From there, Gordon would attack and role up Sheridan's left, while the balance of Early's army attacked from the front.[21]

While Early and his divisional officers studied the plan for a surprise attack on the Federal left, Grimes reveled in the news from home: Charlotte had delivered a baby boy five days earlier. "Thank the Lord for your safe delivery and also that the offering is a boy for I much preferred that surrounded as we are by our great national troubles," began Grimes. "It would have been a source of disquiet and anxiety to know a female would be provided for, but in males it is different. They, if made of character and worth, will soon learn to take care of themselves." The tender side of the warrior revealed itself once again. "Now let me return to you my dearest wife. Thanks for your magnificent present which I value beyond all, and if this wretched war were only over [I] would be supremely happy." Thoughts of family and the ancestral plantation filled Grimes' thoughts, and he openly expressed as much to Charlotte. "My desire to return home increases in the same ratio as my responsibility and my happiness increases so that I can hardly contain myself," he explained to her. "And trust that many months will not elapse before I enjoy the pleasure of being with you and our new treasure. God grant him a long life of usefulness and that he may be a comfort to us in our declining years."[22]

After admonishing Charlotte to "make haste and get well," Grimes remembered to ask about his son: "tell me all about him," he implored. "How he looks and how smart. If he is pretty or ugly, and if he has smiled yet. In the meantime, have your sisters write me daily for I should be very anxious about your welfare for the next two weeks." It was a day of celebration for both Grimes and Dodson Ramseur, who also had just learned he was a father. "I was sent to Ramseur's Headquarters to receive orders," he informed Charlotte," and upon seeing me he exclaimed, 'good news to tell you.' Of course, I thought it relating to war news, when to my surprise he very exalting remarked, 'I am the father of a family,' and seemed to be perfectly carried away with pleasure."[23]

Jubal Early spent much of October 18 finalizing his plan of attack for the next day. General Gordon would lead his three divisions under Ramseur, Pegram, and Evans around the foot of Massanutten Mountain, cross the Shenandoah at Bowman's Ford and take a position near the J. Cooley House. If successful, Gordon's men would be on the left and rear of the unsuspecting Federals. When the attack began, a cavalry brigade would cross the river ahead of the infantry and gallop toward Sheridan's headquarters at Belle Grove mansion two miles to the north and try to capture the Yankee general. The divisions of Joseph Kershaw and Gabriel Wharton would also move forward in conjunction with Gordon. The former would cross Cedar Creek on Gordon's left, while Wharton advanced up the Valley Pike against the center of Sheridan's line. While Early's 10,000 infantry surprised and routed the Union left, General Rosser and his cavalry would attack Federal cavalry on the opposite flank in order to create a diversion and additional confusion. The attack was scheduled for 5:00 a.m. The early hour meant Grimes and the rest of the Second Corps soldiers would have to march most of the night to get around the base of the mountain and be in position before the sun rose.[24]

As the men prepared for the harrowing march, Grimes scribbled a brief letter to Charlotte. He wrote nothing of the forthcoming attack, probably because he did not wish to cause her concern, especially after the birth of Bryan, Jr. "How do you feel with the responsibilities of a mother upon you?" he asked. "I sympathize with you deeply in the trying ordeal through which you have safely passed and know that the pleasure of having something to love will compensate you for all your pain. You must kiss the baby for his father and tell him to make haste and grow fast so as to take my place and let me return to you."[25] As darkness settled on the Valley, Ramseur aligned his four brigades for the march. His division consisted, in order of march, of the brigades of Cullen Battle, Philip Cook, William Cox, and Bryan Grimes. The four brigades formed the middle of Gordon's long and twisting gray column, which snaked its way fitfully through the growing summer autumn twilight toward the enemy. Soon they were across the North Fork of the river and marching along a narrow trail on Massanutten, tramping around Sheridan's flank in a silent, single file. As they made their way over the difficult trail, Gordon later recalled that they were like a "great serpent, glided noiselessly along the dim pathway. . . " The operation consumed the entire night with little time to spare. About 4:30 a.m., the head of Gordon's spear crossed the river at Bowman's Ford in two columns and took up a position on the far side. "The passage was effected with great rapidity and in good order," Grimes later reported, "though the rear necessarily had to double quick for [a] distance to close up." Fog began forming in the low lying areas, hiding the Southerners and aiding them in their plan to catch the Federal VIII and XIX Corps by surprise.[26]

When Ramseur's Division reached a spot about one-half mile from the Valley Pike, he began deploying his brigades, left to right, as follows: Grimes, Cox, Cook, and Battle. "Battle's brigade formed parallel with the [pike]. . . ," wrote Grimes, while the remaining three brigades "continued moving by the flank for about 300 yards, when they were faced to the left." Grimes' jump off point for the assault was near the Cooley house, with the enemy tents and encampment just one-half mile ahead to the northwest. Gordon's old division under Clement Evans took up a position on Ramseur's left, while Pegram's Division formed a second line behind Evans. Somehow, against the odds, Gordon had managed to move his men around Sheridan undetected and align them on time—a remarkable feat in every respect.[27]

The men waited in uncomfortable silence. According to the 32nd North Carolina's Col. David G. Cowand, Grimes' Brigade, "it was quite cold and when the men halted to rest they suffered much, having forded the river and not being able on account of the proximity of the enemy to have fires." They did not have long to wait. About 5:00 a.m. Gordon opened the attack with his three divisions, which swept forward against the unsuspecting slumbering men of the VIII Corps. The Confederate cheers and pattering of small arms fire raised the alarm for General Kershaw's Division, which crossed Cedar Creek northwest of Gordon on his left and likewise bore down in the direction of Belle Grove. Many of the Federals, asleep in their tents, were shot down or captured as they emerged, while others attempted a stand in their night clothes. Most, however, without shoes, uniforms or even arms, simply turned and ran as the veteran lines of Confederate infantry steam rolled through their camps.

Ramseur's Division, complete with a mighty Rebel yell, thrust forward and struck Crook's VIII Corps, routing it completely from the field. The feeble Federal defensive effort allowed the Confederate brigades to continue advancing without much of a loss in either organization or casualties. In fact, Southern momentum increased. Kershaw's attack was similarly successful and his men drove forward toward the Valley Pike, protecting Gordon's left flank. Like a gray tidal wave the Confederates swept through the VIII Corps camps and beyond, routing William Emory's almost equally surprised XIX Corps. Two of Ramseur's brigades, those of Cox and Cook, swept past Belle Grove, while Grimes' and Battle's men moved to the right toward Middletown. "[We] moved by the right flank through the abandoned camp of the Eighth Corps," which had been completely routed," reported Grimes after the battle, "faced to the front, and advanced to the pike, connecting with Battle's right."

It was only about "sunrise," remembered the North Carolinian, and two Federal corps were in wild retreat, attempting to take up a position beyond a small stream called Meadow Brook. Federal artillery "on a high ridge" added a loud accompaniment to the screaming Confederates, but "the smoke and fog obscured the troops so that their fire was inaccurate." Early, meanwhile, was riding with Wharton's Division on the Valley Pike, crossing Cedar Creek on the left of Kershaw's advancing men. The coordinated push continued. In accordance with Ramseur's order, Grimes deployed the 32nd regiment as skirmishers and, together with other skirmishers, drove "the sharpshooters of the enemy from Middletown."[28]

While the attack was thus far successful, Ramseur's Division had split into two wings (Cox and Cook on the left, and Battle and Grimes on the right). John Pegram's Division, which had formed originally behind Evans on the left of the Second Corps, slipped north and advanced into the gap, making it that much more difficult for Ramseur to exercise control over his brigades. The division "remained there for perhaps half an hour," recalled Grimes, awaiting the arrival of artillery support and perhaps Wharton's reinforcements.

Directly in front of Grimes on a strong piece of ground called Cemetery Hill was deployed George Getty's Second Division of Horatio Wright's VI Corps. On Ramseur's order, Grimes advanced against the VI Corps position, his regiments aligned, from left to right, as follows: 45th, 43rd, 53rd, 2nd

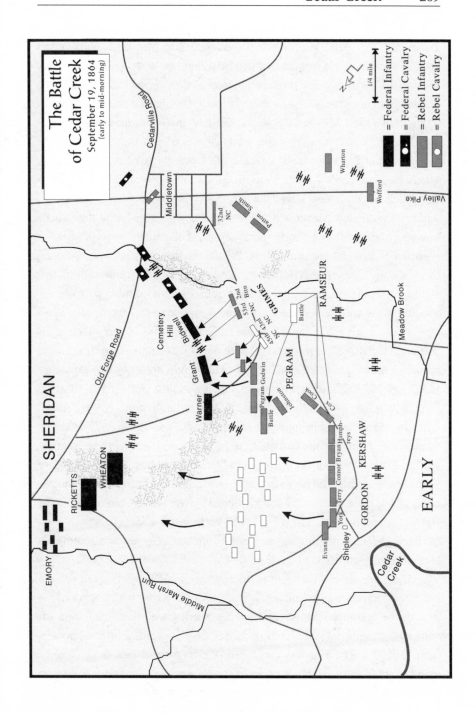

The Battle
of Cedar Creek
September 19, 1864
(early to mid-morning)

Battalion. (The 32nd regiment had advanced into Middletown on orders from Ramseur to clear the town of sharpshooters, and was therefore not available to Grimes). The movement "was made in good order, and with a gallantry never exceeded," he recalled proudly. A number of artillery pieces along the Hottle's Mill Road pounded Grimes' men until they were eventually forced to withdraw by other advancing Southern units, although the heavy ground fog effectively shielded the Confederates from what would otherwise have been a deadly fire. Initially, Grimes exercised great skill as he guided his regiments down the gentle slopes southwest of Middletown and into the shallow Meadow Brook valley. They advanced with skirmishers covering the front about forty yards ahead of the main body of men—a particularly prudent measure given the uncertainty of what was awaiting them ahead. Grimes was no doubt pleased to see (or rather learn) that Battle's Brigade, together with troops from Pegram's Division, were advancing to the west protecting his otherwise exposed left flank.

It was at this point, however, that tactical problems began affecting his brigade. His two left regiments (the 45th and 43rd) continued moving north before turning right to attack Cemetery Hill, while his other two regiments (53rd and 2nd Battalion) continued advancing against Getty's men from the front. Much like Ramseur's Division (at least earlier that morning), Grimes' Brigade had slowly split into two segments and was advancing piecemeal against the enemy. While certainly the fog and confusion of battle contributed to Grimes' losing control of his regiments, another reason may have been the loss of his fifth horse in battle. "I was riding a horse captured in our night attack upon the cavalry [on October 16]," he wrote Charlotte after the fight, ". . .and had him killed by a shell early in the engagement, while on his back, the shell not missing my leg two inches." Grimes was leading his men into a fog-enshrouded battle on foot.[29]

Given the circumstances, it is impossible to know whether Grimes appreciated the precarious situation his brigade was in, or which wing of his brigade he accompanied. Regardless, his North Carolinians continued advancing—straight into the teeth of Lewis Grant's waiting brigade of Vermont veterans. The Federals could hear the tramp and chatter of Grimes' men but could not see them because of the persistent ground mist. A Federal artillerist recalled that the Confederates of the 53rd and 2nd Battalion made it to the crest of the hill and charged forward "with loud yells," artillery shells exploding and throwing "dirt into their faces." The Federal infantry leveled their rifles and shattered the front ranks with a deadly volley of musketry. As they continued advancing the pair of Grimes' left-most regiments, which had swung north along the base of the hill, approached the center and right of the Vermont line. The Confederates were now within just several yards of the main enemy line.

"I could not believe they were really going to close with us," artillerist Pvt. Augustus Buell remembered, "until the men on the remaining gun of our left section abandoned it and retreated toward the old graveyard wall." The front line, he recalled, "was not in order, but there was an officer leading them, and I distinctly heard him shout: 'Rally on the battery! Rally on the battery!'" Whether this officer was Grimes or not is unknown, but the unnamed officer was probably the one who gave the order to spread out to avoid the artillery fire about to be blown against them. Buell, standing by his piece, took the lanyard from the fingers of a dead comrade "and yanked it right in their teeth. . .but they were right on top of us." The single blast of canister had little effect, and within seconds the North Carolinians overran the guns. Many of the cannoneers pulled pistols and "began shooting at the Johnnies coming up out of the ravine." A stand-up affair ensued with the Southern regimental banners flapping just twenty yards from the Vermont line.

The bisected manner of Grimes' attack, simple exhaustion (the men had been up all night marching into position), paucity of numbers, and splendid defensive effort by Getty's division, began to tell on the Southerners. Counterattacks drove them back, and although several localized efforts were made to seize the hill, the attack was over. "The Sixth Corps. . .made a most stubborn defense," praised Grimes in his report of the battle. His men had "charged them most gallantly, but being greatly overlapped on both flanks was forced to fall back and reform after advancing as far as the cemetery [crest]." The presence of the VI Corps troops prompted Early to shift some of Wharton's troops to his left, but the renewed effort met with no greater success than that enjoyed by Grimes' regiments. Only massed fire from some twenty artillery pieces eventually dislodged the resolute Federals from the hill. Ramseur's bloodied and scattered division climbed the body-strewn slopes and "reformed, cartridge boxes [were] refilled, and [we] rested upward of an hour."[30]

By 10:00 a.m., Wright's VI Corps fell back again to a third position north of Middletown and on the west side of the Valley Pike. Substantial portions of the once-routed VIII and XIX Corps were reorganizing and being thrown into line with Wright's men. Confronting the tenuous Federal front was Early's new line of battle, which ran roughly northwest to southeast along the Old Forge Road, into the outskirts of Middletown, and along the Cedarville Road on the right. His left flank, held by the Second Corps under Gordon, extended beyond the Hottle's Mill Road. Grimes' Brigade formed behind a stone fence near Meadow Brook "about 100 yards to the right and rear of Battle's [brigade]." Grimes comprised the far right element of Gordon's line, with an interval "of from 200 to 300 yards between his right and Pegram's left." Beyond Pegram's Division and extending the line to the right was Wharton's Division.

Much of what transpired next, especially from the Confederates' point of view, depends on who you believe. Many of Early's officers, including Gordon, later claimed they wanted to renew the assaults and complete the tactical victory they had thus far achieved. Early, however, disagreed. "Well Gordon," he exclaimed, "this is glory enough for one day." Gordon, however, had already made plans for the attack and told Early as much. "No use in that," replied the usually offensive-minded lieutenant general. "They will all go directly." Gordon demurred, knowing the VI Corps to be well led and composed of veteran soldiers. Early cut off his subordinate's protestations, and the subject was dropped. Instead of attacking, Early decided to consolidate his gains and send the captured wagons, prisoners, and guns to the rear. Hours ticked away and the morning passed into the afternoon, even though Early was receiving messages from atop Massanutten Mountain that the Federals were massing opposite his line.

Unbeknownst to the Confederates, Sheridan had not been on the field when his army suffered its stinging and near-fatal early morning defeat. He had spent the night in Winchester. The early morning fighting was plainly heard in town, and by 9:00 a.m., "Little Phil" was galloping toward his embattled army. Riding through throngs of retreating men, Sheridan initially contemplated reforming his broken divisions near Winchester. Unwilling to accept defeat, however, he decided instead to gallop ahead and attempt to turn the tide of battle in his favor. His arrival was electrifying and the morale of his soldiers immediately soared when word of his arrival reached them.

By 10:30 a.m., Sheridan was conversing with his senior generals, organizing his lines, and preparing for a counterattack. Early's passivity at the moment of decision passed the initiative to the Federals, and Sheridan gladly picked up the dropped gauntlet.[31]

Unlike Early, Sheridan understood how to use his cavalry and could rely on his subordinate officers. George Custer's Division was dispatched northwest to the Federal right flank and took up a threatening position on Early's left flank. Merritt's men, meanwhile, moved to the opposite end of the line and threatened the Confederate right flank. Masses of Federal infantry were now in position for a renewal of the combat. By mid-afternoon it began to dawn on Early that his army was in a precarious situation. He was still badly outnumbered despite his morning victory, his flanks were now threatened, and his defensive alignment was haphazardly arranged and carelessly drawn. Sheridan appreciated these facts as well, and about 3:30 p.m., according to Grimes' official report, the massive Union counterattack began rolling in their direction.[32]

George Getty's veteran division moved directly against Ramseur's line. Grimes' Brigade was "double quicked" up to the line next to Battle's Brigade to meet the enemy advance. Generals Cox and Cook also moved forward. Ramseur's Division, well organized and aligned, poured a heavy fire into the lines of assaulting Federals. Grimes' North Carolinians directed their fire against Brig. Gen. Daniel Bidwell's brigade of New Yorkers and Pennsylvanians, killing several color bearers in the process. The Southerners "repulsed most gallantly" George Getty's attack, "the enemy fleeing in disorder and confusion, throwing down their arms and battle-flags in their retreat." Ramseur's Confederates let loose with a hearty cheer.[33]

While Grimes and his men had reason to feel joyful as they watched the enemy stream rearward, the paradigm that had proven disastrous for them in the past was again taking shape. While Ramseur and Pegram were repulsing Wright's VI Corps, William Emory's XIX Corps was beating back the divisions of Gordon and Kershaw—the Confederate left flank. Although they were putting up a stout defense, neither Gordon nor Kershaw fielded enough troops to hold off the heavy and well-organized Federal attack. Stretched to the breaking point, Gordon's Division (under Evans) began to give ground. This, in turn, unhinged the entire line and caused Kershaw's men to make for the rear as well. Within a few minutes Early's entire left flank was crumbling away, his soldiers running for safety. Like a domino—the same domino that had fallen at Third Winchester and Fisher's Hill—the collapse of the left flank exposed those Confederates next in line to pressure from both the front and flank. In this case the next unfortunates in line were in Ramseur's Division.

The disintegration of almost half of Early's army happened so fast that Grimes' men were still cheering in apparent victory "when the line on our left was seen to give back and the troops to retreat without any organization," wrote a disgusted Grimes. Ramseur, recalled Grimes, quickly grasped the situation and ordered his entire division to "fall back and form [behind] a stone fence [near Miller's Mill] about 200 yards in rear, which was promptly done, and the advance of the enemy in our front prevented." The situation continued to worsen. Custer's cavalry charged into action, and the effect was devastating. While Grimes' men appear to have successfully completed the short withdrawal, others did not, and Ramseur's orderly retrograde slowly inched toward chaos. With the assistance of some of Kershaw's South Carolinians and a handful of artillery pieces, Ramseur continued to hold his line, riding up and down its length and exhorting his men to stand firm and do their duty. Early, attempting to stem the routed elements from his left flank, pointed to "the gallant stand made by Ramseur and his small party."

For about an hour, even as Federal artillery on the right began bombarding his men, Ramseur and his gallant division stood fast behind the low stone walls. Only his defense stood between an semi-orderly withdrawal and a final disastrous rout. But even Ramseur, who was later described as fighting "like a lion at bay," could not prevent the inevitable. Before much longer his horse was killed by a minie ball. A second mount was found and it, too, was struck down. As Ramseur was in the process of mounting yet a third animal a bullet penetrated his right side and sliced through both lungs, lodging in the left chest wall. The mortally wounded general was placed in an ambulance and taken to the rear.[34]

When Ramseur was struck down Grimes assumed temporary command of the division since Cullen Battle had also suffered a wound. He could not have designed a more desperate situation under which to take command. Pressed from three sides, panic spread throughout the four brigades. "The enemy were then in front and to the left and rear of the left flank of this division," he later reported, "when they began to fall back in the same disorderly manner as those on the left." Although he attempted to withdraw the division, "the stampede on the left was caught up, and no threats or entreaties could arrest their flight." The Cedar Creek battle "was the hardest day's work I ever engaged in—trying to rally the men," he sadly informed Charlotte the following day. "Took our flags at different times, begging, commanding, entreating the men to rally, would ride up and down the lines, beseeching them by all they held sacred and dear, to stop and fight, but without success." The contagion of rout had swept through Early' Army of the Valley for a third time in a month, just when victory seemed within grasping distance.[35]

It was as miserable and depressing a night as any endured by Grimes during the war. Together with what was left of his command he reached Fisher's Hill, where Early was regrouping his troops. After a few hours of rest Early moved his demoralized remnants south to New Market. From there on October 20 Grimes penned what was undoubtedly the most difficult letter he wrote during the conflict:

The letters of your sisters announcing the death of our dear little baby was received today while on the retreat from Strasburg. How deeply I regret his loss, and it is only exceeded by my sorrow and sympathy for you my darling wife in this great bereavement, for I, who know how tender in your feelings you are, can appreciate what must be your suffering.

There is no sacrifice that I would not cheerfully make to be with you and comfort you in this, your hour of trouble and trial, and to share and soothe your grief. But the fortunes of war forbid [it], or I should have been with you at this birth.

The will of the Lord be done for it must be best or he would not have taken your dear little baby to himself. Console yourself my dearest, dearest wife with the reflection that which is our loss is his eternal gain. No pleasure on earth would be so great to me as that of being with you now but the rules of discipline prevent it. [It] would be worse than useless for me to apply for a furlough for I should not only be refused, but in all probability reprimanded for making it during an active campaign.

So my darling, please for my sake, try and not be nervous for at all times it makes me unhappy to be separated from you, but when I know that you are in distress and beyond my power to alleviate, my misery is insupportable. So my darling do hold up under your trials as well as possible and the first moment that there is a possibility of my reaching home, it shall be done. I trust that will not be long now as the bad weather will soon set in that will put a stop to active hostilities.

Although my dearest wife the hand of the dead has fallen heavily upon you, there is great deal to be thankful for, fortuitously in my escape from the dangers of yesterday's battlefield when so many others suffered. I was permitted safely to meet the dangers and came out unscathed.

Poor Mrs. Ramseur for instance; how she must suffer when she hears that her husband is not only wounded, supposed to be mortal, but is in the hands of the enemy.

I have only slept two hours in the last fifty, but could not rest until I expressed my grief and sympathy for you in the death of your dear baby. Do my darling, take care of yourself for if I lose you the world has no further dreams for me.[36]

Grimes' poignant and moving letter, perhaps more than any other, reveals much about both the man and his lofty character.

Jubal Early camped his dispirited and pathetically small army at New Market for several weeks in an attempt to recuperate from the debacle at Cedar Creek. Sheridan, fortunately for the Southerners, did not initiate a serious pursuit. Although stragglers drifted back into camp and some conscripts were added, the Army of the Valley remained under strength, poorly equipped, and demoralized. Although exact figures are unknown, Early's losses at Cedar Creek were only about one-half of Sheridan's 6,000 total casualties. Early himself claimed 1,860 killed and wounded, and about 1,000 missing or captured, figures that are almost certainly too small. Casualties in Ramseur's Division are problematical at best. Returns for Grimes' Brigade (which was led by Col. David Cowand after Grimes assumed command of the division) reported only 11 killed, 108 wounded, "and a few prisoners." These figures seem remarkably low given that the North Carolinians were on the tactical offensive for much of the morning against the veteran VI Corps on Cemetery Hill, and again in its stout rearguard action late in the afternoon.

As was his habit, Early generally refused to accept any blame for his latest defeat, attaching it instead to his long-suffering troops. "We had within our grasp a glorious victory," he wrote to General Lee, "and lost it by the uncontrollable propensity of our men for plunder, in the first place, and the subsequent panic among those who had kept their places, which was without sufficient cause." Many generals, including John Gordon and Clement

Evans, took great exception to Early's accusations when they learned of them. Grimes noted in his own report that "the troops of this division, both officers and men, with a few exceptions, behaved most admirably and were kept well in hand, but little plundering and only a few shirking duty."[37]

Regardless of where the fault for the loss rested, the cumulative effect of suffering a string of defeats manifested itself in a variety of disciplinary problems. Early issued strict orders on the subject on October 25 to try to halt the spread of lawlessness and laxity permeating his army. Six days later Grimes explained his own thoughts on the subject. "I see that some of the papers are disposed to censure Genl. Early for the fortunes in the Valley," he wrote Charlotte, "but tis no fault of his; without its want of discipline is attributable to him." Early, at least in Grimes' eyes, had not been a strict enough disciplinarian. Overall, though, Grimes supported Early's efforts in the Valley. "Still we have the utmost confidence in Genl. Early," he wrote a few days after Cedar Creek, "and know that our recent defeats proceeded from want of discipline among the troops." Since his first command as a major serving under Brig. Gen. George B. Anderson, Grimes had held strong views on discipline and the need to constantly drill the troops. To him it was simple: good discipline made good soldiers.[38]

While the army drilled and swelled slowly back to about 11,000 men, Grimes continued to write Charlotte almost daily. Much of this period was taken up with thoughts of Dodson's Ramseur's mortal wounding. "It is reported here that Genl. Ramseur died at Strasburg from his wounds," he lamented on October 23. "How deeply I deplore his loss." Still thinking of the loss of his friend a few days later, he noted: "Poor Mrs. Ramseur, I sympathize with her deeply. I am glad that she has a child, something to direct her thoughts from brooding over her loss. Suppose you write her a letter of condolence."[39]

As the days grew shorter and the nights colder, Grimes turned his thoughts to his own future with the army. "How long I shall remain in command of the Division depends upon the Department at Richmond," he explained. "Genl. Early seems disposed to retain me." One of Grimes' concerns was that another would be elevated over him to command the division. "Major General [Robert] Ransom has requested to be assigned to this Division," he informed Charlotte with palpable displeasure. "While I do not expect to retain permanent command myself, I do seriously object to him as my commander for he is a disagreeable officer to serve under. He's also I believe a coward." Why Grimes believed Ransom was a coward is unclear. His fears about serving under the "disagreeable officer," also a native of North Carolina, proved groundless, however, for after Christmas 1864, Ransom fell ill and did not return to active duty. Despite Ransom's looming shadow, Grimes' optimism slowly returned. "The enemy is keeping very quiet," he related, perhaps with some disbelief. "If we are allowed a month's rest we will be all right again."[40]

The enemy may have been keeping quiet, but a schism was developing within the army that threatened, in the words of one soldier, "a mutiny." Both Generals Early and Gordon attempted to take credit for the brilliant plan to attack the unprotected Union left at Cedar Creek. On October 31, less than two weeks after the battle, Grimes expressed his views on the origins of the plan in a letter to Charlotte. "Some of the correspondents of the papers claim that the plan of our last attack originated with Genl. Gordon. There is no truth at all in it, but on the contrary, if there be any merit in the plan, it is entirely due to Genl. Early and was suggested by the movement that Genl. Rosser and myself made on the night of the 16th, when we marched in their rear and captured their pickets." Grimes' position on the subject seems out of sync with what we know about the pre-battle planning. The historical record (much of it admittedly penned by Early or Gordon) demonstrates that the plan originated with Gordon as he looked down on the Federal camps from high atop Signal Knob. Almost certainly Early modified the plan to some degree. Early and Gordon had the good sense to not allow the issue to split the army asunder, although their professional working relationship was heavily taxed.[41]

November found the army still ensconced at New Market and a number of issues weighing on Grimes' mind. "Tomorrow is my thirty-sixth birthday," he wrote his wife on the first of the month. "This service and the separation from you makes me feel at least ten years older than I really am." The separation from Charlotte had been harder for Grimes than usual because the death of Bryan, Jr., had kept Charlotte from writing her letters. "Again for the first time in three weeks my heart is gladdened by the sight of your dear familiar handwriting," he wrote her on November 3. "You spoke mournfully of our dear little son. If he was to be taken," he wrote rather practically, "far better now than after he had entwined himself around every heartstring." Undoubtedly Grimes wrote these words while painfully recalling the death of his other son, Bryan, who had died in 1863 at age six. In addition to family matters, the issue of divisional command still remained unresolved. "I am still in command of Rodes Division, but it is reported that Genl. Lee, a son of Genl. Lee, will be assigned to this command. I hear that he is a good officer," he wrote without any obvious disappointment, "but has had no experience in the field."[42]

Later in the week, still camped at New Market and with little threat from Sheridan, Grimes observed: "we have been having a very quiet time drilling and disciplining our troops, and the enemy appears to be wanting to recover also from their severe beating of the morning of the 19th." Contemplating the situation, he noted the next day that Early's movements "are entirely dependent upon that of the enemy; if they attempt to reinforce Grant with troops [we will attack them]. Our troops are now better than they have been for past six weeks, but are short of arms." And, he wrote with a tongue-in-cheek jab at Grant, "we will have to fight it out on this line if it takes all Winter."[43]

In addition to everything else, Grimes also was concerned about his half-brother's service (or lack thereof) to the Confederacy. "John Grimes, I think is able to render services somewhere besides as clerk in the Commissary Department," he wrote privately, "but you need not mention that. I had to express myself; let him settle the question with his own conscience." John, it will be recalled, had been captured at South Mountain in September 1862 and exchanged. He returned to Raleigh but had not returned to the battle lines of Virginia.[44]

In addition to bringing in the cold weather, November 1864 also witnessed the important Federal presidential election. After throwing another dig in the direction of William Cox—"[he] is quite jealous of and envious of me. Why he should be so I cannot consider"—Grimes teased Charlotte before turning to politics. "From an article in the Richmond papers I infer that Grant may move down into N.C. What will you do if he goes to Raleigh?" Today, he wrote, "is the election in the United States and which way it is decided is but of little interest here to us for neither of the candidates seems disposed to give us our rights. We can never be conquered and subjected to the Yankee Yoke," he insisted, "which would be far worse than death itself."[45]

Since he was at least temporarily in command of a division, Grimes was now privy to information heretofore inaccessible to him. "Yesterday while at Genl. Early's HQTs. I learned that the enemy [following] the recent battle [Cedar Creek] now has upwards of thirty-six thousand effective men for the field which is more than three times our numbers," he informed Charlotte. "But two of their Corps show an indisposition to fight, and if it were not for their cavalry, we could soon drive their infantry out of the Valley," was his rather optimistic conclusion.[46] The strength of the enemy cavalry again made itself felt when a few days later on November 10, Early dispatched some troops to see if he could provoke Sheridan into fighting him. The Federal general countered by shifting about his cavalry in a move which ultimately forced the Confederates back to New Market.[47] While Grimes respected his enemy's cavalry strength and military prowess, he did not think much of at least one of their leaders. "In capturing a mail bag of the enemy, we found some of the most obscene letters that would disgrace any person," he informed Charlotte on November 9, "and those captured from Genl. [George A.] Custer were vulgar beyond all conversation and even those from his wife would make any honest woman blush for her sex."[48]

"I doubt not I shall come out all safe," wrote Grimes in an issue-filled November 10 letter in response to Charlotte's continued concerns for the safety of her husband, as well as her desires to see him. "If it should be otherwise, you will see by the papers for now I am sufficiently prominent for them to make mention of any accident that should occur." He warned her, though, not to be "too hasty in forming your conclusions for they often make [it] out much worse off than it really is." If I am wounded, he continued, "I will telegraph you immediately." While he also naturally desired to see his wife that winter, Grimes' candid response was less positive than Charlotte hoped it would be. I can't see you, he explained, "unless Genl. Early, with his old bachelor notions of women's demoralization of our army by their presence, shall forbid it, and he is an old bear about such things." Early's negative attitude toward women—he was especially vexed by John Gordon's wife's ubiquitous presence—was legendary within the army's ranks.

In the same November 10 letter Grimes made an interesting admission: "We have been demonstrating against the enemy in order to make them return with their troops to prevent their reinforcement of Grant," he wisely observed. "If we can accomplish that objective we will have done all that can be expected of us." Grimes' statement conceded that victory in the field against Sheridan was no longer possible, but the lesser objective of keeping enemy troops occupied and away from Grant was an acceptable objective.[49]

As the days and weeks passed after Cedar Creek a multitude of voices erupted in Richmond and elsewhere calling for Early's head. It was simply a crisis in confidence, claimed one, and "too free use of ardent spirits both by officers high and low." The public outcry only served to rub raw the Army of the Valley's lingering and multitudinous wounds. The ongoing distraction, coupled with the cold and lack of adequate arms and supplies, guaranteed the 1864-65 winter in the Valley would be arduous one. Even Grimes, who had suffered through three winters in the field, sent notice home on November 15 about the frigid lower Shenandoah. "Now I have a heated sock in my bed each night which makes it comfortable for a few hours, but towards day it loses its warmth and makes me wish for flesh and blood as a bed fellow. You think it a poor substitute don't you?" he asked teasingly. "Were if not for the confounded war, I should not have to respond to such an expedient, but would have you to keep me warm." His desire to share a bed with Charlotte kept the issue of a furlough at the forefront of his thoughts. "Genl. Cox is very anxious and is afraid that I will get home first. He seems to think that I have the knack of knowing how to get a furlough when others cannot, but the secret lies in never asking until you know there is a probability of succeeding and then make a strong case and keep trying."[50]

The middle of November came and went without word of Grimes' permanent status as division commander. Would he retain the command or perhaps be promoted to major general, the appropriate rank for a division commander? Probably not, he believed, although he fervently desired the command (and no doubt the bump in rank as well). Grimes was a proven veteran and trusted brigade commander—but he was not the senior brigadier in the division. "Genl. Battle [Cullen A.] is my senior officer and had command of the Division at Winchester upon the death of Genl. Rodes," he wrote home on November 16. "Genl. Battle is a very dear gentlemen, but little of a military man, and if I had any friends in Richmond there would be little doubt of my having the permanent command of this Division, but as it is, I give myself no trouble about it for I have but small hope of the promotion." As it turned out, Grimes' concerns about his lack of political strings to pull in the Confederate capital were unnecessary, for Battle was not coming back. The gallant Alabamian had been shot in the kneecap at Cedar Creek and came within a whisker of having the limb amputated there. The painful and crippling wound kept the him in the hospital for some two months until he was finally furloughed home in December 1864.[51]

The attitudes toward the Army of the Valley and general war effort exhibited by a segment of the North Carolina citizenry infuriated Grimes, whose passion on the subject was perhaps stimulated to higher levels than usual given his lack of a furlough and suffering in the field. "Some people at home think that we have not done our duty up here," he ranted home in mid-November with some prescience, "but when the history of the war period is to be written and the disparity of the forces employed considered, we will come out with flying colors and honor."[52] The acquisition of a local newspaper did nothing to cool his temper. "I got hold of a Raleigh *Standard* this morning and find that it is at work instilling poison in the minds of the people and ought to be suppressed."[53]

The weeks in mid-late November were especially difficult for the North Carolina soldier, and his letters to Charlotte reflect as much, joking and light on the one hand, sad and pleading on the other. He was without the prospects of a battle and far away from home, unable to personally comfort a woman whose husband was absent and whose first born had recently died. Although Charlotte's letters are, for the most part, nonexistent, it is relatively easy from his correspondence to appreciate that she was writing of her desire to visit him in the field, her loneliness, and other similar feelings. "You must get your good looks on by the time I return," he wrote his wife on the 17th of the month, "for I delight in your beauty, and you must not lose it for it is precious in my sight and there is a giant satisfaction in having a wife admired by others." "You seem to think that it is necessary in each letter to remind me that you are anxiously awaiting the time you can come to the Army," he explained, "but your desire to be here cannot exceed mine to see you." A curious exchange between the couple took place during this period of their separation. "Who or what in the world put such an idea in your head that I loved you less than other men loved their wives?" demanded a hurt Grimes in response to Charlotte's most recent letter. "I know well that I am not perfect and am full of faults, but that of being deficient in love or kindness to you does not lie among them."[54]

The prospects for engagement brightened suddenly on November 22 before dimming again for the foreseeable future. Federal cavalry "in considerable force" prodded Early's mounted pickets and advanced to Mount Jackson. One of Rosser's cavalry brigades, together with a contingent of infantry under Grimes' command met and drove them back. Rosser pursued the Federals beyond Edenburg "in confusion, and compelled him to abandon his killed and wounded," wrote General Lee to the Secretary of War James A. Seddon. "[I] put my men in position and attacked them," Grimes explained the following day, "and you would have thought I had no thoughts of wife and child at home, for my whole heart was for the time being engrossed in whipping them." The running skirmish, considered by someone of Grimes' temperament to be an early Christmas gift, was perhaps all the holiday season had to offer him. "I inquired of Genl. Early yesterday if it was probable that I would be shortly relieved from command of the Division," he explained rather gingerly to Charlotte in early December, "and his reply was that he thought it would not be done until sometime during the spring, and that I was conducting the affairs well and that he was well satisfied with my administration. So you see, he concluded, "there is no possibility of my getting home for the present."[55]

General Early was blamed by many of his soldiers for his refusal to end the campaigning season and take up permanent winter quarters. "We were all anticipating an order to leave in the morning for our winter encampment, but we were sadly disappointed and cannot image what new kink Genl. Early has in his head." Several ideas were circulating through the army at this time as to what, exactly, the "kink" in Early's head consisted of. "Some say Genl. Early is in comfortable quarters himself," related Grimes on December 6. "Others say that he has a sweetheart and cannot leave here and others think he is deeply interested in some book and that he will not leave until he has finished it. I don't believe any of the idle reports and think that he is activated simply and solely by what he considers the good of the service and [is] awaiting more definite information as to what is the intention of the enemy." Sheridan's intentions and Early's options, however, remained something of a mystery. "If we could accomplish any commensurate good, [I] would be willing again to go down the valley and attack Sheridan," Grimes explained, "and if necessary, stay there, although it would interfere with my long-cherished desire to spend a quiet winter, but in my present position the public interest is to be considered before private preferences, and the higher a man rises in the military service the fewer privileges can he enjoy." Duty, regardless of all else, came first.[56]

By early December enough time had passed for some of the leading participants in the Cedar Creek battle to write and submit their reports. Some of these, as was usual after any major engagement, found their way into print, a fact Grimes personally found distasteful. "So Genl. [William] Cox has had his report of the battle of Cedar Creek published," Grimes wrote Charlotte on December 6. "Yes I have seen and read it. We do not think it very soldierly to blow your own trumpet—some others do—Cox had no right to have it published. It is contrary to orders. I have the same right to have mine as Division Commander published. [I mentioned] Cox but not quite in as laudatory terms as he does of himself, but in strict justice to each Brigadier so far as I could discriminate. But I don't mention horses being killed under me."[57]

Lulls in active campaigning allowed Grimes time to attend to administrative affairs, one of which was the meting out of punishment. "I have an unpleasant duty to perform tomorrow, that of supervising the execution of a fellow who is being shot for desertion," explained Grimes on December 12. "It is an awful duty, but must be done. If I had the power, [I] would have men shot, but would not witness their execution if it could be avoided." Grimes remained consistent on the issue throughout the war, accepting the need for executing deserters but disgusted by the necessity of witnessing the act. Other more mundane matters also caused him stress and affected his ability to sleep. Much of his anxiety resulted from the anticipation of pending battle (the army was still not in permanent winter quarters) and his desire to be with his wife. He often awoke in the middle of the night and began planning the day's events, which made it difficult for him to remain in his quarters. Earlier in the war, Sgt. Maj. John G. Young, a member of the 4th North Carolina's Company C and son of Lt. Col. John A. Young, recorded an example of this tendency in his diary: "When the Brigade was on picket duty on the Rapidan River, General [Grimes] would often wake up at midnight, or early morning and have two horses saddled and take me with him, and as we rode along the river bank, some sentinel on his beat would sing out, 'who goes there?' General replied, 'friend with countersign.' So I would dismount, approach the sentinel as he threw his gun with a bayonet on it at my breast that frightened me terribly, and I would whisper in his ear the countersign, and we rode on visiting probably 100 pickets."[58]

General Lee, realizing that Jubal Early had done about all he could do with the troops detached from the Army of Northern Virginia, began calling back his men back to the Richmond and Petersburg region. On December 13, Grimes received his orders to move his brigades to Petersburg, a directive he no doubt relished. In addition to leaving the disaster-filled Shenandoah Valley, the redeployment meant he would be much closer to Charlotte.

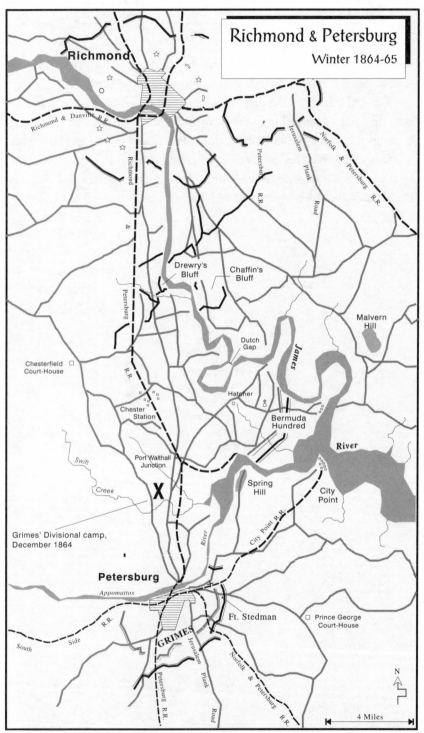

Richmond & Petersburg
Winter 1864-65

Richmond

Richmond & Danville R.R.

Richmond

&

Petersburg

R.R.

Jerusalem

Petersburg

Plank

Norfolk & Petersburg R.R.

R.R.

Road

Drewry's
Bluff

Chaffin's
Bluff

Malvern
Hill

Dutch
Gap

James

Chesterfield ☐
Court-House

Chester
Station

Hatcher

Bermuda
Hundred

River

Swift

Port Walthall
Junction

X

Creek

Spring
Hill

City
Point

City Point R.R.

River

Grimes' Divisional camp,
December 1864

Petersburg

Appomattox

GRIMES

Ft. Stedman

☐ Prince George
Court-House

R.R.

Side

South

Petersburg
R.R.

Jerusalem
Plank

Norfolk & Petersburg R.R.

Road

N

4 Miles

Mark A. Moore & Theodore P. Savas

# Petersburg and Appomattox

## "I expressed very forcibly my dissent to being surrendered"

**T**he proud division once commanded by Dodson Ramseur and Robert Rodes, and now led by Bryan Grimes, departed the Shenandoah Valley for good early on the morning of December 14. Marching from New Market, four under strength brigades tramped their way to Staunton, where they arrived the following afternoon. There they boarded trains for the final leg to Richmond. As Grimes climbed aboard the cars that would forever take him from the war ravaged Shenandoah, one wonders whether he saw and felt what Maj. Gen. John B. Gordon recorded in his memoirs when he embarked on the same train for the Southern capital a week earlier. "As I stood on the back platform of the last car in the train and looked back upon that stricken Valley," recalled the Georgian,

> I could but contrast the aspect of devastation and woe which it then presented, with the bounty and peace in all its homes at the beginning of the war. Heaps of ashes, of half-melted iron axles and bent tires, were the melancholy remains of burnt barns and farm-wagons and implements of husbandry. Stone and brick chimneys, standing alone in the midst of charred trees which once shaded the porches of luxurious and happy homes, told of hostile torches which had left these grim sentinels the only guards of those sacred spots.[1]

Grimes passed through a chilly Richmond early on December 16, where shortly after 10:00 a.m., a simple dispatch from General Lee addressed to the "Commanding Officer Rodes' Division," was received. He was to "proceed to camp [north of Petersburg] between Ashton and Swift Creeks. . .by railroad or turnpike, as most convenient." Thankfully, more detailed information was soon forthcoming, including confirmation on how his men would be transported and news that wagons had been dispatched to handle "the ammunition and baggage," which were to be sent to the front "with the first detachment" of troops. Two days later the division reached its destination about four miles north of Petersburg and near the rail extension running east to Port Walthall Junction on the Appomattox River. One of the first things Grimes did was send for Charlotte to join him.[2]

So much had changed. Since his departure the previous June, the Army of Northern Virginia had dueled with the Army of the Potomac almost daily. After the inconclusive fighting along the North Anna and the infliction of a bloody repulse against the enemy at Cold Harbor, General Grant pulled back and crossed the James River, aiming his spearhead at the vital railroad and logistical center of Petersburg. Hard fighting by "old men and young boys," extraordinarily good fortune, and excessive timidity on the part of the Federals saved the city—and by extension, Richmond, which depended on the railroads feeding into and through Petersburg—from capture.

After the unrelenting bloodshed of May and June, both sides appeared resolved to waging a battle of attrition from behind massive and continually spreading earthworks. Committed to the defense of Richmond and Petersburg, Lee knew it was just a matter of time before his army was too weak to effectively resist the Federals. Grant, meanwhile, continued stretching his left flank in an attempt to break the roads and rail lines running into Petersburg, applying pressure along the whole line to pin Lee in place. By the time Grimes arrived that December, the Petersburg & Weldon Railroad had been cut, army morale was low, and the men were suffering from a host of shortages. The fate of the two cities and the Confederacy itself hinged now on a single line of track running west from Petersburg: the Southside Railroad.

Grimes' arrival provided a small but potent reserve for Lee's thinly-spread army, and that is exactly the role the four-brigade division played for a time. Field returns filed for "Rodes' Division" and dated December 31, 1864, reveal the toll extracted by the ravages of war. By this time Grimes' "aggregate present for duty" was a mere 3,339, with present "effectives" numbering but 3,286. These tired troops had barely had an opportunity to acquaint themselves with their new surroundings, however, before an enemy cavalry raid near Gordonsville, Virginia, caused a reshuffling of several commands north of the Appomattox River. General James Longstreet, back on duty with his First Corps after suffering crippling wounds in the Wilderness, ordered a pair of brigades from as many divisions to vacate the trenches and travel by rail to Gordonsville. This further thinning of the line of defenders resulted in Grimes' reassignment. On December 22, he received a dispatch from General Lee, again addressed to the "Officer Commanding Rodes' Division." "March your command by the shortest route to the pontoon bridge at Chaffin's and report to General Longstreet on the north side," instructed the commanding general. "Obey any orders you may receive from him while on the way." Lee's directive effectively placed Grimes' Division at Longstreet's disposal for whatever task that general deemed necessary.[3]

Grimes put his men on the Richmond and Petersburg Turnpike and marched north about five miles. While on the march another dispatch was received, this one from Osmun Latrobe, Longstreet's Assistant Adjutant General. "Halt your command on Proctor's Creek, between Drewry's Bluff and the railroad," read the order. In an attempt to keep the movement away from prying enemy eyes, Grimes was directed to "select a position as much concealed as possible from the view of the enemy. . . .and report the whereabouts of your camp to Major General Pickett," under whose immediate command Grimes' Division was placed. The North Carolinian stopped his division at Proctor's Creek late on the day of December 22 and awaited developments. For a few harried hours it appeared as though the Federals were making a move in the vicinity of Fort Harrison, and that Grimes' men would be called up for duty north of the James River to reinforce the lines there. The threat failed to materialize to any significant degree, as was the case with the Gordonsville cavalry raid. As a result, Grimes was ordered to return to his recently-vacated camp near Swift Creek. By 5:00 p.m. on Christmas Eve his four brigades had turned around and were marching back through the cold evening air. By sunset they were again in camp.[4]

Fortunately for Grimes' men, their Swift Creek deployment was in a relatively quiet sector known as Bermuda Hundred, behind the right rear of the Howlett Line. Once settled in, the men began to construct winter quarters and Grimes set about improving the division's morale and organization. Lee had ordered as much in a December 29 confidential circular to his generals. "I desire that you will avail yourself of the present period of inactivity to reorganize and recruit the troops in your command as far as practicable." His suggestions were specific: Ascertain what regiments, if any, it would be advantageous to consolidate, and how such vacancies as may exist among the officers can best be filled. In every case in which you think the officer to be promoted unsuitable for the grade," continued the circular, "you will forward a report as to his qualifications, in order that he may be brought before an examining board." These suggestions were to be implemented without delay.[5]

As he and his staff set about implementing Lee's orders, Grimes awaited Charlotte's arrival at Petersburg. It is unclear when she actually joined her husband, but it was probably around Christmas time. Her journey north, accompanied by Brig. Gen. William Cox's wife, was difficult and Charlotte left a full account of her travails in a postwar account:

> We left Raleigh in the afternoon and reached Greensboro before dark. It was very doubtful whether we would be able to get through or not as the trains were filled with furloughed soldiers returning to their commands. About dark, Major Edmundson and several other officers said we should not be disappointed, and they would see that we got on the train. They procured a wagon that had nobody in it, and put us in it and we drove some distance beyond the depot where the train had stopped for a few minutes. They laid a plank from the embankment to the car on which we walked and scrambled into the freight car. I sat all night on a bag of corn. We traveled all that night until the next afternoon. During the night, a heavy snow had fallen and it was very cold and the engine had broken down. We traveled all night and the next day with frequent stoppages and rumors of Yankees blocking the road, but finally reached Petersburg safe and well, but very weary.
>
> General Grimes and General Cox met us at the station. Mrs. Cox stopped at Petersburg to spend the night, but my husband and I drove four miles farther on in an ambulance to Headquarters.[6]

The occasion of her arrival must have been a happy time for both Grimes and Charlotte, for this was the first time they had seen each other since August. Their separation in the interim had entailed military defeats, concern for Grimes' safety (and her own during the pregnancy), and the death of their new baby. "[I] was so exhausted that night," remembered Charlotte, "that I slept the whole night and until three o'clock the next day without waking. Gen. Grimes had been to camp and returned for dinner, when I roused and inquired if it was time to get up, thinking it was early morning, when he said it was three o'clock and dinner time." Charlotte's mid-winter Petersburg sojourn introduced to her the daily regime of siege warfare, as routine Federal shelling made life miserable for the soldiers and civilians alike. She recalled how "at night we could see the shells burst about a hundred fifty yards away."[7]

Although the winter hiatus from serious campaigning continued into the new year, it did not prevent the shifting about of troops. Early in January 1865, General Pickett was ordered to pull one of his brigades from the line and send it north of the James River. "This thins his line somewhat," wrote Lee's Assistant Adjutant General, Walter Taylor to Grimes on the 6th day of the new year. "[Pickett] has been informed that should occasion require that he should have assistance, and should he require it of you, that you would be instructed to move up at once without waiting for orders from here. Govern your actions accordingly." Grimes did not have long to wait. The following day Lee ordered one of Grimes' brigades to "occupy the line formerly held by General [Montgomery] Corse." The position was on the right flank of the Howlett Line. "The General desired me to say to you that great caution would have to be observed to present the movement of the troops from being seen from 'the tower,'" explained E. R. Baird, one of Pickett's staffers, referencing a Federal observation post across the river constructed to observe Confederate operations on the far bank. "He advises you send as large a brigade as possible, as General [William] Terry's line at present covers a great deal of ground." The movement, advised Baird, would be best conducted at night. Grimes dutifully selected a brigade for the task and moved it forward into the vacated trenches on the evening of January 8. Thankfully for the soldiers, General Corse's men had constructed comfortable huts a short distance in the rear.[8]

Despite the cold weather and the constant reminder of war, Grimes and Charlotte enjoyed their time together and the weeks passed relatively uneventfully. On the last day of January, the general was asked to have his division "prepared to move promptly" the following morning. "It may be necessary to send you to the north side of the James river," came the message from Lee's headquarters. Nothing developed, however, and Grimes and his mobile reserve division stood down the following day. On February 5, the prospects of renewed fighting again intruded suddenly into their lives. "One night (5th) we were sitting very cosily by our fire," Charlotte recalled after the war. "General Grimes sorting and signing his papers; suddenly, he stopped and listened and said, 'That's small arms fire and I must go.' I said, 'must you go in all this sleet and rain?' He laughed and said that made no difference and made preparations to go. He immediately called out the division and in a short time had gone." The interruption was caused by a strong Federal movement against the far right of Lee's line designed to interrupt the flow of supplies into Petersburg and test the response of the Southerners. The column consisted of the Second and Fifth Federals corps, together with a division of cavalry.[9]

In the midst of a cold winter storm, Grimes called out his brigades and received an order to march them southwest toward Petersburg. At some point during the march a messenger arrived informing him of the status of the action: "The enemy's cavalry have not passed beyond Dinwiddie Court House. They advanced to that point and then retired." The order directed Grimes to set up camp where he was. "Your men can be made comfortable for the night." If the area he was then in was not suitable, he was to "Move down the Boydton plankroad until you can get to some wood. If you move," concluded the message, "report your location when you halt." Although it was later determined that Grimes was not needed below the Appomattox River, a sharp battle developed from February 5-7. The engagement, known as Hatcher's Run, was fought in bitter cold weather and casualties were high on both sides.

That winter Charlotte and Bryan were living together in a house owned by a Dr. Bragg. When her husband marched away toward the fighting, she remembered, "I had to go too, as I could not stay there alone and would go to a neighboring house where Mrs. Cox boarded." After an uneasy night, Charlotte awoke the next morning. "I thought I heard someone say General Grimes was killed," was her unpleasant recollection. "I jumped out of bed and sent my servant to inquire when Dr. Mitchell, who was in the house, sent me word that it was General Pegram who was killed." The following day Grimes and his weary men returned, unbloodied but freezing. "Many of them," wrote Charlotte, "were barefooted and had icicles hanging in their hair and beards."[10]

Charlotte remained with Grimes until mid-February. Although still winter, ominous signs of a Federal offensive were brewing. It was time for Charlotte to return to North Carolina. "When my husband told me good by," she recalled, looking into his face, "I did not know if I should ever see him alive again." A few days later enemy troops were again discovered angling toward the army's right flank and the Southside Railroad. Major Gen. John

B. Gordon, whose Second Corps command was below the Appomattox River defending Petersburg itself, informed Lee's headquarters on February 15 that if a serious move against the rail line developed, "Grimes' Division [should] keep in readiness to join me should the commanding General think proper to have him report to me in case of battle." Walter Taylor, Lee's A.A.G., passed along Gordon's note to Grimes, adding: "You had better keep your division prepared to move. Though it may not be necessary, it is advisable."[11]

It was also advisable to install a permanent commander for Rodes' Division. With his long and varied experience and stellar field record, there was no one better suited than Bryan Grimes to lead it. Unfortunately, Charlotte was not with him to celebrate his richly-deserved promotion to major general, which was officially set forth in Special Orders No. 55 and dated February 28, 1865 (effective February 15, 1865). "Maj. Gen. Bryan Grimes . . .is hereby assigned to the command of Rodes' old division, Second Corps, and will report accordingly," was how the simple order read. Grimes was thirty-six years old during the war's final February, a man of "quick and fiery temper," wrote Douglas Southall Freeman, "but in action he showed judgment as well as skill and courage." Unbeknownst to everyone, the promotion held a special distinction: Grimes would be the last officer appointed to the rank of major general in the Army of Northern Virginia.[12]

As the command machinery was processing his promotion (and probably before he was officially notified of it), Grimes was ordered to cross with his division below the Appomattox River to support General Gordon and reinforce the far right sector of Lee's extended lines. After a hard march he and his men reached Sutherland's Station, a depot about a dozen miles from Petersburg on the Southside Railroad, on or about February 24. "There was a prospect of a fight," he wrote home that evening, "but heavy rains have delayed it." Grimes set up camp for his division and waited for further orders, again playing the role of a mobile reserve to be plugged into the line whenever and wherever circumstances warranted.

"In accepting the appointment of Major-General, I hope I shall never bring discredit upon myself," he wrote Charlotte two days later on the 26th of the month while still camped at Sutherland's Station. "The higher the position the more there is expected, and like all others who have done their duty in this war, have made enemies, but care little for them, provided I can perform my duties satisfactorily to my superior officers and for the good of the country." The composition of the division remained the same with Grimes' elevation to permanently head the organization. Philip Cook and William R. Cox, both brigadier generals, continued to lead their Georgia and North Carolina veterans, respectively. The brigade of Alabamians once led by Cullen Battle, whose wound would prevent him from ever returning to the field, was in the hands of Col. Samuel B. Pickens. Grimes' own brigade had for some time had been in the temporary but capable hands of the 53rd North Carolina's senior officer, Col. David G. Cowand, and there it remained.[13]

While the composition may not have changed, Grimes' responsibilities as a division commander were exponentially larger than they were as a brigadier. He was now (as he had been for some time as a surrogate commander of the division) accountable for four times as many soldiers, both on and off the field of battle. The winter of 1864-65 was unusually severe, and the lack of food and adequate clothing, coupled with the miserable military circumstances under which he and his men labored, increased his stress level and work load. The lack of adequate rations was of constant concern, for his men were slowly starving. One private in the 43rd North Carolina described his daily diet as consisting of "a hunk of corn bread made with unsifted meal, about as large as a man's fist and less than half a pint of sorghum." Those same circumstances also accounted for a growing rate of desertion in the Army of Northern Virginia. The problem had become so acute that Lee addressed the issue in a report to the authorities in Richmond, claiming that the alarming rates were due to an "insufficiency of food and nonpayment of troops," as well as the urgings of their friends at home to return. According to one estimate, from the middle of February to the middle of March, 1865, nearly three thousand Confederate soldiers fled to the Federal lines. During the last thirty days before the fall of Petersburg, some one hundred men a day were deserting to the enemy. Charlotte herself recalled the depressing situation, commenting after the war that "Forty-five men deserted the night I left."[14]

From the Sutherland's Station area on February 28, Grimes wrote Charlotte concerning what he considered the traitorous rantings of a captain named Tom Settle, who was urging the wives of Confederate soldiers to persuade their husbands to desert and come home. "I wish he [Tom Settle] were in my power for a short time while you may be sure I would stop his mouth forever," wrote an angry Grimes. Settle had enlisted in Company I, 13th North Carolina Infantry on May 3, 1861, and was elected captain. He remained in the army until the following April, when he was reelected but declined the position and "went home." He never returned to the army. Instead, he remained in North Carolina and advocated against the war. Settle's advocacy, which was in line with editor William Holden's anti-Davis administration rhetoric, irked Grimes to no end. He continued to speak out against Settle's position, which obviously weakened morale within his division, and thus the army, as a whole.[15]

Other more personal concerns occupied Grimes' waking hours. Major General William T. Sherman had left Savannah, Georgia, in early January 1865, and was cutting and burning his way through South Carolina. That state's capital at Columbia fell on February 17. Five days later Gen. Joseph E. Johnston was appointed to try to arrest Sherman's progress through the Carolinas. By the end of February, Sherman's armies were poised to enter North Carolina. Both Charlotte and Grimes' ancestral home of Grimesland stood in the path of Sherman's juggernaut. "Sometimes when the thought enters my mind of what indignities you would be subjected to if unfortunately you should fall among those miserable miscreants, the Yankees, my blood curdles," Grimes wrote his wife with some hostility on the 9th of March. "I feel like taking the life of every one who falls in our hands." I am aware of the "violence. . .committed upon females in Sherman's walk through eastern Carolina," he continued, "and I fear that such treatment may fall upon those I love. If they should come to Raleigh always remain in the presence of your father and mother and never, if possible, show yourself to such reptiles."[16]

After the fighting at Hatcher's Run in early February, Grimes Division spent the next several weeks camped near Sutherland's Station along the Southside Railroad. The general spent the first of March "riding all day in order to learn the different roads in the surrounding country, and laying off new ones to enable me to move with rapidity to any point when my services may be required." Heavy rains and cold weather ruined the roads, which Grimes claimed were "in such bad condition that they are impassable." Other than a serenade to "break the monotony," he explained on March 8, all remained the same. Realizing that the weather and military situation were sending morale in the army to lower depths, President Jefferson Davis set aside March 10 as a day "for thanksgiving and prayer," Grimes informed Charlotte, "but the weather is so bad no service can be held out of doors." As a result, the day passed like the others: cold, wet, and miserable. The monotony was broken the next day when a rumor hit the Confederates that General Sheridan and his horsemen were "moving on Richmond." Grimes was shaken from his sleep at 2:00 a.m. with orders to immediately move his division yet again, this time north of the Appomattox River to the Dunlop house near Swift Creek. "Am worn out from fatigue and want of sleep," he scribbled home in a letter when nothing came of the movement other than exhausted soldiers and tired limbs. He had his men on the march by 4:00 a.m., and was nearing the pontoon bridge over the river when a mounted orderly searched him out of the column with orders countermanding the march. "You can move back to your camp," wrote General Gordon, "but keep your command ready; have your wagons so that they can be moved at any time."[17]

Grimes had barely returned to his camp on March 13 when the unwelcome news arrived ordering his brigades into the deadly Petersburg trenches to relieve Maj. Gen. Bushrod R. Johnson's exhausted division. The movement absorbed most of the day, with the weary men filing into the lines about midnight. Grimes himself arrived "sick, with a nervous headache." The general attributed his passing malady to a glass of wine "I took with General Lee, who noticed that I looked pale and fatigued. . .as this was something very unusual with him, I concluded I would take it, and suffered for my consumption."[18]

The section of trenches occupied by Grimes' soldiers bordered the city on the east, stretching from near the Appomattox River on the north past the scene of the July Battle of Crater and down around the Jerusalem Plank Road. His front covered about three miles, which translated into a division perilously extended. Sickness and desertion continued to whittle away soldiers. Colonel Thomas S. Kenan of the 43rd North Carolina claimed the division was down to "about 2,200" men. The winding trench-scared front required that "one-third of the men [serve] on picket duty in front of the trenches and one-third on duty in the trenches, where the mud was frequently more than shoe deep and sometimes knee-deep," he claimed, "while the remaining third caught a broken rest on their arms." The conditions met by Grimes' men were horrible, and the men had not been in combat for some five months. "At night there was almost constant firing between the pickets," explained one officer, which prevented a good night's sleep. "At most points the main lines of the two armies were within easy rifle range, and at some points less than one hundred yards apart." Grimes took stock of the deadly situation by noting to Charlotte that "the bullets fly all around the house which I occupy." Another deadly pastime was artillery shelling, which was made even worse by the use of high-trajectory mortars. Confederate artillerist E. P. Alexander observed that "every man needed a little bombproof [shelter] to sleep in at night and to dodge into in the day when the mortar shells were coming."[19]

Once his men were properly deployed, Grimes spent the morning after his arrival "examining everything on my line. [I] went to each picket post, and at some points so close you could almost see the whites of the Yankees' eyes." The enemy lines, he added, "are in full view." The proximity of the opposing lines and deadly exchange of fire was especially dangerous for the sharpshooters' favorite target: officers. His vulnerability prompted Grimes to cloak his high rank from the wrong set of eyes. "I concealed your handiwork on my collar lest some enterprising Yankee might take it in his head to pick off a Major General," he wrote Charlotte, "and I have no idea of you being a widow if I can help it."[20]

The deteriorating situation in his home state continued to occupy Grimes' attention almost as much as did the close proximity of the Yankees. "I telegraphed yesterday that in case Raleigh was evacuated, I thought it best for you to join me here in Petersburg," he informed his wife. "You can judge for yourself whether it is better to have all the risks with me or stay in Raleigh and take your chances." Grimes' concern was a real one, for that very day Sherman was fighting Lt. Gen. William Hardee at Averasboro in the east central portion of the state—just forty miles below Raleigh. Hardee's delaying action was merely a prelude waged in order to allow Joe Johnston the time he needed to coalesce his forces and fall upon a portion of the separated Federal army and destroy it. Charlotte, however, did not deem a journey north to war-torn Petersburg as a safe option, determining instead to remain in North Carolina with her parents.[21]

As the days of March slipped past, the military situation facing Lee's army continued to worsen. Sherman's presence in North Carolina meant that he was only weeks away from joining forces with General Grant. That junction alone would break the stalemate and end the war quickly in Virginia. The odds were further lengthened against the struggling Southerners when Philip Sheridan and thousands of his troopers were recalled from the Shenandoah Valley to Petersburg, which was now almost completely encircled within the deadly grip of siege warfare. Grant continued to focus on the railroads, appreciating full well that the severing of the Southside line would force Lee to leave his protective trenches within days or starve within them. Even this logistical avenue had lost some of its value for Lee, however, for the critical port of Wilmington, North Carolina, had fallen to the Federals in late February 1865. Its demise ended the city's role as the South's most valuable blockade-running seaport, and fewer supplies were rattling over the rails into Petersburg as a result.[22]

General Lee knew he had to break out of Grant's grasp or face surrender. With Longstreet north defending Richmond and unfamiliar with the situation below the Appomattox, Lee turned to his trusted Second Corps commander to study the Federal lines and suggest a course of action tailored to deal a powerful blow against the enemy and allow the Army of Northern

Virginia to escape the Union stranglehold. After a week of study, John B. Gordon recommended a bold attack upon an earthen redoubt known as Fort Stedman. The target, one in a series of enclosed fortifications, was directly east of Petersburg and about one mile below the

Maj. Gen. John B. Gordon

*Generals in Gray*

Appomattox River—just opposite a protrusion in the Confederate line known as Colquitt's Salient. This bulge narrowed the distance between the opposing enemy lines. A boy with a strong arm, Maj. Henry Kyd Douglas later explained with only a small amount of exaggeration, could have thrown a stone from the Confederate to the Union lines at this point.

Gordon's scheme was nothing short of a desperate gamble. His plan demanded a surprise pre-dawn assault from the Confederate salient, where the opposing trenches were no more than 150 yards apart. The attacking column would run directly into the Federal works, anchored at that point by Fort Stedman (Hare's Hill to the Confederates), which was armed with four guns and supported by artillery batteries on the north (Battery X) and the south (Batteries XI and XII). About a half-mile below Stedman was another Union stronghold called Fort Haskell. Gordon's plan called for his three divisions, supported by another four brigades from other commands, to speed across open ground between the lines in utter darkness and capture the forts and batteries. Once this feat was accomplished, the attackers would fan out left and right and advance up and down the Union lines of trenches. Captured Federal artillery would be turned to enfilade their prior owners, while Confederate reinforcements charged through the gap torn open by Gordon's initial assault.

The terrain fronting Stedman was not conducive to a successful assault. It was crisscrossed with picket trenches and bristling with abatis, felled trees piled together, and strong earthworks. The fort itself was composed of breast-high sharp logs pointing toward the approaching enemy. Gordon developed plans to deal with these problems. The vanguard of the assault would be composed of fifty strong men with sharp axes, who would hack away the obstructions and clear a path for the infantry, which would follow to engulf the fort. Three carefully-selected groups of 100 men, each led by one officer, would rush past Fort Stedman into the Union rear, pretending to be Federals driven rearward by the surprise Southern assault. These three columns would continue and capture three small forts believed to be behind Stedman. Once all this was accomplished, Confederate infantry and cavalry would pour through the gaping hole in the line and collapse Grant's Petersburg wing, cut his army in two, and allow Lee to break out of the deadly encirclement.[23]

According to Gordon, "The tremendous possibility was the disintegration of the whole left wing of the Federal army, or at least the dealing of such a staggering blow upon it as would disable it temporarily, enabling us to withdraw from Petersburg in safety and join Johnston in North Carolina." That the fanciful plan was attempted at all is remarkable, and a clear demonstration that the Army of Northern Virginia would have to risk suicidal attacks simply to remain in existence, an odd irony indeed. Lee had some misgivings about such a mission and asked Gordon if he thought the officers leading the 100-man columns would be able to locate the three forts behind Stedman in unfamiliar terrain and darkness. "That depends, General, upon my ability to get proper guides," hedged Gordon in a rather lawyer-like fashion. "I have no such men in my Corps; and without proper guides my three detachments will be sacrificed after taking Fort Stedman and passing the rear line of infantry."[24]

By 4:00 a.m. on March 25, Gordon's thousands—about one-half of Lee's infantry below the Appomattox River, were arrayed for battle. Bryan Grimes' Division comprised the last of three columns Gordon planned to use during the first phase of the assault. When the signal shot was fired, the men moved forward. "With unloaded muskets and a profound silence, [we] leaped over our breastworks, dash[ing] across the open space in front," recalled Pvt. Henry London. While Grimes' exact location during the assault is not known, he almost certainly advanced with his men into darkness toward Stedman. Tom Devereux, an enlisted man with Grimes' Division, recalled they "went at it in a run and on reaching the fort found that the hundred men sent forward had captured it, or rather were inside, and the Yankees were pouring out at its rear. We were soon in possession, and our half-starved men busy searching the bomb proof [that] had covered ways for rations."[25]

The plan, at least initially, worked better than anyone had a right to hope. Fort Stedman, together with Batteries X and XI fell within a few minutes, leaving a hole in the Union defenses several hundred yards wide. The rapid success of the movement bred confusion, and Gordon soon learned that the guides assigned to lead the three hundred soldiers to the rear had become separated from their columns. The soldiers quickly lost their way in the dark maze of intersecting trenches and earthworks. As the desperate plan began unraveling, Federal gunners opened fire on the mass of milling Confederates. More defenders poured into the area, boxing in the attackers. Unable to advance and facing probable death in retreat, the soldiers held onto Fort Stedman and the surrounding lines. Gordon's expected reinforcements never arrived. Within a few hours General Lee realized the hopelessness of the situation and ordered Gordon to withdraw. It was a difficult and deadly task, for the "no-man's land" between the opposing lines was smothered by shot, shell, and bullets. Hundreds of men were cut down attempting to gain the safety of their trenches. The absence of an official casualty return makes it difficult to determine Southern losses, but one careful estimate placed the number at 2,681 killed, wounded, and missing. Northern losses, which included concurrent and subsequent assaults along the lines, totaled about 2,600.[26]

"This morning we charged the enemy's works and captured them, taking twelve to fifteen pieces of artillery and a good many prisoners," Grimes wrote Charlotte after the close of the Fort Stedman fiasco. "After taking their works they concentrated a large number of cannon upon us, besides several times our number of infantry, and we were obliged to succumb, after fighting two and a half hours and retired to our breastworks." His division suffered heavily with a loss of 478 killed and wounded, or about a quarter of its strength. "As usual I captured a horse to ride during the fight, as I could not get mine over the breastworks." The melancholy aftermath of the battle sickened the tired soldier, who wished "to Heaven this carnage was over, and I [was] permitted to retire from such scenes and live a quiet and domestic life."[27]

The single bright spot of the morning was the undying morale of the men of his division. "It would have done your heart good to hear the men cheer as I rode up and down the line urging them to do their duty." Exactly who was cheering as the general rode his mount along the lines is unclear, but Grimes would have been especially pleased if some of the men issuing the hurrahs were from Cullen Battle's Alabama Brigade. The Alabamians were not especially fond of Grimes, for many of them believed General Battle should have received the promotion to major general. (Although Battle was Grimes' senior, such a grudge conveniently ignores the fact that he was too seriously injured to ever again take the field). The North Carolinian's gallant actions at Stedman, however, where he made himself a conspicuous target, apparently won over Battle's veterans. One impressed

Alabama soldier complimented Grimes, claiming the general "would fight a rattlesnake through a fence and give him the first bite."[28]

Much to his dismay, two days later on March 27 Grimes learned the distressing news that he had been reported killed in the assault on Stedman, and that preparations were underway to recover his corpse. He immediately sent word home that he was well. "[I] trust you did not hear the report of my being killed," he wrote Charlotte with some concern. "When General Gordon saw me, he seemed very much surprised; said he had just sent a flag of truce to recover my body, but I was pleased to know I had brought myself off safe." By the 29th, Grimes had reached the conclusion that someone had bungled the assault. "My loss was heavy [at Fort Stedman]. It was a very badly managed affair, [and] we should have been withdrawn after the failure to capture the other forts on the line." The condition of one of his brigadier's, Philip Cook, also concerned him, for the officer had been severely wounded in the March 25th attack. "General Cook had his arm badly broken," lamented Grimes, "and fears are entertained that it will be have to be amputated."[29]

On the day following the repulse at Fort Stedman, Lee informed President Davis that the time had arrived to evacuate Petersburg and Richmond and unite with Joe Johnston's forces in North Carolina. General Grant, too, appreciated the situation Lee faced and moved promptly to cut the Southside Railroad to guarantee the end of the nine month stalemate. Without that line, Lee's men could not subsist in the trenches for more than a few days. The only direction Lee could move his army was west, and so Grant dispatched General Sheridan and his 13,000 troopers to swing around the Southern flank and cut the roads leading into the interior of the state. Confederate cavalry under Fitz Lee, together with George Pickett's Division, was sent to block the move and hold on until plans to successfully evacuate the cities could be made. Grimes sat down and penned Charlotte the last letter he would write her during the war, probably dated March 31, 1865: "Our troops were to attack the enemy this morning," he informed her, "and I trust that they may whip them. For once I am out of it, and not among the attacking party." Grimes was to be sadly disappointed, however, for these machinations culminated in the disaster of Five Forks on April 1. Under Phil Sheridan, a combined Federal cavalry-infantry column routed Pickett and

Fitz Lee, captured thousands of prisoners, and opened the vital Southside Railroad to destruction.[30]

As Pickett was being mauled at Five Forks, General Lee rode along Grimes' lengthy divisional line south of Petersburg, where the two officers enjoyed what Grimes later described as "a verbal conference." Although exactly what transpired between the two officers is not recorded, Grimes officially sent Lee word later in the day of his "inability to hold this point against any vigorous attack." He may have said as much in person. His lines were simply stretched too thin to withstand a concentrated Federal assault. "On an average throughout the space, from man to man, was at least eight feet in the line of trenches," was his grim estimate of the situation. For some time Grimes had been asking for a force of five hundred men to utilize as a mobile reserve to drive back "the enemy from any point they might capture." Although he "repeatedly urged that such an arrangement be made, knowing well that the enemy, by concentrating a large force on any given point, could press their way through the line," General Lee "informed me that every available man was on duty, and I must do the best I could."[31]

It would not be long before Grimes' appraisal of the deteriorating situation would be seriously put to the test. Realizing the magnitude of the defeat Lee had just suffered at Five Forks, at 9:00 p.m. that evening General Grant ordered a general assault along the lines for the following morning. Artillery opened on the Confederates an hour after his order went out, and Grimes described the night bombardment as "unusually severe." His divisional line at this time stretched over "at least three and a half miles of the trenches around Petersburg," with his left now "resting on Otey's Battery, near the memorable Crater," he explained in a letter written after the war, "my right extending to the dam on a creek beyond Battery Forty-Five." His line, arranged by brigade, from right to left, was as follows: Cox, Cowand (Grimes), Battle, and Cook. Fletcher Archer's Virginia Battalion held the line between Cox and Cowand. My command, explained Grimes, numbered only 2,200 muskets. As Grant's artillery pounded the Southern positions, infantry advanced at 11:00 p.m. and captured Grimes' picket line, "which consisted of pits dug into the earth for protection from sharpshooters, and occupied by my soldiers, varying in distance from one hundred and fifty to three hundred yards in front of our main breastworks." Grimes "took measures immediately to re-establish this line, which was successfully accomplished, and our pits re-occupied." Although Grimes could not have known it, the Petersburg siege had only a few hours of life left in it.[32]

As early as 4:00 a.m. on April 2, Union infantry began rolling forward against the outnumbered Confederate defenders. Grimes' men were on the receiving end of an attack launched by two divisions from Federal Maj. Gen. John G. Parke's IX Corps. Parke's thrust originated from Fort Sedgwick and was directed like a giant spearhead against Fort Mahone (Battery 29), a powerful fortification along the Jerusalem Plank Road. The sweeping and well-delivered assault pushed up against the outer line of works and spilled over into the Confederate trenches, "where Battle's Brigade was posted," reported Grimes, "carrying the works for a few hundred yards on each side of that point, doubling and throwing Cook's Brigade back a short distance."

The fighting was eerily similar to Spotsylvania, beginning in the early-morning mist and spreading along the trenches in a hand-to-hand melee of chaos and bloodshed. And, in a repeat of his Spotsylvania performance, Grimes organized and led a sharp counterattack about 11:00 a.m. The troops he guided forward consisted of his former brigade under Colonel Cowand and Fletcher Archer's band of Virginians. As these soldiers were attempting to stem the mounting tide of defeat, Grimes rode to the rear and sought out artillery support from four guns, which he placed "in our second line of works." The pieces "were invaluable in checking the advance of the enemy," he later explained, "thus confining them by grape and canister to this particular point at the salient, preventing their advancing to attack our lines in flank or rear." Grimes' brilliant defense of Fort Mahone against heavy odds has largely been overlooked by historians of the campaign. With the remnants of Battle's Alabamians and Cook's Georgians "holding them in check on the left," wrote Grimes, "and Cowand and Archer on the right of the captured works, their only point of egress [was] exposed to the fire of the artillery." Grimes' defensive efforts created a Fort Stedman in reverse, with the Federals playing the role of the trapped attackers.[33]

Grimes' men continued to claw their way over the earthworks. "The fight was from traverse to traverse as we slowly drove them back," remembered one of Grimes' survivors. "The Yankees would get on top of them and shoot down at our men, and as we would re-take them our men did the same thing." Sergeant Cyrus B. Watson of the 45th Regiment also described the fierce fighting: "I saw the men of my regiment load their guns behind the traverses, climb to the top, fire down into the ranks of the enemy, roll off and reload and repeat the same throughout the day." A series of localized Federal counter-thrusts, however, finally blunted the Confederate movement. Within 120 minutes Grimes' grueling attempt to throw back the enemy to Fort Sedgwick and stabilize the ruptured line had failed, his troops ground into inaction by sheer exhaustion and mounting casualties. The defensive stand, however, did seal off the breach in the lines and bought Petersburg's occupants a few extra hours.

Other sectors along Lee's front were not doing so well. Although Grimes had managed to stem Parke's thrust, Horatio Wright's VI Corps broke through A. P. Hill's lines right (or west) of Grimes' position, killing Hill and rolling up the defenders. Wright's overpowering attack shattered two Southern divisions and tore a large and growing hole in the lines. Other Federal organizations were also experiencing similar good luck along the Boydton Plank Road and Hatcher's Run. The Confederates had to find a way to hold on until nightfall and utilize the cover of darkness to retreat. Orders were sent for portions of Lee's army north of the Appomattox River to evacuate their lines. The end of the siege was at hand.[34]

But Grimes did not know of the deteriorating situation beyond his flank. With fresh troops from north of the Appomattox River in hand, he studied the enemy positions and formulated a new plan. "My dispositions were soon made to attack the enemy simultaneously at all points," he later reported. "I gave the signal for the infantry advance, when a general charge was made" about 3:00 p.m. Two brigades bore down on the flanks of Parke's equally tired soldiers while a thin line of gray infantry challenged the center of the Federal position. The hard-hitting counterattack, which over the past year had become Grimes' battlefield trademark, further weakened Parke's incursion and turned Fort Mahone into a neutral killing ground owned by no one. As one soldier recalled it, "we had recaptured all of our lines as far as to the left of Fort Mahone." After another hour of small arms fire and reorganization, about sixty soldiers from Robert Johnston's North Carolina Brigade moved into Fort Mahone and captured a large number of prisoners. "After this no general attack was made," reported Grimes after the war, "though we continued slowly but gradually to drive them from traverse to traverse. "I need not say that at this perilous moment he was with the men at the point of greatest danger," wrote one of his soldiers with pride, "for he was always at such places."[35]

Although he had accomplished much, Grimes was particularly displeased with the performance of one of his subordinate officers:

> Through a direct violation of orders on the part of Colonel ——, this attack only partially succeeded, capturing that portion of the line alone upon which the skirmishers advanced, Colonel —— having changed the direction of attack, and charged the point assigned to the skirmishers on the right, thereby leaving a space of three hundred yards unassailed. There is no doubt in my mind if Colonel —— had attacked with vigor at that time, we could have driven the enemy entirely from our works.[36]

Despite his displeasure, Grimes retained control of his lines after turning in one of his finest performances of the war. At the cost of 1,700 killed and wounded, Parke's Federals purchased a few hundred yards of overturned earth. Confederate losses, unfortunately, are unknown but were undoubtedly heavy. "Through no inefficiency or negligence on the part of the officers and men were the works carried," explained Grimes. "but owing to the weakness of the line, its extreme length, and the want of sufficient force to defend it, for they acted most heroically on this trying occasion." If Grimes' account is accurate, his men did indeed do their duty that arduous day. "Only one unwounded man (an officer) did I see seeking the rear," the general recalled, "and he whom I had the previous day ordered under arrest for trafficking with the enemy (exchanging tobacco for coffee)." By this time it is likely Grimes had learned of the Southern failures beyond his right flank. The writing was on the wall: Petersburg and Richmond were doomed.[37]

Even as Grimes' men were fighting for their lives, portions of Lee's army were withdrawing generally west. Lee's first objective was to get his army intact to Amelia Court House, forty miles away, where it would regroup and move south to join Joe Johnston's army in North Carolina. To General Gordon and the Second Corps fell the honor of serving as the army's rearguard as it abandoned Petersburg. For Grimes there was a certain grim irony in the situation, for he had begun his active combat service as part of the rear guard for a retreating Confederate army during the Peninsula

Campaign of 1862; now, three years later, he was executing similar orders, though now without even a glimmer of hope for victory.

After dark on Sunday, April 2, Grimes led his division north through Petersburg, "without the knowledge of the Federals" and across the pontoon bridge spanning the Appomattox River. Following the Hickory Road to Goode's Bridge, his soldiers recrossed the Appomattox and trudged toward Amelia Court House. The roads were muddy and both men and horses had a difficult time. The exhausted and hungry column reached their first objective on the morning of April 5, where Grimes' Division "remained stationary in line of battle, confronting the enemy until about dark, when we followed the army. . ." Nerves were frayed and tempers were understandably short. Taking up the rear of the column, Grimes' men were "being very much impeded on the march by the wagon train and its most miserable management," wrote the general with obvious disgust, "which, as I apprehended, would cause us some disaster."

The danger to the tired and hungry Southerners was growing as the Federal pursuit south and east of them lapped against Grimes' soldiers. In the middle of a spring shower "the enemy showed themselves on Thursday, about 8 a.m. in our rear and on our left flank. . .and in a short time began to press us vigorously." Turning his men to face the enemy, Grimes deployed Cox's and Cowand's brigades north of Flat Creek and astride the road leading from Amelia Springs to Deatonville, placing them "in line of battle, with a heavy skirmish line in front to impede their [the Federals'] progress and to cover our rear." As these men were taking up their positions, a brigade of North Carolina cavalry hovered beyond Grimes' right flank. The brigades of Battle and Cook, together with Archer's Virginia battalion, were similarly deployed about one-half mile west. This second line, Grimes explained, would "allow Cowand and Cox to retreat safely when the enemy had deployed and prepared to attack." Thus situated, Grimes hopscotched his brigades westward throughout the day, "endeavoring to protect the lagging wagon train, which was successfully done up to about 4 p.m., when we approached Sayler's Creek."[38]

This strategy worked well for a time, but the looming disaster Grimes had predicted because of the "mismanagement" of the wagon train was upon them. Late that afternoon on April 6, the North Carolinian took up a position on a ridge running parallel with Sayler's Creek, watching in dismay as the wagons stacked up while attempting to cross the bridge there. Unknown to anyone at the time, a communications mix-up caused Grimes' Division and the balance of the Second Corps under Gordon to take a wrong road. Grimes men were now more than two miles northwest and beyond supporting distance for a large portion of the army under Richard Ewell, which was fighting for its life. As Grimes surveyed the scene, General Lee rode up and ordered him, "if possible, to hold this line of hills until he could have artillery put in position on the opposite hills." The aggressive Federals, who belonged to General Andrew Humphreys' Second Corps, were not about to offer the enemy a reprieve, and "pushed on rapidly, attacking us with very great pertinacity." Although Grimes' veterans were able to repulse several determined attacks, the game of numbers, as it had so often and on so many fields, began to tip the scales against them. By "turning both of our flanks," reported Grimes, "they succeeded in driving us across the creek in confusion." Luckily for the Southerners, artillery had been brought up which "opened on the enemy, and the sun being down they did not cross the creek."[39]

The sharp defeat, however, pressed Grimes and a handful of his men between two converging wings of Humphrey's advancing Federals. "After we broke, personally I was so pressed that the space between the two wings of the enemy was not over two hundred yards when I sought safety in retreat." Appreciating the looming probability of capture (or worse), Grimes "galloped to the creek where the banks were very precipitous, and for protection from their murderous fire, [I] concluded to jump my horse [Warren] in, riding him through the water, and effect my escape by abandoning him on the other side." It was a dangerous ride with "the bullets of the enemy whistling around me like hail all the while." My horse, he continued, "seeming to appreciate the situation, clambered up the height, starting off in a run thus securing my safety." Grimes' account of his perilous escape was witnessed by one of his soldiers, who explained how his general had "stayed with his men until all were over the creek and the bridge destroyed, then plunging his horse, Warren, into the water, crossed over under a perfect storm of bullets and made his escape." Most of the men under Dick Ewell and Richard Anderson, however, were not so fortunate. As Grimes was riding to safety, their trapped soldiers were surrendering by the thousands.

"The Black Day of the Army," as Douglas Southall Freeman called Sayler's Creek, cost Lee about one-third of his men.[40]

That night, Grimes' Division followed the road in the direction of Farmville and crossed over the Appomattox River at High Bridge. Grimes posted a picket force on the south bank to gather "stragglers" and return them to their respective commands. The march continued early Friday morning on April 7. With the enemy hovering nearby, Grimes formed his men into a line of battle on the Lynchburg Road, "still endeavoring to preserve that 'impediment of Caesar's'—the wagon train—marching by the left flank through the woods parallel to the road traveled by the wagon train, and about one hundred or so yards distant from the road." With the Federal Second Corps on the army's heels, Lee ordered his men to entrench around Cumberland Church, about three miles north of Farmville. Grimes' brigades deployed east of the Cumberland Road, although they did not stay there for long. Heavy firing was going on," he later wrote, "when General [William] Mahone came rushing up and reported that the enemy had charged, turning his flank, and driving his men from their guns and the works which he had erected early in the day for the protection of these crossroads." Organizing another of his brilliant (and overlooked) counter-strokes, Grimes double-quicked his brigades a short distance northwest, where they "charged the enemy and [drove] them well off from Mahone's works," he reported with pride, "recapturing the artillery taken by them and capturing a large number of prisoners." His men held this position "until sent for by General Lee, who complimented the troops of the division upon the charge made and the service rendered." Ordered to leave a skirmish line across his front, Grimes was sent "with all possible dispatch" to another threatened crossroads to head off the Federal cavalry and keep them in check while the Confederate wagons passed. He and his men checked the enemy horsemen and spent the rest of the day marching with the wagons.[41]

On Saturday, April 8, the weary and hungry men continued their march westward. "No enemy appeared," wrote Grimes in his report of the campaign, "and we marched undisturbed all day." The sun bathed the Virginia countryside in warmth and light, and the spirits of the men improved somewhat, even if the strategic situation remained grim. It was obvious to almost everyone that Federal infantry was closely pursuing them while strong legions of cavalry were riding west and south on a parallel course to get ahead of the Army of Northern Virginia. If the army was cut off and unable to turn south, a junction with Joe Johnston's army would be impossible. "Up to this time, since the evacuation of Petersburg," Grimes explained, "we had marched day and night, continually followed and harassed by the enemy." The months of siege warfare and the rigors of the retreat had caught up with his soldiers, who were "much jaded and suffering from necessary sustenance, our halts not having been sufficiently long to prepare their food; besides all of our cooking utensils not captured or abandoned were where we could not reach them." As a soldier in Grimes' Division recalled the experience, "we just marched on, the ranks growing thinner and thinner, as the men would fall out exhausted."[42]

General Lee demonstrated his faith in Grimes' abilities when he assigned to him the remnants of Maj. Gen. Bushrod Johnson's Division. Johnson's command had suffered heavily at Sayler's Creek, as had Richard Anderson's corps. Without coherent organizations to lead—Lee may also have been upset by their respective performances—both officers were dismissed from the army. Following in the rear of Gordon's Second Corps, Grimes camped his men a couple miles behind near a small stream. Their slumber was almost immediately disturbed when artillery fire opened in the distance about 9:00 p.m. Grimes roused his men and ordered them to move out once more. The march consumed both their strength and the night hours. Before daylight the division was still fitfully moving forward through the quiet streets of Appomattox Court House. Just on the far side of the village, recalled Grimes, "I found the enemy in my front." The North Carolinian threw forward a skirmish line to test the intentions of the enemy while forming a line of battle in the rear. "[I then] awaited the arrival of General Gordon for instructions," he reported, "who, awhile before day, accompanied by General Fitz Lee, came to my position, when we held a council of war."[43]

Fatigue and stress were both in evidence as the three generals huddled together to discuss their course of action. According to Grimes, "General Gordon was of the opinion that the troops in our front were cavalry, and General Fitz Lee should attack. Fitz Lee thought they were infantry, and that Gordon should attack." The two generals bickered about the issue for some time, which annoyed the decisive-minded Grimes. The subordinate officer lifted his voice and broke the deadlock. "They discussed the matter so long that I became impatient," he explained, "and said it was somebody's duty to attack, and that immediately." Grimes informed his fellow officers that he believed the enemy "could be driven from the cross-roads occupied by them, which was the route it was desirable our wagon train should pursue, and that I would undertake it." Gordon, perhaps relieved that the decision had been made, agreed.

"Well," he told Grimes, "drive them off."

Rethinking the situation for a moment, Grimes replied, "I cannot do it with my division alone, but require assistance."

"You can take the other two divisions of the corps," was Gordon's remarkable reply. In that single sentence, the Georgian turned over the tactical control of his corps to Grimes.[44]

The sun on Palm Sunday, April 9, was just beginning to emerge over the horizon when Grimes rode forward to make his dispositions. He sought out General James Walker, whose division was posted on Grimes' left, and described for him the position of the enemy, explaining "my views and plan of attack." Walker "agreed with me as to its advisability," added Grimes, who was more than a little concerned about "the great responsibility when I took upon myself the charge of making the attack." As a young (and new) major general, Grimes was feeling the full weight of command on his shoulders. At some point during the early morning, perhaps while Grimes was aligning his men for battle, General Lee sent a staff officer to find Gordon and inquire as to whether the corps commander would be able to break through the enemy line. "Tell General Lee I have fought my corps to a frazzle," was Gordon's reply, "and I fear I can do nothing unless I am heavily supported by Longstreet's corps."[45]

The Army of North Virginia's last line of battle, while long and thin, was composed of nothing but exhausted veterans prepared to attempt the impossible yet again. Up ahead the enemy waited at the crossroads. Were they cavalry or infantry? They would soon find out. Grimes directed the remnants of Bushrod Johnson's Division to attack the Federals on their left flank, while his own skirmishers charged their center. The line would be advancing against a fresh stand of light earthworks and a battery of artillery. As his men moved out, "I soon perceived a disposition on their part to attack this division in the flank," recalled Grimes, who took steps to protect his men behind some ditches and fences. Federal shells, meanwhile, began

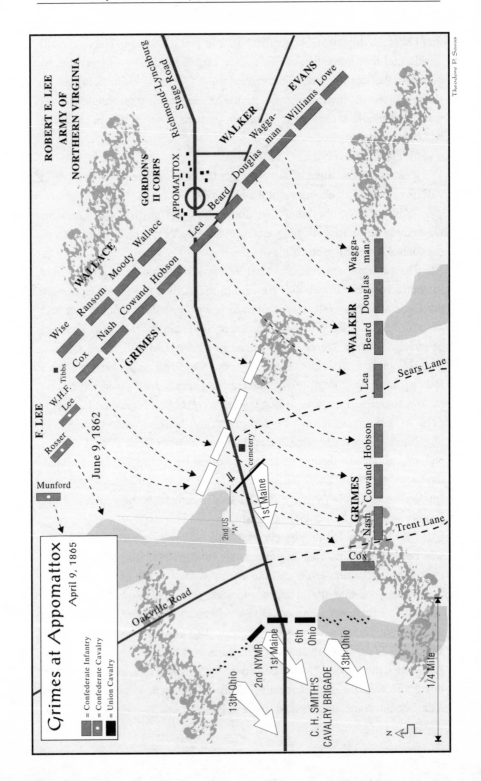

Grimes at Appomattox
April 9, 1865

= Confederate Infantry
= Confederate Cavalry
= Union Cavalry

ROBERT E. LEE
ARMY OF
NORTHERN VIRGINIA

GORDON'S
II CORPS

WALLACE

GRIMES

F. LEE

Munford

Rosser

W.H.F. Tibbs
Lee

Wise    Ransom    Moody    Wallace

Cox    Nash    Cowand    Hobson

June 9, 1862

APPOMATTOX

Richmond-Lynchburg
Stage Road

WALKER    Wagga-
man

Lea    Beard    Douglas    Williams    Lowe

EVANS

Wagga-
man

WALKER    Beard    Douglas

Lea

Sears Lane

GRIMES    Nash    Cowand    Hobson

Cox

Trent Lane

cemetery

1st Maine

2nd US "A"

Oakville Road

13th Ohio    2nd NYMR    1st Maine

6th
Ohio

13th Ohio

C. H. SMITH'S
CAVALRY BRIGADE

N

1/4 Mile

Theodore P. Savas

exploding in the early morning air as Fitz Lee's troopers rode off to get around their left flank and into their rear. Once again Grimes had a brush with death when an artillery round streaked in his direction. "I remember well the appearance of the shell, and how directly it came towards me, exploding and completely enveloping me in smoke." The remarkably fortunate officer avoided being struck by the flying slivers of iron—his last close call of the war.[46]

"I then gave the signal to advance," recalled Grimes, "at the same time Fitz Lee charged. . ." Grimes' infantry quickly captured the line of breastworks "without much loss," together with several pieces of artillery. His division was moved forward to support the skirmish line, advancing by brigade en echelon from right to left, "driving the enemy in confusion for three-quarters of a mile." Learning from prisoners that his right flank was threatened, Grimes stopped the advance and faced General Cox's Brigade in that direction, aligning it at a right angle to his line of advance. With the other two divisions in the corps (Walker's and Clement Evans') marching forward on his left, Grimes sent a message to Gordon that "the Lynchburg road was open for the escape of the wagons," and awaited orders. The directive he received was completely unexpected: Grimes was to withdraw his command immediately.

"This I declined to do," wrote Grimes, "supposing that General Gordon did not understand the commanding position my troops occupied." Gordon, however, "continued to send me order after order to the same effect, which I still disregarded, being under the impression that he did not comprehend our favorable location." An exasperated Gordon sent another withdrawal order accompanied this time with an order from General Lee, "to fall back." A dejected and confused Grimes now had no choice but to obey.[47]

Withdrawing his men after his penetration of the Union lines, however, was a difficult undertaking and required no little tactical finesse. After ordering his skirmishers to conform to the division's retrograde movement, Grimes "ordered Cox to maintain his position in line of battle, and not to show himself until our rear was one hundred yards distant, and then to fall back in line of battle, so as to protect our rear and right flank from assault." When the Federals spied the movement, they "rushed out from under cover with a cheer, when Cox's Brigade, lying concealed at the brow of the hill, rose and fired a volley into them, which drove them back into the woods; the brigade then following their retreating comrades in line of battle unmolested." Grimes' men had just fired the Army of Northern Virginia's last volley of the war.[48]

As his troops walked back to their jump-off point for the morning's assault, Grimes guided his mount over the General Gordon's position and asked where he should form a line of battle. "Anywhere you choose," came the general's odd response. "Struck by the strangeness of the reply, I asked an explanation, whereupon he informed me that we would be surrendered." Grimes, not quite believing what he had heard, and certainly unwilling to accept it, "expressed very forcibly my dissent to being surrendered, and indignantly upbraided him for not giving me notice of such intention, as I could have escaped with my division and joined General Joe Johnston, then in North Carolina." Grimes also told Gordon he was going to inform his men of the pending surrender so that "whomsoever desired to escape that calamity could go with me." His anger vented, the major general galloped off to prepare his exit from the unfolding capitulation. Before Grimes could reach his troops, however, Gordon overtook him and placed a hand his shoulder, asking "If I were going to desert the army, and tarnish my own honor as a soldier; that it would be a reflection upon General Lee, and an indelible disgrace to me, that I, an officer of rank, should escape under a flag of truce, which was then pending."

Grimes suddenly found his combative personality in direct conflict with the deep and abiding respect for authority and honor that had always characterized his army career. "I was in a dilemma," he lamented, "and knew not what to do." Reason and duty won out, and Grimes reluctantly "concluded to say nothing on the subject to my troops."[49]

By the time he reached his troops rumor that the army had or would surrender was winding its way through the ranks. Was it true? asked one of his men? When Grimes answered in the affirmative, the soldier "cast away his musket, and holding his hands aloft, cried in an agonized voice, 'Blow Gabriel, blow! My God, let him blow, I am ready to die!'" Many of the soldiers were speechless and overcome grief. "Sit there, Betsy," uttered one soldier from the 4th North Carolina as he set down his musket, "you've made many of them bite the dust." Another "thrust his musket between a forked sapling, bending the barrel, and said, 'no Yankee will ever shoot at us with you.'" Henry A. London, Grimes' 18-year-old courier, remembered

The tattered kepi worn during the war by Bryan Grimes

*The Museum of the Confederacy (photograph by Katherine Wetzel), Richmond , VA.*

that "strong men wept and battle scarred veterans trembled with emotion too deep for utterance." London recalled that Grimes "resembled a caged lion eager to break loose and scatter his tormentors."

The same emotions probably coursed through Grimes' veins as he marched his men "beyond the creek at Appomattox Court House, stacked arms amid the bitter tears of bronzed veterans, regretting the necessity of capitulation." Appreciating perhaps for the first time that the fighting was indeed over, he guided his faithful horse Warren through the lines in search of his old regiment, the 4th North Carolina. My purpose, he later wrote, "was to shake the hand of each comrade who had followed me through four years of suffering, toil and privation, often worse than death, to bid them a final, affectionate farewell." He vividly recalled the remark of a particular private, "a cadaverous, ragged, bare-footed man [who] grasped me by the hand, and, choking with sobs, said, 'Goodbye, General; God bless you; we will go home, make three more crops, and try them again.'"

The 4th Regiment, Grimes' first command so many years ago, was the first regiment in the brigade to stack its arms. After the men had finished the sad task, Grimes called them to "attention" one last time and had them file past so he could grasp the hands of each man. "With streaming eyes and faltering voice," recalled Major Osborne, he said, 'Go home, boys, and act like men, as you have always done during the war.'"[50]

## "Justice at Last"

After the formalities of the April 12th surrender ceremonies at Appomattox Court House were completed, citizen Bryan Grimes started home to Charlotte in Raleigh. He had not written or received a letter from her in almost two weeks, and it is doubtful whether he knew with any degree of certainty her living circumstances. His traveling party was composed of some close acquaintances, including Maj. W. L. London, an adjutant, his younger brother Pvt. Henry A. London, Grimes's courier, and Pvt. Thomas Devereux.

The travelers spent the first night at the house of an old Baptist preacher who gave them supper and breakfast, but charged them one hundred dollars each in Confederate money, which makes it difficult to determine who got the better end of the deal. "It looks like a big charge," explained the quasi-host, "but you men are going to prison anyway and won't need it." Henry London's horse was so frail and gaunt she could barely bear the weight of her rider. To compensate for the beast's worn condition, London and his companion, Jim Burke, used the "ride and tie" method of transportation. One man rode the horse for about one mile, dismounted and tied the horse to a bush or tree limb, and continued walking. The second man who was walking behind would eventually catch up to horse, ride her for a mile (thereby passing his walking companion), tie the horse up, and repeat the process. By this creative method the pair made their way home to North Carolina, coaxing what little stamina they could squeeze from the exhausted horse.[1]

Grimes' party continued on until it reached a country store, where about one hundred paroled and very hungry Confederates were attempting to extract from the tense storekeeper his good supply of peas. The owner of the vegetables refused to part with them. When Grimes arrived, the soldiers waited for him to take control of the situation. The storekeeper explained to Grimes that if he let them have the peas, his bond would be revoked. Grimes responded by offering to take responsibility and would provide a receipt, but the man still refused. Hungry and tired, Grimes bluntly informed the merchant that he was prepared to use force if necessary to take the peas, a threat which prompted the storekeeper to quickly consent to the arrangement. After devouring the rations, the men—many of them members of Grimes' old 4th Regiment—split apart and headed down whichever road led toward home.

Grim scenes abounded as the homeward-bound North Carolinians rode south. One event in particular must have made Grimes wonder what was in store for him as a defeated soldier without the means to fight back. According to Grimes' astute traveling companion, Thomas Devereux:

> A few miles from the forks of the road we came to an old man, Loftin Terrel, his house was on the roadside and he was knee deep in feathers where the bummers had ripped open the beds, a yearling and a mule colt were lying dead in the lot; they had been wantonly shot. Old man Terrel was sitting on his door step, he said there was not a thing left in the house and every bundle of fodder and grain of corn had been carried off; that he had been stripped of everything he owned and he had not a mouthful to eat. They had even killed his dog which was lying dead near the house.[2]

On Sunday April 16, 1865, Grimes rode into Raleigh atop his trustful horse Warren. Charlotte was "delighted to see him under any conditions," but recalled that, "he would reproach me for want of patriotism when I said so, he was so miserable over the surrender himself." Raleigh was a very different town from the one Grimes left four years earlier. The victorious Yankees seemed everywhere. To make matters worse, Union Maj. Gen. John Schofield had made his headquarters at William Grimes' home. As Charlotte explained it, "The Yankees would walk in and ask how many you had in the family, and if there were any vacant rooms [they] would take possession."

The end of the war found Grimes in difficult straits. He had no money, no income, and little prospects for improving his finances. "He did not have a cent in the world," explained Charlotte, "except for a few gold pieces he had carried all through the war." Fortunately, Grimes' brother William was in a position to assist the destitute couple. Two hundred dollars in gold was "quilted in a belt under my corsets," wrote Charlotte, hidden away from the

Yankees. Although the money belonged to William, he generously gave it to Bryan.[3]

Circumstances beyond Grimes' control added to his financial woes and made life for the former Confederate general unstable and dangerous. On April 15, 1865, at Ford's Theater in Washington D.C., President Abraham Lincoln was assassinated by John Wilkes Booth. As the news spread across the country, Raleigh's streets filled with people. "That afternoon [April 16th]," remembered Charlotte, "an officer came and warned every one to be careful how they behaved and said he would double the guard; (there was one guard for every two or three houses), [and] the soldiers were so infuriated at Lincoln's assassination that he feared they would murder the citizens and burn the town." As a former major general in the Confederate army residing in a state of sharply divided loyalties, Grimes reasonably feared that an angry mob would somehow hold him responsible for Lincoln's death and physically assault or lynch him. "Of course, there was no rest under those circumstances, and we passed a miserable night," explained Charlotte. As the hours passed, however, public anxiety ebbed and the window of potential violence against Grimes and other ex-Confederates closed.[4]

William Grimes, however, suffered an indignity within his own home when he was accosted by a Federal soldier:

> I was met in the passage by a gentleman who demanded my name, asking at the same time if it was Grimes, and placing his hands on my shoulders. I replied that my name was Grimes, [and] he then asked in a rude and authoritative tone what I had done, to which I replied I had done nothing. He then asked where I stood, or what was my opinion or position, or some question of a similar import. I replied that I did not acknowledge his authority to question me. He then drew a pistol and pointed it at me. I stepped to an adjoining door and called Col. Campbell. I think the pistol was put up before Col. Campbell walked in the door.

Colonel Campbell ordered the gentleman to desist and to conduct himself with propriety. Some further conversation then took place in which I remarked that I acknowledged the authority of Gen. Schofield and was under his protection and expressed surprise at such conduct under the circumstances and in my house.[5]

The next week Maj. Gen. William Sherman's troops marched through Raleigh on their way to Washington, D.C. Charlotte observed "bands playing, flags flying with new uniforms and their arms and accouterments burnished and glittering in the sunlight." The Federals garrisoning the city issued orders forbidding former Confederates from wearing their uniforms. For many this directive presented a difficult dilemma, for they had no other clothes to wear and no money to purchase new ones. Charlotte responded to the order by covering her husband's brass uniform buttons with bootblack, a ruse Grimes described made him look as though he was "in mourning for the Confederacy." Still, Grimes needed a new suit of clothes before he could safely return to his Grimesland plantation. The ever resourceful Charlotte, despite Grimes' protestations, sold several of her silk dresses for $100.00 and used the money to purchase his clothes. "It seemed to hurt him to have to use this money," explained Charlotte, "but I would take no denial."[6]

Once Grimes was properly outfitted, he left the state capital and rode ninety miles east to his plantation on his old warhorse, Warren. He did not leave a written record of his feelings as he rode the final miles home, but certainly the former warrior had not anticipated riding home to Grimesland in the wake of utter defeat.

After a few angst-filled days surveying his farm and its deteriorating condition, Grimes rowed across the Tar River and spent the day on a farm owned by his half-brother, John Gray Blount Grimes. When it was time to return home, Grimes discovered his boat was missing. Growing impatient, he stripped and swam the river, returning later for his clothes after he had located a boat on the far side. The cold water chilled him, and before long he came down with a severe cold and fever. "This imprudence," wrote Charlotte, "together with the grief of the surrender, gave him a severe spell of fever, which with chills, lasted all summer. Then he went to Warren County, where he stayed a week and returned much improved."[7]

Grimes dealt with his illness and the "grief of the surrender" amid constant rumors of pending retribution at the hands of the Yankee governors. "There was a report that they would hang all officers above the rank of captain and all their property would be confiscated," Charlotte recalled. "We were living in a 'Reign of Terror.'" They were also living with Charlotte's parents in Raleigh during the summer of 1865, with the former enemy visible everywhere. As the days passed Charlotte's anxiety mounted. "I could not bear to see my husband leave the house to go even as far as his brother's, a short distance off, and would stand at the window and watch until he went in the gate." Charlotte remembered "a Yankee camp just across the street from my father's front gate by which he [Grimes] would have to pass. . .I would see them watch him and hear them say, 'there goes the rebel, Gen. Grimes.'" Knowing that her husband possessed a quick temper and was mired in a melancholy attitude, she feared a violent confrontation with his former enemies. Thankfully, no such thing transpired.[8]

By the first fall after Appomattox, Grimes was ready to return home to Grimesland. Although Charlotte wanted to go with him, her parents convinced her to remain in Raleigh, largely because of her lingering poor health and developing pregnancy. After reaching the farm, Grimes traveled twenty miles south to New Bern, North Carolina. There, he met a former Yankee named C. W. Smith who wanted to lease the land and raise cotton. The offer, which amounted to $11,000, totaled more than he could earn in a year of hard work. Desperate for money, he swallowed his pride and rented the real estate. Perhaps distrusting paper money, Grimes demanded and received the sum in gold. Much to Charlotte's delight, he returned financially secure to Raleigh, where he bought "a large place on New Bern Avenue." Some of the money was used to purchase Charlotte a pair of gentle bay horses from the Yankees. Charlotte's mother, however, had wanted the animals since her horses had been taken by the Yankees. Grimes generously gave them to her, and Charlotte later wrote that her mother used them "a good many years."[9]

On October 19, 1865, Grimes took the Federal Oath of Amnesty, and eight months later on June 27, 1866, was pardoned by the U.S. government for his role on behalf of the Confederacy.[10] It is difficult to determine exactly what Grimes did during this period. In all probability he worked with his brother William, who owned property in Raleigh, and lived on the income from the rental of his plantation. Happily, Charlotte gave birth to a son, Alston, in February 1866. His arrival—their first child since the death of Bryan, Jr. in the fall of 1864—kept them busy during the year while they attempted to reorganize their new lives.[11]

When the lease to C. W. Smith expired in January 1867, Grimes decided to move to Grimesland. Unfortunately, the written record from this period is thin and little is known of his personal activities. Charlotte, who was pregnant again with John Bryan and had young Alston to care for, remained behind with her parents in Raleigh, where the climate was healthier and ready help was nearby. Shuttling between Charlotte and the farm, Grimes spent the next couple of years returning his plantation to the rich and productive estate it had been before the onset of the Civil War. There was much work to be done. The soil had to be readied for planting, buildings needed repair, farm laborers had to be found, and prices for crops negotiated. The separation was especially hard on Charlotte, who longed for her husband to visit the family. In September 1868 she wrote him at Grimesland that baby John Bryan had sprouted his first tooth, and discussed her fear "that he would get sick." She also reminded her husband to write her every day, and wondered when he would be able to visit her in Raleigh. The trip from Grimesland required a lengthy 40-mile buggy or horse ride to Kinston, North Carolina, and a train ride from that point to Raleigh.[12]

A richer supply of Grimes' personal papers detailing his activities from 1869 and beyond exist—perhaps because he had more time to write or perhaps for no other reason than they have survived. Unlike many veterans, his letters during this time do not mention the Civil War or his prominent role therein. Possibly his silence was a way of dealing with his experiences. If there was a constant theme or thread in these letters, it was his anxiety for his family's well-being and the loneliness he felt isolated within the confines of Grimesland. "While down here I am in a constant state of suspense about you and the children," Grimes penned in a June 1869 letter to Charlotte. "Last night the dogs began to bark fiercely at something and woke me up. My first impression was that you or the children were sick and I had been sent for. [I] could not be satisfied such was not the case until rising and calling to know who was at the gate." Although his worst fears were not realized, he observed that worrying about his family was making him "hopelessly nervous and old. I wish it was possible for me to be always near you, but your primary welfare has to be considered before I consult my own preferences and pleasures."[13]

Facing his post-war duty head-on, Grimes remained hard at work at Grimesland for the remainder of the 1869 planting season, cultivating his crops of cotton, corn, and peanuts. Just as he did during the Civil War, he urged Charlotte to write him daily. Much to his chagrin she was not always able to do so, for she had her hands full with two babies to care for. This hard work fed the good luck the family was enjoying. Although still lonesome, Grimes happily wrote home on November 9, 1869, about the recent birth of his daughter. "I wish you were all down here, and I would be much better satisfied for I am intolerably lonesome when in the house and stay indoors as little as possible." He added, "I do not feel like I am living unless your dear face is seen each day." The joy of their new daughter, who was "now fourteen days old," brightened his mood. "I hope the baby will be in every respect, both mental and physical, like you my dear darling." In closing, he wrote that he wished "it was considered healthy down here all the year."[14]

During this period Grimes attempted to allay his wife's fears that he was susceptible to physical injury or worse. "Why do you have unpleasant dreams about me?" he asked. "There is no danger of me fighting duels if I have the Moral Courage to decline. I have always thought it required more courage to refuse to fight than to do so." Grimes' words revealed a side of his personality not readily apparent before or during the Civil War. Charlotte, though, was as aware as anyone of her husband's hot temper and zeal for fighting, both of which had been repeatedly exhibited throughout the conflict. She also knew her husband was not the kind of man who would readily back down if challenged, and that he resided in a region thin on law enforcement but full of robbers, shiftless veterans, and despised carpetbaggers. Perhaps the four long years of bloodshed had drained him of the desire to fight with others, or possibly he resorted to a measured response in an effort to soothe Charlotte's anxiety. It remained to be seen whether his words were written with conviction.[15]

"I received from Dunn [probably an old college friend] a box of old papers and letters from my college days, and I sat up until after one o'clock reading them," wrote Grimes on November 17, 1869. The unexpected cache of papers and his response to them demonstrate just how far he had traveled down the road of maturation. "At some I laughed aloud and at some I was shocked to have testimony before me of what a wild, wicked boy I must have been in the days of my youth, and at some I blushed." Despite being amused and shocked he apparently believed he had not been too bad a youth, for he concluded, "I cannot believe I was any worse for having been wild in those days." Grimes had written poetry from a young age, and the papers contained examples of his efforts. "Among them were several attempts at rhyming," he penned with some self-deprecation. "I presume in those days I called it poetry." He described himself as "a greater nincompoop than I thought possible—I found letters to my father wherein I disclaimed against the practicality of the faculty for not giving me better reports than I received." Some of the more personal written documents, advised Grimes, "I have destroyed," while "others I have kept for your perusal and then they must be destroyed for if our boys in their youth were to get hold of them they might think they were privileged to do like wise."[16]

In a November 21, 1869 letter to Charlotte, he mentioned a legal proceeding that did not go as he wished:

> Jones adjourned court and refused to hear my case in chambers and is planning to spend his time with Smith at his plantation until the Edgecomb Court meets on December 1st. So by this injustice of officers I am [denied] not only my rights, but even of a hearing and there is no appeal or redress. Such is the consequence of Negro suffrage in placing incompetent and corrupt men in office.[17]

Unfortunately, little is known about this court proceeding. This brief passage is one of the few in existence that provide insight into the Reconstruction period in North Carolina from Grimes' perspective.

While earning a living and recouping the splendor that had once been Grimesland's was difficult, so too was living under the rule of Reconstruction and the arbitrary thumb of power wielded by provisional governor William W. Holden. The temporary government was established after the Civil War when Governor Zebulon B. Vance was forced from office and Holden appointed in his place. With the Federal government under the control of the Radical Republicans, a military-style occupation was imposed across what was formerly the Confederacy. North Carolina was in the Second Military District under the command of Maj. Gen. Daniel Sickles. "The military commanders," wrote Woodrow Wilson years later, "used or withheld their hand of power according to their several temperaments. They could deal with the provisional civil governments as they pleased—could remove officials, annul laws, regulate administration, at will."[18]

The situation was made worse in March 1867, when a pair of acts, followed by another four months later, were passed over President Andrew Johnson's vetoes. James A. Garfield boasted that the Reconstruction directives "put the bayonet at the breast of every rebel in the South." In addition, former Confederate leaders were disfranchised by the Fourteenth Amendment. The practical effect of these matters turned military commanders like General Sickles into absolute rulers. As a result, the years in North Carolina immediately following the close of the Civil War witnessed rampant corruption and waste, and a population torn apart by racial strife, bitterness, and distrust.[19]

Partially out of reaction to economic despair, the political chaos brought on by the radicalism of reconstruction—and certainly from a strong desire to preserve their way of life as it had existed before secession—many Southerners began searching for a way to turn back the clock and regain what they believed was theirs. Many feared that Reconstruction politics would bring with it permanent social upheaval and waves of crime from freed blacks against whites. Morals would decay as a result of black freedom, and their religious beliefs, largely based on the Old Testament, supported and prophesied an approaching doom. Few had faith in the administration of justice when the judicial appointees owed more to politics than legal qualifications. In short, the very pillars of their antebellum society had crumbled before new and more democratic timbers could be put in place. Such intense emotional reaction to Republican rule resulted in an unfortunate and emotional defensive response: the formation of the Ku Klux Klan.

The small town of Pulaski, Tennessee, was the cradle of the Klan in late 1865 or early 1866.[20] The movement grew slowly at first, but within a few years it had gathered regional support and was eventually led by famed Confederate general Nathan B. Forrest. In North Carolina, the prevailing attitudes about the destruction of the civilization of the South and the effects of reconstruction were similar to other Southern states and fostered the antecedent conditions that led to the formation of the Klan in the Old North State. It is not clear when the Klan first began in North Carolina, but a reasonable estimate is sometime in early or mid-1868. General Forrest visited the state in early 1868, which already boasted similar local organizations known as the "White Brotherhood" and the "Constitutional Union Guards." The term "Invisible Empire," was also used as a reference for the Klan and Klan activities in North Carolina. Local interest rose as the fall 1868 elections approached.[21]

The Presidential campaign of 1868 offered voters across the country a clear choice over the question of the restoration of all Southern states to the

Union. The Republicans nominated General Ulysses S. Grant, while the Democrats nominated Horatio Seymour. Sharp political differences helped the Klan, which hoped to influence the election and attract new members. For example, John C. Gorman, editor of the Raleigh *Telegram,* was later identified as an organizer of the White Brotherhood during the 1868 campaign. The aim at this time was to deter people from voting through the use of intimidation tactics, and therefore weaken the influence of the Republican party. Despite the Brotherhood's efforts, Grant and the Republicans easily carried the state. To some, the Klan represented an extension of the Confederacy, and thus as a political tool to rid the South of the "evils" of Reconstruction it naturally attracted former Confederate soldiers into its fold. Prominent former generals such as Forrest and John B. Gordon of Georgia were members. One of North Carolina's generals who may have played a role was Bryan Grimes.[22]

Many prominent citizens, including former Governor Zebulon Vance, joined the organization, and Grimes probably did as well. Some reports indicate that Vance was the head of the Klan in the state, but others identified that post as belonging to William L. Saunders, ex-Confederate colonel and associate editor of the Wilmington *Journal.* Interestingly, David Schenck, former brother-in-law of the deceased Dodson Ramseur and a prominent attorney, was also a member. Given the political climate in North Carolina, Grimes' prominence as a high-ranking ex-Confederate major general, and his religious and political beliefs, it should not be surprising that he joined the Klan. In fact, it would have been surprising had he not done so.

Still, Grimes' ties to the Klan are nebulous at best, as are any activities he may have engaged in. He never mentioned the organization in any of his letters, and neither did Charlotte. The only record in existence today linking the general to the Klan is a letter written in 1922 to the Raleigh *News and Observer* by J. J. Laughinghouse, a former head of the Klan in Pitt County, North Carolina. Penned more than a half-century after the events it purports to describe, Laughinghouse identified Grimes as a member of the "honorary advisory committee" of the local Klan, although he was not mentioned as being one of the five men who first approached Laughinghouse in January 1869 about forming a Pitt County branch.[23] Other than advising various individuals who had been issued warrants to plead their cases as a group, the "advisory committee"—and the Klan as a whole in Pitt County—does not appear to have been particularly active.[24]

Insight into how other men similarly situated as Grimes reacted to the Klan can be gleaned by examining the writings of David Schenck, a strong Confederate supporter and attorney. Schenck joined the "Invisible Empire," according to his diary, in October 1868.[25] His reasons for joining appear to be the same as many others: a desire to deny Republican rule and continue antebellum society; a perceived dread of moral decay by blacks following their freedom; and an exaggerated fear of crimes by blacks against whites. Schenck, however, left the Klan in February of 1870 when it was taken over by immoral men who instituted a series of violent acts. "Nine-tenths of the respectable men who had ever had any connection with it left it," he recorded in his diary.[26] Speaking of the Klan in later years, Schenck observed "that men of violent character reorganized it and it was not the original society. It degenerated into a band of robbers, rioters and lynch-law men who deserve the severest punishment. I think it has been very grossly perverted to improper purposes."[27]

In the spring of 1870, ex-Governor Thomas Bragg wrote to some of the prominent men who were in the Klan, including Schenck, urging them to take steps to disband the organization. Schenck replied that he was doing what he could behind the scenes with some success, but "that he was afraid to come out publicly and denounce the Klan as he feared that the lawless men then in control would take personal vengeance on him."[28] By the end of 1870 Klan activities had largely disappeared from North Carolina, and when the Democrats gained control of the legislature in 1871, it largely died. Although we have no way of knowing, it is reasonable to assume that if Grimes had indeed belonged to the Klan, he would have followed Schenck's path and "left it."

The effect of these harsh and turbulent politics on the Grimes family is unknown, although it must have irked the general to no end to see his old enemy, W. W. Holden, elected in 1868 as the state's new civil governor. Although there are no comments attributed to Grimes on this subject, he must have been pleased when Holden was impeached and removed from office in March 1871. Eschewing a public role in political matters, Grimes worked behind the scenes as a member of the Conservative Democratic Party. In 1872, his old nemesis Tom Settle, a vocal peace advocate during the war, emerged as a leading candidate for governor for the Republican Party. However, Settle eventually lost the nomination to Tod R. Caldwell. Like old times, however, Grimes' former military foe, U. S. Grant, carried Grimes' home county of Pitt in the 1872, as well as the national presidential election over Democratic candidate Horace Greeley. Grimes' thoughts on all these important events, unfortunately, are unknown. Throughout these years he spent most of his waking hours working hard to rebuild Grimesland into the productive farm it once was.[29]

"I am getting very tired of being separated from you," complained Charlotte to her husband in August of 1870. "I like being up country and seeing everybody very much, but that doesn't compensate for the separation from you my dearest, precious husband." The hardship of lengthy separations and moving herself and the children twice a year between Raleigh and Grimesland was hard on the family. Despite the separation from his family Grimes remained in the role of provider. The long familial separation finally ended in late 1870 when Charlotte and the children moved to the plantation. Her health must have been excellent, for she was expecting their fourth child. Mary Bryan was born February 15, 1871, the first of six children to be born at Grimesland.[30]

Despite his efforts to put the Civil War behind him, people and events regularly materialized to remind him of those painful years. In 1873 Grimes received a letter from Ellen Ramseur, wife of the late Stephen Dodson Ramseur, who had been mortally wounded at Cedar Creek in the fall of 1864. The correspondence contained a picture of Ramseur's daughter, who was born just days before her father was killed. "I often think of the winter [1863] we passed under the same roof in Virginia. The quiet, happy life Mrs. Grimes and myself led, " reminisced Ellen. "I regress to those days with the saddest pleasure. Please present my kindest remembrances of love to Mrs. Grimes." Grimes of course responded at once, thanking her for:

> . . . including the photograph of your little daughter which I shall prize very highly. I see a very marked, strong resemblance to her father and also to you. How vividly your letter recalls a sad reminiscence of the past in connection with the announcement of your daughter's birth to her father. Tears of sympathy for you filled his eyes upon speaking of you. I remember so well his saying he thought it a boy. That evening's mail brought me a letter from Raleigh announcing the birth of a son, whereupon I went again to tell my glad

Grimesland, the ancestral home of Bryan Grimes. This postwar image includes Grimes (seated), Charlotte (right), and several of their children. Bettie, for whom no known picture has been found, may be seated on the left. *NC Division of Archives and History.*

tidings, and we sat around the roots of an old oak, speaking of our wives, our babies and the future. This was our last interview.

Your husband was a noble expression of God's handiwork—honest and gentle.[31]

The months and years continued to pass for the family at Grimesland. In November 1875, Bettie, to whom Grimes had written so often during the war and who was now a young woman of twenty-two, was married. The proud father gave the bride away in what was described as a "brilliant" wedding at Christ Church in Raleigh. This was the same Episcopal church where Grimes and Charlotte had married in 1863. Bettie, now a college graduate from Saint Mary's, married Samuel Fox Mordecai, an attorney who became the first Dean at Trinity College (now Duke University School of Law).[32]

In 1875, the University of North Carolina undertook a serious effort to restore itself as an academic institution following the setbacks suffered during and after the Civil War. Its greatest need was for money to buy books and pay faculty. According to the minutes of a meeting of the Board of Trustees, the University had a library of about eight thousand volumes, and had begun to appoint faculty at a salary of $1,500 per year. The need for financial assistance was substantial, and the Trustees approved an ambitious plan to raise funds through private donations. Among the very first to respond were William and Bryan Grimes. According to the Trustee's minutes from July 1875, William donated $500, and Bryan $250, both sums pledged over five years in equal installments. These individual pledges were substantially larger than most of the other donations registered in the minutes. Only three individuals offered $1,000, and most offerings were between $50 and $100. The university's drive to raise funds was successful by any measure, and raised over $20,000 over the next five years.[33]

The past continued to tug on Grimes' coat sleeves. In February 1880, the Philanthropic Society at the University of North Carolina, Chapel Hill, requested that he commission a portrait of himself to hang in the hall of their society on campus.[34] Fond memories of his time spent as a member debating with his long-dead friend Johnston Pettigrew flashed past, and he replied that he would have it done as "soon as the services of a competent artist can be found. "Congratulations," he added, "upon the revival of the society."[35] Recalling the fine work artist Garl Browne had performed for him in 1867,

Grimes asked him to make a copy the original. Browne agreed, and by May 18,1880, the price was set at $200. The original painting was sent to Browne in Wilmington, North Carolina, and by August 7, 1880, Browne wrote that "The picture is finished and ready for shipment."[36]   On August 12, Grimes wrote to instruct the artist to put the portrait in a frame and send it to the Society at Chapel Hill. In what was probably the last letter he ever wrote,   Grimes asked Browne to write on the back

Theodora Bryan Grimes, Bryan's and Charlotte's last child, was born in May 1880. She was named after Charlotte's brother, Theodore. *NC Division of Archives and History.*

of the canvas: "Bryan Grimes—Maj Gen, Provisional Army of the Confederate States." It was a fitting epitaph.[37]

Grime rose early on what would be a hot and humid Saturday, August 14, 1880. He planned to ride over to Washington, a small town about eight miles away, to conduct some business, part of which included the posting of his letter to artist Browne. "Don't get up," he whispered to a sleepy Charlotte, who had been awake much of the night with their new baby Theodora, who had been born on May 23, 1880. "Turn over and take a good nap."

Junius Daniel Grimes, born in May 1878, was named after Brig. Gen. Junius Daniel, who was mortally wounded at Spotsylvania. *NC Division of Archives and History.*

Charlotte had her hands full, for a son, Junius Daniel Grimes (after the deceased Confederate general of the same name), had been born in October 1878.[38] Charlotte, however, rose with him and after Grimes dressed for town the pair ate breakfast together. After inquiring whether she needed anything from Washington, he kissed her goodbye and headed for his buggy. He looked "sweet and well," remembered Charlotte, and as usual all the children except the baby followed him to the gate. Charlotte remembered that their Governess, Lou Gilliam, turned from the window and remarked: "I never saw anyone like General Grimes; he is so indulgent to his children." My husband, wrote Charlotte, "had the most smoothing touch of anyone I ever knew. I have seen him take the children and quiet them when no one else could. He was very fond and proud of his children." Often he would "stand them up in a row, the eldest one at the back, coming down in gradation to the youngest, saying, 'look, mother, did anyone ever have a finer lot of children.'" Grimes climbed into his buggy and waved a warm farewell to his family, snapped the reins, and rode away. It was the last time Charlotte and the children would see him alive.[39]

Grimes wrapped up his business in Washington late that afternoon and stowed some purchases in his buggy in preparation for his trip home. Tom Satterthwaite, a fellow Confederate veteran, arranged with Grimes to take his 14-year-old son Bryan to his uncle's (Joseph B. Stickney) home near the Grimesland plantation. By 6:00 p.m. the major general and the boy were on their way, bumping along the narrow road to Bear Creek.

About 7:00 p.m., Grimes stopped the buggy at Bear Creek to allow the horses to drink from the stream.[40] Without warning a shotgun exploded from a copse of trees nearby and large buckshot ripped into the buggy—and into Grimes. "Are you hurt?" stammered the shocked young passenger, to which Grimes replied, "Yes, it will kill me." Within a few seconds the general who had passed virtually unscathed through some of the most desperately fought battles of the Civil War slumped unconscious on the floorboard of his buggy, the victim of an assassin's bullet.[41]

With great presence of mind, the boy grabbed the buggy's reins and urged the horses forward, racing the team through the lengthening shadows to his uncle's home. By the light of a lantern Joe Stickney could easily see that the general was dead. The sorrowful Stickney climbed aboard the buggy to drive Grimes' corpse home.

Stickney brought the carriage to a halt in front of the majestic white home and knocked on the huge front door for Charlotte, urging her to come quickly. When she appeared, he broke the news: her husband had been killed. Charlotte reacted bravely and with simple dignity. "Don't tell the children just now," she whispered. As the tragic news of the general's death spread through the surrounding countryside, friends and neighbors rode to Grimesland to be with the family and express their condolences. A doctor was summoned to examine the body around 10:30 p.m. A single buckshot had traveled through Grimes' left biceps, through his body, and into his heart, inflicting the fatal wound.[42]

The funeral was held at the Episcopal church at Grimesland two days later on Monday, August 16. Behind Grimes' hearse clumped his 26-year-old horse Warren bearing Grimes' military saddle and old gray army coat. The horse who had carried his owner to safety across so many battlefields, was following his master home. Grimes was laid to rest in a simple ceremony in the family burial grounds about three hundred yards from the main house.[43]

A group of men led by Joseph John Laughinghouse, a former Confederate officer who had served under Grimes, was determined to bring the murderer to justice. At the scene of the assassination at Bear Creek they found a small footprint (about size seven), in the mud on a path that had been cleared by an axe for the killer to make a quick escape. There was now little doubt in anyone's mind that Grimes was the victim of a premeditated murder by someone who knew the general would be returning that way late Saturday evening. And Laughinghouse thought he knew who it was: Howell Paramore and his brother W. B. Paramore.[44]

The pair ran a general store at Nelson's Crossroads near Grimesland. The tall and slender Howell reminded some of a river boat gambler. Laughinghouse suspected him because Howell had "quarreled bitterly with Grimes over where a property line lay between their lands." A mysterious fire burned a mill house at Grimesland following the dispute, and livestock died after drinking water from a plantation well that Grimes suspected had been poisoned. According to a newspaper account, Grimes had been gathering evidence in order to accuse and prosecute Howell for perjury involving his previous testimony in a bankruptcy case about to be heard in Federal Court in New Bern, North Carolina. The tension between the two men was so great that Grimes had hired a man to watch his house at night. Three days after Grimes was laid to rest, the Tarboro *Southerner* ran a story in its August 19 edition speculating: "Some say Gen. Grimes and Mr. J. Laughinghouse were witnesses implicating a rather prominent citizen of Pitt [county] in the crimes of arson and well-poisoning alleged against him and this may account for the bloody deed."[45]

There was one problem with this theory, however: the footprint found at the scene was too small to have been made by Howell Paramore. That fact alone might have been enough to exculpate Howell. The Paramores, however, fled Pitt County the next day, which increased speculation regarding their involvement in the killing. Weeks passed without an arrest, although there was plenty of theorizing about who might fit the description of a "small man with a shotgun, seen in the Bear Creek area." A break in the case occurred on Sunday, September 19, when a former Washington policeman named M. J. Fowler questioned Dick Chapman concerning what he knew about the crime. Chapman, a young black man who lived in the area, apparently provided Fowler with a slew of potentially useful information. Fowler responded by placing him in the Washington jail for protection as a material witness.[46]

The next day William Parker was arrested for the murder of Bryan Grimes. Parker was the 23-year-old son of Jesse Parker, whose land was near the Grimesland planation. The suspect was described in the Raleigh *News and Observer* as a "sorry kind of fellow, with no particular occupation and with a reputed bad character." Chapman's testimony was bolstered by the fact that Parker stood 5'5" tall, had small feet, and walked fan-footed—a match for the footprint found in the mud near the creek. While no one could recall any bad feelings between the two families, circumstantial evidence against Parker continued to mount. One resident of the area named Oscar Griffin claimed he had seen Parker near Bear Creek on the afternoon of August 14, while another, Ed Dixon, asserted that Parker owned a shotgun. Others came forward and recalled that Parker, who had no steady job, often hung around the Paramore's store and drank whiskey.[47]

The key to solving the murder mystery rested with the testimony of Dick Chapman. Fowler, who had pretended to be a friend of the Paramores when he interviewed Chapman, testified that the witness told him the following story:

> Parker and himself were in the woods together dipping turpentine on the Saturday evening of the murder, and that Parker told him that he was going down about Bear Creek to kill Gen. Grimes. That he shot a load out of his gun that he said was a squirrel load and then loaded his gun with buck shot and left the woods about 3 o'clock, telling me to continue to work until sunset. The next day I heard at Evonstein's store that Gen. Grimes was killed, and I knew from what Parker told me that it was Parker who had killed him. The evening of the same day I saw Parker and he told me that he had killed Gen. Grimes and that he was afraid that he would be suspicioned of it. If he was, he wanted me to swear that we were together in the woods on the day of the murder until sunset, and that we went to Sam Dixon's house and stayed all night. That Dixon and his wife were going to swear that he was at their house from sunset until the next morning.[48]

Parker's arrest prompted his father to hire a bevy of lawyers, which supposedly forced him to mortgage his farm to pay the legal fees. The lead defense council was James Evans Shepherd, a prominent and powerful attorney from Washington, North Carolina. Two other prestigious attorneys, Senator Charles F. Warren from Beaufort County, and I. A. Sugg of Greenville, North Carolina, were also retained. Parker was visited on a pair of occasions by Shepherd, and prosecuting attorney George Sparrow interviewed witness Chapman in the presence of Sheriff Dixon. Fowler reported later that Sparrow told him Chapman "had been tampered with, that he refused to talk to him, saying that his lawyer told him to keep his mouth shut and not talk to anyone."[49]

Chapman was brought before Justice William P. Campbell on September 25, 1880, for a preliminary hearing on the matter. The defendant denied having said anything to Fowler about the murder, and claimed he knew nothing about the shooting. When Sparrow asked him if he had been told to keep his mouth shut, he replied "yes sir." Sparrow asked him who had instructed him to remain silent. Chapman's reply stunned the courtroom: "that man there advised me to do it," he testified, pointing at Parker's attorney James Shepherd. Ostensibly outraged by the accusation, Shepherd claimed he had given such advice only to his client, William Parker. Chapman, explained Shepherd, had been sitting in an adjacent cell and must have been confused. Unable or unwilling to testify, Chapman was released from custody.[50]

The trial itself opened on December 7, 1880, before Judge David Schenck in the county courthouse in Washington, North Carolina.[51] George Sparrow represented Beaufort County and was assisted by four special prosecutors: D. C. Fowler, L. C. Latham, G. H. Brown and Thomas Sparrow. Parker's defense team was led by chief counsel James E. Shepherd, who was in turn assisted by Senator Charles F. Warren and I. A. Sugg.[52]

Without Chapman's testimony, the trial centered on 14-year-old Bryan Satterthwaite, who had accompanied the general on that fateful evening. Although his testimony was repeatedly interrupted with objections from the defense, no official transcript of his statements or the trial have been found. Newspaper accounts and other notes taken there, however, demonstrate that the defense vigorously cross-examined the boy. Although Satterthwaite testified that Parker shot Grimes, Shepherd challenged his testimony at every turn. Sparrow rested the state's case on December 9.[53]

Parker's defense opened with attorney Sugg calling the witnesses. The court adjourned until Friday, December 10. The defense had hardly begun that morning when Juror Asa Pinkham notified the court that he was sick and in pain, forcing Judge Schenck to take a recess. A doctor examined Pinkham and determined he was suffering from "extreme nervous prostration," and was too ill to continue as a juror. The judge declared a mistrial and ordered the case continued with a new trial date.[54]

Judge Schenck wrote his views of the proceedings in a diary he kept during this period. Inside the journal was pasted a newspaper description of Parker, which he noted was an accurate representation of the defendant. Parker, read the account,

> chewed tobacco during the entire proceedings. He is a troublesome man, particularly when in liquor. Parker is a poor man, but since the murder it is said he has boasted of having 'plenty of money.' Now he also has a horse and a new set of clothes.[55]

On the second day of the trial, December 8, Schenck privately recorded his views of the defendant in his diary:

> [Parker] is one well fitted to a deed of darkness. The almost unlimited challenge allowed a defendant has enabled the counsel to get a jury who has no intelligence and one much [affected] by political propaganda. Much political feeling is [evident] by this case as well as the jealousy of caste. General Grimes was a wealthy gentleman and the prisoner is from the laboring class and poor. Gen Grimes was a stalwart Democrat. The prisoner and his family are Republicans and their party is using the most [extreme] exhortations on his behalf. The testimony yesterday is very strong against the prisoner.
>
> George Brown [prosecutor] said of the jury: 'There is not a clean shirt among them.'
>
> The witnesses for the defense are arrogant, generally ragged and seem to have no particular regard for truth or propriety. There is a conflict between castes and the lower caste is in the jury box. There may be honesty enough under rugged exteriors to vindicate justice, but I doubt it. I am fast losing faith in Republics and the people.[56]

After he had declared a mistrial, Schenck penned in his diary: "My opinion from the testimony is that William Parker is certainly the assassin of Bryan Grimes. The confession to young Keele was conclusive to my mind."

Schenck's reference is to John Keele, a witness who had testified that while in jail Parker confessed to him that he shot General Grimes.[57] Judge Schenck's pronouncement of a mistrial almost certainly avoided an acquittal of Parker. The prosecution was aware of the jury's character and disposition and motioned on December 11 to have the second trial moved from Beaufort to Martin County. The defense opposed the change of venue, arguing that the poverty of the prisoner would make removal burdensome and unfair for his many witnesses. Judge Schenck, however, granted the state's motion and the trial was moved to Martin County. The move was not well received by Grimes' acquaintances, largely because Martin County had not been a strong supporter of the Confederacy. The jury pool, they concluded, would not likely be sympathetic toward a high ranking Confederate general.[58]

Parker's second trial began on June 15, 1881, in Williamston, North Carolina (Martin County) with Judge John A. Gilmer presiding. The prosecution was represented by C. W. Grandy and Thomas and George Sparrow, while the defense, in addition to Shepherd, had added three additional attorneys: J. E. Moore, J. J. Martin and William B. Morton. Moore was a particularly prominent and skilled local litigator. Like the first trial, no formal transcript was recorded. Newspaper accounts, however, recount a torrid effort by Parker's defense lawyers to tear apart the testimony of young Satterthwaite. In spite of the assaults, Satterthwaite remained steadfast in his claim that Parker shot Grimes. The defense challenged this assertion by reminding both the witness and the jury that the young boy was sitting on General Grimes' right side when the assassin fired, and that the shot had come from deep in the woods on Grimes' left. How could he have seen through the general's body, much less get a clear look at the assassin? It was a telling cross-examination of the prosecution's primary witness. The State presented its evidence and witnesses for six days and then rested.[59]

When it was the defense's turn, Attorney Shepherd startled the courtroom by announcing that Parker would not offer any evidence. The implication Shepherd wanted jurors to draw from the daring and unusual tactic was that the State had not carried its burden of proof—and thus no evidence was necessary to rebut what they had presented. After final statements to the jury, deliberations began on June 21 at 2:00 p.m. Within five hours the jury returned with a verdict of "not guilty." Judge Gilmer turned to Parker and admonished, "never allow your conduct to be questioned again," and then dismissed him. Although Parker had been found innocent of the heinous crime, the final chapter in the saga had yet to be written.[60]

Parker walked away from the Martin County courthouse a free man, but many of those connected with the pair of trials continued to be embroiled in controversy. Howell Paramore, who many thought hired Parker to murder Grimes, traveled to South Carolina in May 1881 and was found in a hotel room with his throat slit. His death was ruled a suicide. Howell's brother, W. B. was rumored to have been arrested in a Southern state for poisoning a well, and thereafter disappears from the historical record.[61]

In 1882, Parker's attorney James Shepherd ran for superior court judge. Many of Grimes' supporters never forgave Shepherd for what they believed was tampering with a witness. J. J. Laughinghouse bought an advertisement in the *Raleigh Farmer and Mechanic* in which he accused Shepherd in no uncertain terms of tampering with Dick Chapman and attempting to swing public opinion in support of Parker in Martin County before the trial. Despite these serious allegations, Shepherd was elected. Six years later Laughinghouse and Shepherd clashed again when Shepherd was nominated in May 1888 at the state Democratic convention to fill a vacancy on the State Supreme Court. Laughinghouse attempted a second time to mobilize opposition by attacking Shepherd's veracity in the Hickory, North Carolina *Press and Carolinian*.[62]

Among those offering evidence in the paper was Policeman M. J. Fowler, who repeated his statement that the main witness (Dick Chapman), told him that Parker had shot Grimes and that Shepherd had told him to keep quiet. New allegations came from G. W. Dixon, the Beaufort County sheriff, who claimed that Parker was kept in a downstairs cell while Chapman was kept in an upstairs block (instead of adjacent cells, as Shepherd had stated). The two men were not "upon the same floor at any time," added Dixon. Shepherd, continued the sheriff, had the keys to the jail for a few days following his client's arrest, and thus access to both men. In the same edition of the newspaper, an attorney named Walter S. Dickinson offered a damning indictment against Shepherd. "This is to certify," wrote Dickinson, that:

> about two weeks before the trial of William Parker for the murder of Gen Bryan Grimes at Martin Superior Court that J. E. Shepherd asked me if I

could not go over to Martin County a few days before the Court and create what feeling I could in behalf of Parker among the poor and ignorant classes.

I replied that I did not know how to do it. Mr. Shepherd said, 'why, simply tell them that Parker was an innocent man and that this was a rich man's fight against a poor man's life. Tell them that William Grimes will be down here with $25,000 to buy a verdict against an innocent man.'

I heard Shepherd make this statement several times in the presence of Parker's witnesses.

Just after the suicide of Howell Paramore, Parker told me that he was afraid that Shepherd would go back upon him as Paramore had all the money. That Paramore had already paid Mr. Shepherd over $700 to defend him. It was at this time that Parker made a full confession to me of the murder.[63]

One of the writers opposing Shepherd in the newspaper was the general's son, 20-year-old John Bryan Grimes. John Bryan, who would later become secretary of state for North Carolina, raised some important questions as to Shepherd's ethics and tactics:

Judge Shepherd may have been as he stated, employed by the parents of Parker to defend him, but the father (Jesse Parker) had no money and a mortgage given Judge Shepherd on his land was never foreclosed so where did the attorneys get their pay?

Why did Howell Paramore, who employed the murderer to commit the deed, pay Judge [then defense attorney] Shepherd a day or so after the arrest $150 by a check on the National Park Bank of New York and cashed by W. B. Morton of Washington?[64]

Shepherd responded to these written charges in the same edition by soliciting opinions from attorneys who helped him in the defense or were involved in the trial, along with remarks from both trial judges. David Schenck, the judge in the first trial at Washington (which ended in a mistrial) held that Shepherd's "conduct as a lawyer was unexceptionable." Judge John A. Gilmer, the trial judge in the second hearing in Martin County, wrote that Shepherd's conduct during the trial was proper. Defense attorneys Moore, Morton, and Martin all wrote to say that Shepherd had conducted himself with honor and integrity. Even an attorney for the prosecution, L. C. Latham, wrote: "I know of no unprofessional conduct on your part in the Parker trial, nor do I believe you were guilty of any." George A. Sparrow, the State's Solicitor, said much the same thing when he wrote: "I am confident that nothing was done by Judge Shepherd as counsel for the defense which was inconsistent with an honorable lawyer discharging his duty to his client."[65]

What is to be made of these allegations and rebuttals? It is interesting to note that Shepherd's colleagues do not specifically address Shepherd's *unaccompanied* visits to the jail, nor do they directly challenge the several accounts in existence regarding Shepherd's jailhouse admonition to Chapman that he keep his mouth shut. Instead, the statements carefully describe Shepherd's professional conduct in vague terms or specifically during the trial. Yet, Sheriff Dixon clearly testified that Shepherd went to the jail alone (although why he had keys remains unexplained), and none of the statements offered on Shepherd's behalf have any bearing on what the attorney said to Parker or Chapman during his confirmed visits there. As young John Bryan Grimes astutely pointed out, all the other defense attorneys joined the case days *after* Shepherd had been to the jail. A careful reading shows that most of them said they knew of no improper conduct on his part during the trial, thereby shrewdly avoiding the issue of his behavior before the formal proceedings began. It appears as though the legal establishment of eastern North Carolina was rallying to the defense of one of its own. Certainly James Shepherd's career was not impacted by these tawdry events, for he was later elected to the state Supreme Court in the fall of 1888.[66]

William Parker's acquittal and the unseemly events that followed should have closed the issue. Parker's own character prevailed in the end, however, and sealed his fate. In November 1888, eight years after the assassination, William Parker returned to Washington, North Carolina. It was a Saturday night and Parker wanted to drink whiskey. The alcohol soon loosened his tongue, and before long he was boasting to anyone who would listen that he had indeed murdered General Grimes and that Howell Paramore had hired him to do it to keep Grimes from testifying against him for arson and poisoning a well. With an audience of locals gathered around him, Parker laughingly reminded them that a jury had acquitted him and therefore he could not be retried.

By 7:00 p.m. the boisterous Parker was arrested by a local policeman for drunkenness and disorder and placed in the town jail. Early the next morning around 2:00 a.m., about one dozen masked men overpowered the jailer, placed him in an empty cell, and broke down the cell door holding

Parker. As they carried him out into the street, Parker screamed "murder!" several times before a gag was stuffed in his mouth. An hour later his corpse was discovered by the bridge keeper who had come to open the draw for the passing steamer *Beta*. The sheriff was summoned to the scene, as was the coroner, Arthur Mayo. A large crowd gathered about early that Sunday morning to see the body. Ironically, Parker was swinging from a rope attached to a bridge once owned by Bryan Grimes and used as a toll structure for crossing the Pamlico River near Washington. Someone had placed a placard just above Parker's head with the fitting three-word epitaph: "Justice at Last." A jury seated for the inquest ruled that "the deceased, William Parker, came to his death by hanging at the hands of persons unknown to the jury."[67]

The identify of the vigilantes was never determined. "We very much regret this circumstance and that the fair name of our town has been stained by such a lawless act," the Washington *Progress* editorialized, "but one hears on every side the expression—that this is but the beginning of the end, and that the day is fast approaching when shrewd lawyers and packed juries will be powerless to prevent the punishment of crime in Eastern North Carolina."[68]

Most of the citizens of Beaufort and Pitt Counties were content to drop the matter and move on, believing that at last, the murder of Maj. Gen. Bryan Grimes had been avenged.

Greek philosopher Heraclitus believed that character was destiny. Perhaps Bryan Grimes, who as a young college student read the ancients in their original language, believed it as well.

When Southern society—his way of life as he knew it—was threatened, citizen Grimes quickly pledged his word, honor, and life to defend it. To him, the values handed down through generations of planters and grounded in their interpretation of the teachings of the Old Testament were superior to the secular morals practiced by Northerners. Christianity and the Confederacy were inseparable in his mind. His strength of character, reflected through the prism of battle, admirably revealed itself through impressive courage on most of the war's Eastern battlefields from Seven Pines through Appomattox. And from his character evolved his destiny. When minie balls swarmed like bees and shrapnel and canister tore up the earth and killed horses under him, the only thing that wavered was his sword as he drove his men forward. Grimes was a soldier's soldier. For him, there was no turning back once the battle was joined.

Despite his stellar war record and copious writings, Bryan Grimes has not enjoyed a biography until now. Although he was the last man appointed by Robert E. Lee to hold the rank of major general, Grimes spent the bulk of the war fighting as a colonel. This may be part of the reason why no one has taken the effort to record his remarkable life. His final promotion—like his elevation to the rank of brigadier general in 1864—occurred in the war's final months, and he had little opportunity to exercise the responsibility that came with the position. Still, Grimes was an important figure in the Civil War. Admittedly he did not have the impact of a Lee or Thomas Jackson—or even a John B. Hood or Robert Rodes—but his influence was profound and his achievements deserve recognition. His North Carolina contemporaries Johnston Pettigrew, Dorsey Pender, and Dodson Ramseur have all been the subject of books that have justly elevated them to their proper place in the history of the Civil War. Yet, Grimes fought in more battles than any of them, led the last charge of the Army of Northern Virginia, and survived the war. Dead generals often provide fascinating subjects to write about, and Pettigrew, Pender, and Ramseur all fell on the field of battle. Grimes' career, meanwhile, has floundered in undeserved obscurity. While still in uniform, he once wrote that, at some future time, historians would reveal how the Confederate soldier—including himself, although he was too modest to say it—had fought bravely against long odds, and their record was one of distinction. For over one hundred and thirty years he has waited for his record to be written for everyone to read and understand what he meant.

Few physical images remain of Grimes. Other than a scant handful of photographs, only one painting captured his likeness. The original is owned by a great grandson, Robert Grimes. Three copies from this painting were produced. The first, which was the basis for his last letter, now hangs in the same hall where he debated as a student at the University of North Carolina. The second was unveiled in 1899 and hung for a time in the North Carolina room in the White House of the Confederacy, although it is now in storage at The Museum of the Confederacy. The last copy of the original can be found at East Carolina University, where it has been recently restored through private donations. Thus, his image is not widely available to the general public. Given the modest man he was, Grimes would probably prefer it this way, and simply let his written record speak for itself.

One of the first modern historians who appreciated Grimes' record was Douglas Southall Freeman, the preeminent scholar of the Army of Northern Virginia. According to Freeman, Bryan Grimes was "a man lacking in no soldierly characteristics."[1] This is an extraordinary statement when one considers that Grimes was not trained as a soldier. In stark contrast to so many civilians who wore the wreath and stars, Grimes was an effective leader and an outstanding officer whose conduct in battle proved indeed that "character was destiny." Too often, his civilian counterparts were politicians seeking votes through false glory and little else. Grimes was one of the outstanding exceptions in the Confederate officer corps. His steady string of promotions from major to major general were based solely on his battlefield accomplishments and his strenuous efforts to always see that his men were well cared for.

In his baptism of fire at Seven Pines in May 1862, Grimes' horse was killed under him—the first of six. While pinned under the animal, he raised his sword and yelled "Forward!" His 4th North Carolina Regiment bravely responded and suffered horrendous casualties—thereby earning its lasting sobriquet "Bloody Fourth." Of the twenty nine officers in the regiment, twenty four were either killed or wounded in the bloody attack. Grimes escaped serious injury. One of his officers later claimed Grimes lived a "charmed life." Given his propensity to lead from the front on horseback, his survival—through three years of combat—does indeed seem miraculous. The new lieutenant colonel had displayed sustained courage under fire and capable leadership qualities that marked him for higher command. Lieutenant General Daniel Harvey Hill, a fellow North Carolinian, thought as much as well. "Grimes showed in this, his first serious battle," remembered Hill, "those instinctive qualities of soldiership that led to his promotion through successive grades to major-general."

Grimes' natural inclination to attack did not mean that he was brave to the point of being foolhardy, or aggressive to the point of rashness. One of his officers vividly recalled how he often saw the North Carolinian calmly sitting on his iron-gray horse, one leg hooked over the saddle bow, studying the battle and contemplating his next move. Like all good officers, Grimes developed a feel for the ebb and flow of combat. On field after field he exhibited sound tactical maneuvers, appreciated the necessity of secure flanks against enfilading fire, and knew when it was time to withdraw his men so that they could live to fight another day. Field command came naturally to him despite his lack of formal military training. He handled his brigade as effortlessly as he had his regiment. In the vicious close-quarter Petersburg fighting and during retreat to Appomattox, Grimes directed his division with steadiness and intelligence.

At Appomattox he did what he had never done before in his military career—he refused to immediately obey an order because he believed it was issued in ignorance. When informed of the surrender of the army he wanted to continue fighting—one officer remembered he resembled a "caged lion"—but changed his mind when he realized it would be dishonorable to escape under a flag of truce and thereby discredit General Lee. Years later North Carolina erected a monument to the final campaign inscribed with the words, "Last at Appomattox." The terse statement signified North Carolina's proud heritage in the war and Grimes' role in it. One of his brigades, after all, fired the Army of Northern Virginia's final volley. He was a fighter to the end—he once commented that a good fight made him feel twenty years younger—and his entire life is a statement of that spirit and character.

Indeed, the dominant theme throughout Grimes' life, the cornerstone of his character, was his devotion to duty. From this devotion sprang his firm stance on matters of discipline. To Grimes, orders were orders and they had to be obeyed. As an officer he unfailingly led by example. His heroic charges at Seven Pines, Chancellorsville, and Spotsylvania are well documented. At South Mountain, although unable to walk, he had his men mount him on his horse so that he could fight. Unable to ride his horse during the opening phase of the Gettysburg Campaign and unwilling to miss the action, Grime rode an ambulance into Pennsylvania. It was his duty to go the extra mile to fight for Confederate independence, and it was everyone else's duty to do likewise. Understood in this light, it is easier to appreciate why he had no patience for those who shirked their duty and had nothing but disdain for cowards. At Chancellorsville he demonstrated his contempt for malingerers when he climbed over the back of one officer who refused to go forward and purposely ground the man's face in the dirt.

For those under his command who disobeyed orders or who failed to carry out their duties, he was quick to deliver punishment. It was swift, stern, and just. He personally took no pleasure from it, and he wrote regretfully of having to administer it. Its imposition was, he believed, necessary for the cause they had all pledged to support. His commands benefitted from his firm hand and steady drilling, and since he never asked his men to expose themselves to a danger without doing so himself, they always faithfully followed him. At the height of a battle, an officer who served with Grimes through most of the war remembered, "I need not say at this perilous moment he was with the men at the point of greatest danger, for he was always at such places."

Grimes' vision of duty encompassed more than just fighting the enemy. He and his men endured hardships beyond belief, including scant rations, freezing winters, rampant disease, bloody feet with no shoes to protect them, knee-deep mud in the Petersburg trenches. Yet, in his letters to his beloved wife Charlotte, Grimes rarely mentioned the privations. He never complained that the hardships were so great that the cause should be abandoned.

Never once did he mention to her that he considered quitting. For Grimes, devotion to duty was firmly anchored in his character, and that devotion included handling adversity without complaint.

But what kind of man was Bryan Grimes? The answer—one sought by every biographer—lies beneath the old gray coat and beyond his exemplary military record. He was a first class soldier, but he was also a father when the war began, and a husband before it ended. He had been in the army only a short time when he began writing affectionate and loving letters to his eight-year-old daughter Bettie—letters that were sometimes graphically descriptive when dealing with matters of war. Bettie's mother had died when she was only four, and Grimes understood his special place in her life as her only parent. The fearsome Confederate warrior wrote to her about school, playthings, and even prospective wives. He once scolded her for not writing him, but soon thereafter asked his wife Charlotte to retrieve the letter and destroy it; if something happened to him in battle, he worried, he did not want Bettie's last memories of him to be a rebuke. After the war and while Bettie was attending college, her letters to her father confirm the devoted and loving relationship that had blossomed between them—one he had nurtured so tenderly from the field of battle. Charlotte once wrote that he could "take the children and quiet them when no one else could." His acquiescence to Bettie when she wanted to change schools is reminiscent of his father's behavior toward him and his brother William during their college years. One of the proudest moments of Grimes' life was in 1875, when he walked Bettie down the same aisle at Christ church in Raleigh that he and Charlotte traversed so many years before.

It is his relationship with Charlotte, however, that perhaps helps us truly understand the man, the flesh and blood human being. After their marriage in 1863, Grime wrote her almost daily until the last few days of the war when it was virtually impossible to do so. His letters reveal a deep love for her expressed in his modest way. He was singularly devoted to his wife. To him, the truest test of love is caring more about the other person's feelings than his own, and throughout his copious correspondence he continued to ask, probe, and seek out her emotions and concerns. Would Charlotte be willing to make her home at Grimesland on the old Tar River, isolated from Raleigh society? Would she be safe should the Yankees take Raleigh? What would her fate be should the Confederacy fall? This last concern, voiced near the end of the war, reveals much about Grimes' character. His own predicament was a grim one, and he must have known that the Confederacy was collapsing. Yet, rather than worry about his own safety—whether he would be hanged or imprisoned for treason, for instance—he worried instead that Charlotte's fate had been "doomed" because of her marriage to him. As much as he loved military life, he wrote in one letter that without Charlotte, there were no dreams for him.

His letter penned a few days after the devastating Confederate defeat at Cedar Creek in October 1864 provides an outstanding insight into the man. The battle staggered him. The terrible defeat foretold a bleak future for Southern arms. It also left his dear friend Dodson Ramseur dead, and the responsiblity for his division upon Grimes' shoulders. The most crushing news of all came in the form of a letter from Charlotte's sister, informing him that his little baby Bryan, just a few days old, had died. Though burdened with this sweeping wave of personal and professional tragedy, he sat down after sleeping two hours in the last fifty and wrote Charlotte from his heart. He struggled to find a way with words to ease her pain, to find some ray of hope in the melancholy emotions engulfing her, to reveal a glimpse of a happier tomorrow. The battle, so important to the Confederate cause, he mentioned only generally in a brief paragraph. His duty under those trying circumstances was to her. He found the strength to carry on, eased Charlotte through her grievous loss though separated by hundreds of miles, and paved the way for whatever future awaited them.

When armed conflict resolved the issue of secession, Grime quietly returned to civilian life. At home a new duty awaited him. His task was to make his land productive once again and care for his family. His correspondence to Charlotte from May 1865 until the end of his life spoke of family, farming and the future—and never mentioned the war or expressed any rancor concerning its outcome. Grimes had closed that chapter of his life, and the civilian-turned-soldier was at peace being a planter once again.

As the war years faded and he established himself as an agriculturist, his thoughts turned to the future and to improving North Carolina. He never ran for public office, but he and his brother William became involved in efforts to restore the University of North Carolina, which had been devastated by the war. The Grimes brothers were among the first contributors to a fund aimed at procuring books and hiring faculty for the university. Both were major donors and Bryan Grimes became a University Trustee.

Many lives are surrounded by irony, and the supreme one in Grimes' was his assassination. After having survived so many of the Civil War's bloodiest battles without a serious wound, his fate was to be murdered by a coward hired by unscrupulous men. In a sense, Grimes' character led him to his destiny at Bear Creek. He had stood on principle and acted honestly in the dispute that led to his demise. His strong will and character buoyed him through the criminal acts of intimidation carried out by his opponents, who burned his mill house and poisoned his well. Nothing would deter him from carrying out his duty to testify against the Paramore brothers except a bullet. He was as defenseless as Shakespeare's Caesar, and never dreamed such evil hid in the evening shadows.

The tombstone of Bryan and Charlotte Grimes in the family burial plot at Grimesland near the planation home. *Photo by T. Harrell Allen*

In May 1883, Pulaski Cowper, who collected and edited come of Grimes' correspondence, was coming out of a store in Raleigh when he ran into W. W. Holden, the old anti-war advocate and one of Grimes' few arch enemies. Seeing that Cowper had several copies of his *Extracts of Letters* in his hand, Holden asked he if could have one. Cowper, surprised by the request, nonetheless handed Holden a book. The fiery former editor held it up and examined the title, saying, "It is the record of the bravest man that ever went [to the Civil War] from North Carolina."

A monument to Bryan Grimes erected by his wife in Trinity Cemetery in Beaufort County, near Chcowitney, North Carolina. The marble cenotaph is about twenty feet high and inscribed on all four sides. One side especially captures Grimes' life: an artillery piece and a plow, side by side. *Photo by T. Harrell Allen*

Grimesland today. The plantation, which was built in 1818, was given to Bryan by his father in 1851. It is still occupied as a residence today. *Photo by T. Harrell Allen*

# Notes

Abbreviations of Manuscript Repositories:

DU (Perkins Library, Duke University)

ECU (East Carolina University)

NA (National Archives)

NCDAH (North Carolina Division of Archives and History)

NCC-UNC (North Carolina Collection, Wilson Library, The University of North Carolina at Chapel Hill)

SHC-UNC (Southern Historical Collection, Wilson Library, The University of North Carolina at Chapel Hill)

## Chapter One

1. Ashe, *Biographical History of North Carolina From Colonial Times to the Present,* 7, p. 253.

2. Daniels, *The Civil War Career of Major-General Bryan Grimes,* p.1.

3. Ashe, *Biographical History of North Carolina,* p. 250. Demsie Grimes' gravestone at Grimesland is engraved, "Emigrant from Virginia," reflecting those times and geography.

4. Wheeler, *Reminiscences and Memoirs of North Carolina,* p. 373.

5. Ashe, *Biographical History of North Carolina,* p. 251.

6. Ibid., p. 252.

7. Bryan Grimes, Sr., letter to William, August 8, 1842, personal collection, Alfred L. Purrington, III, great grandson of William Grimes.

8. The author would like to thank Dr. Rick Williams, professor of Classics, Southern Illinois University, for helping translate the obtuse handwriting of Bryan Grimes, particularly this difficult writing.

9. Bryan Grimes, Sr., letter to Bryan, September 18, 1842, Bryan Grimes Papers, NCDAH.

10. As a young man, probably in his teen age years, William suffered a severe head injury when he was thrown from his buggy due to a run away horse. No doubt he suffered a deep concussion along with considerable hearing loss, and due to the injury to his inner-ear, he also suffered from vertigo. His pictures, even as a young man, show

him with a walking cane. It is likely this pronounced deafness caused his "shyness" with young ladies that his father had commented on in an earlier letter to Bryan.

11. Bryan Grimes Papers, SHC. Despite his rather acute health problems, William tried to join the Confederate army in 1862. In fact, he did become a member of the 18th Regiment, Company G—for one day. A "Soldier's Discharge" (honorably) was issued on September 1, 1862, noting that William Grimes had enlisted as a private on August 31, 1862. Clearly he was not fit for military duty, as he could not walk without a cane, but he supported the Confederacy by "having furnished a substitute according to the provisions of the Act of the Confederate Congress—in the person of R. B. Campbell." The discharge papers noted that he was thirty-nine years of age, 5 feet, 10 inches, with light complexion, blue eyes, dark hair and was a farmer by occupation. The discharge paper was signed by Col. Robert H. Cowan, 18th Regiment, North Carolina Troops. In 1864 two family physicians of William wrote statements declaring him unfit for military duty. Dr. F. T. Haywood wrote, "He now suffers [injury] to his limbs so as to render locomotion for a short distance, even for a mile painful, prostrating him entirely." Dr. D. L. Taylor wrote, "he is unfit for military service and I make this statement purely as an act of justice to Mr. Grimes, for I know that very often a man of delicacy in apparent health fails to attract the attention of the examining physician fully to his true condition." These statements probably resulted from the Confederate Congress in 1864 ending the legality of substituting a man for one's place in the army, and thus stating, for the record, medically speaking, that William could not serve because of poor health.

12. Ashe, *Biographical History of North Carolina,* p. 249. Even though he could not serve in the army, William did what he could to support the Confederacy. He probably did more through his actions as a citizen than if he had carried a musket, for his grew abundant crops on his farm land in Pitt County and diverted a substantial amount to Lee's army. In fact, this part of eastern North Carolina served as a granary for the Confederate army. William also grew cotton. When Federal gunboats travelled up the Tar River, William, fearing the $25,000 worth of cotton he had stored on his farms would fall into Yankee hands, set fire to the bales and destroyed the valuable crop.

13. Bryan Grimes, Sr. letter to William, April 10, 1841, personal collection, Alfred L. Purrington, III. The author would like to thank Alfred L. Purrington, III, great grandson of William Grimes, for generously sharing these four insightful letters from his personal collection. These letters provide a rare insight into the relationship between Bryan Grimes Sr. and his two sons. William, five years older than Bryan, had attended the Bingham School and entered the University of North Carolina in 1840. Apparently he did not like it there (the record does not show why) and he asked his father if he could transfer to William & Mary. His father wrote him in April, 1841: "But, why do you make an election of William & Mary? It is true that it is an old and respectable institution and has reared some of the first men of our country, but its reputation has been in the wane for several years and it has by no means its former standing. The

institution, however, may be good enough, but I have strong objections to the education of a son in Virginia. *Suffice it to say, I am not at all the admirer of the Virginia character.*" (Italics added)

14. Ibid. Since the father had attended the University of North Carolina, he wanted William to stay there and graduate. He cited his reasons: "There are many strong reasons to urge me to educate you in my own state—the good old North Carolina. I believe we should patronize our own institutions. . .[and] I conceive the advantages of an education at home to be very considerable in your future course in life." He further advised: "In the first place we form manners, habit and opinions peculiar to our own section of country. In being educated at our own college, you would form an acquaintance with the youth from all parts of the state, the men who are to act a prominent part in the drama of life, who must become leading characters in the affairs of our state." Despite his strong views, Bryan Sr. would often acquiesce to the wishes of his children. He concluded in his letter to William: "If you must go from your own state, I would prefer a northern college to any other. Princeton or Yale afford, I conceive, more advantages to a youth of North Carolina than any institution in Virginia. I think you would more likely form opinions and habits more congenial to North Carolina. I want you to think of the suggestion and if you cannot be reconciled to return to Chapel Hill, make up your mind about a northern college.

15. Bryan Grimes, Sr. letter to William, July 12, 1841, personal collection, Alfred L. Purrington, III. Bryan Sr. wrote him in July, 1841, "I have been thinking seriously about it and I can see many objections to Princeton, or all other institutions of that kind as well as your own. The morals of the youth at Princeton is said to be bad, very bad, and so far as I can ascertain, its standard of scholarship is low and much below that of our University. On the whole I cannot see that your condition would be improved in a location at that college. I have not understood so much of Yale, [as for] its character for morality, I have learned nothing, but its grade of scholarship is certainly higher." However, despite his objections, father Grimes gave in and wrote, "Do make some inquiry as to the latter. . .the necessary preparation for admittance in the Sophomore class, (which you must enter, go where you may) the expenses, etc and let me know the result of your inquiries in your next letter." Finally, Grimes, seemingly resigned to the idea that William would go to Princeton, wrote: "Your promotion, the advancement of your best interest, is my motive of action in the matter, and I shall readily acquiesce in any movement where I can be induced to believe you will be benefited. But on the other hand, if I am not satisfied that you made a proper selection, that you deceive yourself, that you have not the necessary discretion, it is then not only my right, but my duty to enter my dissent and to adhere to it. Write me as soon as you receive this letter."

William returned to UNC for his sophomore year and completed the spring term in 1842. William selected Princeton and entered in the fall of 1842; he graduated in 1844.

16. Carmichael, *Lee's Young Artillerist, William R. J. Pegram,* pp. 1-5. This is an outstanding study of the attitudes of the young men of the planter class during this time period and provides an insight to the strongly-held views of Bryan Grimes

17. Bryan Grimes, Sr., letter to William, June 25, 1843, personal collection, Alfred L. Purrington, III. Bryan Sr. made some career suggestions to William (who was about to enter his senior year at Princeton), and in doing so revealed his desire that his sons distinguish themselves among their peers: "If your mind was of a superior order, I would suggest the profession of law. I have an objection to the profession of physician, and would by no means advise a son if he could do anything else to adopt it as a vocation in life. As to divinity, that is out of the question as you do not seem very devoutly inclined. I wish it were otherwise. The profession of law, as you once heard me remark, I think, is the stepping stone to distinction in our country. You will find most of our great men members of the bar. But I should be very unwilling for you to turn your attention to that profession, unless you could rise above the crowd of young men that swarm about our courts. Most of them are better suited to the common pursuits of life, to be 'hewers of wood and drawers of water.' Now to be a mere pettifogger is the most contemptible station I know. . .but on the other hand, I should be exceedingly gratified to have one [son] distinguished for his learning and ranking high as a barrister."

18. Susan Grimes, letter to Bryan, July 31, 1844, Bryan Grimes Papers, NCDAH.

19. University of North Carolina Faculty Journal, 1844-1848, SHC-UNC.

20. Ibid.

21. Bryan Grimes, Sr. letter to Bryan, March 7, 1845, Bryan Grimes Papers, NCDAH.

22. Bryan Grimes, Sr. letter to Bryan, April 16, 1845, Bryan Grimes Papers, NCDAH.

23. University of North Carolina Faculty Journal, 1844-1848, SHC-UNC

24. Bryan Grimes, Sr. letter to Bryan, October 10, 1846, Bryan Grimes Papers, NCDAH.

25. Bryan Grimes, letter to father, Bryan Sr. no date, but likely 1846, Bryan Grimes Papers, NCDAH.

26. Ibid.

27. Daniels, *The Civil War Career of Major-General Bryan Grimes,* p. 8.

28. Ibid.

29. University of North Carolina Faculty Journal, 1844-1848, SHC-UNC.

30. Ibid.

31. Bryan Grimes, Sr., letter to Bryan, May 12, 1848, Bryan Grimes Papers, NCDAH.

32. Battle, *History of the University of North Carolina,* 1. p. 566.

33. Ibid., p. 568.

34. The Proceedings of the Philanthropic Society, 1844-1848, SHC-UNC.

35. Ibid. In the fall of 1845, Grimes debated twice and lost both times. In the spring of 1846, he argued the affirmative position on an interesting topic for that time period: "Ought a female to hold the reins of government?" Grimes lost, but the minutes described it as a "long debate" and the vote was surprisingly close at 12-9. On April 24 in a debate entitled "Were the Americans justified in employing bloodhounds in driving the Indians from Florida?" Grimes argued that they were not so justified. The minutes show that after an "animated discussion between the debaters" Grimes lost with the majority voting for the affirmative. Despite losing, Grimes was elected treasurer of the Society at the same meeting. During the next year he debated four times, winning two, losing once and one outcome was not recorded in the minutes. During the year he was appointed to the Society's education committee. In his senior year, Grimes was listed on the roll of the Society, but as was the custom, he did not debate during the year in order to give younger members an opportunity.

36. University of North Carolina Faculty Journal, 1844-1848, SHC-UNC.

37. The Proceedings of the Philanthropic Society, 1844-1848, SHC-UNC.

38. Battle, *History of the University of North Carolina,* 1, p. 569.

39. Grimes, Charlotte E., "Sketches of My Life," Grimes-Bryan Papers, East Carolina Manuscript Collection, ECU, p. 10.

40. University of North Carolina Faculty Journal, 1843-1847, SHC-UNC.

41. Wilson, *Carolina Cavalier, The Life and Mind of James Johnston Pettigrew,* p. 12. This is an insightful biography and offers an excellent overview of the highly interesting Pettigrew.

42. J. J. Pettigrew, letter to Bryan Grimes, May 14, 1847. Bryan Grimes Papers, NCDAH.

43. Bryan Grimes, letter to J.J. Pettigrew, June 16, 1847, Bryan Grimes Papers, NCDAH.

44. Bryan Grimes, letter to J.J. Pettigrew, July 27, 1847, Bryan Grimes Papers, NCDAH.

45. Wilson, *Carolina Cavalier,* p. 26.

46. Ibid.

47. Bryan Grimes, letter to J.J. Pettigrew, June 9, 1848, Bryan Grimes Papers, NCDAH.

48. Daniels, *The Civil War Career of Major-General Bryan Grimes,* p. 9.

49. Bryan Grimes, Sr., letter to William, June 25, 1843, personal collection, Alfred L. Purrington, III. In November, 1845, William's father gave him the plantation known as "Yankee Hall," across the Tar River from the ancestral home of Avon and "twenty negroes to help him cultivate it." On the death of his father in 1860, he inherited the Avon plantation. William was successful as a planter, but began to develop business and real estate interests in Raleigh as well. In June of 1851, a happy event occurred in his life when he married Elizabeth Hanrahan. They continued the family custom of living

on the plantation most of the year except during the summer, when it was thought to be unhealthy to stay in the region, and then would move to Raleigh. This lifestyle continued until 1860, when William and his family moved permanently to Raleigh. By now he had considerable real estate holdings there, but he did continue farming the fertile lands in Pitt County. William died in Raleigh in October 1884, and was survived by his wife and five children: Nancy, Elizabeth, William Bryan, Walter, and Nella.

50. Note recording this transaction, Bryan Grimes Papers, NCDAH.

51. Tarboro, *Southerner*, March, 1860. The newspaper also reported that he was in Baltimore to purchase a carriage for a daughter who was recently married. This may not be accurate for family records do not show a Grimes daughter getting married in 1859 or 1860. Family descendants have said that Bryan Sr. was there to seek medical advice.

52. Daniels, *The Civil War Career of Major-General Bryan Grimes*, p. 10.

53. Bryan Grimes, Letter to William, July 14, 1860, Bryan Grimes Papers, NCDAH.

54. Bryan Grimes, Letter to Mollie, July 19, 1860, Bryan Grimes Papers, NCDAH. While travelling he wrote "Cousin Mollie" from Ireland, Scotland, and England. According to the Grimes family genealogy, he did not have a cousin named Mollie. Thus it is unknown who "Cousin Mollie" actually was. "Mollie" could perhaps have been a nickname for Mary. There is some chance that it was the younger sister of his first wife, Bettie Davis.

55. Grimes, Charlotte, *Sketches*, p. 9. An interesting and mysterious event took place at Grimesland while Grimes was abroad. Decades later, Junius Daniel Grimes, Bryan's son, wrote in a letter to his older half-sister Bettie about a clock his father had given him. In seeking to learn more about the history of it, Junius wrote: "It seems to me that sometime in the past someone told me of some incident connected with this clock in connection with the murder of Father's housekeeper by a negro man before the Civil War, but I am not sure whether I am drawing on my imagination about it or not. My impression was that the man made a confession in which he stated that his motive in going into the room was robbery only, but that the striking of the clock awakened her and then is when he committed the murder. In this connection, it seems that I have been told by my Mother [Charlotte Grimes] that Father [Bryan Grimes] was in Europe at that time and that the man had been convicted and hanged before Father returned from Europe, and that as the man was Father's slave the county offered to pay him the value of the slave, which I understand was customary at that time in such instances, but that he declined to take any pay. Tell me what you know about this." Unfortunately, if Bettie replied, it has been lost. Letter, Junius Daniel Grimes to Bettie, March 15, 1939 and given to the author by Bill Mordecai, grandson of Bettie Grimes. The author would like to thank Bill Mordecai for sharing this letter along with other documents from his personal collection.

56. Ashe, *Biographical History*, p. 253.

57. Cowper, *Extracts of Letters of Major-General Bryan Grimes to His Wife*, p. 10 Unless otherwise noted, all references to Cowper are based on the 1986 reprint of this work, edited by Gary Gallagher (Broadfoot Publishing Company, Wilmington, N. C.), hereinafter referred to as Cowper, *Extracts*.

58. Ibid.

59. Original commission in Bryan Grimes Papers, NCDAH.

## Chapter Two

1. Alexander, *Fighting for the Confederacy, The Personal Recollections of General Edward Porter Alexander*, p. 154.

2. Gallagher, *Stephen Dodson Ramseur Lee's Gallant General*, p. 38. This is an outstanding biography.

3. Cowper, *Extracts*, p. 10.

4. Ibid.

5. Mast, *State Troops and Volunteers A Photographic Record of North Carolina's Civil War Soldiers*, p. 240. This work provides an excellent look at North Carolina soldiers and offers insightful statistics concerning them.

6. Ibid., p. 241.

7. Ibid., p. 22.

8. Ibid., p. 311.

9. Ibid., p. 95, 311, 360. For instance, Company A from Iredell County was called the "Blues" because of their unique uniforms. Company B from Rowan County was known as the "Scotch Ireland Grays," and the second company from Iredell County, Company C, was called the "Saltillo Boys." The only company from Wayne County, Company D, was called the "Goldsboro Volunteers." Company E from Beaufort County was nicknamed the "Southern Guards," and Company F from Wilson County was known as the "Wilson Light Infantry." Davie County's only company, Company G, had the unusual nickname of "Davie Sweep Stakes." The third company from Iredell County, Company H, was called the "Iredell Independent Grays." Company I from Beaufort County was nicknamed the "Pamlico Rifles." Company K, the second from Rowan County, was known as the "Rowan Rifles."

10. Steele, "Sketches of the Civil War," p. 17. The author would like to thank John Bass for loaning him a copy of the Steele manuscript to read.

11. Mast, *State Troops*, p. 25.

12. Osborne, "Fourth Regiment," p. 230; For most of the war Osborne served under Grimes.

13. Osborne, "Fourth Regiment," p. 280.

14. Grimes, Bryan, letter to William, July 8, 1861. Personal collection of Alfred L. Purrington III, Raleigh, N.C. The author wishes to thank Mr. Purrington for sharing this important letter which gives insight to Grimes and his early camp life in the army.

15. Grimes, Bryan, letter to William, July 11, 1861, Purrington personal collection.

16. Grimes, Bryan, letter to William, July 15, 1861, Purrington personal collection.

17. Grimes, Bryan, letter to William, July 21, 1861, Grimes Family Papers, SHC.

18. Osborne, "Fourth Regiment," p. 234.

19. Grimes, Bryan, letter to William, August 25, 1861, Purrington personal collection.

20. Ibid.

21. Ibid.

22. Ibid.

23. Ibid.

24. Ibid.

25. Ibid.

26. Grimes, Bryan, letter to William, October 1, 1861, Grimes Family Papers, SHC.

27. Grimes, Bryan, letter to Mollie, October 18, 1861, Bryan Grimes Papers, NCDAH

28. Grimes, Bryan, letter to William, November 13, 1861, Grimes Family Papers, SHC; see Farwell, *Stonewall*, for a discussion of Jackson's attitude on raising the black flag, pp. 374-375. Some accounts disclose that Capt. Rufus Barringer, 1st. N.C. Cavalry, reported that Gen. Jackson said to him that the Confederates should 'raise the black flag'—give no quarter—against Union soldiers. See also *Stonewall Jackson*, James I. Robertson, Jr. for further discussion of Jackson's black flag policy, pp. 234-235. Jackson's widow first mentioned his advocacy of the black flag policy, but on the advice of several ex-confederate officers omitted it from later printings of her book. Other biographies of Jackson do not report this conversation. It is fairly clear from his correspondence written later in the war that Grimes no longer held this extreme view.

29. Ibid.

30. Ibid.

31. David M. Carter and Thomas M. Blount were members of Company E. Carter, age 31, was appointed captain of May 16, 1861, while Blount, a resident of the District of Columbia, enlisted at age 28 on June 15, 1861, mustering in as sergeant. In early July, Blount was appointed a first lieutenant and served as acting quartermaster. By November 1861 he held the rank of captain.

32. Grimes, Bryan, Charges sent to Headquarters, November, 1861, Bryan Grimes Papers, NCDAH,

33. Blount, Thomas, note to Bryan Grimes, November, 20, 1861, Bryan Grimes Papers, NCDAH, p. 64. This series of exchanges between Blount and Grimes are all

found in the Bryan Grimes Papers, NCDAH and hereafter will simply be noted as located in the NCDAH.

34. Carter note to Perry, November 22, 1861, NCDAH.

35. Carter note to Perry, November 23, 1861, NCDAH.

36. Grimes, Bryan, letter to William, November 24, 1861, Bryan Grimes Papers, NCDAH.

37. Carter note to Perry, November 29, 1861, NCDAH.

38. Anderson, George B., letter to Bryan Grimes, November 28, 1861, Bryan Grimes Papers, NCDAH.

39. Grimes, Bryan, note to Thomas M. Blount, January 14, 1862, Bryan Grimes Papers, NCDAH. During that fall when Bryan Grimes experienced the loss of his sister-in-law, who had been taking care of his young daughter Bettie, he requested 30 days leave beginning December 15, 1861. It was granted and he returned to North Carolina to make arrangements for Bettie to live with his brother William in Raleigh.

40. Ibid.

41. Thomas M. Blount, note to Bryan Grimes, January 14, 1862, NCDAH.

42. Thomas M. Blount, note to Bryan Grimes, January 16, 1862, NCDAH.

43. Bryan Grimes, note to Thomas M. Blount, January 16, 1862, NCDAH.

44. Bryan Grimes, letter to Thomas Jordan, January 16, 1862, Bryan Grimes Papers, NCDAH.

45. Thomas M. Blount, note to Bryan Grimes, January 16, 1862, NCDAH.

46. Bryan Grimes, note to Thomas M. Blount, January 17, 1862, NCDAH.

47. Bryan Grimes, letter to John A. Young, January 17, 1862, NCDAH.

48. Bryan Grimes, letter to William, January 17, 1862, NCDAH.

49. Bryan Grimes, letter to William, January 19, 1862, NCDAH.

50. Bryan Grimes, letter to William, January 20, 1862, NCDAH.

51. Bryan Grimes, letter to William, January 24, 1862, NCDAH.

52. Bryan Grimes, letter to William, February 2, 1862, NCDAH.

53. Bryan Grimes, letter to William, June 11, 1862, NCDAH.

54. Bryan Grimes, letter to William, December 8, 1862, Grimes Family Papers, SHC.

55. Grimes, Bryan, letter to William, November 24, 1861, Grimes Family Papers, SHC.

56. Ibid.

57. Pulaski Cowper, letter to Bryan Grimes, November 27, 1861, Bryan Grimes Papers, NCDAH. In closing his letter, Cowper made an interesting reference to the infamous W. W. Holden, editor of the Raleigh *Standard,* peace advocate and head of the anti-war faction in North Carolina, with whom Grimes would later clash politically and publicly in the summer of 1863. Cowper noted, "Holden and Robinson had a street fight

in which Holden got his head badly cut and nearly lost his life by a sword from Robinson's hand."

## Chapter Three

1. Osborne, "Fourth Regiment," p. 235; For most of the war Osborne served under Grimes.

2. Grimes, Bryan, letter to Bettie, February 2, 1862, Grimes Family Papers, SHC.

3. Grimes, Bryan, letter to William, February 28, 1862, Grimes Family Papers, SHC. During most of the war, Grimes had his loyal black servant, Polk, with him.

4. Freeman, *Lee's Lieutenants*, 2, p. 269; *OR* 11, pt. 1, p. 952; ibid., pt. 3, p. 425.

5. Grimes, Bryan, letter to William, March 16, 1862, Grimes Family Papers, SHC.

6. Gallagher, *Ramseur*, pp. 36-37.

7. Grimes, Bryan, letter to Bettie, April 18, 1862, Bryan Grimes Papers, NCDAH.

8. Grimes, Bryan, letter to William, April 27, 1862, Grimes Family Papers, SHC.

9. Steele, *Sketches of the Civil War*, p. 19.

10. Grimes, Bryan, letter to William, April 27, 1862, Grimes Family Papers, SHC.

11. Ibid. Grimes' estimate of the number of men that McClellan had is clearly inaccurate. His estimate of Confederate numbers was much nearer the truth; about 56,500 were under Johnston's command. Freeman, *Lee's Lieutenants*, 1, p. 156.

12. Alexander, *Fighting for the Confederacy*, p. 75. Alexander also noted that "the Federals had an entire regiment armed with rifles with telescopic sights which were wonderfully accurate."

13. Grimes, Bryan, letter to William, April 27, 1862, Grimes Family Papers, SHC.

14. Miller, *The Peninsula Campaign*, vol. 1 p. 185.

15. Cowper, *Extracts*, p. 12.

16. Steele, *Sketches*, p. 20.

17. Cowper, *Extracts*, p. 13.

18. Grimes, Bryan, letter to Bettie, May 10. 1862, Bryan Grimes Papers, NCDAH.

19. Cowper, *Extracts*, p. 13.

18. Osborne, "Fourth Regiment," p. 237.

20. Ibid., p. 191; Sears, *To the Gates of Richmond*, p. 117.

21. Freman, *Lee's Lieutenants*, 2, pp. 212-214.

22. Miller, *The Peninsula Campaign*, vol. 1, p. 191; Sears, To the Gates of Richmond, pp. 117-120.

23. Ibid, p.125.

24. *OR* 11, pt. 1, pp. 943-944

25. Osborne, "Fourth Regiment," p. 238.

26. *OR* 11, pp. 955-956. This is the official report written by Grimes of the Seven Pines battle.

27. Osborne, "Fourth Regiment," pp. 238-239.

28. Cowper, *Extracts*, p. 14.

29. *OR* 11, pp. 955-956.

30. Ibid.

31. Ibid.

32. Cowper, *Extracts*, p. 15.

33. Ibid., pp. 944-945; Sears, *To the Gates of Richmond*, pp. 128-132.

34. Ibid., pp. 138-140.

35. Bryan to William, June 1, 1862, in Grimes Papers; Sears, *To the Gates of Richmond*, pp. 143-145.

36. Welch, *Medical Histories*, pp. 170-171.

37. *OR* 11, p. 952.

38. Hill, D. H., *A History of North Carolina in the War Between the States*, 2, p. 70.

39. *OR* 11, p. 953. Grimes' estimate of the 4th North Carolina losses differs from those found in George B. Anderson's official report. Anderson reported shortly after the battle that 29 officers and 678 men fought at Seven Pines in the 4th North Carolina, and that 24 officers and 369 men were killed, wounded, or missing. See also Cowper, *Extracts*, p. 14

## Chapter Four

1. For more information on the reorganization of the Army of Northern Virginia at this time, see Kevin Ruffner, "Before the Seven Days: The Reorganization of the Confederate Army in the Spring of 1862," in William J. Miller, ed. *The Peninsula Campaign of 1862: Yorktown to the Seven Days*, 3, pp. 47-69.

2. Carter's rank of lieutenant colonel ranked from the date of Grimes' letter to his brother (June 21, 1862). Krick, *Lee's Colonels*, p. 85.

3. Bridges, *Lee's Maverick General* p. 68; *OR* 11, pt. 2, pp. 38-39, 623, 648, 656, 658, 976, 983.

4. Cowper, *Extracts* p. 16.

5. Stikeleather, *Recollections on the Civil War in the United States*, Grimes Family Papers, SHC, p. 3.

6. Ibid., p. 108.

7. Ibid., p. 107.

8. Osborne, "Fourth Regiment," p. 244; Osborne notes that Capt. Thomas Blount, who had earlier defied Grimes' orders and challenged him to a duel, and who was acting as a volunteer aide to Gen. George B. Anderson at Gaines' Mill, was shot during the assault while carrying the flag of one of the regiments.

9. Grimes, Bryan, letter to William, July 5, 1862, Grimes Family Papers, SHC.

10. Cowper, *Extracts,* p. 17. Grimes later named the captured dog "General," and it became the regiment's mascot. The animal accompanied Grimes for two years through many of the army's most difficult campaigns. Unfortunately, during the pursuit of David Hunter's Federals in 1864, General "succumbed to the hard marching, broke down and was lost, not having the endurance of men." The relationship between the dog and Grimes substantiates his wife Charlotte's claim that he had a strong affinity for animals. See Grimes, Charlotte, *"Sketches of My Life,"* p. 14. "My husband always had a great affection for his horse [Warren]. He used to say he had as much sense as a human being. He was a blooded horse and cherished for past services, living many years after the war. He was twenty-seven or twenty-eight years old when he died and was buried on the hillside below the family burying ground at Grimesland."

11. Grimes initially noted that only about 60 men answer the roll call, but he later reported a figure of 150. The difference is likely due to the stragglers and others who for various reasons had become separated from the regiment.

12. Cowper, *Extracts,* p. 17.

13. Cowper, *Extracts,* p. 18.

14. Battle, Walter, letter to Mother, August 23, 1862. The author would like to thank John Bass who generously let the author borrow his personal photocopy of these letters. Battle was a soldier in the 4th N.C. The original letters can be found in Laura Elizabeth Lee's, *Forget-Me-Nots of the Civil War,* 1909.

15. Cowper, *Extracts,* p. 19.

16. For a fascinating and fresh examination of the controversy surrounding Orders 191 and D. H. Hill's role therein, see Wilbur D. Jones, "Who Lost Lee's Lost Orders?" in *Civil War Regiments: A Journal of the American Civil War,* Vol. 5, No. 3 (1997), pp. 1-26.

17. Cowper, *Extracts,* p. 19; *OR,* 19. 1, p.1049; For a good modern treatment of this phase of the battle, see D. Scott Hartwig, "My God! Be Careful!" Morning Battle at Fox's Gap, September 14, 1862," *Civil War Regiments,* Vol. 5, No. 3 (1997), p., 47-48. Grimes' half-brother, John B. Grimes, was captured in this battle and was later exchanged on November 10, 1862, at Aikens Landing, Virginia.

18. *OR* 19, pt. 1, p. 1049.

19. *OR* 19, pt. 1, p. 1049; Osborne, "Fourth Regiment," p. 247.

20. Priest, *Before Antietam: The Battle for South Mountain,* p. 325.

21. Cowper, *Extracts,* p. 19-20.

22. Osborne, "Fourth Regiment," pp. 247-248; *OR* 19, pt. 1, p. 1030. Among the officers of the 4th Regiment killed or wounded were William T. Marsh, D. P. Latham, E. A. Osborne, Jessie F. Stansill, J. C. Cotton, T. M. Allen, T. J. Parker, F. H. Brown, Crawford Weaver, and B. T. Bonner.

23. Osborne, "Fourth Regiment," pp. 247-248; Cowper, *Extracts,* p. 20.

24. Grimes, Bryan, letter to William, October 16, 1862, Grimes Family Papers, SHC.

25. Grimes, Bryan, letter to William, October 22, 1862, Grimes Family Papers, SHC.

26. Cowper, *Extracts,* p. 22.

27. Cowper, *Extracts,* pp. 22-23.

28. Cowper, *Extracts,* pp. 23-24.

29. Battle, Walter, letter to Mother, November 14, 1862.

30. Grimes, Bryan, letter to Bettie, November 27, 1862, Bryan Grimes Papers, NCDAH.

31. Ibid.

32. Battle, Walter, letter to Mother, November 14, 1862. Actually Ramseur was a colonel in the infantry.

33. Gallagher, *Ramseur,* p. 47.

34. Grimes, Bryan, letter to William, December 5, 1862, Grimes Family Papers, SHC; see D.H. Hill's report of this gunboat affair, *OR* 21, pt. 1, p. 36.

35. Cowper, *Extracts,* p. 25.

36. Cowper, *Extracts,* p. 26.

37. Ibid.

38. Cowper, *Extracts,* pp. 26-27.

39. *OR* 21, p. 644.

40. Grimes, Bryan, letter to William, December 18, 1862, Grimes Family Papers, SHC.

41. Grimes, Bryan, letter to Bettie, December 25, 1862, Grimes Family Papers, SHC.

42. Ibid.

## Chapter Five

1. Gallagher, *Ramseur,* p. 48.

2. Hill, D. H. letter of March 10, 1863, Bryan Grimes Papers, NCDAH.

3. Grimes, Charlotte E., *Sketches,* Bryan Grimes Papers, ECU p. 7. Based upon an examination of the time and dates in Charlotte's written recollections with Grimes' visits to North Carolina, it is most likely that the first meeting between Grimes and the beautiful young woman who would become his wife in September 1863, occurred in February 1863, during the time Grimes was in Raleigh on his first furlough.

4. Ibid., p. 8.

5. Ibid., p. 4.

6. Grimes, Bryan, letter to Charlotte, April 9, 1863, Bryan Grimes Papers, SHC.

7. Grimes, Bryan, letter to Bettie, April 24, 1863, Bryan Grimes Papers, NCDAH.

8. *OR* 25, pt. 1, p. 995.

9. Gallagher, *Ramseur,* p. 53.

10. *OR* 25, pt. 1, pp. 797, 940, 995.

11. Cowper, *Extracts,* pp. 28-29; *OR* 25, pt. 1, p. 995; *Ramseur,* p. 57.

12. Gallagher, *Ramseur,* pp. 55-58; Cowper, *Extracts,* p. 29; Furgurson, *Chancellorsville,* p. 171.

13. Gallagher, *Ramseur,* p. 58.

14. Stikeleather, *Recollections,* p. 33.

15. Cowper, *Extracts,* pp. 29-30; *Ramseur,* pp. 58-59.

16. *Ramseur,* p. 59; *Lee's Lieutenants,* pp. 567-570; *OR* 25, pt. 1, p. 942.

17. Cowper, *Extracts,* pp. 31-33; Although Cowper expunged the unit's idenification in his 1884 book, Grimes identified it as the Stonewall Brigade in his original manuscript. In a letter dated March 12, 1883, Cowper wrote to Charlotte, "I have already erased the Stonewall Brigade. . ." Bryan Grimes Papers, NCDAH, p. 364. For further description of this episode, see Gallagher's *Ramseur,* pp. 65-66, p. 186 (n. 46), p. 187(n. 59); also see Freeman, *Lee's Lieutenants,* 2, p. 594; *OR* 25, pt. 1, pp. 943, 996, 1015-16; Osborne, "Fourth Regiment," p. 251.

18. Cowper, *Extracts,* p. 32.

19. Ibid.

20. Gallagher, *Ramseur,* p. 62; Cowper, *Extracts,* pp. 32-33; *OR* 25, pt.1, pp. 944, 966, 1017.

21. Cowper, *Extracts,* p. 33. The frock coat, sword, and belt plate, (the latter twisted by the impact of the minie ball), together with other Grimes-related items, are on display at The Museum of the Confederacy in Richmond.

22. Cowper, *Extracts,* p. 34.

23. Ibid.

24. Gallagher, *Ramseur,* p. 63; *OR* 25, p. 1, pp. 996-997.

25. Gallagher, *Ramseur,* p. 64; Osborne, "Fourth Regiment," p. 252; Cowper, *Extracts,* p. 35. Grimes claimed his regiment numbered "less than three hundred." William Fox, in *Regimental Losses in the Civil War,* p. 568, lists Grimes' casualties as 45 killed, 110 wounded and 58 missing. Captain Osborne's figures, more detailed than Grimes' and somewhat higher than Fox's, are probably the most accurate since he was in a better position to know this type of detail.

26. Cowper, *Extracts,* p. 35; Osborne, "Fourth Regiment," p. 253; Gallagher, *Ramseur,* p. 64; *OR* 25, pt. 1, p. 997.

27. Grimes, Charlotte. *Sketches,* p. 8.

28. Gallagher, *Ramseur,* p. 65; Cowper, *Extracts,* p. 34; Osborne, "Fourth Regiment," p. 251.

29. Grimes, Bryan, letter to Bettie, May 28, 1863, Bryan Grimes Papers, NCDAH. According to a modern medical study, Grimes' wound was so severe that he rode in an

ambulance on the way to Gettysburg except when expecting a fight. Jack Welsh, *Medical Histories of Confederate Generals,* p. 90.

30. Grimes, Bryan, letter to Bettie, May 28, 1863, Bryan Grimes Papers, NCDAH.

31. *OR* 27, pt. 2, pp. 547-549; Gallagher, *Ramseur,* pp. 68-69. Unfortunately, neither Grimes nor Ramseur left an official account of their preliminary actions leading up to the Battle of Gettysburg.

32. Grimes, Bryan, letter to Bettie, June 16, 1863, Bryan Grimes Papers, NCDAH; *OR* 27, pt. 2, pp. 549-550.

33. Grimes, Bryan, letter to Cousin Mollie, June 25, 1863, Bryan Grimes Papers, NCDAH; *OR* 27, pt. 2, p. 551.

34. Cowper, *Extracts,* pp. 133-134. Grimes' account of the engagement with the militia was found scribbled as marginalia in a book in his library after the war in 1884, and is reproduced in full in Cowper, pp. 133-134. Wilbur Nye, in *Here Come the Rebels,* pp. 299-300, describes a remarkably similar incident outside Carlisle at about the same time.

35. Stikeleather, *Recollections,* p. 38. In his manuscript Stikeleather calls him "Hugh H." because he does not want to demean the family name. The regiment record shows the soldier to be Hugh Hall.

36. Stikeleather, *Recollections,* p. 40.

37. Stikeleather, *Recollections,* p. 42; Jordan, *North Carolina Troops 1861-1865: A Roster,* p. 4.

38. For excellent background information on this campaign see, Coddington, *The Gettysburg Campaign.* An interesting account of the North Carolina cavalry in the campaign is found in Hartley, *Stuart's Tarheels.*

39. Gallagher, *Ramseur,* p. 72; Cowper, *Extracts*, p. 36; *OR* 27, pt. 2, pp. 552-554. Excellent recent scholarship has appeared dealing with Robert Rodes' Division and the Oak Ridge engagement, including Robert K. Krick, "Failures of Brigade Leadership," pp. 92-139, in Gary Gallagher, ed., *The First Day at Gettysburg: Essays on Confederate and Union Leadership,* and D. Massy Griffin, "Rodes on Oak Hill: A Study of Rodes' Division on the First Day of Gettysburg," *The Gettysburg Magazine,* No. 4 (January 1991), pp. 33-48.

40. Cowper, *Extracts*, pp. 36-37; Gallagher, *Ramseur,* pp. 72-73; Griffin, "Rodes on Oak Hill," p. 47.

41. Cowper, *Extracts*, p. 37; Stikeleather, *Recollections,* p. 45.

42. Gallagher, *Ramseur;* pp. 73-74; *OR* 27, pt. 2, p. 555.

43. Osborne, "Fourth Regiment," p. 254. Much has been written about the failure to assault Cemetery Hill on the evening of July 1. The best to date is Harry Pfanz, *Gettysburg: Culp's Hill and Cemetery Hill.*

44. The best studies on these assaults were written by Harry Pfanz, see *Gettysburg: The Second Day.*

45. Pfanz, *Culp's Hill,* pp. 277-278; *OR* 27, pt. 2, pp. 556, 587-588. 590.

46. Pfanz, *Culp's Hill,* pp. 277-278

47. Grimes, Bryan, letter to Mollie, July 26, 1863, Bryan Grimes Papers, NCDAH; *OR* 27, pt. 2, pp. 342, 588; Osborne, "Fourth Regiment," p. 254.

48. *Raleigh Register,* September 8, 1863; Gallagher, *Ramseur,* p. 76.

49. Hassler, *The General To His Lady, The Civil War Letters of William Dorsey Pender to Fanny Pender,* p. 227; Gallagher, *Ramseur,* p. 91.

50. *Wilmington Journal,* "Meeting of North Carolina Troops 4th Reg," August 20,1863, Wilmington, N.C. p. 1

51. *Daily Enquirer,* "From Gen Lee's Army," [Richmond] Aug. 15, 1863, p. 1; *Wilmington Journal,* August 20, 1863.

52. *Wilmington Journal,* "Address of the Army," September 10, 1863, Wilmington, N.C. p. 1.

53. Hamilton, J. G. de Reulhac. *Reconstruction in North Carolina,* p. 52.

54. Ashe, *Biographical History,* 6, p. 257.

55. Grimes, Charlotte. *Memoirs,* p. 9.

56. Grimes, Charlotte, letter to Bryan Grimes, September 29, 1863, Bryan Grimes Papers, NCDAH.

57. Cowper, *Extracts,* pp. 40-41.

58. Grimes, Bryan, letter to Charlotte, October 6, 1863, Bryan Grimes Papers, SHC.

59. Ibid.

60. Grimes, Charlotte, letter to Bryan, October 6, 1863, Bryan Grimes Papers, NCDAH.

61. For information on Lee's military operations in October 1863, including the Battle of Bristoe Station, see William D. Henderson, *The Road to Bristoe Station: Campaigning with Lee and Meade, August 1-October 20,* 1863. Although there are numerous letters from Bryan Grimes to Charlotte, few in her own hand have been found. It is likely that Grimes did not preserve them. Charlotte had written him on October 12th, "Please don't let the Yankees get hold of any letters, destroy them when you finish reading them." It was common for both sides to read each other's mail whenever possible. Apparently Grimes honored her request and destroyed them.

62. Grimes, Bryan, letter to Charlotte, October 13, 1863, Bryan Grimes Papers, SHC.

63. Ibid.

64. Gallagher, *Ramseur,* p. 86.

65. Grimes, Bryan, letter to Charlotte, November 21, 1863, Bryan Grimes Papers, SHC.

66. Ibid.

67. Ibid.

68. Ibid.

69. Grimes, Bryan, letter to Charlotte, November 23, 1863, Bryan Grimes Papers, SHC.

70. Ibid.

71. Ibid.

72. Griffith, *Battle Tactics of the Civil War,* p. 50. Ramseur felt the same way as Grimes, and it is likely the two young officers discussed the wisdom of fighting behind entrenchments.

73. Grimes, Bryan, letter to Charlotte, November 23, 1863, Bryan Grimes Papers, SHC.

74. Grimes, Bryan, letter to Bettie, November 25, 1863, Bryan Grimes Papers, SHC.

75. Grimes, Bryan, letter to Charlotte, December 1, 1863, Bryan Grimes Papers, SHC.

76. Ibid.

77. For more information on this understudied and fascinating campaign, see Martin F. Graham and George F. Skoch, *Mine Run: A Campaign of Lost Opportunities, October 21, 1863-May 1,* 1864. A good tactical article on the fighting at Payne's Farm is Theodore P. Savas, "The Musket Balls Flew Very Thick: Holding the Line at Payne's Farm," *Civil War Magazine,* Vol. 10, No. 33 (1994), pp. 20-23, 53-56.

78. Cowper, *Extracts,* p. 43.

79. Grimes, Charlotte, *Sketches,* p. 10.

## Chapter Six

1. Shaffner, Diary of J. F. Shaffner, J. F. Shaffner Papers, NCDAH, p. 17.

2. Ibid. There is confusion over the spelling of the name. There was no "Capt. William F. McRine" in the 4th Regiment. However, there was a "William F. McRorie," Captain, Co., A. It is likely that this is the officer mentioned in the typeset copy of Shaffner's diary. Perhaps this was a typing error in the typeset copy. Shaffner letter to Carrie [L. Fries] January 14, 1864, J. F. Shaffner Papers, NCDAH; Shaffner, Diary, p. 18

3. Shaffner Diary, pp. 21-22.

4. Shaffner letter to Carrie, January 14, 1864, J. F. Shaffner Papers, NCDAH. Note: all the letters to Carrie are in his papers at NCDAH; Shaffner, letter to Carrie, January 21, 1864, Shaffner, Diary, p. 21

5. Shaffner, letter to Carrie, January 23, 1864; Shaffner, Diary, p. 22-23.

6. Shaffner Diary, p. 30. Osborne, in writing the history of the 4th Regiment, made no mention of these charges and neither do several other members of the 4th who kept

diaries or wrote accounts of their service. Interestingly enough, neither did Grimes in his correspondence.

7. Shaffner Diary, pp. 32, 39-40; Shaffner letter to Carrie, April 3, 1864.

8. On January 10, 1865, Surgeon Shaffner asked for leave to return home to marry Carrie. He was worried that General Grimes, who would have to rule on his request, harbored a grudge and would turn his request down. To his surprise, Grimes "wished me success and approved my application."

9. Grimes, Bryan, letter to Charlotte, April 23, 1864, Bryan Grimes Papers, SHC; Grimes, Bryan, letter to Charlotte, April 28, 1864, Bryan Grimes Papers, SHC.

10. *Wilmington Journal,* March 10, 1864.

11. Parris, John, Wilmington, N.C. *Journal,* April 28, 1864. John F. Shaffner, the 4th Regiment's surgeon, described one ghastly scene on a cold January day in 1864 involving two deserters: "the poor criminals passed my tent in an ambulance, seated upon their coffins, in route for the fatal field."

12. Grimes, Bryan, letter to W.H. Taylor, April 25, 1864, Bryan Grimes Papers, SHC.

13. Grimes, Bryan, letter to Charlotte, April 24, 1864, Bryan Grimes Papers, SHC; Allardice, *More Generals in Gray,* p. 3.

14. Cowper, *Extracts,* p. 48.

15. Cowper, *Extracts,* p. 49.

16. Deaderick, *Strategy in the Civil War,* pp. 119-120.

17. Gallagher, *Ramseur,* p. 99; *OR* 51, pt, 2, p. 890; *OR* 36, pt. 1, p. 1081.

18. *OR* 36, pt. 1, p. 1081; Steere, *Wilderness Campaign,* pp. 257-258.

19. Grant was up by 4:00 a.m. and perhaps his breakfast signaled what kind of day he had in mind. His aide, Horace Porter, reported that Grant, "took a cucumber, sliced it, poured some vinegar over it, and partook of nothing else except a cup of strong coffee." Trudeau, *Bloody Roads South,* p. 84. Trudeau's book is an interesting and readable modern study of the Overland Campaign. Another outstanding and more academic study is Gordon C. Rhea's *The Battle of the Wilderness, May 5-6, 1864* (Baton Rouge, 1994).

20. Gallagher, *Ramseur,* p. 103; Steere, *Wilderness Campaign,* p. 324; *OR* 36, pt. 1, p. 1081.

21. Grimes, Bryan, letter to Charlotte, May 6, 1864, Bryan Grimes Papers, SHC.

22. Grimes, Bryan, letter to Charlotte, May 7, 1864, Bryan Grimes Papers, SHC.

23. Alexander, *Fighting for the Confederacy,* p. 363; Trudeau says casualties were 18,000 Federals and 11,000 Confederates. Trudeau, *Bloody Roads South,* p. 341; Steere estimates 17,600 Federals and 8,700 Confederates. Steere, *Wilderness,* pp. 459, 463.

24. Trudeau, *Bloody Roads South,* pp. 125-132.

Chapter Seven

1. *OR* 36, pt. 1, pp. 1071, 1081; Rhea, *Spotsylvania*, pp. 81-83.

2. Osborne, "Fourth Regiment," p. 255; *OR* 36, pt. 1, p. 1081; Rhea, *Spotsylvania*, p. 83; Gallagher, *Ramseur*, pp. 104-105.

3. Trudeau, *Bloody Roads South*, p. 144; *OR* 36, pt. 1, pp. 1081-1082; Gallagher, *Ramseur*, p. 105.

4. Matter, *If It Takes All Summer*, p. 163; Osborne, "Fourth Regiment," p. 255.

5. Matter, *If It Takes All Summer*, pp. 166-167; *OR* 36, pt. 1, pp. 1072, 1082. Rhea notes that recent research suggests that Ewell's losses exceeded Upton's by two or three hundred. Rhea, *Spotsylvania*, p. 176.

6. Grimes, Bryan, letter to Charlotte, May 11, 1864, Bryan Grimes Papers, SHC.

7. Watson, "45th Regiment," p. 50, in Clark.

8. *OR* 36, pt. 1 p. 1082.

9. *OR* 36, pt. 1 p. 1082; Rhea, *Spotsylvania*, pp. 230-242.

10. Osborne, "Fourth Regiment," pp. 256-257; Gallagher, *Ramseur*, pp.107-108; Rhea, *Spotsylvania*, pp. 255-259, *OR* 36, pt.1 p. 1082.

11. Jordan, "53rd Regiment," pp. 29, 50 in Clark; Watson, "45th Regiment," p. 51, in Clark; Gallagher, *Ramseur*, pp. 107-108; Rhea, *Spotsylvania*, pp. 255-259; *OR* 36, pt. 1 p. 1082.

12. Rhea, *Spotsylvania*, p. 257.

13. Cowper, *Extracts*, p. 52.

14. *OR* 36, pt. 1 p. 1082.

15. Rhea, *Spotsylvania*, p. 258.

16. Rhea, *Spotsylvania*, pp. 258-262.

17. Gallagher, *Ramseur*, p. 110.

18. Rhea, *Spotsylvania*, pp. 266-268; Gallagher, *Ramseur*, p. 110; *OR* 36, pt. 1 p. 1082.

19. Rhea, *Spotsylvania*, pp. 305-307; Gallagher, *Ramseur*, pp. 110-111; *OR* 36, pt. 1 p. 1082.

20. Cowper, *Extracts*, p. 52.

21. Freeman, *Lee's Lieutenants*, 3. p. 407; Gallagher, *Ramseur*, p. 111.

22. Grimes, Bryan, letter to Charlotte, May 14, 1864, Bryan Grimes Papers, SHC.

23. Grimes, Bryan, letter to Charlotte, May 17, 1864, Bryan Grimes Papers, SHC.

24. Grimes, Bryan, letter to Charlotte, May 14, 1864, Bryan Grimes Papers, SHC.

25. Cowper, *Extracts*, p. 53.

26. Grimes, Bryan, letter to Charlotte, May 18, 1864, Bryan Grimes Papers, SHC. The author would like to thank John Patterson for helping research this phenomenon and speaking with medical experts on the cause of this condition. Many observers on a variety of fields noted this differentiation between the dead, and some speculate that the rate of decomposition might have had something to do with their respective diets.

27. Grimes, Bryan, letter to Charlotte, May 20, 1864, Bryan Grimes Papers, SHC.

28. Cowper, *Extracts*, p. 55.

29. For an excellent account of the North Anna Campaign, see J. Michael Miller, *The North Anna Campaign: "Even to Hell Itself," May 21-26, 1864* (Lynchburg, 1989).

30. Miller, *North Anna*, pp. 108-110; *OR* 36, pt. 1 p. 450. Miller has William R. Cox in command of Ramseur's Brigade on May 24, although records indicate he did not take command until three days later, on May 27, when Ramseur was given a division and Cox was promoted from his 2nd North Carolina to lead the brigade.

31. Cowper, *Extracts*, p. 54; Miller, *North Anna*, pp. 113-115. Grimes' reference to his brigade as "Daniel's Brigade" highlights the fact that his elevation to command that unit had not yet been made permanent.

32. Grimes, Bryan, letter to Charlotte, May 26, 1864, Bryan Grimes Papers, SHC.

33. Grimes, Bryan, letter to Charlotte, May 28, 1864, Bryan Grimes Papers, SHC..

34. Gallagher, *Ramseur,* p. 115.

35. Gallagher, *Ramseur,* p. 116

36. Grimes, Bryan, letter to Charlotte, June 1, 1864, Bryan Grimes Papers, SHC

37. Grimes, Bryan, letter to Charlotte, June 2, 1864, Bryan Grimes Papers, SHC.

38. Trudeau, *Bloody Rodes South,* pp. 287, 295.

39. Wert, "William R. Cox," in William C. Davis, ed. *The Confederate General,* 2, pp. 39-40.

40. Grimes, Bryan, letter to Charlotte, June 5, 1864, Bryan Grimes Papers, SHC. Charlotte was pregnant at this time, which may account for her sickness that Grimes mentions.

41. Grimes, Bryan, letter to Charlotte, June 6, 1864, Bryan Grimes Papers, SHC

42. Grimes, Bryan, letter to Charlotte, June 8, 1864, Bryan Grimes Papers, SHC.

43. Grimes, Bryan, letter to Charlotte, June 9, 1864, Bryan Grimes Papers, SHC.

44. Grimes, Bryan, letter to Charlotte, June 10, 1864, Bryan Grimes Papers, SHC.

45. Cowper, *Extracts*, pp. 54-56.

46. Grimes, Bryan, letter to Charlotte, June 15, 1864, Bryan Grimes Papers, SHC.

47. Grimes, Bryan, letter to Charlotte, June 18, 1864, Bryan Grimes Papers, SHC.

48. Grimes, Bryan, letter to Charlotte, June 22, 1864, Grimes Family Papers, SHC.

49. Ibid.

## Chapter Eight

1. Grimes, Bryan, letter to Charlotte, August 6, 1864, Bryan Grimes Papers, SHC; see also Lowry, *The Story the Soldiers Wouldn't Tell,* an interesting and insightful study of soldiers' attitudes and behaviors toward sex, which did not often appear in their letters home.

2. Gallagher, *Ramseur,* pp. 123-137.

3. Grimes, Bryan, letter to Charlotte, August 8, 1864, Bryan Grimes Papers, SHC.

4. Grimes, Bryan, letter to Charlotte, August 10, 1864, Bryan Grimes Papers, SHC.

5. Ibid.; Confederate Generals John McCausland and Bradley Johnson burned Chambersburg under orders from Jubal Early. McCausland was instructed to demand $100,000 in gold or $500,000 in greenbacks for the indemnification of the Southerners whose homes and barns had been burned by the Union troops, and if refused, to burn down the town. Early never expressed any regret for this order, and Grimes did not comment on the ethics of it in his letter. Early, *War Memoirs.* The "disaster" suffered by the Confederates is in reference to Union General William W. Averell's surprise attack on Johnson's sleeping troops on August 7. Averell routed them and later reported the capture of four guns, 420 prisoners and over 400 horses. Freeman, *Lee's Lieutenants,* 3, p. 573.

6. Freeman, *Lee's Lieutenants,* 3, p. 574; Lewis, *Guns of Cedar Creek,* pp. 314, 319 and 322; Mahr, *The Battle of Cedar Creek,* p. g. Mahr's book is the best treatment to date.

7. Freeman, *Lee's Lieutenants,* p. 577; Mahr, *Battle of Cedar Creek,* p. i.

8. Grimes, Bryan, letter to Charlotte, August 15, 1864, Bryan Grimes Papers, SHC.

9. Ibid. Ramseur did not mention anything about Johnston not having his guns loaded during the battle, although he did level direct criticism against two other brigade commanders, Robert Lilley (who was captured there) and Gaston Lewis.

10. Cowper, *Extracts,* p. 58.

11. Grimes, Bryan, letter to Charlotte, August 20, 1864, Bryan Grimes Papers, SHC.

12. Grimes, Bryan, letter to Charlotte, August 21, 1864, Bryan Grimes Papers, SHC.

13. Grimes, Bryan, letter to Charlotte, August 23, 1864, Bryan Grimes Papers, SHC. It is interesting to note that Grimes' estimate of the difference in the strength of the two armies essentially reflects the ratio provided by most historians.

14. Grimes, Bryan, letter to Charlotte, August 24, 1864, Bryan Grimes Papers, SHC.

15. Grimes, Bryan, letter to Charlotte, August 27, 1864, Bryan Grimes Papers, SHC.

16. Grimes, Bryan, letter to Charlotte, September 1, 1864, Bryan Grimes Papers, SHC.

17. Grimes, Bryan, letter to Charlotte, August 27, 1864, Bryan Grimes Papers, SHC.

18. Grimes, Bryan, letter to Charlotte, September 1, 1864, Bryan Grimes Papers; Gallagher, *Ramseur,* p. 136.

19. Grimes, Bryan, letter to Charlotte, September 9, 1864, Bryan Grimes Papers, SHC.

20. Grimes, Bryan, letter to Charlotte, September 13, 1864, Bryan Grimes Papers, SHC. A September 8th letter to Charlotte confirms why so few of her letters exist today. Grimes wrote, "I enclose several of your old letters that I do not wish to destroy, nor must you do so, but keep them for me." Apparently, most of the time Grimes honored Charlotte's earlier request and destroyed her letters after reading them. Grimes, Bryan, letter to Charlotte, September 8, 1864, Bryan Grimes Papers, SHC.

21. Grimes, Bryan, letter to Charlotte, September 10, 1864, Bryan Grimes Papers, SHC.

22. Grimes, Bryan, letter to Charlotte, September 11, 1864, Bryan Grimes Papers, SHC.

23. Grimes, Bryan, letter to Charlotte, September 16, 1864, Bryan Grimes Papers, SHC. Grimes' criticisms of some of Raleigh's citizens were left out of Cowper's *Extracts*, which was originally published in 1884.

24. Grimes, Bryan, letter to Charlotte, September 17, 1864, Bryan Grimes Papers, SHC.

25. *OR* 43, pt. 1, p. 697.

26. Wert, *Winchester to Cedar Creek,* pp. 44-45.

27. Wert, *Winchester to Cedar Creek,* pp. 66-70; Osborne, "Fourth Regiment," p. 262; Jubal Early's report, *OR* 43, pt. 1, pp. 554-556, does not discuss the issue of who assumed command of Rodes' Division. "The Diary of Captain Robert E. Park, of Twelfth Alabama Regiment," in *Southern Historical Society Papers*, vol. 2, p. 26, discusses the matter at some length and claims that Rodes' AAG, Major Peyton, told him Cullen Battle assumed command. Given Grimes' silence on the issue, it is probable that Cullen Battle did indeed assume the reins of command. If Grimes had, he would probably have mentioned it.

28. *OR* 43, pt. 1, p. 555; Gallagher, *Ramseur,* p. 143; Wert, *Winchester to Cedar Creek,* pp. 86-92.

29. Cowper, *Extracts,* pp. 65-68; Grimes, Bryan, letter to Charlotte, September 20, 1864, Bryan Grimes Papers, SHC; Grimes, Bryan, letter to Charlotte, September 22, 1864, Bryan Grimes Papers, SHC; Grimes, Bryan, letter to Charlotte, September 26, 1864, Bryan Grimes Papers, SHC; *OR* 43, pt. 1, p. 555. Osborne, "Fourth Regiment," p. 262, puts a rather positive spin on this phase of the battle and claims the men retired "in good order."

30. *OR* 43, pt. 1, pp. 114, 118, 555-557; Wert, *From Winchester to Cedar Creek,* p. 103.

31. Grimes, Bryan, letter to Charlotte, September 22, 1864, Bryan Grimes Papers, SHC

32. The quotes from Grimes are woven together from his letters to Charlotte from September 20 to 26 and describe the action and his participation at Third Winchester. Early seemed to get along with Rodes as well as he got along with any of his subordinate officers. His report on the Rodes' death said simply, "Rodes' division made a very gallant charge, and he was killed conducting it." *OR* 43, pt. 1, p. 555.

33. Wert, *Winchester to Cedar Creek,* pp. 110-111; *OR* 43, pt. 1, p. 556. A concise and witty treatment of Early's relationship with his cavalry and the state of the Valley's mounted is found in Robert K. Krick, "The Cause of All My Disasters," in "Jubal A. Early and the Undisciplined Valley Cavalry," in Gary Gallagher, ed., *The Struggle for the Shenandoah: Essays on the 1864 Valley Campaign,* pp. 77-106.

34. Grimes, Bryan, letter to Charlotte, September 22, 1864, Bryan Grimes Papers, SHC. It is unclear why Grimes believed Battle was "totally unqualified" for the post, although correspondence exists from Battle to Rodes indicating Rodes was not pleased with the subordinate's actions at Spotsylvania (and perhaps in the Wilderness as well). Robert K. Krick, "Cullen Andrews Battle," in *The Confederate General,* 2, p. 75. Battle received a wound at Cedar Creek in October 1864 that ended his wartime career. After the war, Battle eventually moved to North Carolina in 1880 and became editor of the New Bern *Journal* and mayor of the city. New Bern is about forty miles from Grimes' plantation home. For this reason, perhaps, Cowper left out Grimes' negative reference to Battle in his 1884 *Extracts.*

35. Cowper, *Extracts,* p. 69; Wert, *Winchester to Cedar Creek,* pp. 120-121. Grimes urged Ramseur to shift one or two brigades to support Lomax's cavalry. Ramseur would not do this until he talked with Early. Whether Ramseur conferred with Early is unclear. Grimes was right: support was desperately needed to hold the left flank and it was not forthcoming.

36. Jordan, *North Carolina Troops,1861-1865,* 13, p. 46; Wert, *Winchester to Cedar Creek,* p. 120.

37. Cowper, *Extracts,* p. 69.

38. Cowper, *Extracts,* pp. 70-71; Grimes, Bryan, letter to Charlotte, September 30, 1864, Bryan Grimes Papers, SHC.

## Chapter Nine

1. Cowper, *Extracts,* p. 66. It is interesting to note that Cowper edited Grimes' letter of September 25 in his *Extracts* by substituting the word "retreat" for "run." After the battle of Third Winchester, Grimes learned a rumor was circulating that he had been killed. He immediately had a staff officer telegraph Charlotte "for fear the current report in the rear of my being killed might reach you."

2. Trudeau, *Bloody Roads South,* pp. 320-321; Freeman, *Lee's Lieutenants,* 3, pp. 557-568.

3. Grimes, Bryan, letter to Charlotte, September 28, 1864, Bryan Grimes Papers, SHC.

4. Grimes, Bryan, letter to Charlotte, September 30, 1864, Bryan Grimes Papers, SHC. Grimes' gloomy remark about the war's looming defeat was omitted from Cowper's *Extracts*. Grimes probably believed, as Ramseur put it: "Tho' peace may be a long way off, I feel sure that Justice & right will finally triumph." However, it is important for the record to note this first written negative view of the war's outcome by Grimes, because he had expressed such steadfast optimism and positive attitudes in his previous letters.

5. Gordon, *Reminiscences of the Civil War*, p. 327.

6. Grimes, Bryan, letter to Charlotte, October 2, 1864, Bryan Grimes Papers, SHC.

7. Grimes, Bryan, letter to Charlotte, October 3, 1864, Bryan Grimes Papers, SHC.

8. Ibid.

9. Grimes, Bryan, letter to Charlotte, October 3, 1864, Bryan Grimes Papers, SHC.

10. Grimes, Bryan, letter to Charlotte, October 6, 1864, Bryan Grimes Papers, SHC; *OR* 43, p. 2, pp. 882-884. Cox's poor performance at Fisher's Hill is not well known but is well documented. "Another of Ramseur's brigades, under Cox was also sent to the Confederate left but lost its way in the woods and ravines and took itself out of the battle." Jordan, *North Carolina Troops 1861-1865*, 13, p. 46. See also Wert, *From Winchester to Cedar Creek*, pp. 122-123. Cowper in his *Extracts* omits Grimes' criticism of Cox, probably because in 1884, when *Extracts* was published, Cox was a prominent politician and Congressman (1880 to 1886).

11. Grimes, Bryan, letter to Charlotte, October 10, 1864, Bryan Grimes Papers, SHC.

12. Ibid.

13. Wert, *From Winchester to Cedar Creek*, pp. 168-169; Mahr, *Cedar Creek*, pp. 65-69. Some historians describe Early's noisy probe as rash and counter-productive since it resulted in the recall of Horatio Wright's VI Corps (Federal). Theodore Mahr, however, perhaps the most thorough of the Cedar Creek historians, disagrees. Sheridan, claims Mahr, "had decided to recall the VI Corps on the morning of October 13—several hours before Early arrived. Mahr, *Cedar Creek*, p. 69.

14. Grimes, Bryan, letter to Charlotte, October 13, 1864, Bryan Grimes Papers, SHC.

15. Grimes, Bryan, letter to Charlotte, October 14, 1864, Bryan Grimes Papers, SHC.

16. Grimes, Bryan, letter to Charlotte, October 15, 1864, Bryan Grimes Papers, SHC.

17. Ibid. It is difficult to understand why Grimes exhibited so little interest in the naming of their first child. If it was a boy, perhaps Charlotte wanted to name him Bryan, after his father. Grimes' two previous sons were named Bryan, and both had died. She

may have sensed his reluctance to use the name again, although even the thought of doing so appears, at least today, somewhat morbid. Grimes, however, left the decision up to her and Charlotte named the infant Bryan.

18. Mahr, *Cedar Creek,* p. 78.

19. Ibid.

20. Mahr, *Cedar Creek,* pp. 80-81.

21. Wert, From *Winchester to Cedar Creek,* p. 175.

22. Grimes, Bryan, letter to Charlotte, October 17, 1864, Bryan Grimes Papers, SHC.

23. Ibid. Years later after the war, in a letter to Nellie Ramseur, Grimes described the event in more detail for the young widow: "Tears of sympathy for you filled his eyes upon speaking of you. I remember so well his saying he thought it was a boy. That evening mail brought me a letter from Raleigh announcing the birth of a son, whereup I went again to tell my glad tidings and seated around the roots of an old oak speaking of our wives, our babies and the future." Bryan Grimes to Ellen Ramseur, June 27, 1873, Bryan Grimes Papers, NCDAH. Unlike Grimes, Ramseur did not know the gender of his child (it was a girl). In fact, he never learned it, for he was mortally wounded at Cedar Creek the following day and died on October 20. The message Ramseur had received was by wigwag from the signal corps: "The crisis is over and all is well." Gallagher, *Ramseur,* p. 155.

24. *OR* 43, pt. 1, p. 598; Mahr, *Cedar Creek,* pp. 90-92; Gallagher, *Ramseur,* pp. 155-156.

25. Grimes, Bryan, letter to Charlotte, October 18, 1864, Bryan Grimes Papers, SHC.

26. *OR* 43, pt. 1, p. 598 (Grimes official report of Cedar Creek battle).

27. Ibid.

28. Ibid.

29. Cowper, *Extracts,* p. 75; Mahr, *The Battle of Cedar Creek,* p. 222.

30. *OR* 43, pt. 1, p. 599; Gallagher, *Ramseur,* p. 159; Mahr, *Cedar Creek,* pp. 223-226.

31.Mahr, *The Battle of Cedar Creek,* pp. 239-245; *OR* 43, pt. 1, p. 32.

32.*OR* 43, pt. 1, p. 599.

33. Cowper, *Extracts,* p. 81.

34. Welsh, *Medical Histories,* pp. 180-181; Gallagher, *Ramseur,* pp., 164-165. Ramseur predicted his death the previous evening to John Gordon. Following his capture he was taken to the Belle Grove mansion, where he was attended by a captured Confederate surgeon and the chief medical officer of the Union army. Since nothing could be done for him, he was fed copious amounts of laudanum until he lapsed into unconsciousness. George Custer sat by his bedside. Ramseur died the following day,

October 20 without ever seeing his young daughter he had so happily spoken of with his friend Bryan Grimes only a few days earlier.

35. Cowper, *Extracts,* p. 75; *OR* 43, pt. 1, p. 600.

36. Grimes, Bryan, letter to Charlotte, October 20, 1864, Bryan Grimes Papers, SHC.

37. Cowper, *Extracts,* p. 83; Early, *War Memoirs,* p. 111; *OR* 43, pt. 1, p. 607. On October 22, 1864, Early had a formal address read to the soldiers in which he cited their straggling and plundering, noting that they had "yielded to a disgraceful propensity for plunder." Early's accusations (remarkably reminiscent of General Braxton Bragg's comments to his routinely defeated Army of Tennessee) lowered morale and caused many of his men to blame Early for the defeat. Mahr, *Cedar Creek,* pp. 339-346. Early did admit some measure of responsibility when dealing directly with General Lee. See Early's report on the subject, in *OR* 43, pt. 1, pp. 563-564. See also specific references in Charles C. Osborne, *Jubal: The Life and Times of General Jubal A. Early,* for Early's performance in the Valley in general and the Cedar Creek battle in particular.

38. Grimes, Bryan, letter to Charlotte, October 31, 1864, Bryan Grimes Papers, SHC.

39. Grimes, Bryan, letter to Charlotte, October 26, 1864, Bryan Grimes Papers, SHC.

40. Grimes, Bryan, letter to Charlotte, October 25, 1864, Bryan Grimes Papers, SHC. Grimes enclosed an autograph with his October 25 letter from Gen. Lee and sent it home. "Put it away for safe keeping," he advised Charlotte, appreciating its historical significance. Grimes, Bryan, letter to Charlotte, October 27, 1864, Bryan Grimes Papers, SHC.

41. Grimes, Bryan, letter to Charlotte, October 31, 1864, Bryan Grimes Papers, SHC. Mahr, *Cedar Creek,* pp. 344-346, has good discussion on this issue.

42. Grimes, Bryan, letter to Charlotte, November 3, 1864, Bryan Grimes Papers, SHC.

43. Grimes, Bryan, letter to Charlotte, November 5, 1864, Bryan Grimes Papers, SHC.

44. Grimes, Bryan, letter to Charlotte, November 6, 1864, Bryan Grimes Papers, SHC.

45. Grimes, Bryan, letter to Charlotte, November 7, 1864, Bryan Grimes Papers, SHC; Grimes, Bryan, letter to Charlotte, November 8, 1864, Bryan Grimes Papers, SHC;

46. Grimes, Bryan, letter to Charlotte, November 8, 1864, Bryan Grimes Papers, SHC.

47. Mahr, *Cedar Creek,* pp. 347-348; Cowper, *Extracts,* pp. 85-86.

48. Grimes, Bryan, letter to Charlotte, November 9, 1864, Bryan Grimes Papers, SHC. Other references to the nature of Custer's letters include Lewis, *Guns of Cedar*

*Creek:* According to one of Jeb Stuart's officers, Custer's letters "afforded some spicy reading." Ibid., p. 86; Van de Water, *Glory Hunter,* p. 61; Thomas, *Bold Dragoon,* p. 269.

49.Grimes, Bryan, letter to Charlotte, November 10, 1864, Bryan Grimes Papers, SHC.

50. Grimes, Bryan, letter to Charlotte, November 15, 1864, Bryan Grimes Papers, SHC.

51. Grimes, Bryan, letter to Charlotte, November 16, 1864, Bryan Grimes Papers, SHC; see Welsh, *Medical Histories,* p. 16.

52. Grimes, Bryan, letter to Charlotte, November 16, 1864, Bryan Grimes Papers, SHC.

53. Grimes, Bryan, letter to Charlotte, November 18, 1864, Bryan Grimes Papers, SHC.

54. Grimes, Bryan, letter to Charlotte, November 21, 1864, Bryan Grimes Papers, SHC. Charlotte, it seems raised this issue since he was a widower. Grimes later believed one of her sisters, who had also married a widower, had suggested to Charlotte that widowers loved their first wives more than their second. Given Charlotte's state of mind during this difficult time, she may have believed it. Grimes was genuinely upset by her comment, but Charlotte later apologized to him for her earlier remarks.

55. Grimes, Bryan, letter to Charlotte, November 23, 1864, Bryan Grimes Papers, SHC; Grimes, Bryan, letter to Charlotte, December 3, 1864, Bryan Grimes Papers, SHC.

56. Grimes, Bryan, letter to Charlotte, December 6, 1864, Bryan Grimes Papers, SHC.

57. Ibid. Although Grimes carried a personal dislike for William R. Cox through much of the war, his criticisms of him centered on his grating (to Grimes) personality and tendency toward self promotion, and not his military abilities. Grimes viewed him as a braggart. By this late date in the war, Grimes had had six horses killed under him.

58. Young, Diary of John G. 1863, NCDAH.

## Chapter Ten

1.Gordon, John B., *Reminiscences of the Civil War,* pp. 374-375.

2. *OR* 42, pt. 3, p. 1277. Grimes had not been officially promoted to command the division, and thus it was still known as "Rodes' Division." Grimes wrote Charlotte on December 18th and asked her to join him in Petersburg.

3. *OR 42,* pt. 3, pp. 1302, 1287, 1290. It is interesting to note that Lt. Gen. James Longstreet did not place much faith in Grimes' troops, or "troops from the Valley," as he called them. On a number of occasions Longstreet discussed pulling more "reliable" troops out of the works, i.e., George Pickett's Division, and using them as the army's

mobile reserve, and replacing them with Grimes' men or others recently arrived from the Shenandoah. The clear implication is that Longstreet believed that the string of crushing defeats suffered under Jubal Early had ruined the morale and fighting spirit of the Second Corps veterans.

4. *OR* 42, pt. 3, pp. 1292, 1295, 1301, 1362.

5. Cowper, *Extracts,* pp. 90-91.

6. Grimes, Charlotte, *Sketches,* pp. 11-12.

7. Grimes, Charlotte, *Sketches,* p. 13.

8. *OR* 46, pt. 2, p. 1020; Cowper, *Extracts,* pp. 91-93. Cowper, p. 92, mistakenly lists Brig. General William Terry's name as "Tovey." Terry's Brigade was at that time under the command of the 7th Virginia's leader, Col. Charles Conway Flowerree, whom Baird suggested Grimes should see in order to seek assistance "as will most effectually secure the movements of the men from being observed by the enemy." *OR* 46, pt. 2, p. 1020. Colonel Flowerree, according to one soldier writing in 1863, was "the most immodest obscene profane low flung blackguard on this earth." Krick, *Lee's Colonels,* p. 142. The record is unclear as to which of Grimes' brigades were selected to occupy Pickett's section of abandoned trench line.

9. Grimes, Charlotte, *Sketches,* p. 12; Trudeau, *The Last Citadel,* pp. 312-315. Trudeau's book is an excellent and fast-paced study of the siege of Petersburg and fighting at Fort Stedman and Fort Mahone, and often overlooked but important period of the Civil War. Grimes' activities are duly noted.

10. Grimes, Charlotte, *Sketches,* p. 12; Trudeau, *The Last Citadel,* p. 322. Charlotte's reference is to the death of Brig. Gen. John Pegram, who was shot down in the fighting at Hatcher's Run on February 6, 1865.

11. Grimes, Charlotte, *Sketches,* p. 13; Cowper, *Extracts,* p. 95.

12. *OR* 46, pt. 2, p. 1266; Freeman, *Lee's Lieutenants,* 3, pp. 629-630. Freeman states the order was dated February 23, 1865, although *OR* 46, pt. 2, p. 1266, presents the same order with a February 28, 1865 date. Grimes makes reference to his promotion on February 26, 1865 in Cowper, *Extracts,* p. 96. Grimes in a letter to Charlotte, February 23, 1865, wrote his promotion was effective February 15, 1865. Secretary of War, John C. Breckinridge in his letter of February 23 to Grimes wrote Grimes promation ranked from the "FIFTEENTH day of February, 1865." Cowper, *Extracts,* p. 102.

13. Grimes, Bryan, letter to Charlotte, February 26, 1865, Bryan Grimes Papers, SHC; *OR* 46, pt. 2, p. 1270. It is not clear when Charlotte returned to Raleigh, but it must have been by mid-February for Grimes wrote her there on February 24, 1865.

14. Grimes, Charlotte, *Sketches,* p. 13; Trudeau, *The Last Citadel,* p. 294; Alexander, *Fighting for the Confederacy,* p. 509. It is interesting to note that in a report on the subject from Lee to Secretary of War John C. Breckinridge dated February 28, 1865, Grimes' Division suffered 13 desertions from February 15-25, the lowest rate of any division in the army. Cadmus Wilcox's Division, Hill's Third Corps, lost the most men

with 319. *OR* 46, pt. 2, p. 1265. A similar report conducted for the ten days ending March 8, 1865, shows that desertions in Grimes' Division rose to 53, with several divisions suffering fewer desertions. *OR* 46, pt. 2, p. 1292.

15. Grimes, Bryan, letter to Charlotte, February 28, 1865, Bryan Grimes Papers, SHC.

16. Grimes, Bryan, letter to Charlotte, March 9, 1865, Bryan Grimes Papers, SHC.

17. Cowper, *Extracts,* p. 97.

18. Grimes, Bryan, letter to Charlotte, March 14, 1865, Bryan Grimes Papers, SHC.

19. Grimes, Bryan, letter to Charlotte, March 14, 1865, Bryan Grimes Papers, SHC; Devereux, *From Petersburg to Appomattox,* p. 2, SHC; Alexander, *Fighting for the Confederacy,* p. 509.

20. Grimes, Bryan, letter to Charlotte, March 14, 1865, Bryan Grimes Papers, SHC.

21. Grimes, Bryan, letter to Charlotte, March 17, 1865, Bryan Grimes Papers, SHC.

22. Fonvielle, *The Wilmington Campaign,* p. 435. Philip Sheridan defeated Jubal Early yet again at Waynesboro on March 2, 1865, effectively dispersing the small Southern army and ending Early's Civil War career. The Valley by this time was completely denuded of supplies for the South, and thus there was no longer a good reason to keep Sheridan and his veteran cavalry operating in the Shenandoah.

23. Gannon, *Irish Rebels,* offers a good description of the plan of attack on Fort Stedman and fascinating detail on the attack itself from the perspective of the Second Corps' Louisiana Brigade; see also Trudeau, *The Last Citadel,* p. 335. An excellent account and by far the most detailed of Grimes' activities and his role in the attack on Fort Stedman are described in Trudeau.

24. Gordon, *Reminiscences,* pp. 404-405.

25. Devereux, *From Petersburg to Appomattox,* SHC, p. 3.

26. Trudeau, *The Last Citadel,* p. 354.

27. Grimes, Bryan, letter to Charlotte, March 29, 1865, Bryan Grimes Papers, SHC.

28. Jordan, *North Carolina Troops 1861-1865,* 1, p. 29.

29. Grimes, Bryan, letter to Charlotte, March 29, 1865, Bryan Grimes Papers, SHC.

30. Freeman, *Lee's Lieutenants,* 3, pp. 655-656. For more information on Five Forks, see Chris Calkins and Edwin C. Bearss, *The Battle of Five Forks.*

31. Cowper, *Extracts,* p. 109.

32. Cowper, *Extracts,* p. 105. Although Grimes referred to Fletcher Archer's command as a "brigade," it was in fact a battalion. Krick, *Lee's Colonels,* p. 36. It is

unknown when Grimes' Division was shifted south in the trenches to the position it occupied on April 2, 1865.

33. It is most likely that Grimes is referring to the Washington Artillery, Battery 30. Phone interview between the author and historian Chris Calkins, Petersburg National Military Park, August 18, 1998.

34. Trudeau, *The Last Citadel,* pp. 374-375.

35. Watson, "Forty-Fifth Regiment" in Clark, *North Carolina Regiments,* p. 57; Cowper, *Extracts,* p. 108. 36. Cowper, *Extracts,* p. 107. The identity of the colonel Grimes refers to is unknown. It may have been Col. Edwin A Nash (Cook's Brigade), or Col. Edwin L. Hobson (Battle's Brigade).

37. Cowper, *Extracts,* pp. 107-108.

38. Cowper, *Extracts,* p. 110.

39. Cowper, *Extracts,* p. 111.

40. Ibid. In 1879, when Grimes was writing about this incident, he added: "This same animal, Warren, I still own and treasure for his past services." See also Freeman, *Lee's Lieutenants,* 3, pp. 700-711.

41. Cowper, *Extracts,* pp. 112-113; Calkins, *The Appomattox Campaign,* pp. 131-135.

42. Devereux, *Recollections,* p. 10; *OR Supplement,* 7, pp. 799-800.

43. Cowper, *Extracts,* p. 114; *OR Supplement,* 7, p. 800.

44. Cowper, *Extracts,* pp. 114-115; *OR Supplement,* 7, p. 800; Freeman, *Lee Lieutenants,* 3, pp. 727-728. John Gordon, in his often fanciful memoirs written decades later, does not even mention Grimes by name and carefully sidesteps the issue of who commanded his several divisions at Appomattox on the morning of April 9, 1865. Gordon, *Reminiscences,* pp. 436-437. In a letter to Grimes in 1872, Gordon lauds Grimes' role in the fighting but again avoids the issue. Cowper, *Extracts,* pp. 126-127. Gordon's most recent biographer also fails to discuss the matter at any length, stating simply that "Grimes. . . offered to attack," and "Gordon assented and placed his entire corps in line." Eckert, *John Brown Gordon,* p. 118. Grimes, of course, claimed he personally arranged the corps' several divisions that morning and provides considerable detail as to how he did so. *OR Supplement,* 7, p. 800. Given Grimes' pattern of avoiding exaggeration and braggadocio, his account rings true.

45. Cowper, *Extracts,* p. 115.

46. Cowper, *Extracts,* p. 116.

47. Cowper, *Extracts,* p. 117.

48. Cowper, *Extracts,* pp. 117-118. In the November 1898 issue of *Confederate Veteran,* Capt. William Kaigler of Dawson, Georgia, insisted that the last volley at Appomattox was fired by sharpshooters under his command from Clement Evans' Division, *not* by the North Carolinians under Grimes. Kaigler's assertion was refuted in February 1899 by Capt. James I. Metts, 3rd North Carolina Regiment, of Wilmington,

North Carolina, who quoted statements from Brig. Gen. William R. Cox that his brigade had indeed fired the *last* volley. *Confederate Veteran,* February, 1899. In addition, Pvt. Henry A. London, a courier for Grimes, responded to Kaigler's account by noting that he was there on Sunday morning, April 9, and that "it fell to my lot to carry the last order on the field of battle immediately preceding the surrender." As an eyewitness, he added, "I unhesitatingly testify that the last volley at Appomattox Courthouse was fired by Cox's North Carolina Brigade of Grimes' Division." London, "Appomattox Echo," *Southern Historical Society Papers,* 27, 1899, p. 93. Private London also cited Grimes' report of his operations at Appomattox, published in a letter to Maj. J. W. Moore dated November 5, 1879, in which Grimes described in detail the events and battles from April 1 to April 8, 1865. In that document, Grimes stated that Cox's Brigade fired the last volley. Finally, London, pointed out that Kaigler was positioned on the extreme left of the line and was on foot, and thus could not have seen firsthand what was transpiring on the opposite end of the division's line, where Cox's Brigade was fighting. Another officer, Col. Edward A. Osborne of the 4th North Carolina, also recalled the last shots fired at Appomattox: "At one time the enemy, with loud cheers, made a sudden rush as if to overwhelm our little band; but the brigade of General W. R. Cox (which was bringing up the rear) faced about, and with the steadiness of veterans on parade, poured such a sudden and deadly volley into the astonished Federals that they hastily retired in confusion. This was the last volley fired at Appomattox, and the last ever fired by the grand old Army of Northern Virginia." Osborne, "Fourth Regiment," p. 266.

49. Cowper, *Extracts,* pp. 118-119.

50. Cowper, *Extracts,* p. 120; Osborne, "Fourth Regiment," p. 276; London, *The State,* 20, no. 28, June 1933, pp. 4-6.

## Chapter Eleven

1. Devereux, *From Petersburg to Appomattox,* p. 16.

2. Devereux, *From Petersburg to Appomattox,* p. 18.

3. Grimes, Charlotte, *Sketches,* pp. 16-17.

4. Ibid.

5. Grimes, William, in a written recollection of the incident, April 16, 1865. Personal correspondence provided by Alfred L. Purrington III, great grandson of William Grimes. The author thanks him for sharing this information.

6. Grimes, Charlotte, *Sketches,* p. 18.

7. Ibid.

8. Grimes, Charlotte, *Sketches,* p. 19.

9. Ibid.

10. Grimes wrote President Andrew Johnson in November of 1865 requesting that he be pardoned for his participation in the Civil War. Record Group 94, Records of the

Adjutant General's Office, National Archives, microfilm publication M-1003, *Pardon Petitions and Related Papers Submitted in Response to President Andrew Johnson's Amnesty Proclamation of May 29, 1865.*

11. Grimes, Charlotte, *Sketches,* p. 19

12. Grimes, Charlotte, letter to Bryan Grimes, September 17, 1868, Grimes Family Papers, SHC. In the fall of 1867, Charlotte and Grimes had their portraits painted by artist William Garl Browne. Browne, a native of England, had quickly established a national reputation in the United States as a portrait painter. He spent his career in the South (much of it in North Carolina), where he produced several hundred paintings. According to oral history passed down through the Grimes family, Browne had a studio in the backyard of William's home in Raleigh around 1865. R. Little Stokes, *North Carolina Museum of Art* catalog. This original painting is now owned by Robert Grimes, the great-grandson of General Grimes.

13. During this period and for some time after Grimes was dealing with a substantial financial issue regarding a toll bridge on the Pamlico River. In December 1866, the Republican controlled state General Assembly in Raleigh repealed the bridge's charter. The intent of the action was to force a reduction in tolls. A handbill announced that as of January 1867, the toll would be $.05 for one person, $.25 for one person and a horse, and $.50 centers for a two-wheeled carriage. The repealed charter had originally been granted in 1783, and Grimes had obtained rights to the bridge just before the Civil War. The structure was destroyed during the conflict and rebuilt thereafter, and Grimes and Charlotte became its sole owners. It was an important source of revenue for them. About a decade later in December 1877, the Beaufort County Board of Commissioners voted to establish a free ferry across the river. Grimes, of course, protested and in 1878 took legal action against the board. His lawsuit was argued unsuccessfully before the Supreme Court of North Carolina in 1879. Finally, in 1883, the Beaufort County Board bought the bridge for $5,000 and abolished the tolls. Bryan Grimes Papers, NCDAH; *Bridge Co. v. Commissioners*, 81 N.C. 491 (1879).

14. Charlotte did not mention in her memoirs the climate around Grimesland, or "down country," as it was known locally. It is likely her successive pregnancies kept her in Raleigh, where she also had help living with her. Her parents were also getting older, and she may have also felt a need to be with them. In another letter home on November 11, Grimes again wrote Charlotte about their new daughter. While some of his relatives thought the child should be named Mary or Ann, he wrote, "my voice is still for Charlotte." His opinion stands in sharp contrast to his earlier reluctance to suggest a name for their first child, Bryan. He had also once voiced his dislike of the name Charlotte, but he had apparently changed his mind. "[I] regret to learn you think the baby is going to resemble me," he jokingly added, "for it is your image that I prefer transmitted to our daughters." Grimes, Bryan, letter to Charlotte, November 11, 1869, Bryan Grimes Papers, SHC.

15. Grimes, Bryan, letter to Charlotte, November 11, 1869, Bryan Grimes Papers, SHC.

16. Grimes, Bryan, letter to Charlotte, November 17, 1869, Bryan Grimes Papers, SHC.

17. Grimes obviously blamed the votes of freed blacks in electing Jones to office. Grimes, Bryan, letter to Charlotte, November 17, 1869, Bryan Grimes Papers, SHC.

18. Wilson, *The Reconstruction of the Southern States,* p. 10.

19. The first reconstruction Act was passed on March 2, 1867 which "provided for the more efficient Government of the Rebel States." It divided the former Confederate states into five military districts, commanded by a military officer. Each commanding officer was authorized to supervise the election of delegates to state conventions for the purpose to writing new constitutions and setting up new governments. On March 23, 1867, Congress passed the second Reconstruction Act, which presented details by which the military commanders were to reconstruct the southern states. Franklin, *Reconstruction,* pp. 70-72.

20. Wade, *The Fiery Cross,* p. 31.

21. For sources on the Klan and North Carolina, see, generally, Stanley F. Horn, *Invisible Empire*; Allen W. Trelease, *White Terror*; Wyn Craig Wade, *The Fiery Cross;* Charles Reagan Wilson, *Baptized in Blood*; R. D. Connor, "The Ku Klux Klan and Its Operations in North Carolina," in *North Carolina University Magazine;* Otto H. Olsen, "The Ku Klux Klan: A Study in Reconstruction Politics and Propaganda," in *North Carolina Historical Review.*

22. See, generally, Connor, *Klan in North Carolina* and Olsen, *Klan and Reconstruction Politics,* for a good overview of this topic.

23. Laughinghouse letter, to Raleigh *News and Observer,* November, 1922, "Pitt County's Ku Klux Klan of Reconstruction Days."

24. Olsen, Otto H., *"The Ku Klux Klan: A Study In Reconstruction Politics and Propaganda,"*; R. D. Connor, *"The Ku Klux Klan and Its Operations in North Carolina"* pp. 224-234. Both articles identify little Klan activity in eastern North Carolina during the Reconstruction period.

25. Schenck, David, 1880, Personal diary, Schenck Papers, SHC, p. 161.

26. Horn, *Invisible Empire,* p. 210.

27. Horn, *Invisible Empire,* p. 211.

28. Ibid.

29. Typically, Grimes avoided and said little about current politics—as he had done all his life. William Holden was the first governor in American history to be removed from office by impeachment. He left the state and lived in Washington, D.C. but later returned to Raleigh and served as postmaster. Tom Settle was eventually nominated as the Republican candidate for the Fifth Congressional District.

30. Unfortunately there is almost no remaining correspondence or written record regarding Grimes' relationship with his daughter Bettie, now seventeen and in college. An April 1870 letter from Bettie to her father exists discussing spring clothing and other miscellaneous family details. Bettie wrote, "When I go to get my Spring clothes shall I send to you for money or have them charged?" His reply is not recorded, but undoubtedly Bettie got her clothes. Bettie's April letter also contains an interesting reference: "I bought Mollie Davis a dress on Saturday." This is in reference to an earlier January 1870 letter from a "Mollie Davis" to Grimes in which she asked for a "loan of money to attend school." Davis, a young woman about Bettie's age, also mentioned writing "Cousin Bettie," in her letter. Grimes' first wife was Elizabeth Davis and Mollie was probably a relative of hers. Perhaps she was the daughter of his first wife's sister, for she closed her letter as follows: "Ma joins me in love to you and Cousin Bettie." Later letters from Bettie mention Mollie being in school, so apparently Grimes sent her the money she requested. Bettie Grimes, letter to Bryan Grimes, April 12, 1870, Bryan Grimes Papers, SHC.

31. Grimes, Bryan, letter to Ellen Ramseur, June 27, 1873, Bryan Grimes Papers, NCDAH.

32. Raleigh, *Daily Sentinel,* November 10, 1875. The author would like to thank Bill Mordecai, Bettie's grandson, for sharing the newspaper story of the wedding. Bettie graduated from Saint Mary's College in Raleigh.

33. Board of Trustees, University of North Carolina, Minutes, 1875, SHC. Grimes' ties to his alma mater remained close. The state legislature elected him as a University Trustee in February 1877. He began serving in December of 1877 until his death in 1880. Ironically, one of the university's early trustees was David M. Carter, a former Confederate colonel and an old enemy of Grimes, and the man who the general suspected was the deleterious force behind his clash and near duel with Capt. Thomas Blount in 1862. UNC Trustees, minutes, December 1877.

34. Philanthropic Society, letter to Bryan Grimes, February 17, 1880, Bryan Grimes Papers, NCDAH.

35. Bryan Grimes, letter to UNC Philanthropic Society, February 21, 1880, Bryan Grimes Papers, NCDAH.

36. Garl Browne, letter to Pulaski Cowper, August 7, 1880, Bryan Grimes Papers, NCDAH.

37. Bryan Grimes, letter to Garl Browne, August 12, 1880, Bryan Grimes Papers, NCDAH. The letter was postmarked August 14, 1880, the day Grimes was killed.

38. Theodora Grimes was named after Charlotte's brother, Theodore. She was born on May 23, 1880, and was the last child born to them. She was about two months old when Grimes was killed. Writing later about her, Charlotte noted, "Poor little baby, it seemed strange that she should have any life or spirit when her baby face was so often bathed in my tears." Grimes, Charlotte, *Sketches,* p. 22. Charlotte and Bryan Grimes

had ten children beginning with their first, Bryan, who was born and died in October 1864; Alston, born February 1866; John Bryan, June 1868; Charlotte, October 1869; Mary, February, 1871; Susan, September, 1872; William Demsie, February, 1876; George, June, 1877; Junius Daniel, October, 1878; and Theodora, May, 1880.

39. Grimes, Charlotte, *Sketches*,p. 21.

40. Wellman, "The General Dies at Dusk," p. 3.

41. Wellman, "The General Dies at Dusk," p. 4.

42. Welsh, *Medical Histories,* p. 90; Wellman, "The General Dies at Dusk," p. 5.

43. Raleigh, *Farmer and Mechanic,* August 26, 1880.

44. Wellman, "The General Dies at Dusk," pp. 6-7.

45. Tarboro, N.C., *Southerner,* August 19, 1880; Wellman, "The General Dies at Dusk," p. 7.

46. Hickory, N.C., *Press and Carolinian,* August 13, 1888.

47. Wellman, "The General Dies at Dusk," p. 8; Chatham, N.C., *Record,* September 30, 1880, quoting Raleigh, *News and Observer,* undated.

48. "Judge Shepherd and his Vindication (?)," in the Hickory, North Carolina, *Press and Carolinian,* August 13,1888.

49. Ibid.

50. Ibid.

51. The article by Wellman, "The General Dies at Dusk," states that the trial began December 13, 1880. The notes in Judge Schenck's diary, however, show that the trial actually began December 7, 1880, as does the Tarboro *Southerner.*

52. "Judge Shepherd and his Vindication?", in the *Press and Carolinian,*1888: Hickory, N.C.

53. It is unclear who made the unofficial court transcripts taken at the trial, but a typed transcript, based on unidentified hand written notes, exists in the Grimes, Bryan Family Papers, # 16, rare manuscript collection, at ECU. It is likely that the notes were taken by trial Judge Schenck. The author wishes to thank Robert Grimes, great-grandson of Bryan Grimes, for sharing from his private collection the notes of Judge Schenck. The notes begin with a December 7, 1880 entry.

54. Tarboro, N.C., *Southerner,* December 23, 1880.

55. Schenck, Diary, v. 9, pp. 74-75.

56. Ibid., p. 74.

57. Ibid., p. 75.

58. Wellman, "The General Dies at Dusk," p. 12.

59. Ibid. p. 14.

60. Ibid. p. 15.

61. Daniels, *The Civil War Career of Major-General Bryan Grimes,* p. 101; Raleigh, *Farmer and Mechanic,* June 23, 1881; Tarboro, N. C., *Southerner,* June 2, 1881.

62. "Judge Shepherd and his Vindication?", in the *Press and Carolinian*, August 13, 1888: Hickory, N.C.

63. Ibid. Sheriff Dixon's statement is important because it contradicts Shepherd's earlier claim in the first trial that Chapman shared a cell next to Parker's, and that Chapman therefore misunderstood Shepherd's conversation with his client to the effect of "keeping his mouth shut."

64. Ibid. W. B. Morton was a defense attorney for Parker in the second trial in 1881 in Martin County.

65. Ibid. If Policeman M. J. Fowler's earlier claims regarding what George Sparrow told him are true, then Sparrow altered his opinion over the years regarding Shepherd's conduct.

66. Raleigh, *News and Observer,* November 23, 1888. Another local attorney, John B. Respass, later wrote that James Shepherd had told him, "that there were certain things that ought to be suppressed from certain witnesses." "Judge Shepherd and his Vindication?", in the *Press and Carolinian,* August 13, 1888, Hickory, N.C. It is interesting to note that G. H. Brown, one of the prosecutors who wrote in defense of Shepherd's actions, was later identified by John Bryan Grimes as Shepherd's brother-in-law, ibid. It is likely that the alignment of eastern North Carolina lawyers on Shepherd's behalf may have reflected the fact that Bryan Grimes was an outsider to the profession. He had been a wealthy planter with no personal connection to the legal community, no close relatives in the profession, and thus had little influence in that arena.

67. Warrenton, N.C., *Gazette,* November 5, 1888

68. Wellman, "The General Dies at Dusk," p. 21.

## Epilogue

1 Freeman, *Lee's Lieutenants,* 2, p. 594.

# Bibliography

## MANUSCRIPTS

John Bass Collection, Springhope, NC
    James Columbus Steele, "Sketches of the Civil War."
    The Civil War Letters of George Boardman Battle and Walter Raleigh Battle of Wilson, NC
Duke University, Perkins Library, Durham, NC
    Samuel F. Mordecai Papers.
East Carolina University, J. Y. Joyner Library, Greenville, NC, Manuscript Collection
    Charlotte E. Grimes, "Sketches of My Life."
    Grimes-Bryan Papers
    Thomas Sparrow Papers
    George B. Singletary Papers
National Archives, Washington, D.C.
    Microcopy No. 437: Letters Received by Confederate Secretary of War, 1861-1865.
    Record Group 94:
    The Office of the Adjutant General
    Amnesty Papers: North Carolina: Bryan Grimes
    Compiled Service Records
    Bryan Grimes
    Record Group 109:
    War Department Collection of Confederate Records, Letters Received by the Confederate Secretary of War.
    Regimental Records: Muster Rolls, Inspection Reports:
    2nd North Carolina Battalion
    4th Regiment North Carolina Infantry
    32nd Regiment North Carolina Infantry
    43rd Regiment North Carolina Infantry
    45th Regiment North Carolina Infantry
    53rd Regiment North Carolina Infantry
    Rodes Division, 2nd Corps, ANV, Muster Rolls, Inspection Reports
North Carolina Division of Archives and History, Raleigh
    Bryan Grimes Papers
    Stephen Dodson Ramseur Papers
    John F. Shaffner Diary
    John F. Shaffner Papers

John A. Young Diary
John G. Young Diary
University of North Carolina at Chapel Hill, Wilson Library,
    North Carolina Collection: North Carolina Clipping File
    Southern Historical Collection:
    Bryan Grimes Papers
    Grimes Family Papers
    John Bryan Grimes Papers
    Thomas P. Devereux Papers
    Thomas P. Devereux. "From Petersburg to Appomattox." 1912
    Faculty Journal, 1844-1848. University of North Carolina
    Edwin Augustus Osborne Papers
    Johnston J. Pettigrew Papers
    Proceedings of the Philanthropic Society, 1844-1848. UNC
    Stephen Dodson Ramseur Papers
    David Schenck. Diary. David Schenck Papers
    John A. Stikeleather. "Recollections of the Civil War in the United States."

## OFFICIAL PUBLICATIONS & OFFICIAL DOCUMENTS

United States War Department. *The War of Rebellion: A Compilation of the Official Records of the Union and Confederate Armies,* 128 vols. Washington, D.C.: Government Printing Office, 1880-1901.
*Supplement to the Official Records.* Broadfoot Publishing Company, Wilmington, NC, 1995. 50 volumes published to date.

## NEWSPAPERS

Hickory, (N.C.) *Press and Carolinian*
Raleigh *Daily Sentinel*
Raleigh, *Farmer and Mechanic*
Raleigh *News and Observer*
Raleigh *Standard*
Richmond *Daily Enquirer*
Tarboro (N.C.) *Southerner*
Warrenton, (N.C.) *Gazette*
Wilmington (N.C.) *Journal*

## PUBLISHED PRIMARY SOURCES

Ashe, Samuel A'Court. *Biographical History of North Carolina From Colonial Times to the Present*. Greensboro, N.C.: Charles Leonard Van Noppen, 1917.

Battle, Kemp P. *History of the University of North Carolina*. 2 vols. Raleigh: Edwards and Broughton Printing Company, 1907.

Clark, Walter, ed. *Histories of the Several Regiments and Battalions from North Carolina in the Great War 1861-'65*. 5 vols. Goldsboro, N.C.: Nash Brothers, 1901.

Cowper, Pulaski, comp. *Extracts of Letters of Major-General Bryan Grimes to His Wife, Written While in Active Service in The Army of Northern Virginia*. Raleigh, N.C.: Alfred Williams and Co., 1884.

Early, Jubal A. *War Memoirs: Autobiographical Sketch and Narrative of the War Between the States*. Bloomington, IN: 1960.

Gallagher, Gary W., ed. *Extracts of Letters of Major-General Bryan Grimes to His Wife, Written While in Active Service in The Army of Northern Virginia. Compiled from original manuscript by Pulaski Cowper (1884)*. Wilmington, N.C.: Broadfoot Publishing Co. 1986 (Reprint).

—. *Stephen Dodson Ramseur: Lee's Gallant General*. Chapel Hill: The University of North Carolina Press, 1985.

—. *Fighting for the Confederacy, The Personal Recollections of General Edward Porter Alexander*. Chapel Hill: The University of North Carolina Press, 1989.

Green, Wharton J. "Second Battalion," in Walter Clark, ed., *Histories of the Several Regiments and Battalions from North Carolina in the Great War 1861-'65*. 4. pp. 243-260. Goldsboro, N.C.: Nash Brothers, 1901.

—. "General Bryan Grimes," *The University Magazine*, VIII, no. 5 (1889), pp. 195-209.

Grimes, Bryan. "The Surrender at Appomattox." *Southern Historical Society Papers*, 52 vols. (January to December 1899), vol. 27, pp. 93-96.

Jordan, Weymouth T., and Manarin, Louis H., eds. *North Carolina Troops 1861-1865: A Roster*. Raleigh: Division of Archives and History, 1993.

London, Henry A. *Memorial Address on The Life and Services of Bryan Grimes, A Major General in the Provisional Army of The Confederate States, May 10th, 1886 at Raleigh, North Carolina*. Raleigh: E. M. Uzzell, Steam Printer and Binder, 1886.

—. "Great Men of North Carolina. Major General Bryan Grimes," *Carolina and the Southern Cross*, 1, no. 1, (November, 1912), pp. 12-13, 17-18.

—. "Bryan Grimes," in William Joseph Peele, ed., *Lives of Distinguished North Carolinians*, pp. 495-512. Raleigh: The North Carolina Publishing Society, 1898,

—. "Appomattox Echo," *Southern Historical Society Papers*, vol. 27 (1899), p. 93.

Wellman, Manly Wade. "The General Dies at Dusk," in *Dead and Gone: Classic Crimes of North Carolina*, pp. 1-22. Chapel Hill: University of North Carolina Press, 1954.

Wheeler, John Hill. "The Late General Bryan Grimes." *The South Atlantic*. 6, no.2 (September 1880), pp. 139-145.

## PUBLISHED SECONDARY SOURCES

Allardice, Bruce S. *More Generals in Gray*. Baton Rouge: Louisiana State University Press, 1995.

Bradley, Mark L. *Last Stand in the Carolinas: The Battle of Bentonville*. Campbell, CA: Savas Publishing Company, 1996.

Buck, Samuel Dawson. *With the Old Confeds: Actual Experiences of a Captain in the Line*. Baltimore: H.E. Houck & Company, 1925.

Carmichael, Peter. *Lee's Young Artillerist: William R. J. Pegram*. Charlottesville, VA.: University Press of Virginia, 1995.

Calkins, Chris M. and Edward C. Bearss. *The Battle of Five Forks*. Lynchburg, Va.: H. E. Howard, 1985.

—. *The Appomattox Campaign: March 29-April 9, 1865*. Combined Books, 1997.

—. *From Petersburg to Appomattox*. Farmville, Va.: *Farmville Herald*, 1983.

Coddington, Edwin B. *The Gettysburg Campaign: A Study in Command*. New York, 1968.

Connor, R. D. "The Ku Klux Klan and Its Operations in North Carolina." *North Carolina University Magazine*, 30, no. 5 (1900), pp. 224-234.

Coulter, Merton E. "Blackout of Honest Government," in Edwin C. Rozwenc, ed., *Reconstruction in the South*, pp. 92-107. Boston: D. C. Heath, 1952.

Cullen, Joseph P. *The Peninsula Campaign 1862*. New York: Bonanza, 1973.

—. "Cedar Creek," *Civil War Times Illustrated*, 8, no. 8 (December 1969).

Davis, William C. *The Confederate General*. 6 vols. Harrisburg, Penn.: Historical Times, 1991.

Deaderick, Barron. *Strategy in the Civil War*. Harrisburg, Penn.: The Military Service Publishing Co., 1946.

Douglas, Henry Kyd. *I Rode With Stonewall*. Chapel Hill: University of North Carolina Press, 1940.

Dowdey, Clifford. *The Seven Days. The Emergence of Robert E. Lee*. New York: The Fairfax Press, 1978.

Eckert, Ralph L. *John Brown Gordon: Soldier, Southerner, American*. Baton Rouge: Louisiana State University Press, 1989.

Emory, Thomas. *Bold Dragon: The Life of J. E. B. Stuart*. New York: Harper & Row, 1986.

Fletcher, William A. *Rebel Private: Front and Rear. Memoirs of a Confederate Soldier.* New York: Meridian, 1997.

Fox, William F. *Regimental Losses in the American Civil War, 1861-1865.* Albany: Albany Publishing Company, 1889.

Franklin, John Hope. *Reconstruction: After the Civil War.* Daniel J. Boorstin, ed., Chicago: The University of Chicago Press, 1961.

Freeman, Douglas Southall. *Lee's Lieutenants. A Study in Command.* 3 vols. New York: Charles Scribner's Sons, 1942-44.

Furgurson, Ernest B. *Chancellorsville, 1863: The Souls of the Brave.* New York: Knopf, 1992.

Gallagher, Gary W., ed. *The Fredericksburg Campaign.* Chapel Hill: University of North Carolina Press, 1995.

—. *The First Day at Gettysburg: Essays on Union and Confederate Leadership.* Kent, Ohio: Kent State University Press, 1993.

—. *The Second Day at Gettysburg: Essays on Union and Confederate Leadership.* Kent, Ohio: Kent State University Press, 1993.

—. *The Third Day at Gettysburg: & Beyond.* Chapel Hill: University of North Carolina Press, 1997.

—. *The Wilderness Campaign.* Chapel Hill: University of North Carolina Press, 1997.

—. *The Spotsylvania Campaign.* Chapel Hill: University of North Carolina Press, 1998.

—. *The Confederate War.* Cambridge: Harvard University Press, 1997.

Gannon, James P. *Irish Rebels, Confederate Tigers: A History of the 6th Louisiana Volunteers, 1861-1865.* Campbell, CA: Savas Publishing, 1998.

Gordon, John B. *Reminiscences of the Civil War.* Baton Rouge: Louisiana State University Press, 1993.

Graham, Martin F. and George F. Skoch. *Mine Run: A Campaign of Lost Opportunities, October 21, 1863—May 1, 1864.* H.E. Howard, 1987.

Griffin, D. Massy. "Rodes on Oak Hill: A Study of Rodes' Division on the First Day of Gettysburg." *The Gettysburg Magazine,* no. 4 (1991), pp. 33-48.

Griffith, Paddy. *Battle Tactics of the Civil War.* New Haven: Yale University Press, 1987.

Grimes, Bryan. "Official Report of The Battle of Gettysburg," *Southern Historical Society Papers,* XIII (January to December 1885), pp. 175-176.

Hamilton, J. G. de Reulhac. *Reconstruction in North Carolina.* New York: Columbia University Press, 1914.

Hartley, Chris J. *Stuart's Tarheels. James B. Gordon and His North Carolina Cavalry.* Baltimore: Butternut & Blue, 1996.

Hartwig. D. Scott. "My God! Be Careful!" Morning Battle at Fox's Gap, September 14, 1862," *Civil War Regiments: A Journal of the American Civil War*, Vol. 5, No. 3 (1997), pp., 47-48.

Hassler, William W., ed., *The General To His Lady, The Civil War Letters of William Dorsey Pender to Fanny Pender.* Chapel Hill: University of North Carolina Press, 1962.

Henderson, William D. *The Road to Bristoe Station: Campaigning with Lee and Meade, August 1—October 20, 1863.* Lynchburg, Va.: H. E. Howard, 1987.

Hendrick, Burton J. *Statesmen of the Lost Cause.* New York: The Literary Guild of America, Inc., 1939.

Hill, Daniel Harvey. *Bethel to Sharpsburg: A History of North Carolina in the War Between the States.* 2 vols. Raleigh: Edwards & Broughton Co., 1926.

Horn, Stanley F. *Invisible Empire.* Cos Cob, Conn.: John E. Edwards, 1969.

Jones, Wilbur D. "Who Lost Lee's Lost Orders?" *Civil War Regiments: A Journal of the American Civil War,* Vol. 5, No. 3 (1997), pp. 1-26.

Krick, Robert K. "Failures of Brigade Leadership," in Gary Gallagher, ed., *The First Day at Gettysburg: Essays on Union and Confederate Leadership.* Kent, Ohio: Kent State University Press, 1992.

—. *Lee's Colonels: A Biographical Register of the Field Officers of the Army of Northern Virginia.* Dayton, Ohio: Press of Morningside Bookshop, 1979.

Laughinghouse, J. J. "Pitt County's Ku Klux Klan of Reconstruction Days," *Raleigh, News and Observer,* November, 1922.

Lewis, Thomas A. *The Guns of Cedar Creek.* New York: Dell, 1988.

Linderman, Gerald F. *Embattled Courage.* New York: The Free Press, 1987.

London, Henry A. "Appomattox," *The State,* 20, no. 28, (June 1933), pp. 4-6.

Lowry, Thomas P. *The Story the Soldiers Wouldn't Tell.* Mechanicsburg, PA: Stackpole Books, 1994.

Mahr, Theodore. *The Battle of Cedar Creek.* Lynchburg, Va.: H. E. Howard, 1992.

Mast, Greg. *State Troops and Volunteers A Photographic Record of North Carolina's Civil War Soldiers.* Raleigh: North Carolina Department of Cultural Resources, Division of Archives and History, 1995.

Matter, William D. *If It Takes All Summer: The Battle of Spotsylvania.* Chapel Hill: The University of North Carolina Press, 1988.

McPherson, James M. *Drawn with the Sword.* New York: Oxford University Press, 1996.

McWhiney, Grady and Jamieson, Perry D. *Attack and Die. Civil War Military Tactics and the Southern Heritage.* University, Ala.: University of Alabama Press, 1982.

Miller, Michael J. *The North Anna Campaign.* Lynchburg, Va.: H. E. Howard, 1989.

Wilbur Nye. *Here Come the Rebels.* New York, 1969.

Olsen, Otto H. "The Ku Klux Klan: A Study in Reconstruction Politics and Propaganda," *North Carolina Historical Review.* (Summer 1962).

Charles C. Osborne. *Jubal: The Life and Times of General Jubal A. Early.* Chapel Hill, 1992.

Osborne, E. A. "The Fourth North Carolina Regiment." *The Confederate Veteran,* 40 vols. (August 1898), vol. 6.

Parris, John. "On Hanging Deserters," *Wilmington, N.C. Journal,* April 28, 1864.

Peele, William Joseph. "Major General Bryan Grimes, Remarks," *The Confederate Reveille,* May 10, 1898, pp. 20-26. Raleigh: Edwards & Broughton, 1898.

Pfanz, Harry. *Gettysburg: The Second Day.* Chapel Hill: University of North Carolina Press, 1987.

—. *Gettysburg: Culp's Hill and Cemetery Hill.* Chapel Hill: University of North Carolina Press, 1993.

Priest, John M. *Before Antietam: The Battle for South Mountain.* White Mane, 1994.

Raper, Horace W. "William W. Holden and the Peace Movement in North Carolina," *North Carolina Historical Review,* 21, (October 1954).

Reid, Richard. "A Test Case of the 'Crying Evil': Desertion Among North Carolina Troops During the Civil War." *North Carolina Historical Review,* 58 (July 1981).

Rhea, Gordon C. *The Battles for Spotsylvania Courthouse, and the Road to Yellow Tavern, May 7-12, 1864.* Baton Rouge: Louisiana State University Press, 1997.

—. *The Battle of the Wilderness: May 5-6, 1864.* Baton Rouge: Louisiana State University Press, 1994.

Robertson, James I. *Stonewall Jackson.* New York: Macmillan, 1997.

Rozwenc, Edwin C. *Reconstruction in the South.* Boston: D. C. Heath, 1952.

Ruffner, Kevin, "Before the Seven Days: The Reorganization of the Confederate Army in the Spring of 1862," in William J. Miller, ed. *The Peninsula Campaign of 1862: Yorktown to the Seven Days,* 3 vols (1994), Savas Publishing Company, vol. 3.

Savas, Theodore P. "The Musket Balls Flew Very Thick: Holding the Line at Payne's Farm." *Civil War Magazine,* 10, no. 33 (1995) pp. 20-23, 53-56.

Steere, Edward. *The Wilderness Campaign.* Mechanicsburg, PA: Stackpole, 1994.

Sugg, Harold. "Romance and Tragedy of War," *Raleigh News and Observer,* August 28, 1938.

Thomas, Emory. *Bold Dragoon: The Life of J.E.B. Stuart.* New York: Harper & Row, 1986.

Trelease, Allen W. *White Terror.* New York: Harper & Row, 1971.

Trudeau, Noah Andre. *Bloody Roads South.* Boston: Little, Brown and Company, 1989.

—. *The Last Citadel.* Baton Rouge: Louisiana State University Press, 1991.

Van de Water, Frederic F. *Glory Hunter: A Life of General Custer.* New York: Argosy-Antiquarian, 1963.

Wade, Wyn Craig. *The Fiery Cross.* New York: Simon and Schuster, 1987.

Warner, Ezra J. *Generals in Gray: Lives of the Confederate Commanders.* Baton Rouge: Louisiana State University Press, 1959.

Wellman, Manly Wade. *Rebel Boast. First at Bethel—Last At Appomattox.* New York: Henry Holt and Company, 1956.

Welsh, Jack D. *Medical Histories of Confederate Generals.* Kent, Ohio: Kent State University Press, 1995.

Wert, Jeffry D. *From Winchester to Cedar Creek.* Stackpole, 1997.

—. "Spotsylvania: Charge on The Mule Shoe," *Civil War Times Illustrated,* 22, no. 2 (April 1983).

—. "The Third Battle at Winchester," *American History Illustrated,* 15, no. 7 (November 1980).

Wheeler, John Hill, *Reminiscences and Memoirs of North Carolina and Eminent North Carolinians.* Columbus, Ohio: Columbus Printing Works, 1884.

Wilson, Clyde N. *Carolina Cavalier: The Life and Mind of James Johnston Pettigrew.* Athens, Ga.: The University of Georgia Press, 1990.

Wilson, Charles Reagan. *Baptized in Blood.* Athens, Ga.: The University of Georgia Press, 1980.

Wilson, Woodrow. "The Reconstruction of the Southern States," in Edwin C. Rozwenc, ed., *Reconstruction in the South,* pp. 1-10. Boston: D. C. Heath, 1952.

## THESIS

Dailey, Douglas Charles. "The Elections of 1872 in North Carolina." Master's Thesis, University of North Carolina, Chapel Hill, 1953.

Daniels, James Douglas. "The Civil War Career of Major-General Bryan Grimes." Master's Thesis, University of North Carolina, Chapel Hill, 1961.

# INDEX